W9-AYV-716

The
Cold War's
Last
Battlefield

A Global Academic Publishing Book

The
Cold War's
Last
Battlefield

Reagan, the Soviets, and Central America

— EDWARD A. LYNCH —

Published by State University of New York Press, Albany

For information, contact State University of New York Press, Albany, NY
www.sunypress.edu

Production by Eileen Meehan
Marketing by Michael Campochiaro

Library of Congress Cataloging-in-Publication Data

Lynch, Edward A.
    The Cold War's last battlefield : Reagan, the Soviets, and Central America / Edward A. Lynch.
        p. cm. — (Global academic publishing book)
    Includes index.
    ISBN 978-1-4384-3949-5 (hardcover : alk. paper)
    1. United States—Foreign relations—1981–1989.   2. United States—Foreign relations—Central America.   3. Central America—Foreign relations—United States.   4. United States—Foreign relations—Soviet Union.   5. Soviet Union—Foreign relations—United States.   6. Cold War.   I. Title.

E876.L94 2011
973.927—dc22   2011009299

10 9 8 7 6 5 4 3 2 1

Contents

Preface

Why a Book on Central America?

More than twenty years have passed since the nations between Mexico and Panama dominated the headlines of American daily newspapers. Throughout the 1980s, it was barely possible to watch a news report on television, listen to a member of Congress, or pass a magazine rack without being compelled to learn something about El Salvador, Nicaragua, the "contras," the "death squads," or the controversy surrounding U.S. policy in the region. So dominant a place in American consciousness did the region command that the 1984 movie version of science fiction author Arthur C. Clarke's *2010* began with a crisis in Central America that threatened to escalate into World War III.

Having reached Clarke's year of crisis, however, we hear very little about Central America, and we have no foreboding of crisis there. Indeed, one of the two major players in Clarke's fictional crisis, the Soviet Union, no longer exists. Since the 1980s, other crises, from Somalia to Bosnia to Rwanda to Chechnya and ultimately to Ground Zero and the Pentagon have all but erased Central America from the public mind. This is true even as some of the players from the 1980s, such as the presidents of Costa Rica and Nicaragua, have reappeared and regained the offices they held twenty years ago.

The crises in El Salvador and Nicaragua did not have the same dramatic resolutions as crises elsewhere. There was no Berlin Wall to topple. There were no live broadcasts of electronic warfare as there were in both wars in Iraq. Changes in government in Central America did not result in statues of dictators being pulled down. The Americans who contributed to the positive outcomes in Central America never stood under a "Mission Accomplished" banner to receive the congratulations and thanks of a president. Crisis resolution in Central America was decidedly untelegenic, in an age that more and more demanded compelling pictures.

Perhaps that is why, in the twenty years since the end of the Central American crisis, there has not been a book-length treatment of what happened in the region in the 1980s and what it meant for the region, for the United States, and for the world. While many library shelves are filled with books on the civil wars of Central America, virtually all were written while the wars were going on and while U.S. policy toward the region was being formulated. In fact, many of the books on Central America were designed to influence the debate over U.S. policy. While timely, they lack the perspective that two decades can bring.

This is not to say that the researcher is without source materials. There are excellent country studies available on El Salvador, Nicaragua, Grenada, Guatemala, and so on. Some authors have focused on U.S. policy toward Latin America or the developing world as a whole and treat Central America in passing. The major U.S. policy makers, from Ronald Reagan to George Shultz to Oliver North, have all written memoirs in which they devote as least some space to the issues of Central America. There are some very good treatments of U.S. foreign policy in the 1980s, as well as authoritative accounts of the end of the Cold War. Such treatments, for the most part, either do not mention Central America or fail to assign the region its proper place in the global conflict between the United States and the Soviet Union.

I hope to fill a significant (and surprising) gap in the academic and political literature with this book. Starting with the 1979 revolutions in Nicaragua and El Salvador, and working toward the emergence of democracy in both countries in 1990, I present a comprehensive treatment of how the Soviet Union and the United States came to be involved in civil wars in Central America and what especially American involvement was intended to bring about, as contrasted with the actual results of that involvement.

The Argument

President Ronald Reagan perceived a double threat to the United States in the bloody and bitter conflicts in Central America in the 1980s. On the one hand, Reagan believed that the Soviet Union, working mostly through Cuba, had taken a strong interest in Central America and was determined to use the conflicts in the region to weaken, and possibly threaten, the United States. Reagan was determined to stop Soviet intervention in Central America and to reverse the diplomatic and strategic gains that the Soviets had already made when Reagan came into office. Reagan believed that promoting democracy in Central America was the surest way to counter the efforts of the Soviets.

On the other hand, Reagan was similarly determined to implement policies in Central America that were significantly different from those of earlier administrations. Reagan rejected the traditional Cold War notion among American policy makers that the best defense against a Communist threat from the left was a strong dictatorship of the right. For Reagan, the desire for freedom was a universal human aspiration. And this desire for freedom existed not only in the political realm, but also in the economic. Put differently, Salvadorans, Nicaraguans, and others, in Reagan's mind, wanted the opportunity to see prosperity, both for themselves and for their countries. Reagan shared their aspirations.

The president's desire to see free and prosperous nations in Central America, however, put him on a collision course with many members of the foreign policy bureaucracy, including members of his own Cabinet. Some of Reagan's closest advisors had considerably less enthusiasm than Reagan did for democracy, and even less enthusiasm for the prospect of a region filled with countries that were prosperous enough to have no particular need for American assistance. At the same time, Reagan's administration also included those who desired freedom and prosperity for Central America as much as Reagan himself. These divisions, particularly given Reagan's management style, resulted in an internal war in Washington that coexisted with the shooting wars of Central America. Thus, there were two axes of conflict over Central America being played out at the same time. The interplay between these two struggles provides a recurring subplot in the narrative that follows.

Finally, I argue that Reagan saw not only crisis in Central America, but also opportunity. In fact, there were several opportunities. First, the United States could experiment with a new kind of counterinsurgency operation in El Salvador, with possible applications elsewhere. Second, Nicaragua provided an opportunity to remove a nation from the Soviet orbit. Third, promoting democracy in Central America permitted a Republican President to co-opt the language and policy of human rights that Jimmy Carter had hoped to make a Democratic monopoly. Fourth, promoting free market economic policies and, Reagan believed, promoting the prosperity that such policies would surely bring, would weaken the U.S. foreign policy bureaucracy, consistent with Reagan's spoken goal of weakening the federal government overall.

The Plan of the Book

Much of the literature on U.S. foreign policy, and many of the debates over U.S. foreign policy in the 1980s, revolved around the distinction between a "globalist" approach and a "regionalist" approach. For the latter, the problems of Central America, like those of South America, Africa, the Middle East, or almost any other region of the world are best looked at through a focused perspective. Put differently, regionalists believe that crises in El Salvador or Nicaragua are more likely to have a Salvadoran or Nicaraguan set of origins and explanations. Understanding of a current crisis, therefore, is most likely to come from a thorough understanding of the country's specific history and specific current reality. To a large degree, this was the approach of the administration of Jimmy Carter, and his foreign policy aides were particularly adamant about seeing Latin America through a regional lens.

For globalists, Central America was most appropriately seen as a battlefield in the larger worldwide struggle between the United States and the Soviet Union. Globalists, for the most part, paid less attention to the internal roots of conflict in places like El Salvador and Nicaragua than to the efforts of outsiders (Cuba, the Soviet Union, etc.) to exacerbate such problems for their own global purposes. The priority for U.S. foreign policy makers, therefore, was to remove the outside influences first, then tackle the ongoing internal problems, such as poverty, disease, repression and hopelessness. Reagan's rhetoric and policy decisions, for the most part, place him in the globalist camp. In the first chapter, I look at the world in 1980 as Reagan saw it. It was a world filled with challenges to democracy, capitalism, and American power, with many of these challenges either created by Soviet policy or made worse by the Soviets and/ or their surrogates.

But experts in U.S. foreign policy have discovered a cross-cutting dichotomy in the making of that foreign policy, sometimes referred to as the "level of analysis" problem. Especially since the publication of *Remaking Foreign Policy: The Organizational Connection* (Graham Allison & Peter Szanton, 1976), scholars of foreign policy and international organization are less likely to perceive U.S. administrations as unitary actors. Therefore, such analysts are less likely to try to ascribe a single purpose, or even a single set of purposes, to all of the myriad actions of U.S. foreign policy makers.

In the second chapter, I build on the notion that policy making is the result of political struggles between different government officials, who are often motivated to struggle by differences in ideology and/or ultimate goals. The Reagan administration is an excellent laboratory for such study, for two reasons. First, the administration was plagued to an unusual degree by internal disagreement. I was on hand to witness much of this disagreement during a crucial period in the Reagan administration. Second, Reagan never had much success in preventing members of his administration from leaking inside information to the media. Thus, there is a permanent record of clues to the disagreements from the pages of major newspapers.

My own analysis of the divisions within the Reagan administration focused on differences in ultimate goals among the players. Some members of the Reagan administration, including Reagan himself, wished to promote prosperity and autonomy among actual and potential American allies. This goal was based on the ideological stance that prosperous democracies are natural allies of each other and that, in a world largely populated by democracies, the United States will always have numerous allies in time of need. Others in the administration, most notably Secretary of State George Shultz, favored outcomes that left potential American allies dependent on the United States to at least some degree. Shultz did not share Reagan's confidence that other nations would willingly work to achieve American goals and was more comfortable being in a position to use carrots and sticks to secure cooperation.

To a large degree, the internal differences I describe resemble analyses based on IR theory (idealists versus realists), on ideology (conservatives versus pragmatists) or on differences in institutional culture (ideologues versus bureaucrats). Such analyses have been used to explain the divisions within the Reagan administration since the time it began. I believe that the way I categorize the members of Reagan's foreign policy apparatus is more successful in explaining what decisions were made and why. Chapter 2 provides an explanation of the workings of U.S. foreign policy. Along with chapter 1, it provides essential background for the narrative that follows.

The third chapter provides a snapshot of El Salvador at the time of Reagan's inauguration in January 1981. This was a key moment in Salvadoran history, since the leftist rebels in the country had declared that January 10 would be the date for their "Final Offensive" to seize power from the country's military-civilian junta. This chapter provides background on El Salvador to demonstrate what had brought the country to the brink of a rebel victory and what steps Presidents Carter and Reagan took to prevent that victory. Chapter 4 focuses on Nicaragua at the time of Reagan's ascension to power, providing a brief history of the Sandinista movement and the interactions of the Sandinistas and the U.S. government in the late 1970s and early 1980s.

In Chapter 5, we see the U.S. government slowly move from a reactive to a proactive course in Central America. The appearance of the contras in Nicaragua, and the decision of the Reagan administration to provide covert support, as well as the full-scale support for democratization in El Salvador, undertaken at the same time, provide most of the material for this chapter. It was during the early 1980s that the seeds of future conflict were sown, both in Central America and inside the Reagan administration.

The sixth chapter treats the U.S.-led invasion of Grenada in October 1983. While not geographically in Central America, the island nation became an integral part of discussions of the future of Central America, both before and after U.S. troops stormed the island and overthrew its pro-Soviet government. The naked use of U.S. military power against an unfriendly government in the Western Hemisphere, the impotence of the Soviet Union and Cuba in the face of American power, and the muted response from the global community all played their part in future dealings between the Sandinistas and the U.S. government.

Chapter 7 traces the origins of Reagan's most serious blunders in the Central American saga. It begins with the discovery that American agents had mined Nicaraguan harbors, setting off a huge controversy both in Washington and among America's European allies. The fallout changed the political balance in Central America and also within the Reagan Administration. Later in the chapter, we see the maneuverings resulting in the passage of the Boland Amendment, the interpretation of which would be at the center of the Iran-contra scandal.

The mining of the harbors reignited the debate over Central America policy in the United States. Chapter 8 analyzes that debate, showing the major players on both the pro- and antiadministration sides. The chapter treats the goals and methods of Reagan's opponents and also the ways in which the administration and its allies sought to counter the impact of antiadministration groups on public opinion. We will see that, by the end of 1986, administration efforts were paying off, with noticeable swings in public opinion toward Reagan's position.

Then the hammer fell. In chapter 9, the Iran-contra scandal is examined, from its inception with Reagan's miscalculation about congressional seriousness to stop U.S. support for the contras. The breaking of the scandal in November 1986, the months of hearings before the Iran-contra Joint Committee, and the climax of the scandal during the testimony of LTC Oliver North provide the narrative for this chapter. For a time, it seemed that Reagan's preoccupation with Central America and with his desire to find funds for the contras would lead to his impeachment.

Yet Reagan emerged from the scandal unharmed and, to the surprise of many, so did the contras. Chapter 10 chronicles the long process of resolving the Central American crisis, from the various "peace plans" offered by U.S. and Central American officials to the resurgence of the contras, in spite of everything, in 1987 and 1988. Much to the consternation of his own supporters, Reagan seemed willing to settle for a negotiated solution in Nicaragua. Chapter 11 brings the story to a close. Reagan insisted that the Sandinistas uphold their many promises to ease political restrictions and to hold a free election. This constant diplomatic pressure, combined with economic and military pressure (a trade embargo and continued support for the contras) ultimately forced the Sandinistas to hold that election, soon after Reagan left office. In the meantime, El Salvador underwent political changes that emasculated both the extreme left and the extreme right in that country.

The chapter also chronicles how Reagan failed to win the struggle within his own administration and had to settle for an uneasy compromise, which only someone as optimistic as Reagan could view favorably. Chapter 12 brings the story of Central America into the twenty-first century, showing how the events and decisions of more than twenty years ago still affect the region. Among other lasting effects, two of the region's presidents from the 1980s have recently returned to power. Their reappearance shows not only how much is still the same but also how much has changed in Central America.

The final chapter shows that the story is not yet over. The issues over which Reagan and his opponents fought during the 1980s have not yet been resolved. In fact, they reappeared, in only slightly different form, after the terrorist attacks of September 11, 2001. In many ways, the internal struggles of the Reagan administration were replayed in that of George W. Bush, and the epilogue provides some glimpses into the key foreign policy decisions of the latter Bush administration, providing suggestions for further research.

A Note on Sources

This book is the result of many different kinds of research, not all of which permit traditional sourcing methods. My own notes from the time I spent in Reagan's Office of Public Liaison in 1983 and 1984 provided a starting point. Public documents on Central America, from my office, from the State Department Office of Public Affairs, from other agencies of the Executive Branch, and from Congress also provided useful information. I supplemented these research sources with several visits to the Reagan Presidential Library in Simi Valley, California, from 2005 to 2008. Some of my former colleagues were willing to share their memories and ideas. I also compiled and researched virtually every article written on Central America from every major newspaper in the U.S. for the 1980s.

For the most part, I have provided enough information in the text to permit the curious reader to follow up and retrace my steps. It is far less confusing to most readers, and far more conducive to an appealing narrative to say, for example, "A *Washington Post* editorial at the time criticized Reagan's decision . . ." than to end thousands of sentences in this book with a numbered footnote. (Given the advances in electronic and online indices, such allusions will be more than enough to permit double checking.) Where I present information that relies solely on my memory of events, I have said so. I do not think readers will find such information contradicted by written sources. What is more important, where I have drawn conclusions, I have identified them as my own and not presented them as indisputable.

Acknowledgments

This book owes its existence to the assistance of many people, both in the 1980s and in the last few years. I suppose I should start with Ambassador Faith Ryan Whittlesey, who was Ronald Reagan's Assistant for Public Liaison in 1983. She hired me to work in the Office of Public Liaison as a consultant on Central America. In that role, I gave speeches and conducted briefings on Central America for groups that visited the White House. I also wrote a series of newsletters, *The White House Digest*, and managed the vetting of these newsletters through the State Department, Defense Department, and Central Intelligence Agency. Faith's confidence in me permitted me a front-row seat to the internal divisions of the Reagan administration. The experience provided the motivation to learn more about the administration that I briefly served and was the early impetus for this book.

While at the White House, my efforts to understand U.S. foreign policy and, at times, to influence its direction, were assisted by friends and colleagues such as Robert Reilly and Burgess Laird in Public Liaison, Otto Reich in the State Department, Constantine Menges and John Lenczowski in the National Security Council, Antonia Chambers, Dan Fisk, Margaret Calhoun and Saul Singer on Capitol Hill, and all of the officials who anonymously reviewed my *White House Digests* and made useful comments on them. My friends and former colleagues at the Heritage Foundation, the Staunton Group, and the National Forum Foundation also contributed to the experiences and researches that find expression in this volume. Surprising as it may seem to those who were not present, one heard plenty of criticism of Ronald Reagan in these circles, as well as praise, helping to provide the balance I hope my book achieves.

The idea for this book came to me in 2005, as I prepared for my sabbatical leave from the Department of Political Science at Hollins University. Hollins provided generous support for my research, through the

Cabell Fund, the Sowell Fund, and the regular travel and research grants. This book would not have been possible without such support, nor without the conscientious efforts of my faculty colleagues who staff the committees doling out such support. Hollins also provided research assistants and, more importantly, the institutional culture that tolerates a full-time professor spending time on research. If my friends at other colleges and universities are any guide, I have no reason to take that proresearch culture for granted.

At the Reagan Library, Diane Barrie prepared for each of my visits, met me when I arrived to make sure each visit was maximally profitable, and followed up with additional materials when they became available. The staffs at the Hollins University Library and at Alderman Library at the University of Virginia helped me to wade through the thousands of pages of newspaper articles, books, and government documents that were necessary to substantiate my conclusions.

Lori Fuller at Global Academic Publishing is as professional and friendly an editor as I could hope to have examining my work. I am also thankful to two anonymous reviewers retained by Global Academic Publishing for making helpful suggestions. I trust they will see their advice heeded in the chapters that follow. I am, of course, solely responsible for any errors.

Finally, living with a writer is a challenge in itself. For unwavering support, for invaluable perspective and for putting up with it all, thanks to my wife and son.

Prologue

Ronald Reagan Issues a Warning

And suddenly it dawned on me, those who would read this letter a hundred years from now will know whether those missiles were fired. They will know whether we met our challenge. Whether they have the freedoms that we have known up until now will depend on what we do here.

> —*Ronald Reagan*, describing a letter to
> the people of 2076 he was asked to write.

When former California governor Ronald Reagan launched his bid for the Republican nomination for president in 1976, taking on Gerald Ford, the incumbent president, Reagan based his run largely on his dissatisfaction with Ford's foreign policy. Reagan was particularly skeptical of the goals of then secretary of state Henry Kissinger. Foreign policy was the topic of many of his speeches and radio addresses while he was out of office.

These statements by Reagan demonstrate a remarkable consistency with the opinions that Reagan expressed, and the actions he took, while president. Moreover, the Reagan Library has the original drafts of most of Reagan's speeches and radio addresses from the 1970s, and they show that Reagan did his own research and wrote his own speeches, from scratch. For most of that period, he did not have a staff.

While the future president did not speak much about Central America or the Caribbean before January 1981, his words on this area show that he considered the Western Hemisphere an important theater in the ongoing global competition with the Soviet Union. For example, speaking about the leftist government that came to power on the Caribbean island of Grenada in 1979, Reagan said, "Totalitarian Marxists are in control of Grenada where Cuban advisors are now training guerrillas for subversive action against other countries, such as Trinidad and Tobago, Grenada's democratic neighbor."

Reagan's last comment also demonstrated his interest in seeing democratic governments emerge from the authoritarian pasts of countries in Central America and the Caribbean. He commented in the same speech, "In El Salvador, Marxist-totalitarian revolutionaries, supported by Havana and Moscow, are preventing the construction of a democratic government."

While most elected leaders focused on more immediate threats to American security in other parts of the world, Reagan had the advantage of looking toward the future. In that future, he saw the potential for great danger in the actions of Soviet surrogates and other Marxists in the Western Hemisphere. In words that he would repeat, in one form or another, many times during his presidency, Reagan asked in 1980, "Must we let Grenada, Nicaragua, El Salvador all become additional 'Cubas,' eventual outposts for Soviet combat brigades? Will the next push of the Havana-Moscow axis be northward to Guatemala and thence to Mexico, and south to Puerto Rico and Panama?"

Before he became president, Reagan had made several crucial connections in his mind. Soviet aggressiveness was connected with the vulnerability of the United States in its own hemisphere. Cuba's increasingly subversive role in the Caribbean was connected with the global strategic goals of the U.S.S.R. Lack of democracy in places like Nicaragua and El Salvador was connected with the rise of Marxist guerrilla movements. Totalitarianism, in Cuba, Nicaragua, or Grenada was connected with likely aggression toward democratic neighbors. Demonstrations of irresolution by the U.S. government in one part of the world were connected with greater challenges to the United States in another part of the world. Perhaps what is most important, the security of the United States was connected with friendly neighbors to the South.

Reading the original writings of Ronald Reagan, unfiltered by the well-meaning but sometimes heavy-handed staff he would have as president, one is struck by the all-encompassing vision that Reagan had of the world of the 1970s. He saw challenges from the Soviet Union in every corner of the world, including the Caribbean. He believed that the Soviet Union was the implacable enemy of democracy, and it would have to be met with a global response. (His critics would charge that Reagan's world-view was terribly simplistic and unsophisticated and that the connections he made were evidence of a too-rigid ideology.)

Central America may not have been a frequent preoccupation of Reagan's before he became president, but when he did turn his attention to this hemisphere, it was to place the issues and crises of the Western Hemisphere into his vision of a global struggle between Communism and democracy, between the Soviet Union and the United States, and between evil and good. Reagan was determined to have a positive influence on this struggle, and his instinct was to start at the core of the problem, which for him was in Moscow. Reagan probably did not expect that Central America would occupy center stage for so much of his presidency.

Indeed, looking at the world through American eyes as Reagan ran for president, one could easily be forgiven for relegating Central America to the back burner. But it was in Central America that Reagan faced his first foreign crisis as president. It was in Central America that Reagan first saw the opportunity to roll back Soviet influence. And it was in implementing his policies for this region that he would stumble into a crisis that threatened his presidency. Reagan's warnings about Central America in the 1970s are worthy of attention. The region would become, against all odds, the part of the world where Reagan's global crusade to weaken the Soviet Union would first take shape.

1

What Reagan Faced

[O]nce we have Latin America, we won't have to take the United States, the last bastion of capitalism, because it will fall into our outstretched hands like overripe fruit.

—Ronald Reagan, quoting Lenin

Imagine it is 1980, and you have gathered a random selection of five hundred people, made up of political scientists, historians, members of Congress, geopolitical experts, and the first hundred individuals listed in the Boston telephone directory. You have told them that in eleven years' time, the Cold War would be over, that there would be a clear winner of the Cold War, and that one of the two antagonists would no longer exist and then asked them to predict which superpower would be the winner. The overwhelming majority would have predicted the Soviet Union.

The world that Ronald Reagan faced when he ran for president in 1980 seemed to be increasingly hostile to the continued existence of the United States as a free and independent country. As overly dramatic as that statement sounds today, twenty years after the end of the Soviet Union, a look at the world as it existed in 1980 will serve to illustrate just how daunting the geopolitical challenges were for America as its citizens prepared to elect a president.

Among these challenges, a couple of small-scale and low-intensity guerrilla wars in Central America may not appear to loom large. Yet this region would become the site of the first serious effort to roll back the area of Soviet influence in the world, and as such, it would become a vital part of the drama that ended the Cold War in the 1980s and early 1990s. The significance of Central America in 1980, however, was obscured by other contemporary events that seemed more immediate and more threatening to the United States.

On the surface, Latin America, and Central America in particular, would not seem to be a promising area for Soviet intervention. Given Central America's proximity to the American mainland, interference by the Soviets could be expected to bring an immediate and decisive American response that would almost certainly result in an embarrassing Soviet retreat. In 1962, just such an outcome had followed the Soviet attempt to deploy nuclear missiles in Cuba. On other occasions, the U.S. government had used military force to reverse, or forestall, what American officials saw as threatening encroachments by outside powers. (Such uninvited forays by countries outside the Western Hemisphere were exactly what the Monroe Doctrine was designed to prohibit.)

Since the Soviet Union could hardly compete with America at such a geographic disadvantage, the Communist superpower spent the first fifteen years of the Cold War doing not much more than waiting for an indigenous leftist revolution to provide it with an opportunity, a policy that bore fruit with the alliance with Fidel Castro in 1960. While the Cuban Missile Crisis had resulted in the withdrawal of missiles from the island, ending the ability of the Soviets to directly threaten the United States from Cuba, the Castro regime emerged from the crisis with a guarantee that the U.S. government would not try to overthrow it. Thus, Cuba still provided many opportunities and possibilities for the Soviets to threaten U.S. interests indirectly, using the Communist island as a base.

The region had other conditions besides its susceptibility to Cuban interference that recommended it as a suitable place for the Soviets to challenge the United States. In 1978, Latin America boasted only two democratic countries, Venezuela and Colombia. Every country south of the Rio Grande was plagued by poverty, disease, illiteracy, and the despair that comes from decades of wide and seemingly unbridgeable gaps between the tiny wealthy elite and the vast poor majority. Nearly every country in Latin America suffered from chronic political instability. Every country in Latin America contained an intellectual elite and a large percentage of the general population who blamed the United States for its problems. In many cases Latin American countries had recent memories of American military or economic intervention. Many had dictators in power who repeatedly proclaimed their allegiance to the United States.

Societal institutions that had stood for decades as anti-Communist bulwarks in Latin America were growing weaker in the 1970s. Landed aristocracies in several Latin American countries were shrinking in size and waning in political influence, thanks in part to the land reform programs that were a significant (and well-intentioned) part of President John F. Kennedy's Alliance for Progress. Large business owners, as they grew closer and closer to American business interests, also grew less and less influential in their own capital cities. In fact, American-linked businesses grew vulnerable to punitive legislation from governments unwilling to challenge American businesses directly but more than willing to pursue their proxies.

At the same time, reform-minded, non-Communist politicians found themselves the first victims of military dictatorships. Latin American Communists had long experience with acting in secret and going into hiding, an experience that moderate political leaders did not share. Thus, the latter were much more vulnerable to repressive actions. Their vulnerability was heightened by the Communists' practice of betraying their less radical comrades to the military authorities. Military governments in Latin America also found centrist politicians more amenable to taking positions in military governments. For the most part, the centrists were well-intentioned, and in some cases they did serve to soften the harshness of dictatorial rule, but their presence in regimes that menaced human rights discredited them and the parties that they represented. Another anti-Communist bulwark was weakened.

Finally, the Roman Catholic Church in much of Latin America was also sharply divided. While the old-style right-wing Catholic cleric was almost a thing of the past in the 1970s, some specimens still existed. They were opposed by a much larger number of priests, nuns, and hierarchy who were willing to challenge those in power with demands for greater religious freedom and more economic opportunity. A small percentage of activist clergy and religious embraced "liberation theology," an attempt to merge the Gospel with the writings of Karl Marx. Liberation theology would have a great impact on U.S. foreign policy in Nicaragua, where the presence of Marxist priests in the government would confuse, and often totally paralyze, American policy makers. Elsewhere, the new theology divided the Catholic Church so that the institution's voice in the public sphere became garbled, confused, and ineffectual.

As the 1970s progressed, what was surprising was not that there was strong Soviet interest in the continent and the geopolitical opportunities that it contained but that a concerted effort by the Soviets to gain allies in the Western Hemisphere had taken so long to appear. The Soviet Union had never entirely ignored the region, as evidenced by its embrace of Fidel Castro, and its efforts to promote or support revolutionary activity in Guatemala in the 1950s, Bolivia and the Dominican Republic in the 1960s, and Chile in the 1970s. But these earlier Soviet efforts had been halfhearted and tentative. Often, the Soviets seemed more risk-averse in Latin America than elsewhere. Soviet officials evidently considered Latin America an area where they would have to be completely reactive and opportunistic.

But there is another possibility. Soviet geopolitical planners might have seen Latin America as a place where significant intervention would have to wait until the U.S. government was completely preoccupied with crises in other parts of the world. As Reagan prepared to run for president in 1980, America had reached exactly that level of preoccupation, as a tour of the world of 1979–1980 shows.

The World in 1980

Southeast Asia and the "Vietnam Syndrome"

American foreign policy after 1975, when the remaining U.S. forces were driven from Saigon, was dominated by the defeat in Vietnam. No American living in 1975 could remember a time when the United States had even had to settle for a draw in a major military conflict. By 1975, there were no Confederate veterans left, the only Americans to have experienced wartime defeat. The dominant wartime memories of adult Americans in 1975 were the triumphant images of World War II. When Americans thought of how wars ended, they thought of ticker tape parades for returning soldiers, of vanquished enemies, and of grateful, liberated populations. Thus, the photos of Americans fighting for a place on the last helicopter out of Saigon became indelible.

Nor did the nightmare end with the melee on the roof of the American embassy in April. By the beginning of May, Laos and Cambodia had been taken over by Communist forces, and South Vietnam had ceased to exist as an independent country. Even to refer to the largest city in Vietnam meant honoring the founder of Vietnamese Communism, since his heirs renamed Saigon, Ho Chi Minh City. The often-ridiculed domino theory seemed to be coming true, as Thailand and even the Philippines, usually a staunch U.S. ally, found it worthwhile to limit their ties to the United States, and especially to the U.S. military.

Even those who respected and honored the sacrifice of American soldiers in Vietnam were wary of any more such overseas military commitments, no matter how just or urgent the cause seemed to be. For the dominant voices in the American media, in Congress, and in academia, the relevant lesson of the Vietnam disaster was broader and deeper than the mere advent of caution in committing American forces abroad. The "Vietnam Syndrome" became the name for the firmly held belief that the use of American military power, anywhere in the world, would almost certainly lead to failure. Moreover, the nature of the American government and the American military was such that any use of American military force was not only doomed to fail but also bound to be immoral.

The long shadow of Vietnam loomed over all the debates about Central America in the 1980s. Of all the arguments that Reagan's critics used to try to derail his Central America policy, none was repeated more frequently than the charge that Reagan was leading America into "another Vietnam." A popular bumper strip at the time read, "El Salvador Is Spanish for Vietnam." It often seemed that to confront the Soviets effectively in Central America in the 1980s, Reagan had to refight, and try to win, a war left over from the 1960s and 1970s.

Hostages in Iran; Soviets in Afghanistan

As humiliating and tragic as were events in Southeast Asia at the end of the 1970s, events at the other end of Asia seemed to be far more frightening in the short run and more threatening in the long run. The Soviets allied themselves with the Arab states demanding the destruction of Israel and provided states such as Egypt and Syria with weapons and money to attack Israel. In October 1973, the Soviets brought about a nuclear alert by threatening to intervene in the Yom Kippur War between Israel and Egypt.

The U.S.S.R. also seemed to see in the Middle East an opportunity to overturn a fundamental U.S. foreign policy. Since the end of World War II, the core of U.S. policy toward the Soviet Union had been "containing" its imperial ambitions behind a wall of military installations and political alliances. An essential part of the containment strategy was preventing the Soviet Union from gaining access to a warm water port. With the new Vietnamese regime permitting Soviet naval access to the American-built port facilities in Cam Rahn Bay, the Soviets had acquired access to a year-round port, but only indirectly.

In the late 1970s, the leadership of the U.S.S.R. took determined actions to acquire an outlet to the Indian Ocean. This was a goal that had fascinated leaders in the Kremlin since before the October Revolution. In January 1978, the Soviet government sponsored a coup that replaced a neutral government in Afghanistan with one more friendly to the Soviet Union. The coup went largely unnoticed in the West. In 1978, Afghanistan was arguably one of the least familiar countries in the world to Americans, who were blissfully unaware of the fact that the country would rarely leave center stage for the succeeding three decades.

Also in 1978, a popular uprising in Iran threatened the thirty-year-old regime of Shah Reza Pahlavi. The shah had come to power with the aid of the U.S. government and had been returned to power after a 1953 coup, also with U.S. government assistance. Like many client rulers preferred by American policy makers, the shah had limited popular support. Thus, he had to rely heavily on American assistance, both financial and military, to survive. (This situation is what makes clients like the shah attractive to some Washington policy makers in the first place, as we will see in chapter 2.)

Under the Carter administration, U.S. military assistance to the shah's government was significantly reduced. By cutting off aid to a long-time American client, whose regime was in genuine danger, Carter kept a campaign promise to put human rights at the top of America's foreign policy list of priorities. At the same time, the aid reduction also alerted the shah that some of his recent actions, such as joining the oil boycott against the West in 1973 and 1974, were unacceptable to the United States. The cut-off had the desired short-term effect; the shah promised to be more respectful of human rights.

For Iranians who wanted to be rid of the shah, his promises to be more humane did nothing to make the shah seem less autocratic. They did, however, make the shah look like someone willing to take orders from the American embassy. Increasingly, the shah was caught on the horns of a dilemma. Whatever actions he took to appease American policy makers concerned with human rights worsened his image in Iran and crippled his regime. Whatever actions he took to effectively fight the insurgency alienated his only overseas source of support.

In the end, the contradiction became irreconcilable. On January 16, 1979, the shah fled the country. Two weeks later, exiled religious leader Ayatollah Khomeini returned from France to establish the Islamic revolutionary government of Iran. To expedite the shah's departure, the Carter administration promised that he would eventually be allowed to enter the United States, ostensibly for medical treatment. This promise enraged the shah's Iranian enemies, who wanted him returned to Iran for trial. Their anger would explode into the crisis that destroyed the Carter presidency.

In November 1979, demonstrators in Teheran attacked the U.S. Embassy, the visible symbol of American power. The militants made it clear they were prepared to hold the embassy personnel as long as it took for the U.S. government to turn over the shah. The American hostages were paraded through Teheran blindfolded, and the militants threatened to place them on trial for "war crimes."

President Carter responded by closing the Iranian Embassy in the United States and freezing Iranian government assets in American banks. But he made the unfortunate statement a few days after the embassy seizure that "the most important concern for all Americans at this moment is safety of our fellow citizens held in Teheran. . . . None of us would want to do anything that would worsen the danger in which our fellow Americans have been placed. . . . All Americans, public officials and private citizens alike, [should] exercise restraint, and keep the safety of their countrymen uppermost in their minds and hearts."

By stating that securing the release of the hostages, safe and unharmed, would be his top priority in dealing with the crisis, Carter alerted both the militants at the embassy and the Iranian government that no forceful or punitive U.S. military action would be forthcoming. Under the circumstances, the dispatch of an American aircraft carrier battle group to the Persian Gulf seemed almost comically impotent. In April 1980, comedy turned to tragedy when a rescue attempt was aborted, and eight American Marines were killed in the Iranian desert.

Certainly the presence of the American military was no deterrent to the Soviets, who continued their advance toward the Indian Ocean. With the U.S. government paralyzed by the actions of a third-rate power such as Iran, the way seemed open to secure Afghanistan once and for all. On Christmas Eve, 1979, tens of thousands of soldiers from the Soviet Red Army invaded Afghanistan, supposedly at the "invitation" of the country's pro-Soviet leader. Within weeks, the Soviets seemed in control of most of the country. In retrospect, this turned out to be the last advance of the Red Army, but at the time, all that was clear was that the Soviet leadership had achieved a new level of daring and confidence.

Carter's options were extremely limited. The United States would have required the cooperation of Pakistan, at the least, to mount a direct military response to the Soviet invasion, even if Carter had had the luxury of assuming that such direct military confrontation would not have led to a wider superpower war. (The most dramatic option available, the dispatch of American military forces to contest the Soviet invasion, would have put U.S. and Soviet troops in direct confrontation for the first time in all the years of the Cold War.)

Still, Carter's response seemed particularly weak. He announced a boycott of grain sales to the Soviet Union and declared that Americans would not participate in the 1980 Summer Olympics in Moscow. Not surprisingly, neither of these actions induced the Soviets to call off their occupation. Later, Carter would state emphatically that an attempt by any outside force to gain control of the Persian Gulf region would be regarded as an assault on the vital interests of the United States of America, and such an assault would be repelled by any means necessary, including military force. But with the U.S. military seemingly unable even to free fifty-two hostages from Iran, Carter's threat rang hollow.

In the spring of 1980, resistance among the Afghans was stiffening, but the Soviets' hold on the country in 1980 seemed secure enough to permit the Kremlin leaders to make plans to either neutralize or invade Pakistan and finally acquire their warm water port. A major shift in the superpower balance of power seemed imminent, even as the American hostages languished in Teheran.

A statement often attributed to Soviet leader Leonid Brezhnev runs: "We will take the two great treasure chests upon which the west depends: the strategic oil reserves in the Middle East and the strategic minerals in South Africa." The quotation is apocryphal but did not seem outlandish as Reagan prepared to run for the presidency.

Taking Advantage of Upheaval in Southern Africa

Meanwhile, Brezhnev's other "treasure chest" in southern Africa was also undergoing potentially cataclysmic upheavals of direct import to the United States. In 1974, the new socialist government of Portugal announced that it would move to grant its African colonies independence as soon as possible. By 1976, two of these former Portuguese colonies, Angola and Mozambique, were governed by Marxist governments that established friendly relations with the Soviet Union. Both Mozambique, on the east coast of Africa and Angola on the west coast bordered South African territory. (Angola abutted what was then called "South West Africa," a colony of South Africa. It is now the independent country of Namibia.)

South Africa itself was, and remains, one of the world's only two major sources of many minerals vital to both the U.S. defense industry and the U.S. economy. Among South Africa's assets are gold, platinum, iridium, titanium, and diamonds. Since South Africa had the only extensive port facilities in the region, and since virtually all of southern Africa's rail links ran to South African ports, the country was also a major source for cobalt, copper, and uranium from neighboring countries. To make the strategic situation even more serious, the Soviet Union itself was the only source outside of southern Africa for some of these strategically vital minerals.

The whites who ran South Africa in the 1970s reacted to the independence of Angola and Mozambique, and their subsequent embrace of Communism, by helping to fund insurgencies in both countries. The South Africans did not give either UNITA (the Union for the Total Independence of Angola) or RENAMO (Mozambican National Resistance) enough to win their wars against their Marxist rulers. Instead, they gave only enough to keep the wars going, to keep both former Portuguese colonies from rising above the level of abject poverty. This would prevent either country from becoming an example, or a refuge, for South Africa's black population. As an example of cynical statecraft, this South African policy has few equals.

It was also unparalleled in the opportunities that it gave to the Soviets to spread their influence in the region. The Soviet leadership knew it could give huge amounts of weaponry and other aid to Angola and Mozambique virtually without political cost. Any nation that raised objections to Soviet intervention in southern Africa could be accused of being proapartheid. In 1976, the Soviets airlifted Cuban troops to Angola, prompting belated but near-hysterical protests from American secretary of state Henry Kissinger.

It was in Angola that the "Vietnam Syndrome" appeared most obviously. In 1975, Kissinger warned of the danger of Soviet troops in Angola and suggested that the United States might be forced to confront the Soviet effort there. Congress not only rejected Kissinger's warnings but also responded by passing the Clark Amendment, which banned any use of American forces in Angola. The amendment's airtight language also banned financial support to anyone fighting in Angola. (As we will see, the Boland Amendments, which sought to impose a similar ban on aid to the Nicaraguan rebels, were not nearly as ironclad. This fact would lead to some grave political miscalculations during the Reagan years.) Absent American intervention, the main protagonists in southern Africa were Cuba, the Soviet Union, and South Africa.

By 1980, the Soviets had transported fifty thousand Cuban soldiers to Angola to fight alongside the country's Marxist army. A substantially smaller number of Cuban and Soviet troops supported the Mozambican government. With Soviet troops on both coasts of southern Africa, and the internal situation in South Africa becoming more unstable, the possibility of a long-term disruption of strategic mineral supplies loomed large. The Soviets had an enormous advantage in the fact that they did not need to place a pro-Soviet regime in power in South Africa. The Soviets could achieve their geopolitical goals merely by adding to the region's disruption. The danger of a prolonged interruption of strategic mineral supplies took its place alongside American policy makers' growing anxiety about oil supplies from the Middle East. Again, a major shift in the global balance of power was only a step away.

Western Europe: An Alliance in Trouble

As the United States found itself seriously threatened in many parts of the world in 1980, it could not even count on strong support from the members of the NATO alliance. Virtually every NATO country had a strong and growing "peace movement" in place by 1980. Even in Britain, there were calls for unilateral disarmament in the late 1970s. The alliance's resolve to deter and, if necessary, confront a Soviet attack on Western Europe seemed less and less certain. Matters were most serious in the Federal Republic of Germany (West Germany, as it was called at the time) where a succession of Social Democratic Party governments had pursued "Ostpolitik," an effort to improve relations both with the Soviets and with their Eastern European allies. In practice, Ostpolitik seemed invariably to mean a weakening of West German commitment to the NATO alliance.

NATO was weakening just as a new Eastern European crisis was brewing. Since the visit of Pope John Paul II to his homeland in June 1979, Poles had been constantly challenging the legitimacy of the Soviet-backed government and demanding more freedom. In December 1980, it seemed that Soviet patience with the Polish government's efforts to confront the "Solidarity" trade union and its adherents was being exhausted. Under the cover of "routine maneuvers," Soviet troops were moving ominously close to Poland, and the warnings from the Soviet government were growing more stern and uncompromising. The crisis passed without a Soviet military intervention, but not without disturbing questions about what, if anything, NATO could have done in the face of Soviet aggression.

Military Weakness at Home

The late 1970s saw unprecedented tensions in the NATO alliance and myriad threats to U.S. interests around the world. These difficulties were compounded by serious problems with the U.S. military. Yet another manifestation of the "Vietnam Syndrome" was the reluctance of Members of Congress to adequately fund the armed forces. Sharp cutbacks in defense spending from 1973–1979 had left every branch of the military in a precarious condition.

Among the areas in which Congress cut back was pay and benefits for soldiers, especially for enlisted men and women. By 1980, many soldiers' families required food stamps to survive. Maintenance expenditures were also cut, leaving the Navy with ships barely able to leave port, and the other branches with tanks, trucks and planes often immobilized by repair problems and shortages of spare parts.

Even more worrisome, the fitness and morale of the troops were declining. With pay so low, all branches of the service found themselves lowering standards to fulfill recruitment quotas. Poor living conditions and a feeling of disdain from civilians left many soldiers bitter and inclined to direct their bitterness at their officers. In the navy, there were ships in which officers did not enter enlisted quarters without an armed escort. Racial strife and drug addiction, both holdovers of the Vietnam experience, also plagued the military in the 1970s. These signs of weakness were not lost on the Soviet leadership or on America's increasingly nervous allies.

Domestic turmoil of such a prolonged and serious nature has a devastating impact on foreign and military policy, especially when those policies require, above all else, consistent application of principle. The dominant U.S. foreign policy of containment cannot exist without a more or less continuous American commitment to vigilance and determined action, coupled with a well-maintained American military to provide containment's muscle when needed.

While still rhetorically committed to containment, America's leaders in 1980 seemed to have redefined the term. When the word *containment* was coined in 1947, it meant leaving the Soviets in control of what they had already acquired but denying them any additional territory. By 1980, containment seemed to mean conceding to the Soviets all they already had, plus whatever they wanted next. Of all the areas in which the Soviets challenged the United States in the late 1970s, only the thrust into

Afghanistan, where the Soviets' role was absolutely undeniable, brought strong and bipartisan condemnation in the U.S. government. In every other region, the majority of American opinion leaders seemed determined to define Soviet adventurism as something else and to take refuge in the indirectness of the Soviet action to deny that there was any Soviet intervention in the first place.

Latin America: The Cold War Moves Closer to Home

From this willful blindness, the Soviet leadership learned that using proxies, and especially Cuban proxies, was extremely useful in covering their own involvement. Ambiguity about Soviet involvement in the many trouble spots of the late 1970s was a major asset in the Soviets' efforts to overwhelm the U.S. with geopolitical challenges, while simultaneously preventing decisive American action. Since Cuban proxies were obviously of most use in Latin America, it became almost inevitable that Latin America would become a central front in the Cold War in the 1970s and 1980s.

Yet at the very time that the Soviet leadership was turning its eyes toward Latin America, the Carter foreign policy team was turning away. Memos from the early days of the Carter administration reveal that Carter's national security assistant for Latin America stated on March 14, 1977: "[W]e do not need a Latin American policy, and I hope that in the future, we will not have one." Nor was this view limited to one assistant. Summarizing the discussion of foreign policy principals for President Carter, National Security Advisor Zbigniew Brzezinski wrote on 31 March: "The participants agreed that we should *not* have a different policy for the hemisphere than we have for the rest of the world" (emphasis in original.). Carter's top foreign policy advisors saw no special national security requirements for the region closest to the United States.

In 1978, the Soviet Union perceived yet another good reason for thinking that more intensive intervention in Latin America might bear fruit. President Carter's first important policy decision regarding the Western Hemisphere was to press for Senate ratification of the Panama Canal treaties. Carter used every public relations tool at his disposal to press wavering senators for a vote in favor of ratification. The treaties were ratified in the spring of 1978, by close votes, and the Panama Canal issue was one of the few foreign policy "successes" of the Carter years.

The initial reaction in much of Latin America to Carter's effort to disengage the U.S. government from the Panama Canal was positive. But in Havana and Moscow, leaders saw the American effort somewhat differently. The president of Panama in 1978 was Omar Torrijos, a dictator who had close ties to Fidel Castro. During the Senate hearings on ratification of the Canal treaties, it was disclosed that Torrijos had been involved in running guns to Marxist revolutionaries in Central America, smuggling drugs to the United States at the behest of Cuba, and laundering money for extremists of both the Right and the Left. Moreover, Torrijos and Manuel Noriega, his chief lieutenant, had crushed democratic movements in Panama. Even some Americans who supported the eventual restoration of the Canal to Panama resisted returning such a valuable asset to such an unsavory and potentially dangerous dictator.

The Carter administration's apparent lack of scruples about doing business with the thoroughly corrupt and dictatorial Torrijos regime induced Castro and Brezhnev to conclude that the U.S. government was determined to withdraw, at any cost, from its most important strategic asset in Latin America. Such determination indicated that less valuable allies and assets in the region would be jettisoned, too, if the pressure to do so were sufficient. In March 1979, the Soviets closely watched American reaction to the disclosure that a full Soviet combat brigade was stationed in Cuba. In spite of strong and urgent protests from congressmen and senators of both parties, the Carter administration minimized the importance of Soviet combat troops ninety miles from U.S. soil.

In the immediate aftermath of the Panama Canal treaty ratification, Castro got more directly involved in promoting revolution in Latin America, and especially in Central America. While the Castro regime had supported Marxist revolutionary movements in Latin America since the early 1960s, much of this aid had consisted of small amounts of money or weapons and was designed more to induce a repressive response from the targeted government than anything else. Castro himself had usually kept his regime's involvement an official secret. In 1978, however, Castro invited (some of the participants would later say that "summoned" was a better word) revolutionary leaders from El Salvador and Nicaragua to separate meetings in Cuba. In both cases, the revolutionary leaders had been active for more than a decade but had made little headway against the governments of the two Central American republics.

Among the reasons for their lack of progress was disunity. Nicaragua had three separate Marxist rebel movements in 1978; El Salvador had five. At the meetings with Castro, the Cuban dictator insisted that the separate guerrilla movements merge. According to some accounts, Castro threatened death to any revolutionary leader who did not go along. All accounts agree that Castro promised substantial military and financial assistance, once the merger was completed. (Given Castro's complete dependence on the Soviet government at the time, it is unthinkable that he would have made such commitments without Soviet acquiescence.) Soon after receiving Castro's "offer," the Sandinista factions merged, and the Faribundo Martí Front for National Liberation (FMLN) was formed in El Salvador. At the same time, both movements became more serious threats to the pro-American governments they opposed.

Grenada's Marxist Revolution

A combination of long-prevailing conditions, and Castro's intervention, culminated in three crucial revolutions in the Caribbean region in 1979. All of them altered U.S. foreign policy in the region, although this was not evident when they took place. The first revolution occurred in March on the island of Grenada. A Marxist movement overthrew the corrupt and increasingly erratic regime of Eric Gairy, who had ruled Grenada since the country's independence from Great Britain in 1974. Gairy was an almost perfect caricature of a right-wing dictator. He was personally corrupt and encouraged corruption among his subordinates. He sought to protect himself from criticism from democratic countries by professing anti-Communism and support for the United States.

The New Jewel Movement was founded in 1973 by Maurice Bishop, a British-trained lawyer and, later, a Cuban-trained Marxist. After forcing Gairy to flee the country, Bishop installed himself as president and implemented a relatively mild program of Marxist reform in Grenada. However, Bishop's ties with Castro and with the Soviet leadership grew closer very quickly. In early 1980, Bishop visited Castro in Havana and made arrangements to receive economic and military assistance from the Cuban leader. As captured documents later revealed, Bishop used the assistance he received to build a much larger army, capable of threatening his democratic neighbors. Bishop's regime also began work on a large new airstrip, capable of accommodating Soviet troop transports and heavy bombers. With Grenada alongside major sea lanes into the Caribbean, the mere construction of such a large airstrip was worthy of concern. But with the other dramatic developments in other parts of the Caribbean, Bishop's nascent threat in 1979 went virtually unnoticed.

Nicaragua's Sandinista Revolution

On July 19, the second Caribbean Marxist revolution of the year ended with the triumphal march of the Sandinistas into Managua, Nicaragua. The previous day, long-time dictator Anastasio Somoza had fled the country. His departure marked the end of forty-five years of Nicaraguan governments dominated by the Somoza family. Like Gairy in Grenada, the Somozas made much of their supposedly close relationship with the United States government, and the last of the Somozas was invariably referred to as a "pro-American" dictator. The reality was somewhat more complicated. While the Somozas did indeed support the United States, it was less clear that the United States supported the Somozas. It is more accurate to say that the U.S. government tolerated the Somoza family, as it had tolerated the shah of Iran, both for its strong anti-Communism and for pursuing economic policies that prevented genuine economic growth.

Somoza's rule began to unravel in December 1972, after a devastating earthquake hit the capital city of Managua. During the relief operations, Pittsburgh Pirates baseball player Roberto Clemente was killed. His death and the dramatic pictures of the ruined city focused American attention on the plight of Nicaraguans, resulting in large contributions of aid. It soon became clear, however, that Somoza was trying to make money from the disaster, by directing aid funds for reconstruction to areas where he and his friends owned land. There was considerable anger among American members of Congress and Nicaraguan businessmen, two groups that had formerly tolerated the human rights abuses and stultifying economic polices of the Somoza regime.

Somoza had made many other powerful enemies by the late 1970s. His country was the first to send a diplomatic mission to the new state of Israel in 1948, garnering the Somoza family the enduring hatred of the Palestinian Liberation Organization. In 1961, Nicaragua was a staging area for the Bay of Pigs invasion, a fact that Fidel Castro did not forget. During the negotiations over the Panama Canal treaty, Anastasio Somoza tried mightily to interest the U.S. government in a new, sea-level canal through Nicaragua. This earned him the hatred of Omar Torrijos. Somoza continued to believe, however, that his anti-Communist rhetoric and "friendship" with the United States would bring the Americans to his aid if his regime faced real difficulties.

In making this assumption, Somoza lost sight of the fact that, while his relationship with the United States was all-important to him, it was not a high priority for people in the U.S. government. In fact, the Carter administration came into office with plans to use Nicaragua and Iran as showcases for America's new commitment to human rights as a foreign policy priority. Soon after taking the oath of office, Carter cut off military assistance to Nicaragua, citing the regime's poor human rights record. At the same time, several committees of the U.S. House of Representatives began holding hearings on human rights abuses in Nicaragua. These hearings often provided a forum for the most radical opponents of the regime, including members of the Marxist FSLN.

Carter's Nicaragua policy, however, was not consistent. Aid was restored in 1978, as the military threat from the Sandinistas grew more serious. On August 22, 1978, the Sandinistas made their boldest stroke in the war up to that time, an attack on the National Palace in Managua. Shooting their way into the seat of the Nicaraguan government, the guerrillas held 1500 people hostage, including many members of the Nicaraguan Congress. They demanded the release of fifty-nine colleagues from prison, $1 million in cash, and safe passage out of the country. For all of his tough talk about standing up to Communists, Somoza gave in to the FSLN's demands almost immediately. The attackers went to Cuba, where they received a hero's welcome.

The spectacle of Somoza having to give in to the demands of the FSLN after a strike at the very heart of the Nicaraguan government made the dictator look weak, as did the tepid support he received during the crisis from the U.S. government. The following month saw the beginning of a general insurrection in the most populous departments of Nicaragua. Somoza responded with air strikes on civilian population centers suspected of supporting the FSLN. Somoza's heavy-handed response to the insurgency brought another cut-off of U.S. assistance.

Also contributing to the American response was the success of the FSLN in presenting the world with a broad front of opposition to Somoza. While U.S. policy makers, both in Congress and in the Executive Branch, might have shied away from openly supporting a Marxist movement (indeed, the Somoza family had counted on exactly such reluctance for the previous forty-five years), they were reassured by the presence of non-Marxists in the anti-Somoza coalition. Business leaders, church leaders espousing liberation theology, and other seeming moderates stood alongside the Sandinista leadership in denouncing Somoza and promising to work together to build a new government "of neither the right nor the left" for the Nicaraguan people. After Somoza's departure, power rested in the hands of a five-person government of national reconstruction (GNR). The GNR featured prominent non-Communist moderates.

Within months of the Sandinista triumph, however, it was becoming clear that the FSLN leaders had no intention of keeping their promises to bring democracy to Nicaragua. In early 1980, prominent moderates were expelled from the ruling Council of State, and Eden Pastora, who had led the raid on the National Palace, was also in opposition to the Sandinista regime. The regime was increasing its pressure on the country's independent newspaper, on the Catholic Church (in spite of the fact that the Church had supported the revolution, and the Bishop of Managua marked the Sandinista victory by saying a Victory Mass in Managua), and on independent businesses.

Much more ominously for the United States, the FSLN began to strengthen their ties to Cuba and the Soviet Union. The regime also made increasingly obvious efforts to export their revolution to other countries in Central America. Arms shipments and other forms of support began to flow from the Sandinistas to Communist revolutionaries in Honduras and El Salvador.

Much of the debate over Nicaragua in the 1980s revolved around whether the U.S. government, through its supposedly hostile actions, had driven the Sandinistas into the arms of Cuba and the Soviet Union. The actual events show anything but U.S. hostility. American Secretary of State Cyrus Vance himself negotiated Somoza's departure. The U.S. government recognized the Sandinista government immediately. On September 2, 1979, Carter welcomed Sandinista President Daniel Ortega, along with other top-ranking Sandinistas, to the White House. By the end of their meeting with Carter, the Sandinistas had a commitment of $118 million in U.S. aid.

The Sandinistas and their supporters would later contend that the Sandinistas' embrace of Fidel Castro and the Soviet Union came only after Nicaragua was attacked by counterrevolutionaries in the pay of the American Central Intelligence Agency (CIA). This conclusion is not supported by the facts either. High-level contacts between the Sandinistas and Castro began even before the former had come to power. Then in March 1980, Ortega and Tomás Borge, head of Sandinista internal security, traveled to Havana and received firm promises of support from Castro. By the end of 1980, the Sandinistas were supporting Communist guerrilla movements in El Salvador and Honduras, and their leaders were speaking openly of a "revolution without frontiers." The Sandinistas had adopted a policy of hostility to the United States and its allies before Reagan became president.

El Salvador's Democratic Revolution

The Sandinistas' interest in fomenting revolution in El Salvador was particularly revealing of their intentions, since El Salvador in 1980 was not ruled by a typical right-wing military dictatorship like that of Somoza. In October, El Salvador became the site of the third Caribbean revolution of 1979. Unlike the first two, however, the revolution in El Salvador was non-Communist and promised genuine democracy for the small Central American nation.

El Salvador's 1979 revolution was a nightmare for Americans accustomed to easily identifiable, black-and-white characters in stories from Latin America (evil landowners versus dedicated land reformers; evil military dictators versus progressive democratic reformers). The upheaval was, first of all, fairly peaceful, since the departing military regime was sufficiently corrupt and rotten to fall without much violence. But what was more confusing for many Americans, what followed can best be described as a leftist (or at least leftish) civilian-military junta, a seeming contradiction in terms.

The postrevolutionary Salvadoran government was led by José Napoleón Duarte, the former mayor of San Salvador, whose reform credentials were unimpeachable. Duarte had been elected president in 1972 but had been forced into exile by the military. As a political activist for the left-leaning Christian Democratic Party, he had opposed military governments in the past and had been jailed and tortured by members of the Salvadoran military. The junta that took power in 1979 included other reformers with similar antimilitary credentials.

But the junta also contained a number of high-ranking military officers, some of whom had opposed democracy in the past. The division in the Salvadoran military mirrored the divisions in Salvadoran society. Again, for many American experts on Latin America, military officers came in only one variety: right-wing, antidemocratic, personally corrupt caricatures.

Opposing the civilian-military junta was the Faribundo Martí Liberation Front (FMLN), an armed guerrilla group made up of the five revolutionary groups pressured and bribed into unity by Fidel Castro. In large part, it was fear of the progress of the FMLN that prompted a number of military officers to forsake their colleagues in 1979 and join the prodemocracy junta. For some of these defecting military men, support for democracy was merely a cynical tactic, designed to fool the U.S. government into providing military and economic assistance. For others, the motivation was the genuine belief that only democracy could effectively counter the promises of the Marxist FMLN.

By 1979, it was clear to most Salvadorans that if the country were forced to choose between a traditional right-wing military dictatorship and a leftist revolutionary movement such as the FMLN, the latter would be the winner. Thus, when a third option appeared in 1979, in the form of the center-left junta, most analysts expected the threat from the FMLN to diminish. Exactly the opposite occurred. The FMLN leadership, along with their backers in Havana, in Moscow and (after July 1979) in Managua, concluded that the 1979 coup was testimony to their strength and redoubled their efforts to overthrow the Salvadoran regime.

An important part of their effort was to discredit the junta by denying its democratic credentials. Propaganda from Moscow and Havana consistently referred to the government in San Salvador as a "military dictatorship," as though there had been no change at all in October. It was this characterization of the Salvadoran government that dominated American newspaper accounts of events in the country well into 1980. As the visibility of the civilian President Duarte increased, the American media took to describing the government as "military-dominated." Both designations had the effect of making Americans reluctant to support the anti-Communist side.

The Salvadoran government did little to help its own cause. Transforming the Salvadoran military from an instrument of repression for a tiny governing elite, which had been its role for decades, into a force capable of fighting a sophisticated and well-armed guerrilla insurgency was a slow and difficult task. It was made all the more difficult by the tenacity of corrupt generals who enriched themselves while refusing to take the field against the guerrillas. Even senior officers who were not corrupt were unused to the rigors of a full-scale guerrilla war. (Frustrated U.S. military advisors would complain about the "nine-to-five" mentality of the Salvadoran military.)

Also contributing to the cause of the guerrillas were stunning human rights outrages attributed to the military. On March 24, 1980, the archbishop of San Salvador, Oscar Romero, was gunned down while in the act of saying Mass. Romero had been critical of both the Salvadoran government and the FMLN, but since his assassins wore military uniforms, the crime was generally attributed to the army. In December, four American church women, who had been working with Salvadoran peasants opposed to the junta, were raped and murdered. Again, both sides had a motive for killing the women, but the evidence linking the murders to members of the military was stronger.

While President Duarte condemned these actions and promised swift justice to the guilty, he seemed powerless to even insure that the crimes would be investigated, let alone insure punishment for the guilty. Throughout 1979 and 1980, civilian deaths in El Salvador's civil war mounted. *Death squad* became the term commonly used for groups of off-duty military officers and other disgruntled right-wing Salvadorans who killed with impunity. The spectacle of a Salvadoran military unwilling to face armed insurgents, but willing to kill labor leaders, teachers, nuns, and social workers fanned the flames of Marxist revolution in the country and insured that the FMLN would have a strong base of support in the United States.

Preparing for Reagan

Meanwhile, the cooperation of the Sandinistas in Nicaragua made shipment of arms and material to the FMLN easier, and the guerrillas made significant advances in 1979 and 1980. The Carter administration responded to the near-crisis situation in the country with substantial military and economic assistance and increasingly strong statements of support for President Duarte. With the election of Ronald Reagan in November 1980, the FMLN foresaw a much firmer U.S. response to its challenge to the pro-American Salvadoran government. The FMLN leadership decided to present the incoming anti-Communist president with a *fait accompli*. On January 10, 1981, the FMLN launched what it called its "Final Offensive" to overthrow the civilian-military junta. It did so with the full and vocal support of the Nicaraguan Sandinistas. The latter's support prompted the Carter administration to suspend economic assistance to Nicaragua on January 17, 1981.

Thus, Ronald Reagan inherited a Central America already in severe turmoil. From the day that Reagan announced for president, to the day he took office, Nicaragua had gone from being a staunch American ally to being an even more staunch ally of Cuba and the Soviet Union. El Salvador changed from a stable, if not terribly valuable, American ally to a nation under siege from a Communist insurgency that was at least as radical as the Sandinistas. Both Guatemala and Honduras faced the harrowing choice between right-wing governments and left-wing insurgencies. Grenada, situated near the southeastern entry point of the Caribbean Sea, was also a Soviet ally.

And in the middle of 1980, in the midst of the Iranian hostage crisis, the Soviet invasion of Afghanistan, spreading leftist revolution in Central America and southern Africa, and double-digit inflation and gas lines, Fidel Castro unleashed a terrifying new weapon in his ongoing war with the United States. On April 22, Castro opened the port of Mariel to anyone desiring to leave the country. Within days, a flood of refugees was headed toward south Florida. Eventually, 120,000 Cubans would enter the United States. Even under the best of circumstances, such a sudden flood of refugees would have had staggering consequences for the communities bearing the brunt of the human tide.

But in addition to the tens of thousands of honest and freedom-loving Cubans who came to the United States, Castro sent thousands of violent criminals, mental patients, and terrorists. The dictator virtually emptied his prisons and insane asylums and sent the inmates to the unsuspecting, and totally unprepared, residents of south Florida. The impact was devastating and was made more so by the slow and hesitant response from the Carter administration. It was not until May 14 that Carter ordered a blockade of private boats from Cuba. The refugees continued to pour in until Castro closed the port of Mariel in September.

Breaks in the Clouds

In spite of the bleak picture presented above, there were signs of hope in 1980. By the time that Reagan was elected, it was plain that he would have other world leaders to work with who were every bit as anti-Communist as he was. In October 1978, Karol Wojtyla, a Polish cardinal, became Pope John Paul II. His election would sow the seeds of Communism's eventual implosion in Eastern Europe. In May 1979, Conservative Party leader

Margaret Thatcher became prime minister of Great Britain. Like Reagan, she used harsh terms to criticize Soviet Communism, and she foreshadowed in England the orthodox capitalist reform that Reagan brought to the United States.

There were also signs of weakness in the U.S.S.R. Given the aggressiveness and seeming confidence of the Soviet Union in 1980, it was possible to ignore the glaring weaknesses that were beginning to become obvious in that country. In 1981, President Reagan received a top-secret CIA assessment of the Soviet Union (a summary that I saw when I worked in the White House in 1984). The document described appalling conditions in the Soviet Union, including rampant alcoholism and sharply rising abortion rates. Alone among industrialized countries, Soviet citizens in 1981 actually had a declining life expectancy. Food shortages and long lines were becoming endemic. Shortages of medical supplies were so severe that hypodermic needles were delivered to hospitals with instructions for sharpening and derusting.

It is possible that the very seriousness of the problems the Soviets faced in the late 1970s and 1980s prompted their leaders to take such enormous risks as the invasion of Afghanistan. The Soviet Union was by no means doomed in 1981. While it managed to hide many of its weaknesses, its aggression and adventurism were very real. The Soviet leaders worked to provoke a crisis in the United States before their country's own internal crises overwhelmed them.

As he prepared to take the Oath of Office, President-elect Ronald Reagan could barely look at a globe without seeing an area of crisis for the United States or an area in which the country appeared to be in retreat. In his autobiography, Reagan described his first night in the White House: "I peeked into the Oval Office as its official occupant for the first time. I felt a weight come down on my shoulders, and I said a prayer asking God's help in my new job." Certainly few in Latin America doubted that he would need the help of the Almighty to tackle the challenges awaiting him in America's own hemisphere.

And Reagan would face two further challenges, which I will describe in the next chapter. First, Reagan would have to overcome daunting domestic obstacles to creating a strong anti-Soviet foreign policy. These would include a weakened military and devastating economic problems. Even more discouraging was the reluctance of many Americans to criticize the Soviet Union, or even to use the word *Communism*. Before Reagan could act in Central America, he would have to reconquer the language of international relations.

The second challenge would be almost as difficult. For Reagan to impose his vision of a foreign policy based on freedom on his enemies, he would first have to impose that vision on much of the foreign policy bureaucracy of the United States. Throughout his eight years in the White House, Reagan faced not only the possibility of war outside the United States but also the daily reality of war within his own administration.

2

Infighting

Wars Over U.S. Foreign Policy

History is a river that may take us as it will. But we have the power to navigate, to choose direction, and to make our passage together.

—Ronald Reagan

Not only an unenviable international situation, but also unprecedented problems at home greeted Ronald Reagan when he became president. These included economic problems and problems of national morale. Reagan came to the presidency determined to make sweeping changes in the basic direction of both the domestic and foreign policies of the United States. With regard to foreign policy, Reagan faced practical difficulties related to making even minor changes, let alone the radical changes that he had in mind. Among his tasks would be to change the institutional culture of the U.S. foreign policy establishment.

It would take enormous determination for Reagan to press on with his agenda for his administration. It would also take focus, since not even the most determined president can do everything at once. The crisis in Central America was thrust onto Reagan's shoulders in his first days in office, and he decided that the region would be the first step in achieving his global foreign policy goals. It was here, as Secretary of State Alexander Haig stated, that Reagan would "draw a line in the sand." The new president would soon discover, if he did not know already, that he would have to draw some lines in the sand in Washington as well.

Blazing a New Path

In the early 1980s, American intellectuals believed, almost without exception, that the Soviet Union would continue to exist indefinitely and might even become more powerful than the United States. Harvard historian Arthur Schlesinger Jr. was apparently referring to Reagan when he said in 1982 that "those in the United States who think the Soviet Union is on the verge of economic and social collapse, ready with one small push to go over the brink, are wishful thinkers who are only kidding themselves." Another Ivy League expert stated, even more boldly, "The Soviet Union is not now, nor will it be during the next decade, in the throes of a true systematic crisis."

Economist John Kenneth Galbraith asserted as late as 1984 that "the Soviet system has made great material progress in recent years. . . . The Russian system succeeds because, in contrast with the Western industrial economies, it makes full use of its manpower." MIT professor of economics Lester Thurow asked in 1982, "Can economic command significantly compress and accelerate the growth process? The remarkable performance of the Soviet Union suggests that it can." (Neither expert mentioned that Soviet hospitals were sharpening hypodermic needles for reuse.)

By 1980, to call someone a "Communist," even someone in the Soviet Politburo, was considered, at best, behind the times. According to MIT's Paul Samuelson, to believe that Communism made people unhappy was "vulgar." To warn about the dangers of Communist subversion was to invite scorn and derision. In 1979, during all the question-and-answer sessions President Carter had with the media, he got exactly six questions from journalists that began with the assumption that the Soviet Union was an enemy. Carter himself often minimized the Soviet threat. He told graduates at Notre Dame in 1977, "[W]e are now free of that inordinate fear of communism." As late as 1979, on an occasion when he was asked if the Soviets sought world domination, Carter responded, "I don't have any inclination to condemn the Soviets as a people, or even as a government." It was only after the Soviet invasion of Afghanistan that Carter admitted he "no longer trust[ed]" Leonid Brezhnev.

Thus, among Reagan's other tasks would be the reintroduction of the words *Communist* and *Communism* into American political parlance and to turn these words back into pejoratives. Reagan believed that some Americans needed to be reminded that the U.S.S.R. was, in fact, an enemy of the United States, and he took care to do so early in his administration, long before his famous "evil empire" comment in 1983.

In his first news conference, Reagan was asked for his assessment of the Soviets' global intentions. His headline-making answer was, "[The Soviets] have openly and publicly declared that the only morality they recognize is what will further their cause, meaning they reserve unto themselves the right to commit any crime, to lie, to cheat, in order to attain that." Among the first official documents to come from his administration was a State and Defense Department document titled, "Communist Support for Subversion in Central America."

Reagan made clear not only his hostility toward Soviet Communism but also his future plans for it. In May 1981, Reagan told the graduates of Notre Dame, "The years ahead are great ones for this country, for the cause of freedom and the spread of civilization. The West won't contain communism, it will transcend communism. It won't bother to dismiss or denounce it; it will dismiss it as some bizarre chapter in human history whose last pages are even now being written."

At the time, most commentators assumed that Reagan's bellicose comment at South Bend was more of an empty applause line than a concrete statement of policy. In so assuming, the commentators missed the true significance of the new President's statement. Reagan was not just playing to the crowd; he was announcing his Administration's rejection of thirty-five years of American foreign policy, centered on the "containment" of the Soviet Union. Had Reagan understood the obstacles that he and his allies in his administration would have to overcome in Washington to bring about such a fundamental change in foreign policy, the task might have threatened even his eternal optimism.

How Foreign Policy is Made

Political pundits, textbook authors, and, to a large degree, political leaders themselves have given Americans an inaccurate picture of where foreign policy comes from. With most public documents on U.S. foreign policy published over the signature of either the president or the secretary of state, one can easily be misled into thinking first, that the president and secretary of state compose all the documents that they sign; and second, that these documents, and the policies that they contain, are part of a large, overarching, and consistent design.

One of the more misleading habits of commentators on U.S. foreign policy is their use of the pronouns *we, us,* or *our* when they speak or write about U.S. foreign policy. Examples include comments such as, "We tried to overthrow Castro with the Bay of Pigs invasion," or "It was only when Salvador Allende threatened to nationalize our copper companies that we decided to overthrow him," or "Our problem with Saddam Hussein had more to do with oil than with weapons of mass destruction." Closely related to this view is the expectation that U.S. foreign policy, from top to bottom, changes with each change in the U.S. presidency and that there will be particularly sweeping changes if a president from a different political party is inaugurated. This view ignores the larger percentage of American foreign policy that continues unchanged from one administration to the next.

Many textbooks on U.S. foreign policy contain brief acknowledgments that there is, in fact, continuity in the policy but are then divided into chapters titled after presidents. In some cases, authors are so committed to praising or blaming administrations for everything that happens on their watch, they ascribe things to presidents who have not yet taken office. Writing about El Salvador, for example, one author attributed the murder of left-leaning Archbishop Oscar Romero to the hard-line anti-Communist rhetoric of the Reagan administration, conveniently forgetting that the archbishop was killed months before Reagan was even elected.

While such retromonarchical treatments are becoming less usual, those that still exist downplay the vital role that permanent members of the foreign policy elite play, especially entry- to middle-level bureaucrats. Put differently, administration-based analyses assume that all elements of U.S. foreign policy receive the same amount of attention and input from senior policy makers, such as the president or secretary of state, and that the marching orders from the top are always consistent.

Given their basic assumption about the source of U.S. foreign policy decisions, analysts who focus on administrations are hard put to explain inconsistency or incoherence in foreign policy. They take refuge in the idea that foreign policy makers are sometimes irrational, not terribly bright, or simply evil. Former senator J. William Fulbright (D-AR), for example, said of Latin America: "We cannot successfully advance the cause of popular democracy and at the same time align ourselves with corrupt and reactionary oligarchies; yet that is what we seem to be trying to do . . . [T]he approach followed in the Dominican Republic, if consistently pursued, must inevitably make us the enemy of all revolutions and therefore the ally of all the unpopular and corrupt oligarchies of the hemisphere."

Speaking more boldly, foreign policy expert Hans Morgenthau suggested that focusing on the ideology of Communism during the Cold War, "strengthen[ed] another pathological tendency, which is the refusal to acknowledge in thought, and cope effectively with, a threatening reality." This is almost a textbook definition of irrationality. Townsend Hoppes analyzed the U.S. commitment in Vietnam by asking how so many intelligent, experienced, and humane men in government could have failed to understand the "immorality" of the Vietnam intervention and the "cancerous division" it had created in America. His answer, for a time the prevailing view, was that policy makers were emotionally dominated by the "cold war syndrome and its ramified legacy."

For many foreign policy experts, irrationality and evil as explanations for inconsistency are preferred over the possibility that there might be more than one U.S. foreign policy at any given time. Even the portrait of U.S. policy makers as stupid or irrational still requires the assumption that there are a small number of policy makers. In other words, if there are in fact large numbers of people who make foreign policy, and the foreign policy that they make is stupid or irrational, then they must all be stupid or irrational in the same way, at the same time.

Some experts do acknowledge the many-headed nature of U.S. foreign policy by focusing on the bureaucratic process that begets foreign policy. Stephen D. Cohen, for example, writes that in economic matters, foreign policy "emanates not from a centralized, objective decision maker, but from a conglomerate of large organizations and political actors with different missions, different perceptions, and different priorities. . . . More often than not, policy is determined by a committee-bred consensus that everyone can live with." Such analyses are closer to the truth, but these also have a drawback: where the retromonarchist assumes that the same people make every foreign policy decision, the process analyst is too prone to assuming that no one is in charge.

The truth lies between the two extremes. Presidents, national security advisors, secretaries of state, and other top officials do have a major role in creating and directing U.S. foreign policy. However, they are not the only important players. Reagan, like his predecessors, had to learn that he had far less control over foreign policy makers in his administration than he might have expected. Most men and women who create the foreign policy of the United States are not subject to the will of the president. This includes foreign service officers (FSOs), who staff nearly all the entry- and middle-level staff positions at the State Department. FSOs, like most civil servants, are protected by law from dismissal, except "for cause." This phrase has come to mean that, short of embezzling public funds, exhibiting gross incompetence, or committing outright treason, FSOs cannot be fired. Even to discipline a foreign service officer by, for example, transferring him or her to an undesirable overseas post is a difficult process steeped in time-consuming legal requirements.

The same is true of all but a small percentage of analysts and foreign policy makers in the Defense Department, the Central Intelligence Agency, the Treasury Department, the Commerce Department, and the other executive branch agencies that include people who make foreign policy. (Most Americans would probably be surprised to learn that there is an office for foreign policy in the Department of the Interior.) The president has even less sway over members of Congress and their staff members, who, by drafting legislation, also play a vitally important role in making foreign policy.

In fact, there are thousands of government officials who make U.S. foreign policy. Lower level officials can usually make policy without interference, or even supervision, from their nominal superiors in the Cabinet. By necessity, presidents and Cabinet members deal with problems with the greatest and most immediate import. They leave the (supposedly) noncritical policy-making decisions to the FSOs and other bureaucrats. With this reality in mind, it is not remarkable that there are inconsistencies and contradictions in U.S. foreign policy; what is remarkable is that there is any consistency at all. Yet there is consistency, because most of the thousands of anonymous foreign policy makers do have a common world view.

Many Goals, Few Tools

Government officials also have a common daily challenge: multitasking. A surprisingly large number of analyses and explanations of U.S. foreign policy revolve around the notion that a single action can be linked to a single goal. For example, some of Reagan's critics accused him of supporting the Salvadoran government against the guerrillas to please American business interests in El Salvador. Some of his critics said that he tried to overthrow the Sandinistas to send a signal to the Soviet Union. Still others said that Reagan supported democracy in Honduras or Guatemala only to spread U.S. influence in those countries.

Such comments are examples of how analysts can be exactly right, and absolutely wrong, at the same time. Reagan was trying to make El Salvador friendlier to American businesses, he was trying to communicate with the Soviet leadership with his actions in Nicaragua, and he did hope that democracy in Central America would result in more American influence there. However, to suggest that Reagan was taking actions in Central America, or indeed anywhere in the world, for one reason, and for only one reason, no matter what the reason, is to fundamentally misunderstand how foreign policy is made. Single-purpose analyses also misunderstand the much greater challenge of redirecting foreign policy, as Reagan desired to do.

Foreign policy makers, from the El Salvador desk officer up to the president of the United States of America, never do anything for just one reason. Presidential libraries are filled with memos to presidents and other senior policy makers, trying to tell them how to achieve several goals with the same action. Indeed, for a middle-level policy maker, the most certain way to get a senior policy maker to take advice is to convince one's superior that he or she will accomplish several goals by doing so.

Many people without firsthand experience in government do not realize just how opportunistic people in the foreign policy bureaucracy tend to be. Where the average television news viewer may see a guerrilla war in El Salvador, a foreign policy bureaucrat may see an opportunity to use the crisis in El Salvador to advance foreign policy goals in Angola, France, and the Soviet Union, all at the same time.

These are just the overseas arenas of activity, most likely to be seen by a foreign policy professional. A political appointee higher up the ladder, or an elected official, such as a senator or a president, looking at the same guerrilla war in El Salvador, will see opportunities and/or dangers in even more areas. A senator, like a foreign service officer, sees the links between El Salvador and Angola, France and the Soviet Union, but the senator also sees ways to use events in El Salvador to advance a bill on U.S. farm supports or to get a promise from the White House in return for an upcoming vote on military aid to El Salvador. The senator may remember that he or she has a constituent who is an expert on Latin America and see a way to do that constituent a favor. For presidents, the possible linkages are even more numerous.

For foreign policy makers, there are always far more dangers and opportunities than there is power to deal with all of them. The gap between what a president, senator, secretary of state or entry-level State Department official would like to accomplish with any given opportunity, and what he or she has the power to actually accomplish, is usually quite wide.

Under those circumstances, it is preferable, in fact it is absolutely necessary, to accomplish several goals, with the same effort, at the same time. Thus, analyses of U.S. foreign policy that rest on the assumption that decision makers have a single, isolated goal in mind when creating foreign policy are completely unrealistic. A secret 1979 memo to Carter on the meeting of the Policy Review Committee illustrates the determination to accomplish several goals at once. The group had discussed Nicaragua's dictator Anastasio Somoza. The memo summarized the committee's conclusion: "Steps should be taken to signal our displeasure with Somoza's intransigence and to get some distance between us, but without losing the possibility of influencing him in the future." Four days later, the same group met again and added "maintaining credibility with [Venezuelan] President [Carlos Andres] Perez" to the list of goals. A June 1979 secret memo to the secretary of state listed no fewer than nine "U.S. Objectives toward Central America."

Because of the myriad goals and objectives of foreign policy makers, they possess a common desire to extend their control over events around the world. The memo quoted above shows the perceived need in the foreign policy establishment to be able to influence, if not control, foreign governments to insure that the United States gets its way.

Foreign Aid as a Tool

Standing in the way of this desire for control is the fact that the tools with which policy makers can pursue their goals in foreign policy are also more limited than even most presidents expect they will be before taking office. The case of foreign aid is a useful case in point, and one that played a major role in U.S. foreign policy toward Central America during the Reagan years. It is theoretically possible to use foreign aid money as a carrot or stick to accomplish various kinds of foreign policy goals, but the reality is far more complicated.

First, the foreign aid budget of the United States of America in the 1980s totaled less than $5 billion per year, or less than 3 percent of the total budget of the United States. Of that amount, nearly half went to two countries, Egypt and Israel, as the result of promises made to their leaders at the 1978 Camp David meetings. Getting Congress to raise the amount of foreign aid in the budget is a difficult task under any circumstances. Support for increases in foreign aid among Americans is limited, unless it is targeted to a specific, and well-publicized, humanitarian need.

The second obstacle to the efficient use of foreign aid as a foreign policy tool is earmarking. This is reserving foreign aid by law for certain uses, making it not transferable to other uses. Only a small percentage of the small foreign aid budget is discretionary, and this percentage shrank during the Reagan years. The third obstacle to using foreign aid to increase the influence of the United States overseas is precommitment. Managers of foreign aid, both in the Congress and in the Executive Branch, are wary of dispensing large amounts of money to foreign governments without having some security that the money will not be misused. Since there is no effective way to insure the proper use of American aid once it is disbursed, most U.S. aid packages feature multiyear disbursements, with each year's money dependent on the recipient's good behavior (however defined) during the previous year. Discussions of foreign aid in Washington make frequent use of the phrase *money in the pipeline*. This phrase refers to aid that has been appropriated by Congress but not yet given to the recipient.

The fourth obstacle is the fact that the foreign aid "tool" is not only small and limited; it is also clumsy. While there are times when the threat to curtail aid, or the promise to increase aid, can induce a foreign leader to obey commands from the U.S. government, such times are far more rare than those without foreign policy experience might think. The threat to cut off U.S. aid is only useful until the threat actually has to be fulfilled. Once the U.S. government has cut off aid, it can no longer be used as leverage to get a desired outcome. If an aid cut-off does not bring the desired outcome, about the only option policy makers have is to offer to restore aid.

Moreover, the leaders of most U.S. aid recipients know that they would not be receiving aid in the first place if their country were not important to the United States. These leaders also know that only the most significant and blatant departures from U.S. government wishes are likely to make decision makers consider cancelling aid. As one expert on foreign aid put it, for American diplomats, relations with any given foreign country are either improving or deteriorating. Either way, the diplomats are likely to think that more foreign aid is the proper response.

Foreign aid from the United States government is not the only potential source of American economic leverage. U.S. officials hold important positions at the World Bank, the International Monetary Fund (IMF), and other multilateral lending institutions. In addition, private banks in the United States are in the habit of following the advice of U.S. government officials before making loans to foreign governments. In some circumstances, when it is not possible to reduce or cut off direct American aid, foreign policy bureaucrats may be able to threaten punitive action connected with a country's foreign debt.

In some cases, Central American nations did not have much foreign debt and therefore did not have to fear American officials interfering with their financial relationships. Evidence that U.S. officials found this situation objectionable is contained in a secret April 1982 Memorandum of Conversation between a Treasury Department official and the finance minister of Guatemala. According to the memo, Treasury's director of the Office of Developing Nations pressured the Guatemalan government to borrow more money from IMF. "Given its resource base," the official recalled, "Guatemala had a potential for borrowing on a larger scale."

Despite the limitations of foreign aid as a foreign policy tool, it is the preferred method of policy makers to get their way in foreign affairs. Some diplomatic methods are easier to use, such as simple persuasion, but they are seen as even less effective than raising or lowering the amount of foreign aid. Other methods, such as bribery, assassination, sanctions, blockades, or even military force, can be more effective, at least in the short term, but they bring huge risks and complications.

Thus, when Reagan confronted the deepening crisis in Central America when he took office, he did so with a rather limited number of tools at his disposal. Reagan was not daunted by this situation, since he did not discount the value of persuasion in dealing with political opponents. Drawing on his experience as a labor union president, a "pitchman" for General Electric, and a California governor, Reagan came to the presidency with enormous (his critics would say unfounded) confidence in his ability to successfully negotiate with anyone.

Reagan also had a heart-felt faith that political liberty and economic success were universally held aspirations for men and women around the world. Most people, Reagan believed, want to be free and prosperous. The barriers to these goals were leaders who were either ignorant of the benefits of freedom or maliciously standing in the way of freedom. Only with the second group might force be needed. Reagan truly believed that most people, in most of the world, under most circumstances, would be natural allies in his crusade for liberation. Reagan soon learned that, in this regard, he differed from many people in the U.S. foreign policy establishment.

A Preference for "Stability" and a Desire for "Leverage"

Most U.S. foreign policy bureaucrats are well educated in the academic theories of U.S. foreign policy. Most would have read, for example, Norman Graebner's analysis of twentieth-century U.S. foreign policy, which begins with the comment: "Viewing the world from a pinnacle, [American scholars and statesmen] had agreed long before 1914 that the nation's favored position required above all a high degree of international stability." More recently, Robert Tucker summarized U.S. foreign policy this way: "For a period of well over half a century American statesmen effectively pursued an expansionist strategy aimed at 'stabilizing the world in a pro-American equilibrium' and did so on the whole using methods congenial to American power and interests."

Former National Security Adviser and Secretary of State Henry Kissinger was a member of the "realist" school of international theory, and he was most explicit in his preference for stability. Writing before he held a government position, Kissinger said: "The greatest need of the contemporary international system is an agreed concept of order. . . . A new concept of international order is essential; without it stability will prove elusive." That stability is desirable seems self-evident to Kissinger. In the same essay, he underlines the point: "A mature conception of our interest in the world would obviously take into account the widespread interest in stability."

Similar, representative statements by other U.S. secretaries of state are strong evidence of the existence and durability of U.S. foreign policy makers' preference for stability in international affairs. While "stability" can mean a number of different things, for U.S. foreign policy bureaucrats, it almost always refers to the ability of U.S. policymakers to affect outcomes, using "leverage." If one accepts the idea that U.S. officials will, and should, pursue America's self-interest and assumes that the leaders of other countries may not be inclined to pursue America's interest with equal enthusiasm, it naturally follows that U.S. officials will, and should, apply various forms of pressure to get their way.

Kissinger considered the 1970s' oil shocks to be strong evidence of the potentially dangerous divergence of interests between the United States and the OPEC nations. He said in 1977: "[F]or the first time in our history, a small group of nations controlling a scarce resource could over time be tempted to pressure us into foreign policy decisions not dictated by our national interest." Later, he added: "Our prosperity is to some extent hostage to the decisions on raw materials, prices and investment in distant countries whose purposes are not necessarily compatible with ours."

The international system was complicated, Kissinger insisted, by the emergence of new nations that were not part of the traditional international political system. "Today," he wrote in 1969, "statesmen face the unprecedented problem of formulating policy for well over a hundred countries. Every nation, no matter how insignificant (sic), participates in international affairs." Worse, emerging nations see the world so differently, as to make diplomacy almost impossible. Kissinger warned, "A similar outlook about aims and methods eases the tasks of diplomacy—it may even be a precondition for it. In the absence of such a consensus, diplomats can still meet, but they lose the ability to persuade."

John Lewis Gaddis spoke in graver (and more condescending) terms about the likely source of disruption of "the existing distribution of power" in the 1980s. It was not the Soviets whom American officials should fear, Gaddis insisted. "It is, rather, a small and poorly understood group of states, primitive, by most standards, in their economic development, medieval in their subordination of state and even multistate interests to the dictates of religion, unsophisticated in their knowledge of the outside world and for the most part heedless of the effects of their actions upon it, and yet in a position . . . to bring the West to a grinding halt."

In the view of the leading academic voices on U.S. foreign policy, when Americans have to deal with such "primitive," "medieval," and "unsophisticated" leaders, who may control vital natural resources, or command strategic geographic locations, or be in a position to aid enemies of the U.S., American foreign policy makers face the choice of either applying pressure or seeing vital U.S. interests sacrificed. Most FSOs agree that these are the only choices and that the second does not merit serious consideration.

The desire for leverage is also connected to the multiple objectives that foreign policy makers are pursuing at any given time. When there are many goals, and limited tools to achieve them, policy makers will naturally wish to be able to give orders and not to waste time with persuasion.

Leveraged Allies and Natural Allies

Not all members of the foreign policy elite accept the Kissinger-Morgenthau realist view that conflict is endemic to international relations and that the quest for more power is inescapable. Some members of the elite adhere to the "idealist" tradition, harking back to President Woodrow

Wilson. The WWI president insisted upon the existence of universally applicable moral principles, derived from divine sources. Wilson rejected the permanence of conflict, strife, and warfare in international politics. He firmly believed in the necessity and usefulness of a powerful international organization to deter and, if necessary, defeat aggressors. Such international criminals would appear only rarely, in Wilson's view, and most of those who appeared would be deterred by "world opinion," given voice and strength by the League of Nations.

But Wilson had one element in common with Kissinger: the assumption that the United States would occasionally have to use power (or leverage) to achieve desired outcomes. The difference between the followers of Wilson and Kissinger had to do with when the U.S. government should use power, what kind of power ought to be used, and whether such exercises of power would be constant or sporadic. Put differently, both idealists and realists believe that great powers, however defined, will have to use some kind of coercion to get their way.

In the early Cold War policies of the top decision makers in the Truman administration, realism was the theory of choice, and the theory was applied to the goal of containing the Soviet Union. But critics of the realist point of view still saw the desirability of American leverage over developing countries, for different reasons. Senator J. William Fulbright (D-AR), for example, lauded President Lyndon Johnson for comparing John F. Kennedy's Alliance for Progress with his own "enlightened program for a Great Society at home." Fulbright added that the "real friends" of America, in Latin America at least, were "people of the democratic left." Fulbright had no problem with intervention, or with the use of leverage, as long as it was on behalf of "our real friends" in Latin America.

What both Wilsonian idealists and Kissingerian realists seem to fear was the possibility of other countries becoming impervious to American applications of leverage. For foreign policy bureaucrats, such independence of action on the part of foreign leaders is to be avoided. Early in the Carter administration, Robert A. Pastor, who handled Latin American affairs for the National Security Council, lamented recent trends in Latin America that most Americans, had they known about them, would have regarded as positive. In a confidential March 14, 1977, memo to Zbigniew Brzezinski, Pastor wrote: "[R]elatively rapid economic development and increasingly institutionalized governments have made [Latin American countries] more resistant to foreign influence, particularly North American influence."

Viron Vaky, Carter's assistant secretary of state for Latin America, was quoted in an October 1979 secret memo to Brzezinski as saying the U.S. government "should adopt the Cubans' strategy [in El Salvador]: identify a group and give them whatever is necessary to seize power." Some U.S. officials sought leverage over larger and more powerful states as well. In July 1986, Elliot Abrams, Vaky's successor at state, suggested to Secretary of State George Shultz that the U.S. government should "indirectly influence the selection of a successor to [Mexican president Miguel] de la Madrid who will continue reforms, cooperate with the U.S., and maintain stability."

Leverage over the leaders of other countries is useful for another reason. Members of the U.S. foreign policy bureaucracy, for the most part, prefer to face international crises with partners, in order to share the costs (and risks) of exercising power in international relations. On the surface, this would seem to contradict the contention that foreign policy elites fundamentally distrust foreign leaders and prefer coercion to persuasion. In fact, there is no contradiction. Partnerships do not threaten American hegemony if the partners are clearly subordinate partners. Put differently, there is more "stability" in relationships in which "allies" have little or no choice but to follow America's lead. Such nations may be referred to as "leveraged allies."

The desire for stability and leverage is dominant in the foreign policy bureaucracy, but there are members of that bureaucracy with an opposing view. Some officials in the State Department, the CIA, or elsewhere believe, as Reagan did, that coercion was not necessarily a precondition of cooperation in U.S. overseas activities. Reagan's statements on the importance of democracy seemed to be motivated not only by an ideological preference for self-government but also by a confidence that democratic nations will almost invariably be the natural and reliable allies of the United States. With enough democratic nations in the world, the United States will have a selection of potential allies for any given crisis. Provided that the United States adequately maintains its own defense capability, it will be able to protect its interests with a relatively small number of allies.

Allies who follow America's lead because of a common perception of interests and goals, which Reagan believed would usually happen with democracies, are more valuable than allies who follow out of the fear of U.S. "leverage." Moreover, leverage only works on nations that need American assistance in some form or another. Reagan's frequently stated desire for "prosperous" democracies had a double meaning. On the one hand,

Reagan was expressing the ideological view that democracy will naturally and inevitably lead to economic prosperity (at least compared to what is possible under more repressive regimes). On the other hand, Reagan believed that prosperous nations, which can contribute more resources to a joint effort, are more helpful allies than dependent nations, even if the latter are more easily coerced into cooperation.

Loving the Cold War

For foreign policy elites who prefer leveraged allies to natural allies, Reagan's stated desire to end the Cold War was chillingly threatening. His insistence upon that desire guaranteed bloody bureaucratic warfare in the agencies that made foreign policy. (Such warfare will be the recurring subplot of all the chapters that follow.) Removing the menace of Soviet subversion threatened to also remove a major source of leverage for American policy makers.

Nicaragua makes an excellent case in point. Since the 1930s, the Somoza family and its adherents had argued that right-wing dictatorship, backed up with an alliance with the U.S. government, was the country's only protection against Communist subversion. Indeed, the Somozas often gave the impression that Nicaragua was a prime target of the Soviet Politburo. The first Somoza dictator was successful enough in convincing U.S. policy makers of the same thing that Franklin Roosevelt once reportedly described him as: "a son of a bitch, but he's OUR son of a bitch."

As leveraged allies, the Somoza dictators were perfect. The dictatorship had been installed with the assistance of U.S. officials, which meant that none of the Somozas ever had a high level of popular support in Nicaragua. Instead, the Somozas required American support to remain in power. This is the very definition of leverage. The Somozas insured that they would continue to depend on U.S. government assistance by pursuing economic policies that prevented Nicaragua from making real economic progress. The combination of Somoza cronyism, corruption, and incompetence placed heavy shackles on the Nicaraguan economy.

The lack of economic progress, at the same time, guaranteed that there would always be a sizable percentage of Nicaraguans ready and willing to listen to Marxist rhetoric. It was just a matter of time before a Communist insurgency took root in the country, and while the Somoza dictatorship could contain a strictly home-grown revolutionary movement indefinitely, it would need additional American support to fend off serious intervention from the Soviet Union or Cuba. Moreover, the threat of outside Communist intervention made some Nicaraguans acquiesce in the Somoza dictatorship, even Nicaraguans who would otherwise insist on a free society and a free economy.

Absent the Soviet threat, neither democratically inclined Nicaraguans nor human-rights-minded North Americans would have any incentive to tolerate a dictatorship. For Somoza, this would mean the loss of his bargaining position with U.S. officials. For those officials, accustomed to having leverage available if needed to influence Somoza's actions, the disappearance of the Soviet threat could mean the end of their leverage. Absent the Soviet threat, it would no longer be possible to persuade human rights organizations or concerned members of Congress that Somoza was necessary to U.S. national security and in need of American funds. Without those funds at their disposal, the leverage of U.S. officials would disappear.

Without holding the presidency, the Somoza clan would no longer be able to manage the country's economic policy, which it did to its own benefit, but to Nicaragua's detriment. Nicaragua in the 1970s was actually fairly well off, as developing countries go. The nation is not without natural resources, and, before the destruction of the civil war, and a decade of Sandinista economic incompetence, Nicaragua had a reasonably good infrastructure, a sizeable middle class of businesspeople, and a productive agricultural sector. Despite the Somozas, it was possible to envision a self-sufficient Nicaragua in the 1970s. Looking one step further, it is also possible to envision a strong Nicaraguan economy lifting up the other economies in the region, moving more U.S. aid recipients, such as Honduras and Guatemala, toward self-sufficiency. Self-sufficiency means no more need for foreign aid, which means no more leverage. It was this future that Pastor warned against in his 1977 memo to Brzezinski.

Somoza was hardly alone in the world as a dictator leveraged by U.S. government support. He was not even alone in the region. Dozens of right-wing dictators used the threat of Communism, and the Cold War, as a method of staying in power and, simultaneously, of giving leverage to American officials. Reagan's crusade to end the Cold War was almost as large a threat to right-wing dictators as it was to left-wing dictators. Minimally, it meant a sizeable disruption of long-established and mutually beneficial relationships between dictators and U.S. foreign policy bureaucrats.

However, reducing the threat of outside Communist intervention, replacing dictators with democratic leaders, and bolstering the economies of developing nations all promised to create more natural allies for the United States. While the dominant preference in the foreign policy bureaucracy might have been for a dependent and leveraged Nicaragua under Somoza, it was at least possible to envision a democratic Nicaragua, with a growing economy, freely making common cause with the United States in the region.

The Reagan administration was an unusually divided one. Moreover, its divisions were often out in the open, thanks to the propensity of officials to leak information to the media. Scholars and analysts have taken great pains to categorize and explain the multiplicity of voices emanating from the Reagan administration. Some analysts have focused on the conflicts between conservatives and liberals, between "hawks" and "doves," between "true believers" and "moderates," between the State Department and the Defense Department, and between presidential appointees and permanent bureaucrats. In the internal wars of the Reagan administration over Central America policy, it was the conflict between those who preferred leveraged allies and those who preferred natural allies that best explained the sometimes bewildering cacophony of voices from the administration.

Reagan's Offensive

It is not clear whether or not Reagan realized all of the forces he was challenging when he made his Notre Dame speech and followed it up with concrete actions to challenge the existence of the U.S.S.R. Except for one or two tantalizing hints, he makes no mention of this aspect of foreign policy making in his autobiography. Nevertheless, it is clear from the nature of the opposition Reagan faced from his own foreign policy bureaucracy, which will be detailed in the succeeding chapters, that not everyone in his administration supported his efforts to permanently weaken the Soviet Union.

In spite of the widespread opposition it generated, inside and outside the administration, Reagan gradually unveiled a four-pronged attack on the Soviet Union during the first two years of his presidency. The details of his offensive have been much more fully treated elsewhere, so a brief summary will suffice, to show the pivotal role played by Reagan's policy for Central America.

The first prong of the attack was rhetorical and psychological. It included statements such as the ones at Reagan's first news conference and at Notre Dame. Reagan continued this part of his attack by telling the

British Parliament in 1982: "It is the Soviet Union that runs against the tide of history. . . . [It is] the march of freedom and democracy which will leave Marxism-Leninism on the ash heap of history as it has left other tyrannies which stifle the freedom and muzzle the self-expression of the people." Most famously, he told the National Association of Evangelicals in 1983 that the Soviet Union was an "evil empire."

Like foreign policy makers, Reagan rarely did things for just one reason. Rhetoric of this kind was designed to threaten the Soviet Union, to reclaim the anti-Communist vocabulary that had fallen into disrepute, to assure his conservative supporters that he was unchanged by the presidency, to get news coverage, and to signal his own bureaucracy that he would be the spokesman for his administration's foreign policy.

Aggressive oratory was not the only part of Reagan's psychological offensive against the Soviet Union. Soon after taking office, Secretary of State Haig discontinued a long-standing privilege of the Soviet ambassador. Anatoly Dobrynin had been accustomed to entering the State Department via a private entrance, thus avoiding the gauntlet of media that sometimes congregated at the Department's main entrance. Under Reagan, the Soviet ambassador received the same treatment as other foreign representatives, which the Soviets interpreted as a denial of their special status as the only other superpower. This is exactly the psychological effect that Reagan and Haig desired.

The second prong of Reagan's offensive was economic. The first element of the economic attack was to deny the Soviets hard currency. Reagan brought enormous pressure to bear on Western European countries to postpone or cancel work on a natural gas pipeline from the U.S.S.R. Reagan was determined enough to prevent the Soviets from profiting from the sale of natural gas that he was willing to put new strains on the NATO alliance. Reagan also ordered U.S. representatives at multi-national banking organizations to use whatever means possible to deny the Soviets access to hard currency loans.

The second part of the economic offensive was to create the conditions for an economic boom in the United States. Strong, sustained expansion of the American economy would, among other things, provide the tax revenues necessary for a large buildup of American military forces. In fact, Reagan was committed to the military buildup regardless of the pace of economic growth. His critics would charge he was gambling, recklessly, that the Soviets would bankrupt themselves just before America did. By blocking the flow of hard currency, and compelling the Soviets to spend more and more money, Reagan was squeezing at both ends.

The final piece of the economic plan was to toughen the U.S. line on technology transfer to the U.S.S.R. The wherewithal for modernization of the Soviets' military hardware, not to mention the modernization of their civilian economy, came largely from the West. Defense Secretary Caspar Weinberger sought to pinch off this route to economic survival for the Soviet Union. Reagan's critics again charged he was acting contrary to American economic interests, by preventing American companies from doing high-technology business with the Soviets.

The third prong of the offensive was technological. As a 1981 CIA assessment showed, the Soviet economy was in serious trouble, and its social indicators were appalling. By 1981, the Soviet Union was barely able to continue its subsidy to Fidel Castro, and it was rapidly losing its ability to act the part of superpower by using money. Its economic model was increasingly rejected by developing nations (even if it was still admired by some Harvard economists). About the only instrument the Soviets had that kept them a superpower was their massive nuclear arsenal.

In March 1983, the same month as the "Evil Empire" speech, Reagan proposed the Strategic Defense Initiative, usually called the "Star Wars" plan. Without going into details, Reagan called upon American scientists to create a way to destroy nuclear missiles before they could reach the United States. While there was great skepticism about the practical possibility of deploying such a system, there can be no question about its political and diplomatic impact. Reagan repeatedly expressed the hope that nuclear weapons could be made obsolete. For the Soviets, this meant losing their superpower status.

The Star Wars proposal generated almost as much opposition in Washington as it did in Moscow. Few observers were quite sure what impact the proposal would have on continuing arms control talks with the Soviets. One expert described the Strategic Defense Initiative (SDI) as a decision by Reagan to take the most basic question of national security, survival in the nuclear age, out of the hands of American diplomats and to place it in the hands of American scientists and technicians, who were the best in the world. It is not surprising that the diplomats took a dim view of their replacement. Moreover, by denying the Soviets the use of nuclear weapons, Reagan was implicitly rejecting containment once again and looking toward the day when the U.S.S.R. would no longer exist. Many foreign policy professionals either rejected that vision or were simply unable to imagine it.

The most optimistic estimate of the time when SDI might be deployable was the early 1990s. In the meantime, Reagan moved to implement the fourth prong of his anti-Soviet offensive, which was a military challenge to the Soviets. As we saw in chapter 1, the Soviets and their allies were militarily active in Afghanistan, Southeast Asia, the Horn of Africa, southern Africa, and Central America. Since the 1960s, the Soviets had been on the offensive in the small-scale proxy wars that marked the middle years of the Cold War.

By the middle of the 1980s, the Soviets and their allies would be facing anti-Communist guerrilla movements. But in 1981, except for assistance to the Afghan resistance, the United States was not yet able to turn the tables on the Soviets. They would retain the initiative a while longer, but in the meantime, Reagan was determined to counter the attacks of guerrilla armies funded and supplied by the U.S.S.R. more forcefully and effectively. Put differently, Reagan intended first to stop the forward momentum of Communism, preparatory to reversing that momentum. As usual, Reagan had other goals in mind as well: promoting democracy, freeing developing economies, and shrinking the power of the U.S. foreign policy bureaucracy. Confronting Soviet expansion was, however, the primary goal.

Reagan was much in the same position as U.S. war planners in 1942, after the Japanese had launched successful offensives at Pearl Harbor, the Philippines, Singapore, Guam, Hong Kong, and the Dutch East Indies. By July, Australia itself was threatened by the Japanese offensive at Guadalcanal. It was not the most auspicious place for the United States to begin its counterattack. The Japanese knew the area, they were already entrenched, and they were beginning their final offensive to seize the rest of the island. Japanese troops were able to present themselves as the liberators from colonialism. Few Americans, on the other hand, knew or cared about Guadalcanal, and some of those who did questioned its importance in the war's overall strategy. Fighting in a Dutch colony would bring political complications also. Finally, there were serious problems of logistics and supply, especially with the U.S. military stretched to the breaking point by commitments elsewhere in the world. A counteroffensive at Guadalcanal promised to be long, difficult, and risky.

In 1981, an eerily analogous situation existed in Central America. The Soviets and Cubans were already there, and the Cubans knew the region. The Salvadoran guerrillas had just begun their Final Offensive to take over the country. Leftist guerrillas portrayed themselves as anti-imperialists. Few Americans were familiar with the conflicts in Central

America, and fewer still were convinced of the wisdom of confronting the Soviets there, with the American military facing challenges all over the globe. Like Guadalcanal, Central America was the key to a continent, in this case, North America. Assistance to the Salvadoran government promised to be fraught with political difficulties. The American presence in El Salvador would be long, difficult, and risky.

Yet, like the Japanese in Guadalcanal, the Soviet proxies in El Salvador were at the extreme end of a long and tenuous supply line and an even more tenuous political alliance. Moreover, El Salvador, for all of the political and logistical challenges it posed, was the place where confronting the Soviets was most urgent. While continuing to prepare for other offensives in other places, the Reagan administration ignored the skeptics and openly confronted the Soviets for the first time in Central America. El Salvador would become the Cold War's Guadalcanal.

3

Opening Moves

The "Final Offensive," 1981

The uprising's object is to seize power. Its political task will be clarified after the seizure. . . . The people have the right and duty to solve such questions, not by voting, but by force.

—*Lenin*, 1917

On December 30, 1980, the "government-in-exile" of the Salvadoran guerrillas made an announcement at its headquarters in Mexico City. The Faribundo Martí Liberation Front (FMLN) proclaimed that the rebels had their answer to the staunchly anti-Communist Ronald Reagan, now president-elect of the United States. The leaders of the FMLN were determined not to give Reagan the chance to demonstrate what his new hemispheric anti-Communist policy might look like. Instead, the guerrilla spokesman promised to present Reagan with an "irreversible situation in El Salvador by the time he reaches the presidency." The guerrillas, he promised, would soon begin their "Final Offensive" against the U.S.-backed government. So confident were the FMLN guerrillas at this stage that they gave themselves a scant three weeks after their dramatic announcement to overthrow the Salvadoran government.

Background: El Salvador in 1981

The guerrillas and their backers had good reason for confidence as Reagan prepared for the presidency. El Salvador, the smallest and most densely populated country in Central America, seemed on the brink of collapse. The Salvadoran army was small, largely corrupt, and largely incompetent. There were almost as many guerrillas under arms as soldiers. The civilian-military junta was wracked by infighting and inexperience. Some of its most prominent members were defecting to join the opposition. U.S. military aid had been cut off since 1977, and in the waning days of his presidency, Carter seemed understandably reluctant to take time away from crises in Iran, Afghanistan, and the Middle East to direct attention to Central America.

In many ways El Salvador was not the typically dependent "banana republic" of Latin American lore. Unlike many of its neighbors, El Salvador never once in its history saw armed U.S. Marines arrive. The people of El Salvador did not exhibit any particularly strong anti-U.S. feelings until the late 1970s. While the country was a nominal ally of the United States in the Cold War, neither side seemed to believe that El Salvador would contribute anything to the Cold War struggle except an occasional pro-United States vote at the United Nations (UN) or Organization of American States (OAS). There were no U.S. military bases in El Salvador. U.S. Navy ships stopped there only very rarely. The country's economic assistance from the United States was also minimal.

El Salvador never had large parts of its natural resources or arable land owned by foreigners. While coffee was its largest and most important export, the country also raised and sold cotton, sugar, beef, and indigo for export. During the 1970s, El Salvador's exports expanded most years, as did its Gross Domestic Product (GDP). In 1980, while some still circulated stories of the oligarchy of the "Fourteen Families," who supposedly controlled the national wealth, 1,139 people controlled about two-thirds of El Salvador's economic assets. (To be a true "oligarchy," each of the "Fourteen Families" would have to have eighty-one people directly involved in ownership, and all eighty-one of these family members would have to have the same economic interests.) While land ownership in El Salvador was certainly concentrated, it was not any more concentrated than in Mexico, where there was not widespread discontent

But El Salvador's success as an export economy, and especially its success in raising and exporting coffee, was sowing the seeds for a peasant uprising. Compared to its Central American neighbors, El Salvador is crowded, with a population density of nearly three hundred persons per square kilometer. The countryside had long harbored tensions and conflicts between subsistence farmers and export farmers. Until the 1960s, while El Salvador's overall economy remained small and weak, subsistence farmers dominated the countryside. When coffee became a profitable export, and sugar, cotton, and beef joined it, the drive for consolidation in the rural areas of the country accelerated.

Occasionally, tensions in the countryside erupted into violence. Most Salvadoran peasants remembered, or had heard about, the 1932 peasant uprising that was brutally suppressed by the Salvadoran government, at the cost of more than thirty thousand lives. Wealthy Salvadorans never forgot 1932 either but focused their memories on the fact that the rebellion was led by members of El Salvador's Communist Party. Since 1932, the specter of Communism was a convenient method of condemning all attempts to ameliorate living conditions in rural El Salvador.

Stirrings of Change: The October 1979 Coup

A ruling class that routinely names its opponents Communists and constantly warns of violent revolution, while at the same time preventing any noticeable positive evolution in the status of the majority, is also likely to be frightened by democracy. For most of the country's history, El Salvador has been ruled by military dictatorship. At times, the military would hold fraudulent elections to mask the true nature of the regime. At other times, the military would hold free elections but ignore the results if the winners were people the military considered dangerous or Communistic.

As late as 1979, it was possible to believe that this system would serve El Salvador's rulers indefinitely. Still, there were warning signs. By the late 1970s, a number of Latin American countries were beginning the transformation to democracy, setting an example to which Salvadoran dictators would eventually have to pay attention. In 1972 and 1977, the ruling class had used fraud to steal elections, again, and called upon the military to enforce its wishes, but the level of repression necessary was increasing. In July 1979, the Sandinistas came to power in Nicaragua, overthrowing a pro-American dictator.

All of these trends gave hope to the Salvadoran leftists, and the number willing to take up arms against the government of El Salvador grew rapidly. The government of General Carlos Humberto Romero, however, was unwilling to take the steps necessary to quell the growing rebellion in the rural areas. Romero responded to the challenge with old-style repression, which was inadequate for dealing with a new and much more sophisticated threat. Moreover, unlike anti-Communist Latin American governments in the past, Romero could not take the support of the U.S.

government for granted. President Jimmy Carter had cut off military aid to El Salvador in 1977 to protest the repression of human rights.

Some of Romero's colleagues in the army concluded that the traditional manner of confronting Marxist revolution was doomed to fail. In their view, significant political and economic changes would have to come to El Salvador to counter the leftists. On October 15, 1979, a group of reform-minded military officers, mostly colonels, placed President Romero under arrest and advised him to leave the country immediately. The rebellious officers also gained control of the government radio station and the key military garrisons around the capital city. U.S. Embassy officials had been informed in advance of the coup by some of its leaders, who asked the Americans what their attitude would be to a civilian-military government committed to reform. Upon receiving vague assurances that the U.S. government would look favorably on such a development, the plotters permitted the coup to go forward.

Within hours of the seizure of power, the army announced that some prominent civilians would be added to the ruling junta. The leader of the government was Román Mayorga Quiroz, the rector of the Jesuit Central American University. Within days, the hybrid interim government announced a series of significant reforms. El Salvador's banks were nationalized, and the junta unveiled a three-stage proposal for radical land redistribution. On the political side, the new government promised to end human rights abuses by the military and to bring the perpetrators of past abuses to justice. The junta also promised elections for a Constituent Assembly to write a new constitution.

Some on the left, like Guillermo Ungo, long-time supporter of the revolutionary groups attempting to overthrow the government, concluded that the time had come to try to change El Salvador from the inside. Ungo accepted an appointment to the junta. The armed guerrillas, for their part, insisted that nothing had really changed in El Salvador, except the faces of a few people nominally in charge. The military, insisted the rebels, still held the real power, and thus the armed struggle, they argued, was still the only viable alternative to military governments.

For those military officers who genuinely desired reform, some had high hopes for the political and economic success of land reform, bank nationalization, and other basic reforms. Others viewed these policies much more skeptically and believed that they were more likely to bring severe economic hardship to the country. Many of those who supported the reforms also hoped that they would bring financial and political support from the U.S. government. Many of those who were wary of the reforms agreed that the Americans were now more likely to send money, but they wondered what level of American interference would accompany the American aid.

˙Thus, beyond wanting to be rid of the old dictator and to score political points against the guerrillas, the members of the October 1979 junta had very little in common. It is not surprising, therefore, that the junta did not last long. Disagreements over the pace of land reform, over the prosecution of military officers, and over the relative strengths of military officers and civilians in the Cabinet prompted the resignation of all the civilian members of the junta on January 3, 1980.

Three days later, the Christian Democratic Party, the largest civilian, centrist party in El Salvador, held a party congress to nominate replacements for the party members who had just resigned. Some Christian Democrats were already convinced that collaboration with the military, even the officers ostensibly committed to reform, was a mistake. These members wished to have no representation on the junta, and they were convinced that the party's withdrawal would cause the junta to collapse, paving the way for a completely civilian regime. Other Christian Democrats were just as strongly convinced that it was their responsibility to continue working from the inside. Eventually, a compromise was reached. The Christian Democrats would reenter the junta, on the condition that the army publicly commit itself to reform and that no representatives of the Salvadoran business community be included on the junta or in the Cabinet.

Not surprisingly, the business community feared the effects of its exclusion. From their point of view, businessmen were necessary to rein in the more economically risky moves that the Christian Democrats had in mind. For groups such as the National Association for Private Enterprise (ANEP), the junta's reform program was likely to cripple the Salvadoran economy, at least in the short term, and make the country more and more dependent on foreign assistance. Avoiding dependence was also a priority for many military officers, so San Salvador became rife with rumors of another coup.

In February 1980, the rumors prompted strong pressure from the U.S. Embassy, directed at ranking military officers, warning that a rightist coup could easily erupt into civil war, and in that case, the U.S. government would not intervene. Without U.S. help, some generals feared, the rebels would win outright. As it happened, the extraordinary U.S.

pressure only postponed the coup attempt until the night of April 30, 1980. Although the attempt to topple the government failed, it did bring prominence to Major Roberto D'Aubuisson, who would play a major part in El Salvador's political infighting for the next eight years. D'Aubuisson was arrested but later freed when a judge declared there was insufficient evidence to prosecute him.

In the process, D'Aubuisson became a hero to Salvadorans concerned not only about the threat from the Communists but also about the threat of domination by the United States. For many Salvadorans, D'Aubuisson's actions were not seen as evidence of his hatred for democracy but rather as proof that he would stand up to the American embassy. D'Aubuisson built his future political career on giving exactly this impression. It was a part of his appeal that continually baffled American policy makers.

Meanwhile, another major political figure was emerging. In March, a raucous two-day Christian Democrat Party congress took place. José Napoleon Duarte emerged as the new party delegate to the ruling junta. Duarte was a former mayor of San Salvador and the apparent winner of the 1972 presidential election. Members of the military, including some members who would now be Duarte's governing partners, had prevented Duarte from taking office in 1972.

Duarte was a favorite of American embassy officials and State Department officials in Washington. Even before he joined the junta, U.S. representatives initiated talks with him in November 1979, with an eye toward insuring Christian Democratic participation in the Salvadoran government. Duarte was personally committed to the land reform program, to bank nationalization, to cutting the power of the military, and to taking advice from the U.S. Embassy. The Americans made it clear that U.S. aid to El Salvador was largely dependent on Duarte's presence in the government.

The Insurgents in 1979–1980

From October 1979 to December 1980, El Salvador underwent a successful military coup, an unsuccessful military coup, rumors of military coups, and three major shake-ups in the military-civilian junta that was attempting to govern the country. If ever there was a time when the rebels had a chance to overthrow the regime and march triumphantly into San Salvador, it was during this period.

But the rebels were having their own problems with internal division. It was not until late 1980 that a united guerrilla organization came into existence. Prior to that, there were five separate rebel groups, all with different leaders, all with different interpretations of Marxism-Leninism, and all committed to different ways of acquiring power.

For years, groups such as the People's Revolutionary Army (ERP) and the People's Liberation Forces (FPL) had spent almost as much time attacking each other as they did attacking the Salvadoran army. The Salvadoran Communist Party had existed since the 1930s, led by Cayetano Carpio and Shafik Handal, and had acquired the blessing of the Soviet government but failed to make serious inroads among the peasants of El Salvador. In the 1970s, Carpio left the Communists to form the FPL, and the group undertook a series of spectacular kidnappings of government officials and businessmen.

While the various leftist organizations in El Salvador argued among themselves, Cuban dictator Fidel Castro decided to take action. In April 1980, Castro helped to arrange a meeting at the Hungarian Embassy in Mexico City between members of three Salvadoran guerrilla groups and the representatives of the Soviet Union, Cuba, Bulgaria, East Germany, and Vietnam. He summoned the leaders of four guerrilla organizations to Havana in June 1980 and oversaw the formation of the United Revolutionary Directorate (DRU). Finally, in November 1980, a fifth organization was added, and the Faribundo Martí Liberation Front (FMLN) was born.

Assistance from the Soviet bloc increased, with the Sandinistas as intermediaries. The FMLN headquarters in Managua became an extremely sophisticated command-and-control center—more elaborate, in fact, than that used by the Sandinistas against Somoza. Nicaraguan Foreign Minister Miguel D'Escoto said in an interview with an American religious magazine, "You [Americans] may look at us as five countries, six now with Panama, but we regard ourselves as six different states of a single nation, in the process of reunification." This statement was consistent with other Sandinista statements that theirs was a "revolution without frontiers." The Sandinistas served as the main conduit for weapons into El Salvador. Nicaragua also provided a base for training, usually done by Cuban instructors. In the course of a government raid on a Communist Party safehouse in December 1980, soldiers found documents relating to a June 1980 deal that Handal had made to import arms from the U.S.S.R., Vietnam, and Ethiopia.

Jimmy Carter and the Salvadoran Crisis

For most of his administration, Carter's foreign policy toward El Salvador was inconsistent and confusing. In 1977, Carter imposed human rights' restrictions on military aid to a number of countries, El Salvador included. The Salvadoran regime responded by refusing all aid, and the country received nothing from the United States in 1978 and 1979. The U.S. Embassy in San Salvador had warnings of a possible coup against the Romero government in June 1979 and tacitly supported the coup plotters by failing to report the warnings to the government.

After the October coup brought a number of prominent reformers to power, embassy officials initiated talks with José Napoleon Duarte, who was not a part of the junta, but whose presence on the junta, the embassy made clear, would mean more money from the U.S. government. The administration was as good as its word. In January 1980, after Duarte joined the junta, U.S. Secretary of State Cyrus Vance unveiled a $54.3 million aid package for El Salvador, which included both economic and military assistance.

The path of the money from Vance's promise to El Salvador's treasury was not smooth. The Foreign Operations Subcommittee of the U.S. House of Representatives considered part of Carter's request on March 25, 1980. At issue was Carter's proposed $5.7 million in "nonlethal" military aid. (This aid would include trucks, jeeps, communications gear, and night vision goggles.) Overshadowing the subcommittee hearing was the murder, the previous day, of Salvadoran Archbishop Oscar Romero. Under intense pressure from administration officials, the subcommittee voted in favor of the military aid on April 1, 1980.

Carter immediately intervened in El Salvador's politics by appointing Robert White as ambassador. White made it clear that he considered himself a sort of proconsul for the country. Before taking up his new position, he stated boldly: "Washington wants something [in El Salvador] to the right of Nicaragua. My job is to make that happen." Leverage and influence were important to him. In 1980, for example, White said that the U.S. government had to give El Salvador military aid to prevent a rebel victory but added, "On the other hand, there is the problem that we do not want to give the impression that we totally support the armed forces as presently constituted."

A glance at the public statements of Carter administration officials, or a perusal of their internal documents, reveals an administration with deep divisions over how to proceed as El Salvador's condition became more and more critical. Occasionally, differences between officials would emerge into the public eye. In mid-1980, for example, National Security Advisor Zbigniew Brzezinski and Defense Secretary Harold Brown both recommended the dispatch of a small contingent of troops from the U.S. Army's Special Forces. Defying two Cabinet officials, Robert White threatened to resign if the Green Berets landed in El Salvador.

The ambassador did not have everything his own way, however. After D'Aubuisson's unsuccessful coup attempt, White declared the major "persona non grata" at the U.S. Embassy and said that no U.S. officials would have anything to do with him. However, D'Aubuisson made several trips to the United States after White made this statement. Foreigners traveling to the United States require a visa, and the only place to get such a document is from a consular official at the U.S. Embassy. White, who aspired to run El Salvador from the U.S. Embassy, was evidently not even able to control the embassy staff.

The Salvadoran Land Reform Program

There was, however, one area of strong and unquestioned agreement among U.S. officials dealing with El Salvador, and that was that the Salvadoran government had to proceed with the land reform program as quickly and as thoroughly as possible. This rare show of unity is revealing of a larger consensus within the Carter administration. The purported reason for the unfailing support for land reform was the belief that if more peasants owned their own land, they would be less susceptible to the promises of Communist rebels. Ownership was the ostensible goal of the land reform program.

The facts do not support this justification. The Salvadoran program did not originate with the Salvadoran government, but with a group of North American experts, including University of Washington law professor Roy Prosterman, whose career included developing a land reform program for South Vietnam. Prosterman's plan for El Salvador was for a three-phase land reform program. In phase 1, announced by the Salvadoran government on March 6, 1980, the government seized 376 farms and ranches of more than 500 hectares (1,235 acres), compensating the owners at a value set by the government, and paid over 30 years in government bonds, at interest rates well below the Salvadoran rate of inflation.

In theory, the land was to be turned over to the peasants who had previously worked on it. But the land reform did not produce owners. Peasants did not receive a deed to their land. They received a government document that gave them the use of the land, as long as they remained part of a rural cooperative run by government officials. In effect, the peasants merely traded servitude to the landowners for servitude to the government. This situation, plus the forced communal nature of the land, caused production on the confiscated farms to plummet. What production did take place was largely small-plot subsistence farming, causing El Salvador's export earnings to fall. In 1981, an official from the U.S. Agency for International Development (USAID) noted that while El Salvador had seen a marginal increase in maize production since the reform started, it had also seen a precipitous drop in export crops.

Phase 2 of the program called for the confiscation, under similar conditions, of farms ranging in size from 100–500 hectares (247–1235 acres). Farms of this size were vital to the Salvadoran economy. Almost all of the country's export crops, including coffee, cotton, and sugar, were raised on farms of the size targeted by phase 2 of the land reform. The Salvadoran government, having had to institute a nationwide state of emergency to implement phase 1, decided to postpone phase 2. The decision may well have saved El Salvador from Haiti-like levels of rural poverty.

Phase 3 of the program was a relatively benign effort to provide land to sharecroppers and day laborers. The land, for the most part, was idle or of questionable ownership, so few working farms were affected. Moreover, this phase of the program was most clearly directed at the poorest rural Salvadorans, so it enjoyed widespread political support in El Salvador. Again, however, very few new owners were created. Like the peasants affected by phase 1, they received only a preliminary permission to use the land, which did not include the right to sell the land, to borrow against the value of the land, or to bequeath the land to heirs.

There are a limited number of plausible ways to explain how a failure of this magnitude could have received the support of so many otherwise intelligent American officials. One explanation is that the officials did not bother learning the reality of the reform but based their enthusiasm on the general theory of land reform. This is undoubtedly the explanation that applies to ranking officials who spent only a fraction of their time on Salvadoran issues.

For those with more familiarity with the program, however, such blindness would have to be willful. Moreover, blind adherence to theory is rarely internally consistent. A more plausible explanation is that American officials did not see the devastation of Salvadoran export agriculture as necessarily a bad thing. As noted above, El Salvador was in a position as recently as 1977 to refuse all U.S. aid and, in so doing, to be able to ignore the wishes of U.S. officials. Robert White was clearly not the only U.S. official who found such an independent attitude intolerable.

Economic leverage was the least visible, and consequently the least controversial, method of overcoming this independence. To exercise leverage, however, requires a nation that requires aid. By the end of 1980, El Salvador's requirements were huge. The woes accompanying the land reform were only part of El Salvador's disastrous economic news in 1979–1980. A report from the Inter-American Development Bank described the collapse of El Salvador's economy during this period. Strikes, harvest interruptions brought about by land reform, and capital flight all devastated the country. El Salvador's GDP fell 1.5 percent in 1979, 5 percent in 1980, and a crippling 9.5 percent in 1981, compared to a 4.8 percent increase in 1978 and average annual growth of 5.2 percent from 1975 through 1977.

In addition, the country experienced a "stampede" of capital flight. Besides land reform, the post-October 1979 junta also promised to nationalize the country's banks. To the holders of bank accounts in El Salvador, bank nationalization meant government control of their assets, with the near certainty of political interference with those assets. These fears led to eight hundred thousand dollars per day leaving the country for banks overseas, especially banks in the U.S. By 1981, at least half a billion dollars in savings had left the country. At the same time, large industrial employers, uncertain whether or not they would meet the same fate as their landholding counterparts, moved operations out of El Salvador as well. The Salvadoran business newspaper *Prensa Gráfica* reported in January 1980 that twenty businesses, with eighty-two hundred workers, had ceased operations since October 1979. By February, another seven thousand workers had been laid off. (During the "good" economic times before 1979, Salvadoran businesses only employed thirty-five thousand industrial workers.)

Such economic devastation paved the way for greater American influence, through the provision of aid. As El Salvador required more and more American assistance, U.S. economic advisers became permanent fixtures in its finance and economics ministries. Military advisers, USAID personnel and contractors, intelligence agents, diplomats, and other officials flooded the country. While these officials were uncertain whether or not they could prevent the FMLN from winning the war, they could prevent the Salvadoran government from defying American officials. As one expert put it, "For some U.S. officials, U.S. aid to El Salvador was no longer perceived primarily as support for the Salvadoran regime, but as leverage upon it, enabling the U.S. government to push for a political opening."

To make matters even worse, the FMLN had a particular predilection for attacks on El Salvador's economic infrastructure. Assets such as bridges, power lines, switching stations, railroads, and dams were all fragile and vulnerable to attack by fast-moving, well-armed guerrilla forces. In 1981, the rebels systematically destroyed 1300 power pylons, leaving one-third of the country without electricity. Bridges were another preferred target, since their destruction allowed the physical isolation of parts of the country, which the FMLN immediately declared to be "liberated zones."

The Final Offensive

On the morning of January 10, 1981, the rebel offensive began. The plan was to strike all the country's main military garrisons at once. At the same time, the FMLN and its civilian counterpart, the FRD, called a general strike. The leadership of the FMLN hoped that defeat at some military garrisons, defections to the rebel army at others, and mutiny among the troops at still others, combined with the economic disruption of a general strike, plus the publication of a political platform and the announcement of diplomatic recognition, would be an unbeatable combination.

At the very least, the rebels expected to control a large portion of El Salvador and at least one major city, perhaps even San Salvador itself. From the "liberated" territory, the FMLN could announce the formation of a provisional government, welcome ambassadors from friendly nations, petition for El Salvador's seat at the United Nations, and compel the Americans and conservative Salvadorans to acknowledge, minimally, that the U.S.-supported government did not control the national territory. With a secure zone in which weapons and other support could be delivered from the Soviet bloc countries that had promised aid in 1980, the FMLN could continue the war from a stronger footing, even if the Final Offensive should fail.

In the event, the dreams of the FMLN leadership far outstripped the reality of the offensive. While attacks on every military garrison were an essential part of the plan, in reality, there were FMLN attacks on military posts in only about two-thirds of the country. No garrison was actually taken. There was only one mutiny in a military garrison, and it was quickly put down.

In the cities, the general strike call proved not much more successful than the military part of the offensive. Either because they feared reprisals from the government and the business community, or because they did not support an economic attack on a country that had already had its share of economic dislocation, workers and city dwellers in El Salvador largely went about their business as usual.

Within hours of the start of the offensive, the U.S. government responded. The divisions and hesitation of the Carter administration finally disappeared, and the Americans immediately reopened the flow of economic and military assistance, including machine guns, grenade launchers, ammunition, and most important, helicopters. Carter also sent twenty U.S. military advisors with expertise in antiguerrilla warfare to assist the Salvadoran military. The amounts involved were small, but the symbolism of Carter's response was important. Carter was demonstrating that his administration, while in its last days, and preoccupied with the Iranian hostage crisis, the Soviet invasion of Afghanistan, and the transition to Reagan, was still capable of forceful intervention in the Western Hemisphere.

But even before the resumed American aid could arrive in El Salvador to make an appreciable difference, the offensive was running out of steam. In the days following the failure of the Final Offensive, most observers agreed that the Salvadoran army had actually acquitted itself fairly well on the battlefield, in spite of all its inadequacies. Also responsible for the rebel defeat, however, were serious, ongoing divisions in the rebel coalition itself. Of the five guerrilla groups that made up the FMLN, only the Communist Party was fully committed to the offensive. One faction was willing to take part in the offensive but announced that under no circumstances would the group share weapons or information with any other guerrilla group.

In spite of these differences, and the overall disappointment that the Final Offensive represented for leftist Salvadorans, it was not a total failure. Many of the secondary goals were met. The FMLN-led insurrection was consolidated and fortified in the eastern third of the country, and lasting arrangements were made to transfer arms, ammunition, transport, and other support from Nicaragua to El Salvador. Indeed, strong evidence of Nicaraguan intervention in El Salvador prompted the Carter administration to cut off U.S. aid to that country three days before leaving office. The Sandinistas remained unchastized, and their assistance continued to flow into El Salvador.

Many in the ruling junta in El Salvador ascribed the temporary defeat of the rebels to divisions within the FMLN and feared that if these were overcome, a new offensive would be launched. The junta made the decision that vastly increased amounts of American aid were absolutely necessary if disaster were to be avoided. But some senior military officials, and civilian leaders such as ex-Major Roberto D'Aubuisson, drew a different lesson from the January rebel offensive. To them, the most important development was that El Salvador had successfully defended itself from a major Communist effort to take over the country and had done so before the restored American aid had actually arrived. It would lead D'Aubuisson and others to believe that El Salvador's dependence on the U.S. government was not a necessity. His conclusion would vastly complicate U.S. policy toward El Salvador over the next several years.

Reagan Takes Over

Reagan did not regard El Salvador as a sideshow, unworthy of his attention. Rather, he saw the country as an important area of confrontation between the United States and the Soviet Union. He made this clear early on in his campaign for president, asking the Chicago Council of World Affairs in March 1980: "Must we let . . . Grenada, Nicaragua, El Salvador, all become additional Cubas, new outposts for Soviet combat brigades? . . . These humiliations and symbols of weakness add up." With this and other, similar statements during the campaign, Reagan made it plain that El Salvador would be part of his global struggle against Communism. (Indeed, some authors blame Reagan's fiery rhetoric for emboldening military and right-wing elements in El Salvador in 1980. Even the deaths of Archbishop Romero and the four American churchwomen would be laid at Reagan's feet, although they all took place before he became president.)

As we saw in chapter 1, El Salvador was only one of many difficult global challenges Reagan faced when he became president. But for the new president, most of the challenges had the same cause, which was Soviet interference, driven by the Soviets' determination to decisively swing the global balance of power in their direction. It was, in Reagan's opinion, Carter's naïve assumption that the Soviets were worthwhile global partners that had led to significant strategic reverses for the United States in such far-flung sites as Ethiopia, Yemen, Afghanistan, and Nicaragua. These reverses were not, in Reagan's eyes, evidence of a coming shift in the cycle of hegemonic dominance. They were, much more simply, the results of bad U.S. policies, which Reagan was determined to change.

The administration began its effort carefully. Some additional military advisers were sent to El Salvador, and the administration indicated that there would be no more than fifty-five in the country at any given time. The U.S. aircraft carriers *Eisenhower* and *Kennedy* staged routine (and temporary) maneuvers in the Caribbean, near Cuba. The U.S. Army practiced amphibious landings at the American military base at Vieques, in Puerto Rico. The American military task force stationed at Key West was renamed "Caribbean Command." In addition, the Reagan administration tried to raise the cost of anti-Americanism for Fidel Castro. The embargo of Cuba was tightened, a propaganda offensive against Cuba was begun, and Reagan directed Voice of America to prepare a plan for starting regular American broadcasts to Cuba, on the model of Radio Free Europe.

As these measures were put into place, they seemed to bear fruit almost immediately. The administration's initial objective, stopping the flow of arms from Nicaragua into El Salvador, was met. With two American carriers in the Caribbean, Castro found it temporarily impossible to send contraband weapons to Nicaragua. It was even deemed too risky for the Soviets to send more arms to Cuba. The *New York Times*, decidedly unfriendly to Reagan's hard line during the campaign, ran two articles in March 1981 saying that the government of El Salvador was gaining the upper hand, while the FMLN was losing popular support. During this period of early optimism, Sen. Charles Percy (D-IL), chair of the Senate Foreign Relations Committee, promised support for Reagan's Central America initiatives and said boldly that the United States should do "whatever was necessary" to prevent a Communist takeover in El Salvador.

But this initial success was deceptive. U.S. officials did not know if the halt in the arms flow was due to American actions or simply a planned pause, as the Salvadoran guerrillas and their supporters absorbed the failure of the Final Offensive. The evidence is that neither Reagan nor his secretary of state, Alexander Haig, thought that fending off Communist attacks on El Salvador would be quick or easy. Reagan received the Pentagon's bleak assessment of the military situation in the spring of 1981. The guerrillas, according to the report, in spite of their failure in

January, were strongly supported in some parts of the country. El Salvador's economic woes were crippling the military.

Worst of all, the Salvadoran army itself was completely unprepared, strategically and psychologically, for the demands of a nationwide counterinsurgency campaign. Most of its soldiers were underpaid, undertrained draftees. The officers, with some noteworthy exceptions, were less able and far less willing, to confront armed guerrillas than they were able and willing to threaten unarmed villagers and peasants, which had been the role of the Salvadoran military for decades. The army operated on a nine-to-five timetable, with most of the officers leaving their posts and heading for San Salvador every Friday. Turning the Salvadoran army into an effective counter to the Cuban and Soviet supported and trained FMLN would take time.

Division Early on in the Reagan Administration

Some in the military's top leadership were reluctant to escalate the war before knowing exactly what the intentions of the new American administration were. Unfortunately, in spite of very clear language from Reagan and Haig, who said that the United States would "draw a line in the sand" in El Salvador, there were other voices in the administration that sounded very different.

At first, these voices were heard only in the secret, internal discussions of foreign policy in the White House Cabinet Room. Some Cabinet members opposed risky and forceful action on El Salvador, which, they said, would detract from attention to Reagan's domestic agenda of tax cuts and budget changes. Success on these domestic issues, some argued, was crucial to Reagan's presidency and threatened by action on an issue as potentially unpopular as military aid to El Salvador. Secretary of Defense Casper Weinberger repeatedly expressed concern that El Salvador could become an area where the United States ended up committing troops, without the requisite popular support. The furor in Congress and the Washington media over the assignment of 55 U.S. advisors to El Salvador seemed to justify the worst fears of Reagan's political advisors.

While no one in the Cabinet suggested abandoning El Salvador, powerful members of the administration backed a step-by-step policy. Vice President George H. W. Bush, CIA Director William Casey, and National Security Advisor Richard Allen, along with Chief of Staff Jim Baker and Deputy Chief of Staff Michael Deaver, all supported the slow approach, with frequent pauses in U.S. actions to permit rethinking and reevaluating what was happening in El Salvador. Even presidential counselor Ed Meese, who frequently sided with conservatives outside the administration, was unenthusiastic about involving the Reagan administration in El Salvador.

Sometimes the differences of opinion resulted in contradictory policies being pursued simultaneously. While Haig was ratcheting up U.S. pressure on the FMLN, and its backers in Managua and Havana, Allen met in Miami with an official of the Cuban government, at the invitation of columnist Jack Anderson, who was a friend of the Cuban official. When word of the Allen meeting leaked out, including the fact that the Cuban official said Castro was eager to improve relations with the United States, it seriously undermined Haig's ongoing effort to portray Castro as an unrepentant and dangerous neighbor.

Other divisions in the administration also made it out into the open. Some of the differences were over the basic ideological underpinnings of the Reagan policy. Richard Hallaway, undersecretary of defense, for example, made the statement: "Democracy means something different to Central Americans than to North Americans. They never practice 'liberal democracy' in the true sense of the word; instead the Iberian heritage had created a much more traditional society, so you cannot expect the Central Americans to adopt our kind of political system." Elliott Abrams, assistant secretary of state for human rights, later inter-American assistant secretary, justified dictatorship in a 1985 interview: "It is perfectly plausible that you have an efficient and effective dictatorial government which is quite ruthless and effective in putting down all opposition, reformist and revolutionary. When these regimes loosen up their control, revolutionary pressure grows rather than reduces."

Other differences emerged over methods to achieve desired goals in El Salvador. Early in the Reagan administration, Haig received an offer to talk secretly with the FMLN from Mexico's ambassador to the United States. Haig, according to his account of the exchange, "exploded." " 'No longer,' I said, 'would Washington deal secretly with insurgents seeking to overthrow legal governments in the Western Hemisphere. Moreover,' I continued, 'in the next four years, the Americas would see a determined U.S. effort to stamp out Cuban-supported subversion.' "

Yet within weeks of making this pronouncement, Haig's top deputy for Latin America, Thomas O. Enders, gave a speech in Philadelphia in which he pledged that the United States would pursue goals in El Salvador virtually identical with those of the Carter administration. Reagan administration priorities, he said, would include human rights, democracy, land reform, and a negotiated end to the "civil war" in El Salvador. Enders insisted that El Salvador was not primarily a part of the East-West competition. Instead, "just as the conflict was Salvadoran in its origins, so its ultimate resolution must be Salvadoran," meaning the sort of negotiations that Haig had angrily rejected with the Mexican ambassador.

Earlier that same spring of 1981, the Reagan administration published an inch-thick White Paper on Communist interference in El Salvador that sought to prove that the conflict in El Salvador was anything but "Salvadoran in its origins," as Enders insisted. Copies of the White Paper were delivered to every office on Capitol Hill, to every Latin American Embassy in Washington, to every U.S. Embassy in Latin America, and to every NATO country. Administration officials traveled to Western European capitals to hand deliver the bound evidence of Soviet, Cuban, and Nicaraguan intervention in El Salvador and to solicit support for administration efforts to stop the intervention and to punish those responsible for it.

Although the White Paper received considerable criticism, and did contain some errors, it was a remarkable effort not only to demonstrate outside interference in El Salvador but also (perhaps unintentionally) to educate the American people on the difficulty of interpreting raw intelligence data. Americans patient enough to read the White Paper, and to listen to the criticisms, learned that satellite photos are subject to interpretation, that accounts from defectors are often suspect, and that even official statements from Communist officials can be read in different ways. The White Paper was not conclusive; the paper itself noted that most sensitive intelligence information was not included. At best, it was a request for trust from the American people in the fact that Reagan did have a strong basis for his actions in El Salvador and was not making up reasons for hostility to the Salvadoran rebels.

In this regard, it was unfortunate that the *Wall Street Journal*, normally reasonably friendly to Reagan, ran an article in early June 1981 in which Jon Glassman, the State Department official principally responsible for drafting the White Paper said that the document was "misleading and over embellished." He added that when Haig had told the House Foreign Affairs committee in mid-May that massive shipments of arms were coming to El Salvador, he did so against the advice of State Department and CIA officials, who later insisted that Haig had exaggerated.

Reagan's hard line did have its proponents in the administration as well. Jeane Kirkpatrick, U.S. ambassador to the UN, was unstinting in her efforts to draw attention to Communist interference in El Salvador and the necessity of doing something forceful about it. She was joined by Edwin Meese, Undersecretary of Defense Fred Iklé and, after Richard Allen's departure in January 1982, by new National Security Advisor William Clark. Iklé made perhaps the most bellicose statement when he said in December 1981 that Nicaragua's frequent violations of Honduran territory, for the purpose of delivering arms to El Salvador, could be construed as a violation of the Rio Treaty's ban on intervention. The treaty, Iklé reminded his listeners, provided for "joint action against an aggressor nation in the case of an external attack."

National Security Advisor Clark, for his part, brought to the NSC staff Constantine Menges, a former CIA analyst and known hard-liner on Central America. Under Clark, the NSC would become the center of hardline anti-Communism in the Reagan administration. As such, the staff would fight long and bitter wars against other Executive Branch agencies inclined to take a less belligerent line. Such internecine conflict would become one of the hallmarks of the Reagan administration.

Explaining the Confusion

There are various factors that partly explain the inconsistency and infighting inside the Reagan administration. First, Reagan was simply not a good manager, and he had an intense dislike of personal confrontation, as he repeatedly demonstrated as governor of California. Second, when George Bush agreed to be on the ticket, and brought in the more moderate wing of the Republican Party, his price was the selection of James Baker as chief of staff. Baker strongly disagreed with many of Reagan's policies, both foreign and domestic, and used his vast connections and unmatched bureaucratic skills to both place obstacles in front of those policies and insure damaging leaks to the anti-Reagan media.

Third, Reagan presided over a Republican Party that was bitterly divided between conservatives and moderates. Conservatives believed that since they shared an ideology with Reagan, and since it was this ideology that won Reagan his landslide victory in 1980, they should receive the choice policy-making positions. Moderates, led by Baker and by many Republican senators, believed with equal fervor that "ideologues" had no place in Washington and certainly should have no prominent place in the Reagan White House. It was left to Reagan himself to try to balance these antagonistic factions in his party while also trying to push his legislative agenda through a House of Representatives dominated by Democrats and a Senate dominated by moderate Republicans. To succeed, Reagan needed the loyalty and hard work of both factions. Thus, both had to be given positions and perks, which they used alternatively to advance Reagan's agenda and to undercut one another.

But none of these general explanations fully clarifies the dizzying inconsistency of Reagan's early El Salvador policy. A full explanation requires the analysis we saw in chapter 2, regarding those who desire leveraged allies for the United States and those who prefer strong and independent allies. Much of the internal debate over El Salvador focused on just how subservient El Salvador should be to American wishes.

One of the major differences between the Carter and Reagan administrations was that in the latter, there was not universal support for the Salvadoran land reform program. In fact, this program became the early focus of conflict between the factions in Reagan's Executive Branch. As occurred elsewhere, disagreements between Reagan's aides led to an apparent confusion of policy. During the transition in 1980, Reagan officials told representatives of the Salvadoran government that the incoming administration would not tolerate any attempt to reverse the bank nationalization or the land reform. In July 1981, newly appointed U.S. Ambassador Deane Hinton told the American Chambers of Commerce in Washington that El Salvador did not have to undertake new reforms until the existing reforms had been "consolidated." Hinton's listeners knew that this meant that the Reagan administration would not insist on the implementation of phase 2 of the land reform, which was the phase that threatened the greatest economic chaos.

There was actually no contradiction here. Reagan was merely trying to avoid a head-on collision between those who wanted to see El Salvador completely subservient to the United States and those who wanted a stronger and more prosperous El Salvador. Trying to undo phase 1 of the land reform would have pulverized congressional support for Reagan's attempts to give El Salvador military and economic assistance. Proceeding with phase 2 would have meant economic prostration for the country. Reagan split the difference, kept alive the possibility of U.S. aid, and gave Salvadorans the opportunity to win the war and start to rebuild their economy. What seemed like confusion was a deft political stroke.

It was only the opening skirmish in what promised to be a long war within the Reagan administration. Reagan took other steps to try to accomplish the related goals of winning the war and encouraging El Salvador's economic growth. Reagan found that he had more allies in the Defense Department than in the State Department. As the result of constant persuasion from U.S. military advisers, the army of El Salvador changed tactics. Before the Americans took a hand, the Salvadoran army relied heavily on large-scale sweeps. These usually resulted in human rights abuses and rarely did more than inconvenience the FMLN.

Starting in 1981, the army deployed smaller units, which were more mobile, more effective, and less disruptive to civilian life. In addition, the Salvadoran military learned to fight a seven-day war. Under Casper Weinberger's direction, the U.S. government got better at supplying the Salvadorans with useful weapons and somewhat more reliable supplies of ammunition. The U.S. military also supplied significant amounts of communications equipment, finally giving the Salvadoran army an edge over the guerrillas in this area. Finally, the Pentagon supplied additional air power, especially helicopters. The cumulative effect of these changes, inspired by the U.S. military, was to take the war to the guerrillas, with less random destruction.

Reagan also turned more and more of the primary decision-making power on Central American policy to the National Security Council and the conservative staff that William Clark had hired there. The NSC's top Latin America policy maker was Constantine Menges, who shared Reagan's desire for a strong and prosperous El Salvador. Menges had told a conference of Latin America experts during the transition period that there were certain "essential tasks" of an effective U.S. policy for Latin America. The most important of these, Menges said, was to "provide help for successful adaptation to global economic pressures, as a way of promoting continued economic growth."

Menges also broke with normal State Department thinking by praising the role of private groups such as the West German Friedrich Ebert and Konrad Adenauer Foundations. These two, among others, forged links between private business and civil organizations, gave money for publication and travel of democratically minded citizens, spread the word about the success of democracies, provided democratic governments with reliable information about extremists, and gave advice on holding free elections, establishing independent political parties, and promoting the emergence of a professional media.

For an American official even to acknowledge, let alone encourage, the participation of other potential donors in a country such as El Salvador was close to heresy in the State Department. The point of giving aid was to spread American influence. Aid from elsewhere diluted that influence and reminded recipients that USAID was not their only option. Menges courted opposition by embracing any outside aid. To highlight the work of the Ebert and Adenauer Foundations, which encouraged growing economies and healthy civil societies, was far worse. During most of the Reagan administration, the professional diplomats in the State Department regarded the NSC staff as almost as threatening to American success as the enemies in El Salvador and Nicaragua. With few exceptions, the ill feeling was returned.

The Demand for Power Sharing

For the most part, professional diplomats wished to see El Salvador with a more or less permanent need for American aid. For policy makers with this preference, the essential goal was to keep the war in El Salvador going. Salvadorans had proved their ability to get along without American assistance for years before the guerrilla war started; to have them do so again, especially under the leadership of someone such as D'Aubuisson, was intolerable.

It would have been extremely dangerous politically for anyone in Washington to openly state that their goal was a dependent El Salvador or that their short-term goal was a prolonging of the Salvadoran conflict. A coalition government, however, which sought to bring together elements of the Salvadoran democratic center with the military, and the guerrillas, would have exactly the desired effect. Even better, phrases such as *negotiated solution* and *coalition government* played well politically.

No one with even a passing familiarity with the bitter passions that underlay the Salvadoran conflict, or of the shocking violence and hatred that had been unleashed since 1979, could possibly believe that a coalition government could actually work. At best, such an arrangement would require the constant and heavy-handed intervention of an outside power to keep the coalition from falling apart. At worst, the coalition would come under the control of the Communists as was occurring at the same time next door in Nicaragua. The most likely scenario was that factions of both the Left and the Right would reject the coalition and continue the war under slightly different auspices.

For the guerrillas, the failure of the Final Offensive brought signs of impatience and even defeatism from some of their outside supporters. The FMLN needed time to rearm, and also to reassess its strategy. The Sandinistas, successful in using a coalition strategy themselves, began to strongly suggest a similar path for the Salvadoran guerrillas. In fact, in February 1981, the Nicaraguan government leaked a document of the joint Diplomatic-Political Commission of the FMLN and the FDR proposing that the Left offer to negotiate with the Salvadoran junta if the United States would first terminate military assistance.

After a face-saving interval, the Salvadoran guerrillas took the Sandinistas' advice. On January 27, 1982, the FMLN commanders sent Reagan a letter calling for a negotiated end to the war. The following month, Mexican president José López Portillo, an FMLN supporter, offered a three-point plan: mediation in El Salvador, leading to a coalition government; a nonaggression pact between the United States and Nicaragua; and talks between the United States and Cuba. Both of these sensitive diplomatic feelers were made public, to put pressure on Reagan to accept. The initiatives prompted 104 members of Congress, including twelve Republicans, to write to Reagan urging him to support López Portillo's initiative.

Realizing the importance of Congress to their future, the FMLN and the FDR began to lobby the delegations of congressmen and senators who frequently visited El Salvador on fact-finding missions. Leftist spokesmen in El Salvador, such as exjunta member Guillermo Ungo and FMLN Directorate member Rubén Zamora, repeatedly told visiting American congressional delegations that the U.S. government should insist upon negotiations and a coalition government. American influence, the Salvadoran assured the lawmakers, would permit El Salvador to avoid the outcome in Nicaragua, in which anti-American elements dominated. The Sandinista outcome, Ungo and Zamora contended, came about because the United States waited too long before taking the side of the "moderate" Left and thus had no influence after the "hard" Left won. A political settlement now, they said, would mean more clout for moderates and more clout for the United States in El Salvador's new government.

No appeal could possibly have sounded more melodious in the ears of U.S. congressmen, accustomed as they are to deference and as deserving as they think they are of influence. To sweeten the offer further, the FMLN reminded listeners of its December 1980 "six-point platform of principles," which included such language as: "[The revolutionary democratic government] will guarantee democratic representation of all popular democratic and revolutionary sectors that actively contribute to the overthrow of the military dictatorship." In the same statement, the FMLN promised to "support all private businessmen who cooperate and promote the economic development of the country and the revolutionary government's program."

Close analysis of these lofty-sounding promises, however, reveals only a determination by the FMLN members to purge anyone from the coalition government that disagreed with them. The first part of the statement, for example, promises representation only to "revolutionary sectors that actively contribute to the overthrow of the military dictatorship." Similarly, only businessmen who "cooperate" will receive support. Again, no one familiar with the FMLN, or with experience in reading political statements, could honestly believe that a coalition government would bring peace.

Even the FMLN leadership itself was divided on the question of negotiating with the government as a means of gaining power. Caytano Carpio, founder of the Salvadoran Communist Party, vehemently opposed the strategy. He sought ways to liberate the FMLN from the dominance of the Sandinistas, who were insisting that the FMLN follow the same path to power that they did. Carpio made a trip to Libya in early 1983, seeking arms and support from Muammar Qaddafi, in case Nicaragua and Cuba cut the Salvadoran rebels off. For his trouble, Carpio was framed by the Sandinistas for the murder of an associate (who backed the coalition government strategy) and "encouraged" to commit suicide.

Reagan continuously resisted calls for both direct negotiations with the guerrillas and for pressuring El Salvador to accept a coalition government. He reminded listeners that the U.S. government had insisted on a coalition government in Laos in the 1970s, only to see the Communists seize total control. Reagan also pointed out that the Sandinistas had been part of a coalition in Nicaragua but had begun consolidating power almost immediately. In a speech on Central America to the National Association of Manufacturers in March 1983, Reagan said, "What we oppose are negotiations that would be used as a cynical device for dividing up power behind the people's back. We cannot support negotiations which, instead of expanding democracy, try to destroy it."

The dispute over whether or not to put pressure on El Salvador's government to permit a coalition government with the guerrillas is illustrative. At best, a coalition between Communists and non-Communists in El Salvador would require external policing to work. Since only the U.S. had the resources for such a commitment, a coalition would increase American leverage over El Salvador. In addition, a coalition government could do little in the way of creating coherent government of the type necessary for potential investors to risk opening businesses in El Salvador. Without such investment, sustained development, which could ultimately lead to a return to economic independence for El Salvador, simply would not take place.

There is absolutely no evidence to indicate that even those American officials most strongly committed to a coalition government desired a Communist victory. There is strong evidence, however, that White, Enders, and others wanted badly to maintain American leverage in El Salvador. Thus they desired an outcome with two crucial features: first, that the Salvadoran guerrillas did not win and create a new pro-Soviet government in Central America; and second, that the Salvadoran government did not emerge from its dependence on U.S. aid.

Reagan and the "hard liners" in his administration, for their part, also had overlapping goals for El Salvador. They wished to see the guerrillas defeated, and defeated outright. They also desired the process toward democratic rule in El Salvador to continue. In addition, they wished to see genuine and sustained economic development in El Salvador, ideally leading to the emergence of a free, prosperous, democratic, and capitalist country in Central America.

The goals of the two factions in the administration had just enough in common to permit them to work together on projects such as getting military and economic aid passed by Congress and reining in the violent Right in El Salvador. But these common goals, while immediate and vital, were not enough to mask the serious disagreements that the two sides had over the preferred final outcome in El Salvador. For those outside the Executive Branch, it did not take long for it to become clear that disagreements existed in the Reagan administration, although it was the rare commentator who guessed correctly at the true nature of these disagreements.

Reagan himself may have been surprised at the depth of disagreement over policy toward Central America. For him, it was a clear-cut struggle between Soviet-backed Communists and freedom-loving Salvadorans. Reagan could have argued that he was doing what every U.S. administration since Truman's had done when faced with a new Soviet threat. By shoring up the Salvadoran government, the United States was containing Soviet expansionism. For Reagan, the threat was clear, the Soviets' involvement indisputable, and the stakes higher than in Korea and Vietnam. There should have been consensus, not disagreement.

But for Reagan, containment was not enough. He wanted to reverse the long trend of Soviet expansion. This meant defeating the Salvadoran guerrillas by stopping the support that they were getting from Nicaragua.

Reagan concluded that Nicaragua's pro-Soviet government could be the starting point for reversing Soviet geopolitical gains. In pursuing this ambitious goal, Reagan would end up dealing with disagreements far more significant than those over El Salvador. For most of Reagan's presidency, it was hard to tell which civil war resulted in more bitterness: the one in Nicaragua or the one in his administration over what to do about Nicaragua.

4

Making Enemies in Nicaragua, 1979–1982

They accused us of suppressing freedom of expression. This was a
lie and we could not let them publish it.

—Sandinista censor to the *New York Times*, 1983

The Sandinista Revolution in Nicaragua occurred at the most propitious
time imaginable for an anti-American, leftist revolution in Latin America.
On past occasions, the U.S. government has used armed intervention to
crush revolutionary movements threatening to U.S. interests. The Sandinistas, however, took over during a time of other crises, which prevented
the American people from paying close, sustained attention to events in
Nicaragua, while distraction and irresolution paralyzed the response of
the Carter administration.

For American news consumers, 1979 began with the flight of the
shah of Iran, ushering in the rule of the Ayatollah Khomeini. It ended
with the Iranian hostage crisis and the Christmas Eve Soviet invasion of
Afghanistan. In between, the American people watched news broadcasts
concerning a failed arms control treaty between the United States and
the U.S.S.R.; a new war in Southeast Asia; the signing of the Camp David
Accords; Pope John Paul II's visit to Poland; and the election of Britain's first
woman prime minister. At home, Americans contended with the disaster
at the Three Mile Island nuclear plant and the onset of crippling inflation.
On July 15, four days before the Sandinistas marched triumphantly into
Managua, President Carter gave his "crisis of confidence" speech.

The only time that the Sandinistas were on the front pages of American newspapers in 1979, they were showing their best face to the world. Americans gained a lasting impression of a romantic, almost perfect Latin American revolution. An unsavory dictator had been overthrown. The people of Nicaragua were shown on American television celebrating and attending Mass. The revolutionaries, while some of them occasionally spoke in positive terms of Marxism and in negative terms about the United States, were a mix of sober moderates and more photogenic hard liners. The latter, favoring fatigues and sunglasses, seemed to have been sent not from Moscow, but from Hollywood's central casting office.

The impression that the Sandinistas had led a moderate, nationalist, nonaligned revolution, opening a "new era" in Latin American politics, was a lasting one. Later the world would learn that even in its early days, the Sandinista leadership was planning to trample human rights, align themselves with Cuba and the Soviet Union, and attack their neighbors. But the Sandinistas sustained their moderate, nonthreatening image until the news spotlight had shifted. It would be left to President Ronald Reagan to formulate an American policy to counter the Sandinistas' accelerating drive toward totalitarianism.

By the time Sandinista Nicaragua returned to the headlines in the early weeks of the Reagan administration, the reality behind the positive images of July 1979 was gone. Most of the prominent non-Communist moderates who had marched into Managua with the Sandinistas were out of power, in exile, or even in prison. The promises of democracy were a bitter memory for many Nicaraguans, while nonalignment disappeared in a rush to align with the Soviet Union and Cuba and to use these connections to support a Marxist-Leninist insurgency in El Salvador.

Among the myriad other tasks of Reagan's first weeks in office, he would have to reintroduce Americans to Nicaragua. Reagan had little success in this effort, which would last for most of his presidency. His failure to change perceptions of Sandinista Nicaragua would repeatedly threaten his goals in Central America. Even given the enormous difficulties in El Salvador, it was U.S. relations with Nicaragua that would become the driving force in Reagan's Central America policy.

Carter and the Sandinistas

In the early days of his term, Jimmy Carter decided to use Nicaragua and Iran as showpieces for his stated belief that U.S. foreign policy should focus on the protection of human rights. In 1977, Carter cut off military aid to the Somoza dictatorship and signaled that the U.S. government was open to regime change in Managua. Some Carter administration officials believed that a forceful demonstration of U.S. pressure would induce Somoza to cease his regime's human rights abuses. Other officials foresaw violent revolution in Nicaragua and hoped to prevent it by emboldening moderate reformers. Still others desired to make contacts with and establish leverage over the Sandinistas, with an eye to influencing them if they seized power.

By May 1979, it was becoming increasingly clear that the Broad Opposition Front (FAO) would take power in Nicaragua. The Front consisted of the Marxist-Leninist Sandinista Party and a number of non-Communist organizations, including the Roman Catholic Church, which were all united in their determination to oust pro-American dictator Anastasio Somoza. By mid-1979, the Carter administration's support for Somoza had dried up. Instead, the American government focused on claiming a role in the actual departure of Somoza, to preserve American influence with the successor government. Central to this policy was the hope that the non-Communist elements of the Front would prevail in the coming struggle for power.

Thus, it was Cyrus Vance, Carter's secretary of state; William Bowdler, assistant secretary of state for inter-American affairs; and Lawrence Pezullo, U.S. ambassador to Nicaragua, who persuaded Somoza to leave the country on July 17, 1979. Vance had also brought the Organization of American States (OAS) into the process, persuading the international body to recognize the FAO as the legitimate government of Nicaragua. In return for the blessing of the OAS, the Sandinistas promised to establish a "pluralistic" society, respect human rights, and hold free elections.

The official rulers of Nicaragua were the five members of the Council of State, three of whom (Daniel Ortega, Sergio Ramirez, and Moises Hassan) were also members of the Sandinista Front. The other two members were Violeta Chamorro, widow of the slain editor of *La Prensa*, an anti-Somoza newspaper, and Adolfo Robelo, leader of the Nicaraguan Democratic Party. The first public event of the post-Somoza era was a victory Mass, celebrated by Monsignor Miguel Obando y Bravo, the highest-ranking Roman Catholic cleric in Nicaragua, who had clashed repeatedly with Somoza.

Jimmy Carter's initial reaction to the Sandinista takeover was positive. At a news conference a week later, Carter said, "We have a good relationship with the new government [of Nicaragua]. We hope to improve it." In September, in a joint statement with Mexican president Jorge López Portillo, Carter added that he and López Portillo "agreed that progress toward a democracy in Nicaragua had improved the prospects for peace in the region, and a greater respect for human rights." Robert Pastor, Latin America expert for the National Security Council (NSC), predicted that the Sandinistas would bring Mexican-style one-party democracy to Nicaragua.

Just weeks after the Sandinista triumph, Ortega, Ramirez, and Robelo were invited to the White House for a private meeting with Carter. At that meeting, Carter promised $118 million in U.S. aid would be forthcoming, to repair the ravages of the civil war and facilitate the building of a new society. For their part, the Nicaraguan leaders had nothing but praise and gratitude for the American president.

Some members of the U.S. Congress, however, including some prominent Democrats, had reservations about providing aid, and it became clear that Carter's original promise of $118 million would be substantially reduced. Indeed, Carter and his aides had to fight to get Congress to provide $75 million in aid. Just as the aid package was sent to Congress, allegations surfaced that the FSLN was assisting Communist rebels in neighboring El Salvador. Deputy Secretary of State Viron Vaky acknowledged the presence of weapons from Nicaragua in El Salvador but suggested that it was the work of rogue military officers. In the end, Congress passed $75 million in aid, but the legislators attached an amendment requiring Carter to urge the Sandinistas to hold free elections as soon as possible.

Even after Congress acted, Carter hesitated to actually release the money, concerned that the American people might see his policy of accommodating the Sandinistas, in the context of the hostage crisis and the Soviet invasion of Afghanistan, as evidence of weakness in foreign policy. Early in September 1980, Deputy Secretary of State Warren Christopher, along with Senator Edward Zorinsky (D-NE), wrote to Carter urging him to release the funds and counseling him to ignore the Republicans' efforts to make the aid into a campaign issue. On September 15, Carter finally did so, after certifying to Congress that the Sandinistas were not supporting international violence or terror. (Two days later, Anastasio Somoza was killed in Asunción, Paraguay, with a bazooka.) In the meantime, Carter had also ordered U.S. representatives at the World Bank to provide the Sandinistas with $250 million in new credits, at below-market rates of interest.

Nicaragua's Path toward Totalitarianism

One of the enduring myths about the Sandinista revolution, and one that would bedevil Reagan during his presidency, was that the Sandinistas did not intend to impose one-party rule or to become dictators, and certainly did not intend to form a Soviet satellite. These things occurred, according to the myth, because hostility from the United States, and especially from Reagan, drove the Sandinistas "into the arms of the Soviets." Even a brief summary of the facts will demonstrate the emptiness of this myth.

As early as 1977, fully two years before they even took power, the leaders of the FSLN described themselves as Marxist-Leninist. A fifteen-thousand-word party program published that year called for the overthrow of Somoza and the establishment of a "revolutionary democratic state" that would "assure the structural and superstructural bases for revolutionary progress toward socialism." The 1977 program also acknowledged that deception would be a major factor in revolutionary success. National and international factors, the program said, "do not allow for the formulation of socialism in an open way at this stage."

The program asserted that there must be two faces to the Sandinistas, one for internal use and one for external use. At the same time, the Sandinistas were committed to presenting themselves as the only alternative to Somoza. To maintain this illusion, the FSLN had to embrace some non-Communist leaders, such as Eden Pastora, leader of the August 1978 attack on the National Palace, but without giving non-Communists any actual power. Pastora himself was never allowed to sit on the FSLN National Directorate.

In addition, the FSLN had to derail efforts to democratize Nicaragua under non-Sandinista leadership. One such effort, sponsored by the United States in 1977, was met with a renewed FSLN military offensive around the country. The offensive, explained one prominent Sandinista, was intended "to prevent sections of the bourgeoisie and petty bourgeoisie from . . . convert[ing] themselves into an alternative to Somoza."

After taking power, the FSLN leaders were no less devoted to the twin goals of establishing communism in Nicaragua and lying about doing so. Two months after marching into Managua, the leaders of the FSLN held a secret, three-day meeting to discuss ways to consolidate their power. The record of this meeting, called the "Seventy-Two-Hour Document," was intended by the Sandinistas only for internal use, but leaked in 1984. In the document, the Sandinistas laid out their plans to repress human rights, gain control of the Catholic Church, co-opt the business community, ally themselves with Cuba and the U.S.S.R. and, most important of all, deceive the Americans and their own countrymen about their intentions. (Part of this deception was to prevent publication of the Seventy-Two-Hour Document.)

FSLN leaders asserted that "the alliance [with non-Communists] that took the form of the National Reconstruction Government, the cabinet and, to a major extent, the FSLN's basic program . . . was designed to neutralize Yankee interventionist policies." Daniel Ortega also made efforts to neutralize opposition to the Sandinistas from the major American newspapers. *Washington Post* columnist Jack Anderson was one of those convinced of the Sandinistas moderate credentials, writing: "Left-wing influence on the Sandinistas is minimal. Of the three main guerrilla groups [factions] that make up the rebel camp, the only avowedly leftist group . . . appears to have little or no influence."

Even those who believed that the FSLN was divided into Communist and non-Communist factions, however, should have been concerned when Tomás Borge was named interior minister. Borge was from the "avowedly leftist group" that Jack Anderson insisted "had little or no influence." The Interior Ministry in Nicaragua, as in other communist countries, was charged with internal security. Borge, in other words, was put in charge of the secret police and given the power to decide which human rights Nicaraguans would be allowed to have.

These rights turned out to be few. Well before the end of the Carter administration, arbitrary arrests became common. Prisoners were denied legal representation and sometimes tried by "tribunals of conscience," in which the rights of the accused were virtually nonexistent. Protests and demonstrations were banned and sometimes broken up by force. In 1980, Nicaragua witnessed the first appearance of the "divine mobs" (*turbas divinas*), which were groups of Sandinista youths, often armed with everything from iron pipes to rifles. The Sandinistas diverted attention from their legal abuses by announcing that they had abolished the death penalty in Nicaragua.

By May 1980, the two non-Communist members of the Council of State, Violeta Chamorro and Alfonso Robelo, had resigned. Increasingly, power in Nicaragua was held by the nine-man FSLN National Directorate. In November 1980, Jorge Salazar, president of the Nicaraguan Coffee Growers' Association, and a critic of the Sandinistas' increasingly antibusiness policies, was killed by Sandinista security forces, who claimed he was shot while "resisting arrest." The Sandinistas arrested several other private-sector leaders, alleging that all the men were involved in a plot to overthrow the government. On December 10, the Catholic Church signaled its impatience with the Sandinistas' repression by ordering all Catholic priests out of the Nicaraguan government by the end of December. Catholic priests were prominent in the Sandinista revolution, and three served in the Cabinet. One of these, Miguel D'Escoto, was foreign minister.

In February 1981, the government closed the anti-Somoza Human Rights Commission and arrested its leader, José Esteban Gonzalez, charging him with "lying" to Pope John Paul II about torture in Nicaragua. After three weeks in prison, Gonzalez submitted a letter recognizing his "errors" and was acquitted. The government also began putting pressure on *La Prensa*, in spite of the paper's anti-Somoza history. *La Prensa* was closed three times in August 1981 and again in October. Its editors were required to submit copy for review by government censors.

Even during the worst years of the Somoza dictatorship, Nicaragua was a society with a surprisingly low level of militarization. The hated Somoza National Guard usually numbered only seventy-five hundred, and that number included both military and police. At its height, the Guard increased to fifteen thousand. This would be the smallest number of people in uniform that Nicaragua would see for more than a decade. As early as February 1981, the *New York Times* reported that the Sandinistas had established "militias," consisting of factory workers, bureaucrats, and other Sandinista supporters. Nicaraguan government officials told the *Times* that they planned to deploy a militia of two hundred thousand.

The Sandinistas also moved early in their revolution to forge ties with Cuba, the Soviet Union, and other enemies of the United States. As we saw above, the Sandinista party was never a mass movement, and its leaders never wanted it to be. This complicated the task of governing after the revolution. The FSLN simply did not include enough people to run necessary government agencies. The Sandinistas' partial solution to this problem was to depend heavily on foreign Communists. By the middle of 1980, there were thousands of Cubans and hundreds of Soviets providing "technical advice" to the Sandinistas. The foreigners focused their efforts on expanding the military, strengthening the forces of the Interior Ministry, and taking over Nicaraguan schools.

In return for the "advice," the Sandinistas provided significant diplomatic and political assistance to the Soviets and Cubans. Just three weeks after taking power, Daniel Ortega appeared to a hero's welcome at the conference of the Nonaligned Movement and was crucial in that body's decision to support the Soviet line in foreign affairs. Early in 1980, the Sandinistas signed a joint communiqué with the U.S.S.R., supporting the latter's invasion of Afghanistan.

This remarkable statement of support came at a time when Nicaragua was receiving more aid from the United States than from the U.S.S.R. and when even some Eastern European Soviet satellites were hesitant about supporting the Afghan invasion. In December 1981, after the Polish military, with Soviet support, declared martial law in Poland, FSLN news outlets were ordered to publish only information "confirmed by TASS and by the Cuban Prensa Latina News Service." Soon after, the Sandinista government denied entry to a delegation from Solidarity visiting the Americas.

Nor did American aid turn out to be a deterrent to pro-Soviet activities by the Sandinistas. Far from providing leverage for the American government, the passage of the Carter aid package seemed to embolden the Sandinistas. Less than two weeks after the initial House vote for the $75 million in February 1980, Sandinista Directorate member Moesis Hassan and other Sandinistas traveled to Moscow, where they spent six days in meetings with Soviet officials. Hassan went from Moscow to several Eastern European capitals. Three days after a second positive House vote on aid in July, Sandinista leaders were in Havana, thanking Fidel Castro for his support and accepting Castro's offer of "teachers" for Nicaragua. Castro made his first extended visit to Nicaragua in July also, attending celebrations marking the first anniversary of the Sandinista triumph.

The Sandinistas also welcomed Yasser Arafat to Nicaragua for the first anniversary celebrations in 1980. The leader of the Palestinian Liberation Organization, which had not yet renounced terrorism nor acknowledged the right of Israel to exist, was treated as a head of state. Borge embraced not only Arafat, but also his crusade against Israel, proclaiming, "We say to our brother Arafat that Nicaragua is his land and the PLO cause is the cause of the Sandinistas." Arafat returned the compliment, insisting that "the triumph of the Nicaraguans is the PLO's triumph." He added: "The links between us are not new. Your comrades did not come to our country just to train, but also to fight. Your enemies are our enemies."

Later in the day, Arafat warned, "Anyone who threatens Nicaragua will have to face Palestinian combatants."

Reagan Tries Business as Usual

The purge of the moderates from the Sandinista government, the suppression of civil rights, the subversion of their neighbors (especially El Salvador), and the creation of strong links with America's enemies all took place before Ronald Reagan took office. Nevertheless, the initial contacts between the Reagan administration and the Sandinistas were not of an overtly hostile nature. While Reagan did suspend economic assistance to the Sandinistas two days after coming into office, this was merely the culmination of efforts in the last days of the Carter administration to do the same thing, based on the conclusion of the Carter administration that the Sandinistas were providing arms to the guerrillas in El Salvador. At the same time, Reagan ordered contacts with the Sandinistas to determine their intentions and thus determine appropriate U.S. responses.

Reagan's initial cool but correct attitude toward the Sandinistas received encouragement from Nicaraguan moderates. Just days after Reagan took office, Robelo Callejas, a critic of the Sandinistas, told the *New York Times* that, in his opinion, the Sandinistas were Communists. He added the claim that there were five thousand Cubans in his country. At the same time, he urged Reagan not to suspend U.S. aid but to find a way to send the money to private groups, rather than to the Nicaraguan government. Later, Arturo Cruz, Nicaraguan ambassador to the United States, criticized the aid suspension and expressed his hope that the United States would not force the Sandinistas to the left. The anti-Sandinista newspaper *La Prensa* also advised Reagan to keep the door open to the Sandinistas.

Reagan Sees a Larger Threat

For Reagan, as for Carter, however, the insurmountable barrier to normal relations was the Sandinistas' determination to aid guerrillas in neighboring countries. The Carter administration knew that the weapons that the Salvadoran guerrillas used for their January 1981 "Final Offensive" came from Nicaragua, but Carter officials hesitated to do anything about it, other than provide more assistance to El Salvador. They laid the groundwork for a suspension of U.S. aid, but left the process for Reagan to complete.

As early as his confirmation hearings before the U.S. Senate, Al Haig expressed concern about Sandinista activities in Central America. At an encounter with Rita Delia Casco, "the fiery young ambassador of the Sandinista regime," at a reception, the ambassador reminded Haig of the pending $75 million U.S. aid package, and she expressed confidence that there would no change in relations as a result of Reagan's election. Haig said Nicaragua's aggression against its neighbors would have to stop for the United States to even consider normal relations.

Meanwhile, the evidence mounted of Sandinista support for guerrillas in El Salvador, Guatemala, and Honduras. In June, U.S. intelligence agencies spotted large shipments of Soviet arms entering Nicaragua, including T-55 tanks. Three weeks later, a group of Nicaraguans seeking asylum in Honduras told the same story of "hundreds" of Soviets working alongside Sandinista government officials, particularly in the army. Although U.S. ambassador Pezzullo minimized the importance of the Soviet armor, he failed to allay the fears of the Hondurans, who immediately requested antitank weapons from the United States.

Armed with this evidence, the Reagan administration terminated all aid to Nicaragua on April 1. Even at this point, however, the administration did not slam the door completely shut. It followed the advice of the Nicaraguan private-sector representatives and provided $5.6 million to a variety of private humanitarian groups in the country. Also, the administration did nothing to interfere with the loans and credits that the Nicaraguans were due to receive from the World Bank.

The Internal Wars over Nicaragua Begin

The decision to cut off assistance did not have unanimous support from Reagan's aides. Reagan's first ambassador to Nicaragua, Lawrence Pezullo, was particularly outraged. Bringing official word of the decision to Sandinista junta member Sergio Ramirez, Pezullo added an apology: "Look, I'm sorry. This was not the way it was supposed to be." He later told one of Reagan's critics, "We dealt ourselves out of the game for no reason in April 1981, because of small-mindedness on our side." Pezullo later said the aid cutoff convinced him to resign his post. After all, he asked later, "[Without aid], how could you really think you could do anything?" A career Foreign Service officer, Pezullo's perception of policy began and ended with using aid.

Such dissension in the Reagan administration over the April 1 decision was only the first shot in what was to become an endless war over

U.S. policy toward Nicaragua. Constantine Menges, a major player in the war, entered the administration in April 1983, joining the Central Intelligence Agency (CIA). Late in the year, he was transferred to the staff of the National Security Council. Menges recounted a meeting with Robert "Bud" McFarlane in which the new National Security advisor "didn't really grasp the international implications of having a new Communist regime on our doorstep."

It is implausible that McFarlane was really as blasé as Menges suggests, but he may have had another agenda. Latin American governments, facing guerrilla organizations funded and armed by Castro and the Sandinistas, are likely to conclude that they need much larger military establishments. To fulfill this need, El Salvador, along with Guatemala, Honduras, and Costa Rica, would have very little choice but to come, hat in hand, to the U.S. government for help. And their dependency would be driven not only by the need for more soldiers, but also by the economic consequences of taking so many young men out of the productive economy. In addition, a larger military would likely strengthen the antidemocratic forces on the right in Central America, postponing (at least) the advent of democracy. Since dictatorships involved in guerrilla wars pay scant attention to economic development, this would also be postponed, and in fact crippled by the likely capital flight that accompanies civil war.

In short, it is possible for an American policy maker who prefers leveraged allies to natural allies to see a Communist Nicaragua not as a disaster, but as an opportunity. While there would be minimal American leverage over a pro-Soviet Nicaragua, the danger from Nicaragua could force its neighbors to accept dependence on the United States as a necessary evil. Viewed that way, the "loss" of Nicaragua could be more than balanced by the gain in leverage over the remainder of Central America. Such thinking was repellent to Reagan's more conservative allies.

The Players Take Sides

Secretary of State Al Haig was far more determined than most members of the administration to deal with the problem of Communism in Central America, but his solutions, for the most part, were directed toward Cuba. Haig had talked in his confirmation hearings of "going to the source" to counter Central American Communism.

Haig's statements on Cuba generated immediate, and public, response from Casper Weinberger, secretary of defense, who believed that an important part of his job was to protect the American military from any repeat of Vietnam. For Weinberger, this meant opposing any military action that did not meet strict criteria of public support, clarity of mission, feasibility of exit strategy, and so on. But while in other administrations, such a disagreement between Cabinet officials might have been aired in the Cabinet Room, during a Cabinet meeting, Haig and Weinberger voiced their conflicting views in public, a pattern that Reagan administration officials would largely follow throughout Reagan's eight years in the White House.

Pressed by Reagan for a policy on Nicaragua, Haig ordered the State Department staff to analyze the situation and present policy options. The resulting paper was largely the work of then State Department counselor Bud McFarlane. In it, McFarlane focused largely on the role of Cuba in supplying arms and support to the Sandinista government and the Salvadoran rebels. The paper's policy options all involved putting more diplomatic, economic, and perhaps, military pressure on Cuba, to induce Fidel Castro to curtail this activity. Weinberger responded with public statements about the difficulty and undesirability of a naval blockade of Cuba, an option the McFarlane paper did not include.

Reagan rejected all of the options presented in the McFarlane paper and directed Haig and his staff to try again. This time, Haig entrusted the task to Thomas O. Enders, newly appointed assistant secretary of state for inter-American affairs. From May 1981, until his departure from his post in May 1983, Enders would be the flashpoint in the internal Reagan administration wars over Central America.

Enders had no particular expertise in Latin America. A career Foreign Service officer (which was enough to make him suspect to many of Reagan's conservative supporters), Enders had had assignments in Southeast Asia (which was enough to make him suspect to many of Reagan's liberal critics) and, most recently, as U.S. ambassador to the European Economic Community. As he began to formulate a plan for Central America, he drew two crucial conclusions. The first was that the lynchpin of U.S. Central America policy had to be the interdiction of arms from Nicaragua.

Enders' second conclusion was that the president's political advisors, and perhaps President Reagan himself, preferred to see Central America off the front pages as much as possible. Consequently, he referred the matter to the CIA and asked for a covert plan to use military force to cut off the supply of Sandinista arms to the Salvadoran rebels. Given Reagan's repeated promises not to send American combat forces into Central America, this military force would have to be made up of non-U.S. nationals.

Enders might have gone the covert route even without the perceived preference from the White House. A journalist who covered the Reagan White House described Enders as possessing "a passion for secret diplomacy and a conviction that the United States could impose its terms on smaller powers by combining the promise of economic aid with the threat of military intervention." Under U.S. law, a covert interdiction program would require Reagan to sign a National Security finding that the Sandinistas' activities constituted a danger to the security of the U.S. The State Department and the CIA began compiling the evidence for this finding, and also making contact with the anti-Sandinista groups already in existence.

The Birth of the Contras

Meanwhile, anti-Sandinista Nicaraguans declined to wait for the Reagan administration to make a decision about assisting them. Early in 1981, groups of Nicaraguans began training in camps in the United States. Some attended camps in Florida, where, for the most part, the training was done by Cuban exiles. There was also at least one training camp in southern California, where the Nicaraguans would later state openly that they were training for an invasion to liberate Nicaragua.

These early attempts to organize, train, and equip an armed force to take on the Sandinistas were rudimentary to the point of being pathetic. (The CIA estimated that by the end of 1981, there were no more than five hundred rebels facing the twenty-thousand-man Sandinista army.) Their attempts occurred under the radar, largely guided and funded by private individuals. In no way were the camps initiated or even endorsed by the Reagan administration. Richard Allen, Reagan's National Security Advisor in 1981, said later that Reagan never approved a plan to create a Nicaraguan rebel army. Haig also said he did not know about it and added that the rebels were "the wrong medicine for the wrong disease."

As rudimentary as these early efforts at armed resistance were, they left lasting impressions, all of them negative. The involvement of anti-Castro Cuban exiles gave the impression of weakness, since the Cubans had been singularly unable to mount an effective resistance to Castro for more than twenty years. The small numbers of rebels reinforced the impression that the armed resistance to the Sandinistas would never amount to anything really effective. At the same time, many of the early recruits who came to the Florida and California training camps were former members of Somoza's National Guard. The presence of the exguardsmen gave the rebels a reputation from which they would not recover for years.

The one bright light in the rebels' early days was the decision of former National Guard colonel Enrique Bermúdez to play a leadership role. Besides being one of the few genuinely effective combat leaders in Somoza's army, Bermúdez also had a reputation for personal probity and for respecting human rights. He was also known to be industrious, conscientious, and committed to the needs of the men under his command.

While his leadership helped the rebels to become a more effective fighting force, it did nothing to assuage concerns over the rebels' commitment to fighting for democracy. For most of the 1980s, American newspapers would routinely refer to the Nicaraguan rebel army as "mostly" made up of ex-National Guardsmen. This habit would even continue when the rebel army was much larger than the National Guard ever had been. American media outlets, in the main, also adopted the Sandinistas' name for the rebels: the *Contras*, an abbreviation of the Spanish word for counterrevolutionary. This name gave the impression that the rebels simply wanted to turn the clock back and had no positive agenda for Nicaragua.

Disagreements over What the Contras Are For

While the Nicaraguans gathered in their training camps and dreamed of returning to their homeland, the Reagan administration continued to wrestle with the decision about how to handle the Sandinistas. As 1981 progressed, the revolutionary government of Nicaragua grew more repressive at home, more aggressive with its neighbors, and more anti-American in its rhetoric. Though many Latin Americans may view the U.S. government as an all-powerful institution that can impose its will on smaller, poorer countries at will, Reagan's options for dealing with the Nicaraguan challenge were few.

Reagan himself had repeatedly ruled out a direct invasion by American forces. Such a move, he believed, would have virtually no support in the United States. In addition, Reagan was acutely aware of Latin Americans' visceral resentment of American military interventions of the past, and he even peppered his pledges not to intervene with the phrase *Colos-*

sus of the North, a pejorative Latin American nickname that Reagan was determined the United States would not earn on his watch.

Short of military force, the U.S. government was left only with more indirect options. Economic sanctions, a favorite of U.S. foreign policy professionals, largely because sanctions usually create more dependence on the United States, were not likely to garner much more public support in the United States than an invasion. Americans who were opposed to shooting Nicaraguans, Reagan included, were not much more enthusiastic about starving them.

A less drastic option, but also a less effective one, was creating and assembling more diplomatic and political opposition to the Sandinistas among Latin Americans. The FSLN leaders, after all, had signed written pledges to the Organization of American States (OAS) that they would respect human rights and hold elections, in return for the regional body's recognition of them as the legal government of Nicaragua. A diplomatic effort would involve, at the extreme, withdrawing OAS recognition. On a parallel track, the administration could try to convince other Latin American states to cool their relations with Managua and isolate the Sandinistas, while publicizing their record of broken promises. While the above actions are significant, and indeed became integral parts of the Reagan administration's offensive against the Sandinistas, the only action likely to produce any short-term change in Sandinista domestic or foreign policies was to support and deploy a Nicaraguan armed force, which the administration eventually did.

The discussions leading up to this decision revealed divisions within the administration even deeper and more bitter than those that existed over Salvadoran policy. On El Salvador, the argument within the administration was over the best means for attaining a similar end. Everyone in Reagan's White House wished to prevent a Communist victory in El Salvador. They disagreed over things such as timing, level of publicity, importance of one tactic over another, which agencies should be involved, and similar matters of detail. On Nicaragua, by contrast, the argument was over not means, but ends. Some very high-ranking officials working for Reagan did not wish to see the contras succeed.

The primary drafter of Reagan's Nicaragua policy was Thomas Enders, assistant secretary of state for inter-American affairs. As we have seen, in May 1981, while still very new to his position, and while spending much more time drafting what would become Reagan's Caribbean

Basin Initiative, Enders tasked the CIA to develop policy options. During the CIA drafting process, the agency's director, William Casey, acquired an interest in the project and made sure Enders' request was acted upon promptly.

Still, it was not until November that the full National Security Council discussed Enders' report, which included the option of secretly funding the Nicaraguan rebels. According to Lou Cannon, White House reporter for the *Washington Post*, Enders attended a NSC meeting on November 16, 1981, and presented the case for the covert action. Both Enders and Casey told Reagan that the primary purpose of funding the contras was to induce the Sandinistas to halt their arms shipments to El Salvador. Failing that, the rebels would be able to intercept the arms themselves. What Enders apparently did not say at the meeting was that the U.S. level of support would be paltry enough to provide incentive for the Nicaraguan rebels to steal arms from the Sandinistas that were intended for the Salvadoran guerrillas.

Cannon describes the eventual decision, taken at the November 16 meeting, to begin funding the rebels as "the most negative consensus imaginable." While the hard-liners in the administration, such as UN Ambassador Jeane Kirkpatrick and National Security Advisor William Clark, backed the idea enthusiastically, the others on the NSC were much less sanguine. Haig went along with the covert funding program because all the other, more forceful options for dealing with the Sandinistas had been rejected. Chief of Staff James Baker and Michael Deaver (his chief aide) agreed largely to prevent any more forceful option from being adopted, especially Haig's stated goal of wanting to "go to the source," meaning Cuba.

Reagan's instincts were against a covert program. He felt no shame whatever in using forceful means to stop the Soviets' surrogates from gaining ground on the American mainland. His political instincts told him that he still had much hard work to do to convince the American people that the Salvadoran rebels and the Sandinistas were serious threats to the country's security and well-being. Moreover, Reagan saw guerrillas fighting a Communist government as forces for freedom and had a hard time understanding why his advisors did not want him to talk about it. A covert program, by its very nature, would be one for which Reagan was giving away his greatest asset, his ability to communicate persuasively. (Reagan would not publicly make the case for supporting the Nicaraguan rebels until May 1984. The delay would be disastrous.)

Disagreements over Democracy

Enders' inner thoughts about the covert funding program are fairly easy to read. The assistant secretary saw the rebels solely as a means to pressure the Sandinistas into improving their human rights record and stopping their support of the Salvadoran guerrillas. He had no desire to see the Sandinistas overthrown. For Enders, a covert program meant very little involvement from senior members of the administration. Instead, the program would actually be run by middle-level bureaucrats like Enders himself.

In the actual National Security finding that authorized the covert funding, Reagan directed that an interagency task force, including representatives from the State Department, Defense Department, National Security Council staff, and CIA, handle the day-to-day details of the program. This arrangement meant more power for Enders also, since Reagan had earlier directed that all interagency task forces concerned with foreign policy be chaired by their State Department representative. Thus, at its inception, the Nicaraguan rebels found themselves the dubious beneficiaries of an American program run by a man who did not want them to win.

Enders had made it clear over the summer of 1981 that he had no opposition to the Sandinistas remaining in power, nor even with their abysmal human rights' record. While the options paper Haig ordered was being drafted in August 1981, Enders tried some secret diplomacy with the Sandinistas. Earlier in the summer, Enders had accepted an invitation to see Senator Jesse Helms (R-NC), who had been vocal in his demands for more concerted action against the Sandinistas by the Reagan administration. Enders asked if the influential conservative senator would give him six months to try to alter the Sandinistas' policies through diplomacy. Helms agreed.

August 1981 was significant for U.S.-Nicaraguan relations for another reason. Clark brought in an expert to the NSC staff to assist with the negotiations surrounding the sale of sophisticated spy planes (AWACS) to Saudi Arabia. After the sale was authorized by Congress, Clark kept the Marine major on staff. His name was Oliver North.

While North settled into his new job, Enders made a trip to Managua, without telling anyone from any other agency outside the State Department. At meetings with Daniel Ortega and other hard-line Sandinista leaders, and alongside the U.S. ambassador to Nicaragua, Lawrence Pezzullo, Enders told the Sandinistas that normal relations with the United States depended only on the Sandinistas' promise that they would end the subversion of their neighbors, reduce the size of their armed forces, and cut their ties to Cuba and the Soviet Union. Enders then backed off from the demand that the Sandinistas reduce their armed forces and said that the U.S. government had no objection to the tanks, helicopters, aircraft, armored personnel carriers and howitzers that the Sandinistas had by then acquired from Cuba.

Enders did not even request that the Sandinistas adopt democracy. In fact, at a private meeting with Daniel Ortega and Sandinista foreign minister Miguel D'Escoto, Enders said, "You see your revolution as irreversible, and so do we." Enders even offered to "look at" the training camps in the United States for Nicaraguan rebels and to reexamine the possibility of food aid and a resumption of the Peace Corps program. "You can do your thing," Enders said, "but do it within your borders." While it is doubtful that Enders would have been able to persuade Reagan to go along with the offer, the fact that Enders made it at all is instructive. Friendship with the Sandinista leadership was important to him.

However, democracy for Nicaragua was not one of Enders' goals. Soon after taking over the Inter-American Bureau at State, as he was starting to draft administration policy on Central America, Enders considered adding language about the importance of democracy, but he noted later that there was considerable resistance to this. Free elections, Enders insisted, were simply too risky. "Who'll win?" he asked. "How can we tell?" Constantine Menges recounted a meeting that he had with Enders in September 1981. Menges gave Enders a one-page document on restoring democracy to Nicaragua. "Enders read my plan," Menges wrote, "looked angrily at me, crumpled the page in his fist, and smashed it down on his table saying: 'Constantine, this is the real world. Get serious. There is no chance for democracy in Nicaragua.' "

President Reagan, for his part, believed that the U.S. government should increase the region's chance for democracy and that economic prosperity would follow. In a speech to the OAS in February 1982, Reagan reminded the organization of the Sandinistas' promises of free elections and respect for human rights. The United States, Reagan insisted, was committed to making sure that the Sandinistas kept their promises. The speech was also noteworthy because in it Reagan did not use the words *stable* or *stability* at all. By contrast, he used the word *freedom* twelve times and *democracy* or *democratic* eleven times.

When Reagan wrote in his autobiography about his decision to confront the Soviet Union in Central America, he said, "If Communism prevailed in Latin America, it would end any hope of achieving the social and economic progress needed to bring prosperity to the region." He added, "The only long-term solution [to Communist subversion] was economic development of these countries, a better standard of living for their people, democratic rule, and more social justice."

Interfering with the Nicaraguan Rebels

One factor in the decision to secretly support the Nicaraguan rebels that did not seem to receive much discussion was the goal and motivation of the rebels themselves. It did not seem to occur to anyone that, whatever goals the U.S. government might have, the Nicaraguans risking their lives fighting the Sandinistas were not primarily concerned with arms flows to El Salvador. U.S. officials, however, were bent on exercising tight control over the rebels once the decision was made to provide them with funds.

Prior to the start of American covert aid, the rebels had been receiving aid from Argentina. When Argentina invaded the Malvinas-Falkland Islands in April 1982, however, the State Department moved immediately to use the war to stop the Argentine aid funds. While the U.S. government was officially neutral in the Falklands conflict, U.S. officials used the unspoken threat that the United States would side with Britain if Argentina ignored the officials' wishes. In fact, Argentina had no choice but to cut off the Nicaraguans, given Britain's unexpected decision to fight.

The State Department also tried to replace the contras' leader with one more to its liking. Since Enrique Bermúdez, leader of the largest rebel army, was fairly well known and not completely beholden to the U.S. government, some U.S. officials tried to supplant him with Eden Pastora, an ex-Sandinista who formed his own rebel group in early 1982. At the same time that U.S. officials were pressuring Argentina to discontinue its support, they were also trying to force Bermúdez to accept Pastora as a partner. Honduras scuttled these plans by refusing to permit Pastora onto Honduran soil.

Pastora would eventually take his small force to Costa Rica, where it remained only a fraction of the size of the Honduran-based rebel army led by Bermúdez. Since Pastora had been a member of the Sandinista junta, he lacked the trust of many Nicaraguans taking up arms against the

Sandinistas. He was also a committed socialist. Both of these factors made him an attractive substitute for Bermúdez in the eyes of some U.S. officials. With less popular support than Bermúdez, Pastora would have to lean on support from American officials that much more. If, by some miracle, he did win, his socialist policies would hurt the Nicaraguan economy and make post-Sandinista Nicaragua dependent on outside assistance.

Liberal members of Congress also desired to prevent a rebel victory, if such a victory meant less control and influence for the U.S. government. In December 1981, five days after Casey briefed congressmen on the intelligence committees, Edward Boland (D-MA), chair of the House Select Committee on Intelligence, wrote to Casey with what he called "serious concerns" about the covert funding program. Among other things, Boland wanted assurances that the rebels would be under U.S. control. In the spring of 1982, Boland's committee voted to limit aid to the purpose of interdicting arms.

The Battle Lines Harden

By the time the House Intelligence Committee had cast this vote, the Reagan administration had become two warring camps on the issue of Nicaragua. At the Cabinet level, National Security advisor Clark backed the rebels, along with Kirkpatrick and Casey. All three embraced the goal of a Nicaragua freed from Sandinista control. Haig, Baker and Deaver, for their part, had no enthusiasm for the rebel program and even less for democracy in Nicaragua. At the lower levels of the administration, more battle lines were drawn. For the most part, Reagan appointees championed the rebels and soon became known as the "hard-liners" or "Reaganites." Careerists, however, worried most about losing control of Nicaragua. Members of this faction were called "pragmatists."

The war between these two factions would dominate the remainder of the Reagan administration. The hard liners were firm in their belief that they were carrying out Reagan's wishes and equally firm in their belief that global Communism could be reversed, starting in Central America. They preferred to speak and act publicly about their goals for democracy in Central America, and they made common cause with the hundreds of young conservatives who flocked to Washington after Reagan's victory and who, for the most part, worked for private think tanks and lobbying firms committed to victory in the Cold War.

The pragmatists, for their part, firmly believed that in controlling and hamstringing the rebels, they were saving Reagan from himself. They preferred the largely secret methods of bureaucratic warfare, which Menges described in his memoirs: "bypassing normal channels, making secret diplomatic contacts, suppressing and withholding information, delaying the release of key documents, holding private parallel meetings instead of doing business at regular ones, furtive networking, leaking to the press, dealing opponents within the administration out of the action, undercutting responsible officials, and, of course, simple backbiting." The combatants rarely met in face-to-face combat and, in fact, rarely met at all. Even within the small and closed social scene in Washington, DC, they managed to avoid one another, although they never took their eyes off each other.

Since the rebel aid program was covert, many administration officials, on both sides, first learned about it, along with the rest of the country, when the *Washington Post* reported on the plan in early 1982. Much of official Washington suspected that Casey himself was the leak and that he was insuring that the administration did not have the option of abandoning the rebels once they started receiving U.S. aid. Remarkably, in light of what followed, the *Post* story did not generate much controversy. It was not until *Newsweek*, the *Post*'s sister publication, ran the story in its November 8 issue that the story took over the front pages.

By then, the contras had erupted onto the Nicaraguan scene. On March 15, 1982, the contras staged their first major action in Nicaragua, blowing up two bridges in the north. The action isolated the far northwestern part of Nicaragua from the rest of the country, which both prevented Sandinista arms from going to El Salvador, at least overland, and permitted the rebels to organize themselves inside Nicaragua itself.

As major conduits for supplies and troops, the bridges were, by any reasonable measure, legitimate military targets. The Sandinistas, however, portrayed the action as evidence that the Reagan administration was making war on Nicaraguan peasants, who needed the bridges to get their produce to market. In what would become a pattern, the Sandinistas would make their case and have their case reported in the American media, without rebuttal, since administration officials were prohibited from commenting on ongoing intelligence efforts. The president was included in this prohibition. His enemies in Congress, however, were not; nor were the Sandinistas. As the contras opened their war on March

15, they discovered that the fight to influence American public opinion had already been ceded to the enemy.

March 1982 was a watershed month for other reasons as well. On March 11, the Reagan administration released aerial photographs that showed the Sandinistas engaging in a huge military buildup, with Soviet and Cuban help. On the same day, the Sandinistas gave credence to Reagan's warnings by protesting U.S. reconnaissance flights and indicating that they might attempt to acquire MiGs from the Soviet Union. On March 14, the Sandinistas welcomed the prime minister of North Korea to Nicaragua. Premier Li Chong brought promises of more Soviet-bloc aid to the Sandinistas.

The next day, the Sandinistas suspended all rights and guarantees under the constitution for thirty days, citing "U.S. aggression." For the next six years, the Sandinistas would refuse to deal with the contras directly and would never refer to them as anything except agents of U.S. aggression. They would also insist that their suspension of rights (which lasted for much longer than thirty days) was reactive, although the March 15 declaration merely ratified repression that had started much earlier.

Also on March 15, U.S. Congressman Michael Barnes (D-MD), chair of the Latin America Subcommittee, introduced a bill to prevent any U.S. government aid from being used to support any covert effort to overthrow the Sandinistas. Barnes' bill mirrored the later and much better known efforts of Representitive Boland. Their measures were the first of many attempts by Democrats in Congress to prevent the overthrow of the Sandinistas.

Finally, Thomas Enders made yet another foray into personal diplomacy in March 1982. He persuaded Haig to hold two long meetings with the Mexican foreign minister Jorge Casteneda, who was known throughout Central America as a strong supporter of the Sandinistas. At same time, roving U.S. ambassador Vernon Walters was sent to Havana to meet "secretly" with Castro. Within two days, every head of state in Central America knew about both meetings. To leaders friendly to the United States, the Haig and Walters meetings seemed like repetitions of U.S. diplomacy just before the 1973 Vietnam "peace" accords. Casteneda, for his part, claimed that Haig had brought specific proposals for "normalization" of U.S. relations with Nicaragua and Cuba. According to Menges, the leaders assumed that another American sellout was coming, and they started thinking about making their own deal with Castro and the Sandinistas.

Enders' machinations outraged administration officials who were preparing for the March 25 elections in El Salvador and trying to bring some semblance of democracy to Central America. The civil wars, in Central America and in the Reagan administration, had only begun.

5

The Wars Escalate, 1982–1983

The national security of all the Americas is at stake in Central America. If we cannot defend ourselves there, we cannot expect to prevail elsewhere.

—*Ronald Reagan*, April 1983

Regaining the Initiative

In the early days of his presidency, Reagan's policies toward Central America had been primarily reactive. In El Salvador, he reacted to the guerrillas' "Final Offensive" by rushing supplies to the Salvadoran army and stationing fifty-five U.S. military advisors in the country. He reacted to congressional opposition by agreeing to certify progress on human rights at regular intervals. He reacted to unexpectedly high levels of infighting in his administration by focusing on the slender areas of agreement. Mostly, he bought time and encouraged the democratic process the Salvadoran government had started in 1979.

In Nicaragua, Reagan reacted to Sandinista interference in El Salvador by cutting off economic assistance to the country and by asking for policy options to stop the flow of arms to the Salvadoran guerrillas. Reagan responded to the accelerating trend toward totalitarianism under the Sandinistas by reminding as many listeners as he could of the Sandinistas' 1979 promises to bring pluralism and democracy to Nicaragua. Eventually, Reagan supported the anti-Sandinista guerrillas.

By the beginning of 1982, Reagan was ready for a bold stroke. He wished to do something that would immediately change the terms of the

Central America debate while fundamentally changing conditions in the region for the better. At the same time, he also wanted to clear out some of the bureaucratic resistance to his objectives in Central America. On February 24, he unveiled his idea for accomplishing all of these goals.

The Caribbean Basin Initiative

Had Reagan been satisfied with simply blunting Cuban and Soviet inroads into Central America, he could have chosen more direct ways of doing so, such as a massive increase in U.S. military aid, a naval quarantine, or a deal with the Soviet Union over the heads of the Caribbean leaders. There were precedents for such actions, and Reagan would not have had to face measurably greater political opposition. But Reagan wanted to start the process of liberating Central America not just from the Communists, but also from U.S. bureaucrats who were determined to make the countries of the region into leveraged allies. His speech to the Organization of American States was the equivalent of laying down a gauntlet.

The speech began with a series of rhetorical swipes at Cuba and the Soviet Union, such as: "We know that a nation cannot be liberated by depriving its people of liberty." But when Reagan shifted the topic of the speech to the countries of the Caribbean Basin, he began to send some unmistakable signals. "We all seek to insure that the people of this area," he said, "have the right to preserve their national identities, to improve their economic lot, and to develop their political institutions." Rather than focusing on stability, Reagan focused on nationalism and economic independence. It was clear to seasoned listeners that something new and unusual would follow.

Reagan described the Caribbean Basin Initiative (CBI), which would increase U.S. aid to the region, streamline trade relationships, and create a new State Department Bureau for the region, combining the work of several State Department agencies. The central goal of the CBI would be to encourage the nations of the region to "use the magic of the marketplace, the market of the Americas, to earn their own way toward self-sustaining growth." Most commentators latched onto the free market references (this may have been what Reagan wanted the media to do) and missed the really key phrase, which was "self-sustaining growth." Such growth means, in time, the end to American foreign aid. Reagan also referred to the positive role that trade and investment would play, in addition to U.S. aid. To underline the point, Reagan stated boldly: "But [U.S.] aid will encourage private-sector activities, not displace them." He added, "We will offer technical assistance and training to assist the private sector." This commitment was significant because it meant that agencies other than the State Department would be involved, including private contractors, who could provide the actual technical assistance and training.

By lifting American trade barriers regionwide, Reagan deprived the State Department of the leverage that comes from negotiating bilateral trade concessions with individual countries. Reagan emphasized that such a regional approach to free trade was unprecedented for the United States and again broke radically new ground by saying, "This commitment makes unmistakably clear our determination to help our neighbors grow strong." Reagan also linked his initiative with the wars in Central America: "Our economic and social program cannot work if our neighbors cannot pursue their own economic and political future in peace, but must divert their resources, instead, to fight imported terrorism and armed attack."

There was a bureaucratic element to the Caribbean Basin Initiative as well. By creating a new region, which had previously been dealt with piecemeal in the State Department and other U.S. agencies, Reagan provided himself with opportunities to appoint new people, reward bureaucrats in line with his thinking, and marginalize potential enemies. Reagan not only knew what he wanted for the Caribbean, but he also knew how to compel the foreign policy bureaucracy to share his goals, at least outwardly.

Elections and Offensives in El Salvador

While Washington digested Reagan's initiative, the political and military wars went on in El Salvador. On the political front, El Salvador made ready for elections, in part to fend off demands for power sharing. An elected government, after all, could not be expected to share power with those who did not participate in the election. In addition, both Reagan and Salvadoran president Duarte were personally and ideologically committed to elections. Duarte announced on May 10, 1981, that the first round of elections would take place in March 1982. These elections would be for members of a Constituent Assembly. This body would write a new constitution, while simultaneously serving as a national parliament.

Soon after Duarte announced the elections, his government invited the left-wing Social Democratic Party and the National Democratic Union, which was the political arm of the Communist Party of El Salvador, to compete openly in the elections. Duarte recognized the legitimate fear that leftists in El Salvador had of identifying themselves, and thus making themselves a target for the military and the death squads, although his own Christian Democratic Party had suffered many such killings itself without going underground. To assuage the leftists' fear, Duarte offered the protection of international observers throughout the election process.

All the factions associated with the FMLN rejected Duarte's offer. The FMLN said early in 1982 that it was not opposed, in theory, to elections but that the scheduled elections took place "in the shadow of too much violence." The guerrillas repeated their demand for negotiations on power sharing. In the short term, the promise of elections gave the Reagan administration an argument for rejecting power sharing. With this backing, the Duarte government was also able to withstand pressure from liberals in the United States and leftists in El Salvador to postpone the elections or to replace them with direct talks with the guerrillas. The FMLN, once it became clear that the elections would go on as scheduled, turned to disrupting the elections.

American officials, and Duarte himself, fully expected the Christian Democratic Party to coast to victory, especially with much of the Left refusing to participate. But a new political power was rising in El Salvador. In September 1981, several conservative parties merged to form the Nationalist Republican Alliance (ARENA), led by exarmy major Roberto D'Aubuisson. In spite of D'Aubuisson's background, ARENA insisted that it was separate from the military and was running to provide an electoral alternative to the left-leaning policies of Duarte's Christian Democrats.

Land reform was at the center of the ARENA platform. D'Aubuisson promised that phase 2 would never take place if he were in power but that the phase 3 "land to the tiller" program would proceed as soon as possible. In general, ARENA embraced a free-market approach to El Salvador's economic problems, and its spokesmen constantly made reference to the success of Chile's economy in the late 1970s. More striking was the promise from ARENA that a growing economy would permit El Salvador to do without American assistance. D'Aubuisson told cheering audiences that there were other possible aid donors available and reminded his countrymen that he had connections in Argentina. D'Aubuisson spoke in angry terms about Duarte, promising to try the president for treason for his subservience to America.

The party also promised a far more vigorous prosecution of the war against the FMLN. At one point, D'Aubuisson promised that El Salvador would become "the tomb of the Reds" and that he would "exterminate" the rebels in three months. Putting his life where his mouth was, D'Aubuisson campaigned throughout El Salvador. Duarte, for his part, did not enter FMLN strongholds, citing security concerns.

U.S. officials left little doubt that Duarte was their favored candidate. U.S. Ambassador Deane Hinton, for example, told Salvadoran officials at a diplomatic gathering in San Salvador that his main worry about the elections was a strong showing by ARENA. Two weeks before the elections, Hinton spoke up again, warning that a victory for the "right-wingers" could jeopardize U.S. aid, although he added that his embassy would work closely with the winners of the election, whoever they were. The day before the election, Haig told reporters that the Reagan administration had a preference for a government in El Salvador that would continue the economic and political reforms that Duarte had begun as head of the junta.

Meanwhile, the FMLN pursued its campaign of intimidation against Salvadorans who cast votes. In December 1981, Castro summoned the guerrilla leaders to a meeting in Havana, where they discussed ways to prevent or disrupt the elections. Arms shipments to the Communists in El Salvador increased, almost doubling what they had received in the previous six months. In February, with their new Cuban arms in hand, the Communists promised that a "Final Offensive" would take place before the elections and accompanied the promise with a call for a general uprising.

When this uprising failed to appear, the guerrillas focused on punishing Salvadorans who dared to vote. To help prevent voter fraud, the government planned to have voters dip their fingers in indelible ink as a mark of their participation. The FMLN promised to sever any stained fingers they found. They threatened to put land mines on the roads leading to the polling places and shut down the power. On election day, the FMLN repeatedly broadcast the slogan, Vote today, die tonight.

These threats turned into a military and political disaster for the rebels. About three-quarters of the eligible Salvadorans voted on election day. Most stood in long lines to do so, enduring heat and boredom for up to ten hours. They persisted through deplorable levels of disorganization. Except in a few areas already under rebel control, the effect of the guerrillas' threats was negligible. The myth of the guerrillas' invincibility was shattered.

Even worse for the rebels, the determination of Salvadorans to vote was witnessed by hundreds of international observers and thousands of journalists. Images of long lines of voters pulverized the guerrillas' international support, especially among Americans. The failure of the promised Final Offensive was all the more embarrassing. Salvadorans began making jokes about the rebels' "annual final offensive." The FMLN was the clear loser of the March 1982 elections.

It was also clear, after a few days, who the winner was. While the Christian Democrats won a plurality of the votes, ARENA formed a coalition with two smaller conservative parties to claim a majority of seats in the new Constituent Assembly. D'Aubuisson declared himself the winner and prepared to take office as both prime minister and provisional president.

Initial Reagan administration reaction was euphoric, when the turnout figures were announced and the impotence of the rebels to disrupt the elections was made clear. Euphoria quickly turned to concern, however, when D'Aubuisson emerged as the new head of government. D'Aubuisson was despised by liberals in Congress, who were likely to suspend all military aid to El Salvador with him at the helm. His outspoken disdain for U.S. government officials alone guaranteed opposition to assistance to El Salvador from those who believed U.S. officials should dominate the country.

Ironically, the emergence of D'Aubuisson's coalition blunted one of the emerging criticisms of the elections. When the extent of the rebel failure became clear, the FMLN's supporters, in the United States and elsewhere, insisted that the results were fraudulent and accused the CIA of working with Duarte's junta to stage manage the entire election. (The criticism prompted CIA director William Casey to take the unusual step of acknowledging that the agency did indeed play a role. He insisted, however, that the CIA limited itself to providing indelible ink for the voters' fingers and providing the Salvadoran government with intelligence on rebel activities.) With Duarte's party having lost, however, the credibility of rumors about the CIA disappeared.

Rather, in an election certified by international observers, D'Aubuisson's coalition was the legitimate winner of an election that both Duarte and Reagan had promoted as the next step in El Salvador's political development. To have insisted on D'Aubuisson's exclusion from political power would have been to admit failure in holding the elections in the first place. Moreover, many of Reagan's conservative aides, and conservative backers, were overjoyed at the emergence of D'Aubuisson and his free-market prescriptions for El Salvador. It is likely that Reagan himself at this point had more confidence in D'Aubuisson's leadership than in Duarte's.

D'Aubuisson himself was aware of the controversy surrounding his past and the disappointment that some Americans felt when his conservative coalition won the elections. He addressed their concerns by initially promising to include some Christian Democrats in his government, although he absolutely vetoed the idea of permitting Duarte to remain as provisional president. Indeed, a "grand coalition" of conservatives and Christian Democrats might have been possible, had not American officials started acting like the de facto rulers of El Salvador.

Ten days after the elections, a congressional delegation, led by House majority leader Jim Wright (D-TX), visited El Salvador and held a meeting with Salvadoran leaders in the U.S. Embassy. At the meeting, the congressmen invited themselves into the process of selecting a new government and warned the Salvadorans that, to continue getting U.S. assistance, they had to form a "broad-based, moderate government, committed to economic and social justice." If continued leverage over El Salvador was the goal, U.S. officials would have done better to speak more softly. Far from acquiescing to the demands for a broad-based government, the ARENA leadership took control of the new Constituent Assembly on April 22, shutting out the Christian Democrats completely. In addition, ARENA had the Constituent Assembly declare itself the sovereign government of El Salvador, a role well beyond drafting a new constitution. Ambassador Hinton seemed to accept the setback with good grace, insisting that the election of a right-wing government would not affect Reagan administration policy toward El Salvador.

On May 2, Alvaro Magaña, an international banker, was chosen provisional president by the Constituent Assembly. Magaña was fluent in English and familiar with the ways of Washington. More important, he was colorless enough not to be a challenger for president when elections for that office were held in 1984. Thus, both Duarte and D'Aubuisson could accept his choice, knowing that they would soon have another chance at the top job.

Perhaps more significant than what the Reagan administration did to intervene in El Salvador after the 1982 election was what it did not do. Reagan made no attempt to dislodge D'Aubuisson as head of the Constituent Assembly, nor did the administration react when, as assembly president, D'Aubuisson announced that phase 2 of the land reform program would be postponed indefinitely. This announcement came only a few days after a warning from Senate Foreign Relations Committee chair Charles Percy (D-IL) that funds would be cut off if any part of the land reform were discontinued. D'Aubuisson cleverly did not abandon the entire program, just the part that threatened to be most disruptive to El Salvador's export economy.

Reagan dealt with both Magaña and D'Aubuisson as legitimate leaders and continued to press Congress for more military and economic aid. The American advisors stayed in the country and continued to work to make the Salvadoran army into an effective fighting force. The U.S. Congress also seemed resigned to D'Aubuisson's position. On May 12, the House Foreign Affairs Committee voted overwhelmingly to provide Reagan's request for $60 million in additional military aid for El Salvador.

The FMLN responded to the elections with a military campaign against economic targets. The effort had a remarkably sophisticated purpose, which showed the rebel leaders' understanding of the fissures in the U.S. administration. Widespread and serious economic disruption in El Salvador forced the newly elected government of Roberto D'Aubuisson to request more economic aid from the United States, an onerous task for the independent-minded president of the Constituent Assembly. (In fact, D'Aubuisson wisely left the task of begging for money to Magaña.) Either way, the increasing dependence of the Salvadoran government on American money reinforced the rebels' propaganda image of the government as nothing more than an American client.

At the same time, the rebels knew well that for some officials in the U.S. State Department and aid agencies, El Salvador's dependence was a godsend, since it increased their leverage. Indeed, by attacking economic targets, the guerrillas could insure that Reagan's plans for the elimination of the rebel threat would be implemented half-heartedly, at best, by key U.S. officials. In the meantime, the FMLN could wait for American officials to make some heavy-handed use of this leverage to gain an even greater political payoff from their attacks on El Salvador's economy.

They did not have long to wait. At the end of October, Ambassador Deane Hinton addressed the Salvadoran chamber of commerce. Using decidedly undiplomatic language, he portrayed the U.S.-backed government as unwilling or unable to curb the abuses of right-wing death squads. He equated violence from the Right and the Left, pointedly denouncing the "guerrillas" of the Left and the "gorillas" of the Right. The Salvadoran legal system, he announced, was "rotten," echoing a frequent rebel claim.

He concluded by boldly threatening to stop U.S. military and economic assistance if human rights abuses were not stopped and the death squads brought under control.

Hinton's speech bolstered everything that the Left, both in El Salvador and in the U.S., had been saying about the subservience of the Salvadoran government and the imperial designs of the U.S. government. Radio Venceremos, the radio station of the FMLN, quoted the speech repeatedly, as did Reagan's political enemies in Washington. In the space of an evening, one U.S. official had undermined much of the progress that Reagan had made in garnering support for the defeat of Communism in El Salvador. Instead, the battle in Washington, like that in El Salvador, merely entered a new phase.

The Sandinistas Tighten their Grip

As El Salvador was making giant steps toward democracy, Nicaragua was headed in the opposite direction. Internal repression grew worse and became centered on religious leaders. Just days before the Salvadoran elections, the Sandinistas arrested eighteen Jehovah's Witnesses and expelled nine of them on charges of "antirevolutionary activity." Pressure on other foreign missionaries increased, and the Nicaraguan Catholic Church came under greater scrutiny as well. The leftist government began to demand that the country's highest-ranking Catholic official, Archbishop Miguel Obando y Bravo, provide government censors with an advance copy of his Sunday sermon every week. The demand marked a turning point; Obando y Bravo had been willing to work with the Sandinistas up to that point.

There were other turning points for the Sandinistas that spring. On April 15, former Sandinista junta member Eden Pastora denounced the FSLN as a betrayer of the revolution. He denounced the growing dependence on the Soviets and called for the expulsion of Soviet and Cuban officials from Nicaragua. Less than a month later, Daniel Ortega was in Moscow, where he announced a five-year $166 million agreement for Soviet military and economic aid. Soviet leader Leonid Brezhnev publicly accepted an invitation to visit Nicaragua and also announced new trade pacts between the two countries.

Back in Nicaragua, political and social conditions continued to deteriorate. The first large-scale incursions by the contras took place over the summer of 1982. In some cases, the Sandinistas attributed the contra attacks not to the American CIA, but to evangelical groups in the United

States. Linking the contra attacks to religious groups gave the Sandinistas an excuse to increase repression. It was not long before their actions produced a backlash. In August, a group of Roman Catholic high school students briefly seized control of their Catholic school to show support for Obando y Bravo, who was rapidly becoming a national hero.

Three days later, the Sandinistas struck back in a dramatic, though backhanded, way. Obando y Bravo's chief aide was Monsignor Bismarck Carballo. On August 21, Carballo was called to the home of a young woman who said that she wanted to confess. On entering her home, the priest was seized by Sandinista supporters, who forced him to strip naked. He was then dragged out of the house, where Sandinista news cameramen were waiting. The photographs of the nude priest appeared on television and in print, accompanied by rumors that he had been caught in bed with the woman (who turned out to be a Sandinista also).

The clumsy and shocking treatment of a Catholic priest turned into a public-relations nightmare for the FSLN. No one in Nicaragua, except for committed Sandinistas, believed the story about the priest's alleged tryst. In the United States, the Carballo incident provided graphic and attention-grabbing evidence of the hostility of the Sandinistas for religion in general, and for Catholics in particular. The mistreatment of Carballo undid years of careful image making by the Sandinistas, who had portrayed themselves as pro-Christian, often touting their support from socialist liberation theologians. More than any single event in 1982, the Sandinistas' failed attempt to intimidate and discredit Obando y Bravo, through his aide, hardened the battle lines over the Sandinista Revolution, in Washington and in Nicaragua. It would not be the last time the Sandinistas hurt their own cause by insulting a Catholic churchman.

The Contra War in Nicaragua Goes Public

But the Sandinistas were not the only ones suffering self-inflicted wounds in 1982. On November 1, *Newsweek* magazine's cover story asserted that the U.S. government, more specifically the CIA, had been providing funding and advice to the anti-Sandinista rebels in Nicaragua. The story provided details of the contra operations that had occurred with U.S. help, named some of the Americans and Nicaraguans involved, and purported to quote secret government documents establishing the program.

The reaction to the *Newsweek* story was immediate and almost wholly negative. In the minds of Reagan's political opponents, his anti-

Communist rhetoric was barely tolerable even when it remained nothing more than rhetoric. For Reagan to turn his anti-Communism into policy, by attempting to overthrow a leftist government, one that most of Reagan's enemies did not even acknowledge to be Communist, was completely out of bounds. Democratic leaders in Congress, joined by some moderate Republicans, denounced the program in apocalyptic terms, comparing the actions of the CIA to their actions in the Bay of Pigs, to the overthrow of a leftist government in Guatemala in 1954 and, of course, to their actions in Vietnam.

The public relations battle over the CIA program was almost completely one-sided. Reagan's critics freely quoted the *Newsweek* article, as well as earlier articles that had hitherto been ignored. They waved secret documents around, quoted unnamed intelligence and foreign policy officials, cited purported witnesses to contra attacks in Nicaragua, and wholly controlled the discussion. Reagan administration officials, for their part, responded with refusals to discuss the subject. Reagan himself, confronted at a news conference, evaded questions about the program by saying that he could not discuss an ongoing intelligence matter. Other administration officials took his lead and said nothing (with the exception of unnamed officials who opposed the program and used leaks to the media to try to kill it).

The leaders of the contra movement, however, were not secretive at all. On December 8, contra leaders announced the formation of the Nicaraguan Democratic Front (using the Spanish acronym FDN) and issued a call to arms to the people of Nicaragua. On the same day, however, Congress made the contra war more complicated. By 411–0, the House of Representatives voted to bar the CIA and the Defense Department from using government funds "for the purpose of overthrowing the Government of Nicaragua." The author of the amendment was Rep. Edward Boland (D-MA). It was the first of the Boland Amendments.

When the contra war became public knowledge, it revealed fissures and divisions in the U.S. government that had been widening since Reagan took office and set the stage for much of the acrimony, controversy, and wrangling over Central America that would almost cost him his presidency in 1987. The funding for the contras had followed a lengthy debate in the administration over whether or not U.S. assistance should be covert. To Jeane Kirkpatrick, and to many of Reagan's conservative supporters, a covert program simply did not make sense. It would make Reagan seem ashamed to be supporting anti-Communist guerrillas fighting to bring freedom to their homeland. Moreover, the conservatives foresaw that an ongoing, complex, and controversial program was unlikely to remain secret. They foresaw that when (not if) the contra program became known, the administration would be powerless to defend itself.

The supporters of an overt program proved to be prophetic, but the covert side of the argument was strong also. To support the contras, the U.S. government would require the support of Honduras. Nicaragua only had two land borders, and Costa Rica, its other neighbor, would have nothing to do with a CIA program involving armed Nicaraguans. Honduras' government insisted on what intelligence officials call "plausible deniability." They wanted to be able to say publicly that no hostile actions toward the Sandinistas were being launched from their territory. With considerable justification, the Honduran leadership did not trust the Americans to protect them from the wrath of the Sandinistas.

The first Boland Amendment also brought confusion to Washington, made worse by the already strained relations between the Reagan administration and Democrats in Congress. In spite of the lopsided vote in favor of the 1982 Boland Amendment, it was not clear to the administration exactly what the House of Representatives was saying with its vote. The amendment was actually rather limited in scope. It referred only to the CIA and the Defense Department. It did not limit the actions of any other agency of the U.S. government.

At the same time, it barred using U.S. government funds for the purpose of overthrowing the Sandinistas. It did not bar funding for a program to harass the Sandinistas, to discomfort them, to weaken them, or to impede them in exporting revolution to other parts of Central America. Thus, a contra program that was officially intended to stop the flow of arms from Nicaragua to El Salvador was not in violation of the Boland Amendment. One way of reading the 411–0 vote, therefore, was as a statement by Congress that the Reagan administration should continue the program but talk about it differently.

Democrat members of Congress would later insist that they intended to stop the contra program with the various Boland Amendments, and they would express shock that the Reagan administration would try to find loopholes in the legislation. Such statements were either disingenuous or evidence of serious short-term memory loss. In the 1970s, Congress had reacted to rumors of U.S. support for anti-Communist rebels in Angola with the Clark Amendment. Unlike the Boland Amendment, the Clark Amendment was ironclad and comprehensive. Had Boland and his colleagues genuinely desired to put an end to U.S. intervention, all they had to do was rewrite the Clark Amendment.

That they did not do so indicated that they did not wish to do so. Thus, Reagan administration officials were wholly justified in concluding that Congress wished to have it both ways: to publicly condemn a program that was unpopular and avoid responsibility for any negative results that might come from actually stopping it. Had the communications between the White House and Congress been more open and built on a stronger layer of trust, administration reaction to this first Boland Amendment might have been different. As it was, White House officials had long since concluded that they could not trust the words of congressional leaders, so they drew conclusions from their actions instead.

Using Leverage in El Salvador

As 1983 opened, the situation in El Salvador was deteriorating rapidly. Many Salvadorans greeted New Year's Day in the dark, after rebels attacked power lines throughout the country, blacking out the capital of San Salvador and other cities. After U.S. pressure on El Salvador to remove military officers with bad human rights records, the Magaña administration transferred LTC Sigifredo Ochoa Pérez, commander of the northern province of Cabanas. Instead of leaving his post, however, Ochoa declared himself "in rebellion" and sealed off roads leading to the province. His rebellion lasted for a week and added a new note of chaos to El Salvador's political situation.

By the end of January, liberal members of Congress were proposing cutting off aid to El Salvador unless the government opened negotiations with the rebels. Since FMLN members had said that they were only interested in discussing power sharing, a demand for negotiations was tantamount to a demand for surrender. The FMLN, for its part, expanded its operations from the northeast of the country, where it was strongest, to the southeast, trying to cut the country in two. On January 31, it captured the city of Berlin against heavy resistance from government troops.

Two days later, Assistant Secretary of State Thomas Enders sounded a distinctly pessimistic note at a congressional hearing. He said that the administration was "anxious" about El Salvador after the fall of Berlin and hinted that military means were not working to manage the conflict. Enders complained that U.S. policy was "confused" and that the government of El Salvador was receiving "mixed signals." The solution he suggested, not surprisingly, was more control by the State Department over U.S. policy toward El Salvador.

The impact of this State Department control became visible on February 10, when a DOS spokesperson said that the U.S. government rejected power sharing but did support "reconciliation" between the government and the rebels. Reaction from conservatives in Congress and in the administration was strong, and negative, forcing George Shultz to pull back and tell Congress that the administration would not back any solution that allowed the FMLN to "shoot [its] way into power." Instead, Shultz and the State Department took a more indirect route to their goal of a "negotiated" end to the civil war. Shultz made secret preparations to meet with the FMLN leadership, a fact he denied to the *New York Times*.

At the same time, some officials single-mindedly stressed the bad news from El Salvador. In late February, in several public hearings on Capitol Hill, officials from the State and Defense Departments told reporters the situation in El Salvador was "discouraging" and that a major increase in both U.S. military aid and the number of advisors would be necessary. The latter prediction was nearly certain to encourage comparisons with Vietnam and increase pressure from Congress and from the American people for a quick, negotiated end to U.S. involvement. With some U.S. senators, the strategy worked perfectly. In late March, Christopher Dodd (D-RI), Daniel Inouye (D-HI), and Nancy Kassebaum (R-KS) called for a sharp reduction in U.S. aid to El Salvador and demanded that future aid be tied to El Salvador's elected government entering into "unconditional negotiations" with the FMLN. (The three senators insisted, however, that they did not wish to see power sharing in El Salvador.) The rebels sought to increase the pressure for negotiations by beginning a major offensive.

The drive toward power sharing, however, was dealt a severe setback by the visit of Pope John Paul II to San Salvador on March 6. In his homily to hundreds of thousands of Salvadorans at an outdoor Mass, the pontiff rejected power sharing and gave strong support to the country's elected officials. The pope left no doubt that he believed that elections and democracy were the proper basis for El Salvador's future, not backroom negotiations. His visit provided a needed dose of confidence and determination to the government of El Salvador, beleaguered by pressure from both the rebels and U.S. officials to surrender their democratic mandate. To show that he also rejected the violence of the right in El Salvador, the pope prayed at the tomb of murdered Archbishop Oscar Romero.

Tightening the Screws in Nicaragua

Two days earlier, the pope had been in Managua, where one of his most dramatic visits took place. The moment John Paul II got off his plane and kissed the ground of Nicaragua, the Sandinista government sought to embarrass him. Ernesto Cardenal, culture minister for the Sandinistas and a Trappist monk, appeared in the receiving line of government officials. Earlier, Vatican officials had been assured that Cardenal would not be at the airport, since he had ignored a Vatican directive to give up either his priesthood or his political office.

Cardenal's appearance was a ploy to get photographed with the pope, ideally in a pose that would neutralize Vatican opposition to his political activities. Cardenal even knelt and tried to kiss the pope's ring as the pontiff got to him in line. John Paul recognized the renegade priest immediately, however, and pulled his hand away. With Cardenal still on his knees, the pope delivered a stern rebuke, insisting that Cardenal had to comply with the Vatican's rules for priests. The image of the two, broadcast worldwide, was an embarrassment for Cardenal.

The real challenge for the pope would come later in the day at an outdoor Mass in Managua's main square. Well before the pope's visit, Sandinista officials confiscated yellow paper, so Nicaraguans could not make replicas of the Vatican flag. On the day of the visit, space in the square was allocated on the basis of loyalty to the Sandinistas, with their strongest supporters nearest the altar. The altar itself was devoid of a cross and decorated instead with murals of Sandinista heroes. The nine members of the Sandinista junta attended the Mass on the altar itself, just off center.

During John Paul's homily, the pontiff called for reconciliation and peace, asking both sides in Nicaragua's spreading civil war to choose nonviolent means of settling their differences. The Sandinistas, however, wanted a statement from the pope condemning only contra violence and blessing the victims of contra attacks. The FSLN referred to the contras' victims as saints, a practice the pope did not wish to seem to endorse. When he failed to verbally canonize the victims of only one side, hard-line Sandinista supporters in the front rows began to chant slogans, drowning out the pope's words. As the pope asked for silence, the nine junta members led the crowd in even more chanting. The heckling was loudest during the Consecration, which for Catholics is the most sacred part of the Mass. After Mass, one final insult remained: the pope's plane was kept on the tarmac an extra twenty minutes before being given clearance to take off.

Unknown to the Sandinistas at the time, a Venezuelan television crew was recording the entire papal Mass. Before the day was over, pictures from Managua were being broadcast all over the world, with the additional credibility of coming not from a U.S. news source, but from a Latin American independent television station. Conservatives in the United States soon obtained copies (a complicated process in 1983, when videocassettes were still novel) and played the tape repeatedly to American audiences.

The mistreatment of Pope John Paul II, far worse than anything the Polish Communists had tried, offended Americans of all faiths. Reagan denounced the mistreatment of the pope in his radio address some weeks later, and the Vatican itself used unusually harsh language to condemn the pope's treatment. The reputation of the Sandinistas among American Catholics never fully recovered. Nicaragua's leaders were embarrassed again when Brazilian authorities conducted a routine search of four Libyan aircraft that had stopped for refueling on their way to Nicaragua. Although the planes' manifests said they were carrying medical supplies, the Brazilians found that all four were loaded with tons of weapons and other military equipment.

But if the Sandinistas felt chastened by these incidents, they did not alter their behavior because of them. On March 13, Nicaragua signed a three-year trade and assistance pact with Bulgaria, whose agents were widely believed at the time to be involved in the 1981 attempt on the pope's life. By the end of March, the Sandinistas had seized the businesses of some of their political opponents, bombed an Indian village near the country's east coast, and hosted a visit from the defense minister of Communist South Yemen, reportedly to talk about providing Soviet-built MiG-17 fighters to the Sandinistas. On April 3, the Nicaraguan government censored Easter Mass. Soon afterward, the Sandinistas created "popular tribunals" to try suspected contras, before which even Nicaragua's limited human rights protections did not apply.

As the Sandinistas tightened their grip on their own people, the Reagan administration hardened its attitude toward the junta. Reagan ordered a review of Caribbean sugar quotas in early April, an explicit threat to discontinue Nicaragua's ability to export the vital commodity to the United States. A month later, the administration followed through on the threat, cutting Nicaragua's export quota to the United States by 90 percent. Reagan administration officials wanted to reduce the hard currency available to the Sandinistas for supporting guerrillas in other countries.

Taking the Case to the American People

In spite of these events, the public debate over U.S. policy in Central America was going against the administration in the spring of 1983. On April 28, Reagan took the unusual step of asking to discuss Central America before a Joint Session of Congress. That Reagan wanted to talk about a single topic was also unusual, and the setting was intended to underline the importance that the president attached to the issue.

The speech was divided into three parts. In the first, Reagan emphasized the strategic and military importance of the Caribbean. He pointed out that two-thirds of America's oil passed through the region and that half of the supplies and reinforcements for NATO were transported through the Gulf of Mexico. He recalled that in the first six months of 1942, the Nazis sank more shipping in the Caribbean than in the entire Atlantic Ocean and did so without having Cuba as a base. He asked his audience, "If the Nazis during World War II and the Soviets today could recognize the Caribbean and Central America as vital to our interests, shouldn't we also?" Reagan compared the stakes of the conflict to those that faced President Harry Truman at the start of the Cold War. Indeed, Reagan quoted extensively from Truman's 1947 Marshall Plan speech and averred that he was taking similar steps to confront a similar problem.

In the second part of the speech, Reagan contrasted the budding democracy in El Salvador with the onset of Communist-style dictatorship in Nicaragua. He touted the success of the March 1982 elections in El Salvador, asserted that the country was addressing long-standing problems of human rights and the rule of law, and insisted that the U.S. government could not possibly turn its back on the hundreds of thousands of Salvadorans who risked the wrath of the guerrillas to vote in the country's first free election. El Salvador's democracy, however, was threatened by the determination of the Sandinistas to export their revolution. (Interestingly enough, Reagan did not refer to the contras as "freedom fighters," reserving that term instead for the Salvadorans who had cast votes.)

As the Reagan continued to the third part of his speech, on U.S. policy toward the region, he did not call for the overthrow of the Nicaraguan government. With the strictures of the Boland Amendment firmly in mind, Reagan explicitly stated that his administration did not seek the overthrow of the Sandinistas. Rather, he wanted the FSLN to adhere to its 1979 promises of democracy and nonalignment and cease its interference in the affairs of its neighbors.

Reagan's speech was followed by an appreciable but very short-lived bump in the popularity of his Central America policies with the American people. Faith Ryan Whittlesey, Reagan's assistant for public liaison, realized that a more sustained and multifaceted effort would be needed to bring about stronger and more lasting support for the president's policies in the region. She decided to initiate a series of weekly briefings on the area, with exactly this goal in mind.

What Are the Contras For?

Although it was far from obvious at the time, Reagan's pledge not to try to overthrow the Sandinistas would unleash a new flurry of infighting in his administration. Secretary of State George Shultz used the president's words as a rationale for making sure that the U.S.-funded contras did not win. CIA director Casey, for his part, joined with other conservatives in the administration in concluding that, if the Sandinistas were to keep their promise of a free election, they would be overthrown at the ballot box. For Reagan's conservative supporters, the contras were a method of bringing democracy to Nicaragua. For Shultz and the "pragmatists," they were, at most, a way of stopping arms shipments to El Salvador and a lever for bringing the Sandinistas to the bargaining table.

The latter goal, however, was completely at odds with what the contras themselves desired. Not surprisingly, very few Nicaraguans were willing to risk their lives and their families to stabilize El Salvador or to make the Sandinista regime slightly more moderate. Shultz must have been aware of this. Perhaps he simply disregarded what the contras wanted and saw them as nothing more than a tool of U.S. foreign policy. Such an attitude would be consistent with Shultz's prevailing desire for leveraged allies.

A more intriguing possibility, and one more suited to an accomplished political player like George Shultz, is that Shultz was well aware that the contras would not fight simply to protect El Salvador, and might have trouble recruiting if it became clear that the U.S. government would not give them enough funding to win. Under those circumstances, the contra movement could simply disappear, leaving Shultz in charge of more traditional methods of applying leverage, such as reducing Nicaragua's sugar quota. With the contras out of the way, the State Department could negotiate a settlement with the Sandinistas that would leave them in power, but with weaker ties to the Cubans and Soviets, and with less hostile designs on their neighbors. Even by 1983, it was obvious that the longer the Sandinistas held power, the more economically weak Nicaragua would become and the more it would need outside help. A negotiated "solution" that promised U.S. aid to replace Soviet aid, and that kept the Sandinistas in power, would cement U.S. leverage in place.

Presidential Elections in El Salvador

The leveraged ally faction had been bitterly disappointed in the victory of Roberto D'Aubuisson's coalition in 1982 and his elevation to head of the Constituent Assembly. D'Aubuisson was a free marketer and had made the military defeat of the guerrillas a priority, hoping to end his country's dependence on U.S. military aid as quickly as possible. There was little doubt that Christian Democratic leader José Napoleón Duarte would pursue economic policies less likely to result in real economic growth for El Salvador, nor was there much doubt that he would place more restraints on the military. Thus, for Shultz and his allies in the administration, Duarte was the more attractive candidate for president. They would move mountains to have him elected.

The leveraged ally faction took advantage of events in El Salvador to ease the path to the presidency for Duarte, who was officially nominated Christian Democratic Party candidate for president on April 19, 1983. Six days later, the *New York Times* quoted "U.S. officials" who warned that the previous six months (the time since D'Aubuisson had taken over) were "a time of steady progress for the FMLN." The guerrillas, the officials said, were now able to attack civilian and military targets without substantial casualties. The FMLN, in fact, had made fewer and fewer attacks on military targets since the beginning of the year. Days after the officials talked to the *Times*, however, the rebels did attack important civilian targets, including bridges linking El Salvador to Honduras. These attacks slowed El Salvador's exports even more. The attacks also drew the Honduran army away from contra bases, permitting Sandinista raids against the contras. The attacks suggested that the Salvadoran rebels and the Sandinistas were coordinating their activities. As spring turned to summer, the guerrillas focused their attacks on El Salvador's railroads, crippling what had been an important trade artery for the country.

On the political front, Shultz and the State Department had been pressing for a special ambassador to the region, to further insure that the State Department would dominate U.S. foreign policy in the region. (The ostensible reason for the appointment was to insure that elections took place in El Salvador on time and in good order.) Reagan went along with this request in late April 1983 but dealt Shultz a rare setback when he announced that the new official would be a White House ambassador, reporting directly to Reagan. (As a practical matter, this meant that the special ambassador would send reports to the National Security Council.) Shultz fumes about this designation in his memoirs, but in reality it did little to slow down his drive to make sure Duarte was elected.

A seemingly larger, but ultimately temporary setback to Shultz's plans for total control of Central America policy came in May 1983. Earlier in the year, UN ambassador Jeane Kirkpatrick had been sent to the capitals of U.S. allies in Central America with a letter from Reagan. In the letter, the president reasserted his support for democracy throughout the region, including Nicaragua. On her return to Washington, Kirkpatrick met with Constantine Menges and showed him a cable smuggled to her by a friendly U.S. ambassador. The cable was from Assistant Secretary of State Thomas Enders, and it had been sent to coincide with Kirkpatrick's visit to the region. In the cable, Enders advised U.S. diplomats to ignore both Kirkpatrick and the presidential message that she carried. Soon after her return, Enders said, there would be a new diplomatic initiative launched, which would supersede previous U.S. policy.

Enders had undermined Reagan's close supporters before and had always gotten away with it, in large part because of the unswerving support he received from Shultz. In this incident, however, Enders clearly sought to undercut Reagan himself. Shultz threw his aide overboard; he had turned into a liability in Shultz's dealings with Reagan. However, Shultz managed to spare Enders any genuine punishment; he was assigned to the largely ceremonial, but exceedingly pleasant, post of U.S. ambassador to Spain. Enders' replacement was Langhorne A. Motley, whom Reagan had appointed U.S. ambassador to Brazil in 1981. Conservatives were initially pleased by the choice, since Motley had supported democratization and economic development while in Brazil. Reagan's supporters were soon to have reason for disappointment, however.

On the same day that Enders was "reassigned," Reagan fired Deane Hinton, the American ambassador to El Salvador who had angered conservatives with his insistence on the continuation of phase 2 of the land reform proposal and his outspoken support for Duarte over D'Aubuisson. Again, conservatives saw an opportunity to replace a career Foreign Service officer with someone more in tune with Reagan's wishes and less enthusiastic about creating a leveraged ally in El Salvador. Reagan officials leaked that the replacement for Hinton would be Ambassador Gerald E. Thomas, a Reagan appointee to Guyana.

Shultz reacted immediately, and angrily, both to the selection and to what he considered the supreme affront of having someone appointed without his approval. He wanted to give the post to Thomas Pickering, a careerist then serving in Nigeria. Shultz decided to make the matter a test case of his power to run U.S. foreign policy without interference from the president's other appointees. He was especially eager to show that he could win a bureaucratic battle against William Clark, who was pushing for Thomas' appointment. Among Shultz's many strengths was an impeccable sense of timing. He initiated the showdown over Pickering's appointment in the middle of the Williamsburg economic summit, when Reagan and Clark were completely engaged with other matters. Shultz won the battle, only to find a new battle over Pickering brewing. U.S. senator Jesse Helms (R-NC), chair of the Senate subcommittee on Latin America, vowed to delay and possibly defeat the nomination in the Foreign Relations Committee.

On May 25, LTCM Albert A. Schaufelberger, one of the U.S. military advisors, was shot while waiting in his car outside Central American University in San Salvador. Schaufelberger was the first American soldier to be killed in El Salvador, and Reagan's enemies immediately seized upon his death to make comparisons between El Salvador and Vietnam. (A cartoon in the *Washington Post* depicted a wall, identical to the Vietnam Veterans' Memorial, with Schuafelberger's name carved on it and with plenty of room for more names.) In the meantime, members of Congress from both houses seemed to be losing patience with democracy in El Salvador. In May, the House Foreign Affairs Committee approved $65 million in aid but spread the money out over three years and made it conditional on the elected government opening talks with the guerrillas. Reagan's goal of a democratic and prosperous El Salvador seemed further off than ever.

The Contra Wars Escalate

Violence was also spreading in Nicaragua. The Sandinistas' reaction to the growing guerrilla movement dedicated to their overthrow was inconsistent through most of 1982 and early 1983. On the one hand, Sandinista officials wished to claim that there was no significant armed opposition. When they acknowledged the contras' existence at all, the Sandinistas would refer to them as "cattle rustlers" or a few disgruntled National Guardsmen. However, after U.S. government support for the contras became public in November 1982, the Sandinistas had every reason to inflate the importance of the guerrilla movement and even to backdate that inflation. Suddenly, the same officials who had been dismissive began to speak of large and frightfully destructive force, made of wholly of ex-National Guardsmen, and malevolently funded by the United States.

By the summer of 1983, the contras had made themselves into a force to be reckoned with. U.S. officials estimated in June that there were eight thousand men under arms against the Sandinistas. As the contras' numbers grew, the cover story that they were all ex-National Guard became less credible, since Somoza's National Guard had only numbered seventy-five hundred for most of his dictatorship. Of them, many had been killed in the 1979 civil war, and many more were still in Sandinista prisons in 1983. Even the *New York Times* acknowledged on June 28 that there were "many decent men" among the contras. (However, since the *Times* made this admission on page 26, the myth of ex–National Guard bogeymen persisted.)

In response to the growing contra threat, the number of Cuban and Soviet advisors increased, and they were joined by military advisors from North Korea and East Germany. Rather than try to hide their growing dependence of the Communist bloc, Ortega acknowledged that a major arms buildup was going on. He insisted, predictably, that the buildup was wholly defensive, forced upon his country by Reagan's support for the contras.

The Sandinistas also used the contra threat to justify suspending human and civil rights in the country. The Sandinista army moved in large numbers into the sparsely populated Atlantic Coast region of the country, home to Nicaragua's Native American population. The Indians were divided into three ethnic groups, the largest of which was the Miskito, numbering about fifteen thousand. In the summer of 1983, the Sandinistas began forcibly relocating the Native Americans into "model villages," from which the residents were not allowed to depart. In response to an unconfirmed report that Israel might supply arms to the contras, the Sandinistas also began mistreating Managua's small Jewish community.

Heavy-handed actions such as these complicated the actions of Congress, which was rapidly becoming the inside-the-beltway front of the Nicaraguan civil war. Reagan knew, from the intense storm that was generated when U.S. support for the contras was revealed, that the program was unpopular. Moreover, he also chafed visibly under the rules that prevented him from discussing a covert operation. The program's unpopularity made it reasonable to expect that Democrats in Congress would try to look like they were shutting the program down. At the same time, Reagan's insistence that Central America was a central front in the Cold War made even the most liberal Democrats skittish about seeming to side with a Soviet-supported government. When the Sandinistas closed synagogues and accepted Soviet arms, they made Reagan's job easier.

On July 28, however, the House voted to end funding for the contras. The administration could find reasons for hope even in this seemingly disastrous event. First, the vote was close (228–195). Changing the minds of only seventeen congressmen, a not insurmountable task, would reverse the outcome. Second, there was still the chance of restoring the contra funding in the Senate version of the budget. Third, the House vote did not make the cutoff of funds effective until the end of September. The only thing the House vote made certain was that the issue would not go away.

Muddying the Waters

The Kissinger Commission

By summer, it was clear that Reagan was losing the battle for democracy and economic independence in Central America. Reagan needed to buy time, broaden the base of support for his Central America policy, and neutralize opposition from the "leveraged ally" faction of his administration. It was time for a bold gamble, and Reagan took one. On July 19, he appointed former secretary of state Henry Kissinger to chair the Bipartisan Commission on Central America. Conservatives were stunned. As far back as 1976, Reagan had always seemed to regard Kissinger as an enemy. Indeed, a major rationale for Reagan's spirited challenge to President Gerald Ford that year was Reagan's oft-stated opposition to Henry Kissinger. Kissinger, for his part, made no secret of his lack of regard for Reagan.

The Kissinger Commission, as it soon came to be called, was charged with studying every aspect of the crisis in Central America, to develop a series of recommendations for the president and report to him no later than December 1, 1983. The commission included some prominent Americans from both parties, including AFL-CIO president Lane Kirkland, Boston University president John Silber and San Antonio mayor Henry G. Cisneros. Except for the appointment of UN ambassador Jeane Kirkpatrick and Congressman Jack Kemp (R-NY) as the senior counselors to the commission, none of Reagan's close allies was included.

Reagan, for his part, was fully aware of the deep and unbridgeable differences between himself and the architect of détente. But Reagan also knew that Kissinger had always ignored Central America. Thus Kissinger would not have to repudiate his own actions to support Reagan in Central America. And, much more significantly, Kissinger knew, and Reagan knew he knew, that the only way Kissinger would ever play a role in the Reagan administration was to produce a set of recommendations on Central America that bolstered Reagan's goals for the region.

More Interference from Mexico

As the ground wars in El Salvador and Nicaragua worsened in the fall of 1983, the Reagan administration faced a new and potentially much more damaging diplomatic and political challenge. In January, the foreign ministers of Mexico, Venezuela, Colombia, and Panama had met on the Panamanian resort island of Contadora and began what came to be known as the Contadora peace process.

The U.S. media paid little attention to the Contadora meetings when they took place (the *New York Times* did not mention them at all), but the "Contadora process" would cause no end of trouble for Ronald Reagan in the mid-1980s. As public opposition to Reagan's policies became more vocal in 1983 and 1984, some members of Congress hesitated to support Reagan, but these wavering legislators also feared looking wholly negative and being blamed for a mistake that could lead to a Communist Central America.

"Contadora," which came to refer more to a state of mind than to any actual set of proposals, provided perfect political cover. A congressman could vote against aid to El Salvador, for example, and justify the vote by saying he or she was merely giving Contadora a chance to work. A senator could appease angry constituents by denouncing Reagan's policies and stave off charges of isolationism or softness on Communism by wrapping his or her denunciation in an insistence that what Reagan wanted was inconsistent with Contadora. Indeed, the very word *Contadora* became something like an incantation, used by legislators and their staff members to ward off difficult questions about U.S. policy in Central America.

The situation was made considerably worse by Secretary of State Shultz's immediate and thorough embrace of the Contadora group's Document of Objectives. Rather that point out the flaws and omissions it contained, Shultz insisted that the objectives were entirely consistent with U.S. policy and a useful starting point for negotiations. He did so in the face of opposition from the National Security Council staff. Shultz would later write that he had to endorse Contadora, since seeming to fall in with the Mexican-inspired document was the only way to insure that Congress would not cut off aid completely to El Salvador. His hasty decision set up yet another bitter division within the Reagan administration.

Portents

Whatever hope the Contadora process may have brought, and however genuine or appropriate that hope may have been, 1982 and 1983 brought far more bad news than good news from Central America. As the Kissinger Commission members began their work, and the foreign ministers of the Contadora nations held their press conferences, the people of Central America continued to suffer. In El Salvador, as the new ambassador Pickering was presenting his credentials to the Magaña government on September 5, the guerrillas of the FMLN were attacking San Miguel, the third largest city in the country, and being repelled only after heavy fighting. This attack showed that the rebels had a sophisticated intelligence network and a capacity to operate in several parts of the country at once.

An even more ominous event took place in Nicaragua in early October. The FDN, largest of the contra groups, announced that it had laid mines in the waters around Puerto Sandino, Nicaragua's busiest port. The contras announced that Mexican oil tankers were the specific target of the mines. Exxon announced that it would no longer carry Mexican oil to Nicaragua. The day after Exxon's announcement, Langhorne Motley arrived in Managua for talks with the Sandinista leaders and immediately found himself dealing with the repercussions of a contra raid on oil importing facilities. U.S. officials confirmed, off the record, that the contras had used American assistance in the raids. Surprisingly, in the light of what would follow, the story received little attention at the time.

Events in Central America in the fall of 1983 were arranging themselves into a tangled Gordian knot that would not be cut by political ploys like the Kissinger Commission, as useful as that was. Somehow the real stakes of the conflict had to be brought home to the American people, and American resolve had to be demonstrated. Somehow the myth of Communist invincibility had to be shattered, and the reality of Communist intervention in the Western Hemisphere had to be established. And somehow the governments of Cuba and the Soviet Union had to be sufficiently intimidated to make them rethink the wisdom of interfering in Central America.

In October, Reagan would be presented with a completely unexpected opportunity to accomplish all these goals. The end of the beginning was at hand.

6

The End of the
Brezhnev Doctrine, 1983

The weakening of any of the links in the world system of socialism directly affects all the socialist countries, which cannot look [at such weakening] indifferently.

—*Leonid Brezhnev*, speaking to Polish workers, November 1968

Grenada's "New Jewel Movement"

The world paid little notice to the events in Grenada when, in March 1979, the island nation's corrupt and venial dictator, Eric Gairy, traveled to the United Nations to try to interest the world body in an effort to find, and contact, extraterrestrials. Like many brutish and ineffective dictators of his stripe, Gairy found that leaving the country was a fatal undertaking. The New Jewel Movement (NJM), a leftist organization, took the opportunity to overthrow Gairy. His successor, Maurice Bishop, leader of the NJM, initiated programs designed to improve education, health care, and social security for Grenadians.

At the start of his time in office, Bishop promised an end to the repression of the Gairy regime. He also promised free elections, and indeed, the NJM had participated in elections under Gairy in 1976, winning six of the parliament's fifteen seats. His party's showing made Bishop official head of the opposition (a position he would not tolerate once he had power himself). Even at this early date, the NJM had secretly decided to be an elite party, based on Marxist-Leninist principles. To most Grenadians, however, the most pressing economic issue was how to obtain more land and how to acquire more secure title to the land. Grenadian farmers were decidedly, and unabashedly, capitalist. Bishop knew this and knew he would have to move carefully to impose socialism on an unwilling population.

Like the Sandinistas, Bishop included non-Communists in his first ruling council. But also like the Sandinistas, the moderates in the government had no real power. Bishop acknowledged this in 1982, telling an audience of party activists that including moderates "was done deliberately so that imperialism won't get too excited and would say, 'well, they have some nice fellas in that thing; everything allright.'"

By the time that Bishop made this statement, elections had been postponed indefinitely, more than one hundred political prisoners were being held, and the right of habeas corpus had disappeared. As early as May 1980, Bishop had established a secret police force, whose methods were patterned on those of the Soviets and Cubans. In a meeting that month with Bishop, the Grenadian minister of national security said that he had specifically rejected democratic methods of intelligence gathering. Such methods, the minister told Bishop, "have proven, after experimentation, not to be effective enough."

During his first year in power, Bishop also persecuted and imprisoned many democratic, civic, and trade union leaders and created what the NJM called "mass organizations." These were groups of organized and radicalized teenagers, which Bishop used to intimidate and attack opponents. Under Gairy, the Grenadian police and armed forces, combined, numbered about three hundred men. By 1980, Bishop had raised this number to more than four thousand. Also in 1980, Bishop made a national radio broadcast in which he promised to organize a "people's militia" of twenty- to thirty-thousand people, more than one-fourth of the island's total population. Bishop's portrayal of an American threat was belied by the Carter administration's wholly positive view of Gairy's ouster and Bishop's revolution.

At the time of Bishop's appeal for militia recruits, the people of Grenada probably did not know that the government of the United States was generally supportive. Indeed, Grenadians knew only what Bishop wanted them to know. Only five months after taking power, the NJM forcibly closed *The Torchlight*, a newspaper that was critical of Bishop (and that had also been critical of Gairy). In June 1981, the government arrested the editor of a new opposition paper, *The Grenadian View*. Finally, in June 1982, a decree from Bishop, called "People's Law Number 18" banned all opposition newspapers.

NJM members paid close attention to what was said about them in the American media and responded quickly to what they perceived as unfair or damaging information. Bishop received advice in this area from the U.S.-born wife of Cuba's ambassador. Erroneously believing that the mainstream American media would look askance at the rise of an obviously Communist regime in Grenada, Bishop's government busily cultivated an image of moderation well into his time in power, even trying to look, in one expert's eyes, "like a group of somewhat fuzzy-headed reformers."

A Complex Relationship

Bishop also began to forge ties with Castro and with the Soviet Union. Cuban advisors began to arrive and made themselves at home in the Grenadian Ministries of Education, Defense, and Internal Security. At the beginning of the Bishop regime, the Soviet leaders' attitude was somewhat reserved and wary. While they were certainly pleased that the ostensibly pro-Western dictator Gairy had been replaced, they were not sure at first what to make of the Bishop regime. The Soviets did not even establish diplomatic relations with the new Grenadian regime for six months (well after the United States had done so). When Bishop finally established relations with the Soviets, the communiqué that codified the new relationship was signed in Havana, signaling the dominant role that Fidel Castro intended to play in the foreign policy of the Bishop regime. A large part of the history of Grenadian foreign relations between 1979 and 1983 was the effort by Bishop and the NJM to exploit the Cuban-Soviet rivalry.

The complementary roles of the two Communist powers was illustrated in the first major arms deal that Bishop undertook, in October 1980. In secret treaties and protocols found after the invasion, the Soviets agreed to supply eight armored personnel carriers, thirty thousand bullets, one thousand AK-47s, one thousand grenades, and much more, a list filling seven type-written pages. The treaty stipulated, however, that while the Soviet Union would supply the arms, they would be transported to Grenada through Cuba. Had Castro decided to shortchange Bishop, he would not have been in a position even to complain about it.

Using Cuba as the transshipment point also gave the Soviets plausible deniability on the entire arms deal. Indeed, for the Soviets, the great riddle of the relationship with Bishop was how to make the potential benefits outweigh the costs. The latter were considerable. The Soviet leadership knew that they could not defend Grenada from an attack from the United States (or, for that matter, from an attack from Venezuela).

The Soviets also knew that while such an outright attack was unlikely, especially with Carter in the White House, there were other forms of U.S. political and economic pressure that the Soviets were also unable to match. Thus, to have Bishop identified as a Soviet ally, and then have his government overthrown, would have damaged Soviet prestige.

Bishop and his colleagues knew that the Soviets needed concrete evidence of Grenada's value, and they did their best to provide it. From the beginning, the NJM worked much harder to cultivate the Soviets than vice versa. The Bishop government carefully phrased its foreign policy pronouncements to match those of Soviet news outlets. In January 1980, Grenada became the only country in Latin America other than Cuba to vote with the Soviets against a resolution condemning the invasion of Afghanistan.

Such diplomatic gestures were appreciated in Moscow, but they did not constitute any strategic benefit to the Soviets. Moreover, the actions most likely to bring such benefits, such as opening a Soviet air base, or submarine base, or missile base, were also the actions most likely to bring swift U.S. retaliation. The relationship remained somewhat cool. Even as late as Brezhnev's funeral in November 1982, Maurice Bishop was politely but firmly denied an opportunity to meet with Yuri Andropov, the incoming Soviet premier, although Daniel Ortega was given a lengthy audience.

The Grenadian foreign minister decided that the country needed to "play a more active role at the United Nations." Given the already close adherence to Soviet initiatives that Grenada was following, this could only mean persuading other states to join the Soviet bloc. About the only other states in the UN over which the NJM could hope to have influence were other small, Eastern Caribbean states.

Given the conservative and tourist-dependent nature of their governments and economies, countries such as Dominica, St. Kitts-Nevis, or St. Vincent had no use for Communism. After 1981, the staunchly anti-Communist Reagan administration had to be considered also. Nor could Grenadian authorities disguise from themselves the fact that, of the three Communist Caribbean countries, Grenada was by far the most vulnerable. The U.S. government undoubtedly had the ability to intervene in Grenada, so Bishop and the NJM would have to find ways to convince the United States not to do so.

Thus, by the start of 1983, Bishop's government faced four policy imperatives: first, it needed to impress the Soviet leadership with its usefulness, to avoid becoming a Cuban colony; second, it needed some way to threaten its Caribbean neighbors, since persuasion to join the Soviet bloc was not working (put differently, it needed some way to make its neighbors into leveraged allies); third, it needed enough influence in the United States to prevent a U.S. invasion; and fourth, it needed hard currency, since the U.S. administration was not inclined to provide economic aid.

This was a large and complex agenda for a small country, and virtually everything that Bishop did, up to the moment that he was overthrown, was designed to address one or more of these imperatives. In most cases, the Grenadian Communists were able to address more than one agenda item at a time. The first three imperatives could all be addressed by increasing the number of Grenadians under arms and fortifying the island. As we have seen, the Bishop government moved to accomplish these goals by the middle of 1980, with the first large-scale arms deal with the U.S.S.R. Other arms transfers followed, with an additional 15 million roubles' worth of equipment by 1982.

For the most part, the weapons that the Soviets gave to the Bishop regime were small arms, such as AK-47 rifles, hand-grenade launchers, and pistols. In small quantities, such weapons were most useful in controlling the largely unarmed population of Grenada and arming the NJM militia. By 1982, however, the types of weapons had changed and become more ominous to Grenada's Caribbean neighbors. The 1982 arms transfer included antiaircraft guns, howitzers, and cannons, in addition to armored vehicles and coastal patrol boats. Also in 1982, the Soviets promised to equip paratroopers for Grenada and provide a plane that could carry them. At the beginning of 1983, the Bishop regime, with Cuban help, began building a large new airport, a development watched with growing apprehension by the peaceful states of the Eastern Caribbean.

A critical part of Grenada's relationship with its Soviet arms suppliers was training Grenadians in the use of the Soviet equipment. For this purpose, squads of Grenadians were taken to the Soviet Union for instruction (and for political indoctrination as well). Of greater concern to the United States was the stationing of Soviet agents and advisors in Grenada. The Soviet presence was substantial, and the Soviets appointed a four-star general, with experience in Angola, as ambassador.

Bishop and the Enemies of the United States

In April 1981, an NJM member went to the Congress of the World Peace Council in Havana, where he met with representatives from the U.S.S.R.,

Bulgaria, East Germany, Hungary, and even a terror group from Quebec. The NJM delegate later reported to Bishop that assistance would soon be forthcoming from the Soviets, the Hungarians, and the East Germans. By the end of 1981, American officials were hearing concerns from Eastern Caribbean states about growing numbers of Soviets, East Germans, Cubans, Bulgarians, and North Koreans in Grenada. As one expert on the region put it, "[T]he division of labor among the communist countries aiding Grenada was quite impressive." In addition, Bishop permitted the regime of Muammar Qaddafi in Libya to open an embassy.

The burgeoning relationship between Bishop and anti-American leaders eventually became more difficult to hide and to have more of an impact on the lives of Grenadians. People on the island later reported that when ships arrived from either Cuba or the Soviet Union, which invariably happened at night, the entire island was blacked out, and a shoot-on-sight curfew was imposed, while the ships were unloaded. Roads from the docks to the capital were guarded by uniformed Cubans.

As early as 1981, Grenada's growing military might and increasingly hostile rhetoric toward its Caribbean neighbors prompted other independent states in the Eastern Caribbean to form the Organization of Eastern Caribbean States, a mutual defense organization. While Grenadian Communists, and other of Reagan's enemies, would later characterize this organization as implacably anti-Bishop, Grenada was actually a charter member of the OECS. The democratic members of the new organization hoped to demonstrate to Bishop the tangible advantages of maintaining cordial relations with his Caribbean neighbors.

It was not long before such hopes were dashed; in 1982, the NJM sponsored an unsuccessful coup attempt against the government of Dominica, whose prime minister was the leader of the OECS. The failure of this first attempt at regional power projection unmasked Bishop's deceptions but in so doing, only served to accelerate Grenada's drive to arm itself, finish the new runway, and insure that the next attempt would not fail.

Danger to the United States in Grenada

With a population of fewer than ninety thousand, and a land area comparable to Rhode Island, even the most paranoid Cold Warrior might have had difficulty seeing Grenada as much of a threat to the United States. But there was indeed danger in Grenada, which took two forms.

First, Grenada's location, off the coast of Venezuela near the eastern tip of the South American continent, placed the country astride important trade routes coming from the Atlantic. Oil tankers from Nigeria and the Persian Gulf (and from Venezuela) and cargo ships laden with strategic minerals from southern Africa all sailed past Grenada.

Throughout the 1980s, Cuba had a large contingent of combat troops helping the Communist government of Angola to fend off an anti-Communist revolution. There were no large transport planes in either the Soviet or Cuban air forces that could fly fully loaded from Cuba to Angola without stopping for fuel. However, any likely stopping point between Cuba and Angola was a country that did not allow military aircraft to land or refuel. This involved a lot of time-consuming deception on the part of the Cuban military and complicated the Cuban war effort in Angola. Grenada, however, is just within reach of Angola.

In addition, a Grenada with two airports would have made an ideal transit point for Cuban and Soviet agents traveling to Suriname or Guyana, both of which had governments that the Soviets and Cubans were courting, and both of which, being on the mainland of South America, would have provided myriad opportunities for further subversion. Moreover, Grenada was in a perfect position to act as a transit point for arms shipments to Central America, either by the Soviets or by Muammar Qaddafi, who also had close ties to the Bishop regime.

The second threat emanating from Grenada was less direct but serious enough to place Ronald Reagan's plans for the Caribbean in jeopardy. A heavily armed Grenada, closely allied with the Soviets and Cubans, and taking advantage of the Communist countries' logistical and power-projection capabilities, was a serious threat to the other small island nations of the eastern Caribbean. These were some of the countries that Reagan hoped could pull themselves out of dependency on the United States with the help of the Caribbean Basin Initiative.

If nations such as Dominica, St. Kitts-Nevis, or St. Lucia had to suddenly create armed forces large enough to defend themselves from a new regional threat, they would be forced to beg the U.S. government for help and would sink even further into subservience. This was directly counter to Reagan's hopes for the region. Such a threat fit nicely into the plans of some foreign policy professionals in the Reagan administration, however. As we will see, Reagan's eventual decision to invade Grenada would divide his administration along familiar lines.

Bishop Visits Washington

The Bishop regime might have proceeded much faster with its plans for becoming a regional military power had it not been for the fourth policy imperative of the NJM: gaining hard currency. By 1983, Reagan had succeeded in cutting off what little economic aid the U.S. government had provided. However, mismanagement, inexperience, and the contradictions of applied Marxism, along with falling commodity prices and the devaluation of the British pound had done much more to bring Grenada to the brink of economic disaster. Faced with this looming economic meltdown, Bishop learned to his disappointment that the Soviets had limited ability to provide economic aid and even less interest in doing so. Castro, himself an economic thrall of the Soviets, provided only minimal aid to Grenada. Bishop would have to find other sources of funds, which meant attempting a rapprochement with the United States.

The Grenadian dictator approached this project from two angles. As we saw, the NJM kept a careful watch on North American news outlets and quickly responded to negative information. The regime also provided positive information, especially about the popularity of Maurice Bishop, the laudable goals of the NJM, and its peacefulness and "independent" foreign policy. Bishop's government actively cultivated friends in the U.S. Congress, especially the more liberal members of the Congressional Black Caucus. They were most successful in befriending staff members of Congressman Ron Dellums, a black Democrat from Marin County, California.

Bishop's government, with advice from its friends in Washington, presented itself as a high-minded, fiercely independent revolution, committed to human rights (while suppressing these rights in Grenada), economic justice (while providing poverty for all Grenadians but the privileged few), and international nonalignment (while becoming more closely aligned with Cuba and the Soviet Union). The NJM skillfully played on the desire of many on the left in the United States, especially journalists, to believe only the best of leftist revolutions, especially in the Western Hemisphere. The same journalists that covered every death squad killing in El Salvador, while ignoring human rights violations in Nicaragua, and devoted innumerable articles to repression in Chile, while ignoring far worse repression in Cuba, were inclined to believe most of what Bishop's officials told them about the Grenadian revolution.

The Bishop regime also played on the ingrained belief of State Department officials that all differences between governments can be resolved through negotiation. For officials accustomed to dealing with leveraged allies, this belief was largely true, and the experience of American diplomats impelled them to try to make Grenada dependent on U.S. aid. Thus, for Foreign Service Officers, the NJM's plan for a new airport, capable of accommodating Soviet cargo and troop transport planes, was not a threat. It was an opportunity to bribe or dupe Bishop into dependence.

By the spring of 1983, both the State Department and the Bishop regime desired face-to-face negotiations. For Bishop, such negotiations meant the possibility of American money to balance the influence of the Cubans and Soviets, and perhaps even to induce his Communist supporters to provide more military aid. In addition, a trip to the United States would permit Bishop to present himself to the American people. If Bishop made a good impression, through the reporting of friendly journalists, he could raise the political cost of forceful U.S. action against him.

Bishop made his visit to the United States in May 1983. There is a certain amount of mystery connected with this visit, even to this day. Some histories of the Bishop regime give the impression that Bishop simply turned up in Washington unexpectedly and embarrassed the Reagan White House by asking for an immediate appointment with the president. When the appointment was refused, Bishop and his American supporters were able to claim that the "snub," combined with threatening rhetoric about Bishop from Reagan, demonstrated his implacable hostility toward Bishop.

There was nothing unexpected about Bishop's visit, nor did he arrive unannounced. Heads of state do not simply get off an airplane at Dulles Airport. All foreigners, heads of state included, require a visa to enter the United States, and heads of state require an official invitation. Then U.S. secretary of state George Shultz recounts in his memoirs that Bishop "was invited to Washington in an effort on our part to size him up and see how committed he was to his present course." While in D.C., Bishop met with National Security Advisor William Clark and Assistant Secretary of Defense Kenneth Dam. He did request an appointment with Reagan, which was declined.

Shultz does not explain Bishop's interlocutors. It is strange, to say the least, for the State Department to issue an invitation to a foreign head of state and then not have him meet with a high-ranking State Department official. As secretary of state, Shultz was strongly, almost single-mindedly, determined to protect and expand the prerogatives of the State Department, especially against what he saw as encroachments from the National Security Council and the Defense Department. Yet the two ranking officials who met with Bishop were the National Security advisor and an assistant secretary of defense. Shultz might have been playing a "good-cop, bad-cop" game, permitting Bishop to hear threats (in one form or another) from Clark and Dam, with an eye to permitting him to hear inducements to better relations from State Department officials later. In any event, Bishop left the United States empty-handed.

Events Leading up to the Invasion

Bishop's visit helped to widen a split in his own government. Among the NJM's top leadership were those who rejected Bishop's hope to use better relations with the United States to wring more support from the Soviet Union. By 1983, the U.S.S.R. had placed agents of influence in the top echelon of the Bishop regime. These agents, such as Bernard Coard and Hudson Austin, expressed Moscow's view that the Washington visit was a direct challenge to Soviet influence in Grenada.

Bishop's visit seriously heightened tensions with the Soviets. Ian Jacobs, the Grenadian ambassador to Moscow, found out about it only after Bishop arrived in Washington. The Soviet government did not know about it in advance either. Vladimir Kazimirov, director of the Soviet Foreign Ministry's Latin American Department and the official responsible for Soviet relations with Grenada, angrily told Jacobs that he "first read of the visit in the newspapers." Bishop was either disappointed enough with his Washington visit, which yielded not even the faint promise of aid or reduced hostility, or fearful enough of the Soviets' anger at being bypassed, that he followed up his trip to the United States with a trip to Eastern European capitals in early fall 1983 and a visit to Fidel Castro in October. Cuba responded to Bishop's American visit by stationing more "advisors" and "construction workers" on Grenada.

Bishop also faced a fight for leadership of the NJM, which to varying degrees had been brewing since the movement's founding. Bernard Coard was originally a partner with Bishop, but as early as 1981, Coard attempted to make himself the darling of the Soviets, biding his time until they should lose patience with Bishop. Coard happened to be in Moscow when Bishop was in Washington, and Coard no doubt used the coincidence to persuade the Soviets that their interests would be better served with him at the helm.

Soon after Bishop returned from Cuba, the fight for leadership broke into the open. On Wednesday, October 12, after a long and stormy meeting of the NJM leadership council, Bishop was placed under house arrest by Coard and his supporters. Coard announced the formation of the Revolutionary Military Council (RMC) and began consolidating his power. Bishop's supporters, for their part, began making plans to return him to power. On October 19, a large crowd of Bishop's supporters overpowered guards at Bishop's house and freed the former leader.

The crowd then marched in triumph to Fort Rupert, which was Coard's headquarters, with the intention of forcing Coard out and restoring Bishop to power. What the crowd did not know was that Coard himself was no longer in charge. When Bishop was freed, Coard had been placed under "protective custody" by NJM army chief Hudson Austin, who was backed up by the island's large contingent from the U.S.S.R. The crowd marching with Bishop was surprised by troops of the RMC, who took Bishop, his wife, and members of the Bishop Cabinet from the crowd. Once inside the fort, Bishop and the others were shot. The RCM soldiers, on orders from Austin, then fired into the crowd, killing between fifty and sixty people.

The violence at Fort Rupert sent shock waves throughout the region. The Austin government, fearing that there might be more demonstrations, imposed a twenty-four-hour shoot-on-sight curfew on the entire country. Among those affected by the curfew were the one thousand Americans on Grenada, most of whom were students at the Medical College of St. George's.

Reaction, and Action, in Washington

It did not take long for the significance of events in Grenada to register among officials in the Reagan administration. Whether the violence was due to genuine policy differences, as some said, or represented factional fighting between Cuba and the Soviet Union, as others insisted, it was clear that Grenada's new rulers, whoever they were, were friendly to Moscow. The most likely outcome of the coup and the accompanying violence was an increase in Soviet power on Grenada, with all the attendant dangers to U.S. interests in the Caribbean. Reagan administration officials also knew that the new pro-Soviet regime could not possibly be unaware of the importance of Grenada to the United States and of the consequent danger of U.S. intervention to prevent Grenada from becoming a Soviet colony. The new leaders of the small island also knew that there was a very limited number of ways that they could protect themselves from a

U.S. invasion. Over time, the presence of Soviet soldiers and warplanes at the new airport might deter the Americans, and the deployment of Soviet missiles certainly would do so, as it had for Cuba. In addition, continuing their public relations effort with the U.S. media and Congress might protect Grenada from invasion.

But on October 19, 1983, none of these possible deterrents was in place. For the Austin regime, there was only one way to forestall an American invasion, and that was to seize the American medical students as hostages. Officials at the White House and at Fort Rupert probably realized the precarious position of the American students within minutes of each other. Under different circumstances, the Austin regime might have moved immediately to round up the Americans and use them as bargaining chips with Reagan. However, Austin simply did not have sufficient control of his own soldiers to do so. Moreover, living under a shoot-on-sight curfew, cut off from the outside world and dependent on NJM members for food and water, the students were, in effect, already hostages. But Austin and his colleagues were also aware of the political implications of a hostage crisis for the Reagan administration. Having been elected on the anniversary of the Teheran hostage crisis, and in large part because of that crisis, Reagan knew the potentially devastating fallout of American hostages, and the Grenadian knew also just how sensitive he would be about the possibility and how quickly the American people would rally behind Reagan if they were confronted with another Teheran. Thus, for Austin, the goal was to use the Americans as hostages without calling them hostages.

Consequently, Austin's junta quickly sent reassuring messages to American officials that the students were safe and repeated these assurances to whatever intermediaries might be persuaded to listen. (They were assisted in this effort by the head of the medical school, who, from the safety of his Long Island office, insisted that the students were not endangered by a shoot-on-sight curfew and that they were content living under such conditions.) At the same time, Grenadian officials also prevented the departure of the students. The State Department offered to evacuate the students by air. The request for landing rights was turned down. The State Department offered to charter a cruise ship, only to have docking rights refused also. It quickly became clear that Austin did not want to lose the only bargaining chips he had.

With Bishop's death, and the resulting confusion and threat to the American students, various parts of the U.S. government began to seriously consider options for dealing with the crisis. Almost immediately, existing divisions within the Reagan administration reappeared. The specific areas of disagreement were first, whether or not to mount a military operation in Grenada, and second, how to define the goals of such an operation. The first was decided fairly quickly, in favor of an invasion, but the second matter, the purpose of the invasion, resulted in intense infighting.

Among the first to recognize the multifaceted danger of a consolidated pro-Soviet regime in Grenada was National Security Council staff member Constantine Menges. According to his own account of the matter, Menges began preparing for a possible U.S. invasion of Grenada on October 13, the day after Bishop's ouster and incarceration. He wrote what he described as a "one-page plan for the protection of U.S. citizens and the restoration of democracy to the island." Presumably, Menges would have immediately shared his plan with his superior, National Security Advisor William Clark, but for the fact that on the same day, Clark announced his resignation.

Recognizing the quickly shifting conditions in Grenada, and unwilling to let the matter drop until a new NSA was in place, Menges showed his one-page plan to the NSC's military attaché, LTC Oliver North, on Friday, October 14. Menges asked North to determine what military assets would be needed for the plan and, above all, to keep the matter quiet. Menges also discussed the plan with "a senior Defense Department official." Menges said that an invasion, aimed at the restoration of democracy in Grenada, would not only protect Americans, and stop Communism at one of its Caribbean bases, but also have a "positive political effect in Central America and throughout the Caribbean, encouraging our friends and demoralizing the violent communist groups." Finally, Menges saw the invasion as insurance that the Soviets would not try to station nuclear weapons in Grenada, which they might be tempted to do to deter or to match proposed U.S. missile deployments in Europe.

By the time Menges talked to his friend at the Pentagon, Reagan had announced that Robert "Bud" McFarlane would take over as national Security advisor. Widely rumored to have been appointed at Shultz's insistence, McFarlane was expected to largely follow the State Department's lead and substantially reduce the independence of the NSC staff. As Menges outlined his Grenada plan to the Defense Department official, the latter warned him to tread lightly. McFarlane, the Defense official said, was probably already looking for a reason to remove Menges from the NSC staff. "You're too Reaganite," Menges was told. The official also told him that there was no chance that the United States would use military force.

On Tuesday, October 17, McFarlane held his first staff meeting as national security advisor. He asked the regional specialists, Menges included, to summarize the salient issues in their respective areas. Menges told the group that he had a plan for restoring democracy to Grenada and that he intended to discuss it with William Middendorf, U.S. ambassador to the Organization of American States (OAS) and a staunch Reaganite. "Well," said McFarlane, "that's okay." McFarlane's laconic style left it unclear (probably intentionally) whether he was giving his "okay" to the plan or just to the meeting with Middendorf.

Menges next checked to see what actions the Department of State had taken in the wake of Bishop's overthrow and the looming threat to the students. He discovered that Grenada had been the subject of high-level attention at the State Department for only a few days, in spite of the fact that the U.S. ambassador had been warning for months of increasing Soviet and Cuban influence on the island. (Shultz confirmed Menges' contention. Shultz said he did not appoint a Grenada task force until October 18, six days after Bishop's ouster.) When the State Department did turn its attention to Grenada, it was not with the intention of restoring democracy.

On October 19, the day that Bishop was killed, the Grenada Task Force created a plan to use the military for a "quick in and out" operation to evacuate the medical students. Two days later, Shultz says, the task force chair, Assistant Secretary of State Langhorne Motley, briefed Shultz on the danger to the students and the proposed military operation. "I want to make sure you're on board," Motley said. Shultz replied with an endorsement of a limited operation: "If we can bring this student rescue off, it would be a damn good thing."

Once again, clashing foreign policy views were on display. At a crisis preplanning meeting on October 20, the issue of a quick rescue versus a government takeover was discussed. Even at this point, however, a State Department official suggested negotiating with Hudson Austin, "to see what kind of a person he is." Menges, who attended the meeting, replied, "I think his killing fifty people yesterday told us what kind of person he is." Menges learned later that the State Department had already sent a negotiating team but that the Revolutionary Military Council had refused to meet with them.

A military operation to rescue the students would not change the political status quo, except to give the Austin regime the perfect excuse to forge even closer ties with Cuba and the Soviet Union, much in the same way the Bay of Pigs gave Castro political cover to invite Soviet protection for Cuba. Menges told Motley on October 20 that Austin would see even a limited U.S. invasion as a humiliation, and that he could only respond by becoming an even more implacable enemy of the United States. "I believe it might then offer its territory as a base for Soviet-bloc forces."

State officials must also have known that Austin's closer ties with the Soviets would not be without price; they would want something in return. Since 1982, the Soviets had made it plain that the value of a Communist regime on Grenada was the possible subversion of its neighbors. The leaders of Grenada's neighbors knew this, and knew that they were more vulnerable than ever. With small or nonexistent armies of their own, the democracies of the Eastern Caribbean would have little choice but to beg the U.S. government for economic and military aid. The State Department would have a brand new group of leveraged allies.

Shultz did make contingency plans in case Reagan made the decision to overthrow the Austin regime. As early as October 20, Assistant Secretary of State Motley and Lawrence Eagleburger (another close Shultz confidant) met with the British ambassador to discuss the permissibility of transferring authority in Grenada to Sir Paul Scoon, the governor general of the island under the Commonwealth of Nations. Shultz says he had his staff prepare a list of acceptable democratic leaders, to whom U.S. forces could cede power, should it come to that.

That Shultz wanted his own list of acceptable leaders is illustrative of his determination that he and no one on Grenada (least of all the Grenadian people) choose the post-Austin government. In addition, Constantine Menges had already presented a list to the Grenada Task Force. Unlike the people on Menges' list, the Grenadians on Shultz's list were all living in America. As such, they would have only weak and tenuous ties to the people of Grenada. Since it would be obvious to the entire Caribbean that the "leaders" on Shultz's list were American puppets, they would quickly become completely dependent on the U.S. government: the perfect leveraged ally.

The OECS Takes the Initiative

In the event, Shultz ended up being outmaneuvered. Grenada's neighbors decided upon a supremely risky gamble. Article 8 of the OECS treaty permitted the defense ministers of the members to form the Defense and Security Committee, which could request assistance from outside powers to counter a regional threat. On October 21, the heads of state of the OECS met, and under the provisions of the treaty, the Defense and Security Committee was formed.

It made its first requests for help from France and Great Britain, lending credence to the notion that a central objective of the OECS action was to avoid entanglements with the U.S. government. Both European countries, however, refused to help. (Margaret Thatcher, in her memoirs, insists that there was never an OECS request for help from the United Kingdom, but this is not necessarily incompatible with others' recollections. Thatcher makes it clear that there was never an official request; there might have been more discreet overtures.) Having made even discreet overtures for assistance, however, OECS head Eugenia Charles and her colleagues knew that, for them, the danger had significantly increased, since word of their discussions with French and British officials might leak out, providing Austin with a pretext for aggression.

Having nowhere to turn but to the United States, Charles transmitted the request for military assistance to the national security advisor, gambling that it would go directly to President Reagan. Making the request of the U.S. government, however, also increased the likelihood of a leak, with the danger such publicity entailed. The Defense and Security Committee finally transmitted its request at 2:00 A.M., October 22.

Reagan Opts for Freedom

The OECS request reached Washington while Reagan was asleep at the Eisenhower Cottage at the Augusta National golf course. He was awakened by Shultz and National Security Advisor Bud McFarlane. With supreme irony, Reagan would make his decision to liberate Grenada in a house named after the president who failed to do anything when faced with Soviet aggression in Hungary. Eisenhower's inaction helped to establish the Brezhnev Doctrine; Reagan's actions would demolish it.

Reagan had little time for such historical musings, however, as he weighed the various options placed before him. Shultz emphasized the danger to the students and told Reagan that plans were in place for a rescue. Reagan, however, was fully aware of the horrifying risk that the OECS leaders, now joined by Barbados and Jamaica, had taken in placing the call to McFarlane. Reagan's entire vision of a free and prosperous Caribbean was flickering before his eyes. The diplomatic risk connected with any military action was likely to be the same, whether it was a surgical rescue or a more comprehensive invasion and overthrow mission. Only the latter, however, contained any promise of permanent change and greater security. Reagan made his decision: "Under these circumstances, there was only one answer I could give to McFarlane and Shultz and those six countries who asked for our help."

Another Reagan Administration Split

Having made his decision, Reagan found that he had to defend it from members of his own administration. He would have to do so quickly, and in circumstances that left no room for leaks, neither of which were Reagan strengths. Although the U.S. invasion of Grenada would have additional goals, rescuing the students was still a prime objective. This required absolute secrecy; any hint of forceful U.S. action could prompt the Grenadian regime to remove the students to secret locations, as the Iranians did after the unsuccessful April 1980 rescue attempt.

At five o'clock Saturday morning, a secure conference call from the White House to the Eisenhower cottage permitted Reagan, Bush, Shultz, Weinberger, McFarlane, and some staff members to discuss the situation. Vice President Bush was initially opposed and cleverly masked his opposition by suggesting that an invasion by all English-speaking countries might provoke a hostile reaction from Latin America. Bush suggested asking the Venezuelan government to contribute troops, knowing full well that such a request would delay the operation. Reagan vetoed the suggestion immediately and firmly.

Weinberger's opposition was not cleverly concealed at all. The military, he insisted, needed time to compile the necessary maps, intelligence, options, plans, and other contingencies before he could contemplate going into action. Yet in his memoirs, Weinberger writes that on October 20, he had given the order to recall the U.S.S. *Independence* carrier group, then on its way to Lebanon with Marine reinforcements, to move to the eastern Caribbean. At Weinberger's request, the Joint Chiefs of Staff began to "prepare options as to how to evacuate American citizens from Grenada in a hostile environment." Weinberger, like Shultz, envisioned a limited military operation. He raised objections only when Reagan broadened the mission.

After the conference call ended, with a decision to invade on Tuesday morning, Weinberger spent much of Saturday and Sunday trying to get the decision reversed. On Monday afternoon with Reagan back at the White House, Weinberger and the Joint Chiefs met with the president. Reagan polled the Chiefs and asked each to summarize how his part of the plan would work. Each said he was concerned about the lack of time to gather intelligence and to rehearse and practice several of the more difficult aspects of the operation. To make his decision stick, Reagan had to overcome considerable opposition.

Interestingly enough, Shultz was no longer part of this opposition. He evidently switched his thinking, at least outwardly, and became, even according to his nemesis Menges, "completely on board." Perhaps Shultz, having just won a huge victory in getting Reagan to fire his old friend William Clark as NSA, guessed that opposing Reagan on Grenada would permanently damage their relationship. Meeting with Reagan in person, whereas the others only heard his voice on the telephone (and probably a scratchy and static-filled voice, if the secure link was up to its normal, early 1980s standards), Shultz may have been something in Reagan's eyes that demonstrated that he would brook no opposition. Shultz decided to survive and to fight another day.

Reagan's memoirs contain evidence that did not trust everyone at the State Department. Reagan notes that even though Grenada was a former British colony and a member of the Commonwealth of Nations, "We did not even inform the British beforehand, because I thought it would increase *the possibility of a leak at our end* and elevate the risk to our students" (emphasis added). Such communications with a foreign head of government would necessarily involve the State Department.

Even on the morning of the invasion, it was clear that not all of Shultz's colleagues embraced the larger purpose of the mission. The DOS prepared Reagan's announcement of what was now codenamed Operation Urgent Fury. On a hunch, Menges looked over the draft announcement and noticed that "restore democracy" had been deleted as one of the mission's objectives. It was replaced before Reagan spoke. Shultz himself was not adverse to a small rearguard action on that momentous Tuesday morning. Shultz himself told the State Department press spokesman, first, that his emphasis should be on "the restoration of law and order and the safety of our students," and second, that "this was not an East-West confrontation." Shultz made no mention of democracy or of insuring the safety of the surrounding democracies.

The Invasion

Reagan later described Operation Urgent Fury as "a textbook success." It was nothing of the kind. Throughout the mission, there was confusion, miscommunication, and unnecessary danger to American forces.

Gen. Norman Schwarzkopf, deputy commander of the American invasion force, recalled initial briefings about the mission from the experts at Atlantic Force Command. They emphatically stated that there would be little or no resistance. "Don't worry," Schwarzkopf was told, "When the [Grenadian] army sees we're Americans, they'll give up." When one of the commanders noted that there were antiaircraft batteries near the airstrip at Port Salinas and St. George's, the capital, he was assured, "Don't worry. The gunners are poorly trained and don't represent a real threat." Regarding the estimated one thousand Cubans on the island, Schwarzkopf heard, "Don't worry. They're not going to fight." Every one of these predictions turned out to be wrong.

The first stage of the mission was to land the army's Green Berets in St. George's in the dead of night on October 25. Their mission was to find Sir Paul Scoon and make sure nothing happened to him. The Green Berets were also supposed to seize Fort Frederick, Austin's headquarters, and Fort Rupert, where the massacre had taken place on October 19. The planners reckoned that these two forts would be most difficult to take by storm, so they intended to take them by surprise. Every one of the Berets' missions went awry. While the Special Forces did find Scoon, they soon found themselves surrounded by dozens of armed and hostile Grenadian soldiers. Neither Fort Frederick nor Fort Rupert was seized easily.

The next stage of the operation was similarly plagued with problems. The chief military concern of the United States, from the first discussions of a possible invasion, was the possibility of reinforcements coming from Cuba. Reagan was told that between five and ten thousand additional Cuban troops could be landing in Grenada in a couple of days, unless American forces seized the island's two airfields, Pearls and Port Salines. In one of the few bright spots for the U.S. military on October 25, Pearls Airport fell without a fight. U.S. Army Rangers were given the task of seizing Port Salines.

At the time that the Rangers left their base in Savannah in the early morning hours of October 25, however, they still had no idea what they would find when they landed in Grenada. Originally, Navy SEALS were to make a night landing near the airstrip and check on its condition. Rough seas forced the cancellation of the SEALS' landing, prompting the navy commander to suggest that the entire operation be postponed twenty-four hours. The Green Berets' landing was already in motion by that time, however, and the postponement was denied. With Grenadian and Cuban troops defending the airstrip, the Rangers did not succeed in taking it until 10:00 a.m., several hours behind schedule.

Once the Port Salines airstrip was secured, American reinforcements began to arrive, along with soldiers and police from the participating OECS countries. The latter quickly took over the guarding of the Cuban and Grenadian prisoners. With the airstrips taken, preventing reinforcement from Cuba, and with the Cubans on the island engaged, the American troops could turn their attention to the rescue of the medical students. This turned out to be more complicated and difficult than expected.

The Army Rangers moved to the True Blue campus of the medical school, near Port Salines, at midmorning. Before they were able to congratulate themselves, however, the True Blue students told the Rangers that there was a second campus, housing an additional 224 students, located at Grand Anse, two miles away on the road to St. George's. Fortunately, one of the Grand Anse students had kept a phone line open, and the Rangers learned that the other campus was surrounded by Grenadian troops. The rescuers would have to fight their way in. The chances for heavy casualties were high.

It was Schwarzkopf who made the tactical decision that saved the situation. He suggested using Marine helicopters to land troops at Grand Anse, behind the Grenadian defenders, and then using the same helicopters to ferry the students out. This part of Operation Urgent Fury took place on Wednesday morning. By the end of the day, all the students were rescued, the capital and airstrips were secured, Scoon and the Navy Seals had been rescued from St. George's, more reinforcements were arriving, and all of the major objectives of the operation had been achieved.

Overall, there were 19 American deaths in Operation Urgent Fury, along with 116 wounded. Seventy Grenadians were killed, of whom 25 were civilians. Among the 750 Cuban "construction workers," 25 died and 59 were wounded. There was not a single U.S. civilian casualty. By Thursday afternoon, less than 72 hours after the Navy Seals landed, the fighting on Grenada was over.

Fallout: The Shots Heard around the World

Soon after combat operations ended, Shultz launched a successful bureaucratic offensive. He replaced the position of ambassador to the eastern Caribbean, which had been filled by Milan Bish, a friend and appointee of Ronald Reagan, with a full-time ambassador to Grenada. Shultz immediately filled this new position with his own appointee, a career Foreign Service officer and someone who shared Shultz's view of the desirability of leveraged allies. While the rest of the Reagan Cabinet was celebrating a U.S. victory over Soviet Communism, Shultz was thinking primarily of how to establish State Department control over the newly liberated Grenada.

Initial reaction to the invasion of Grenada, from members of Congress, from the British, from the United Nations, and from Ronald Reagan's political enemies was wholly and loudly negative. The reaction from those most directly affected, however, was completely and wholeheartedly positive. U.S. and OECS troops were greeted with garlands of flowers, with fruit, with wild cheering, and with tears of joy. For the citizens released from days of confinement, following years of oppression, no questions of international law or geopolitics clouded their exhilaration.

Grenada's neighbors were also thrilled. In a stunning public relations coup, the administration brought Prime Minister Eugenia Charles to Washington, and she accompanied Reagan as he went before reporters to announce the beginning of Operation Urgent Fury. Charles spoke after the president, and made the case that, with a Soviet ally in Grenada, no one in the eastern Caribbean was safe. Charles, not Reagan, insisted that the operation was not an invasion, but rather a rescue, of Grenada and of Grenada's neighbors. An articulate black woman, defending Reagan, was a powerful symbol and helped to convince Americans of the need for the operation.

The students at the medical college began to arrive back in the United States on Thursday afternoon, October 27. With the entire U.S. media watching, the students came down the steps of the transport planes at a base near Charleston, South Carolina. Once off the planes, some of the students knelt and kissed the ground. In multiple interviews with the three major television networks, reporters tried to get the students to confirm what the college president had said, that they were in no danger. Instead, the students had nothing but praise for the U.S. military and nothing but gratitude and relief to be home safe.

The impact of the students' emotional arrival in the United States was heightened by the fact that the military did not take any reporters with them to Grenada and in fact imposed a quarantine on the island to make sure no one came or left once the operation began. (In fact, a ship full of reporters that tried to land on the island on Wednesday was turned back by U.S. warplanes.) The purpose of the quarantine was to maintain the element of surprise and to keep Hudson Austin and his colleagues from leaving the island. But it had the effect of making the returning students the first Americans, other than military spokesmen, to speak to the American people about the invasion.

First impressions are lasting ones. To this day, when Americans think of Grenada, they think of students kissing the tarmac in South Carolina. Major media representatives, furious at being denied the opportunity to shape a major news story, tried to turn their exclusion into a major controversy. To their consternation, they found that most Americans had serious doubts about trusting the media with sensitive military information. One *Washington Post* reporter later said at a forum that I attended on media bias that had she known about the pending invasion, it would have been on the front page the next day. Many in the media reacted to this unwelcome dose of reality by becoming even more adversarial toward Reagan. (Three years later, when the Iran-contra scandal broke, I saw two TV reporters high-fiving one another in a Senate office building and saying, "It's payback time for Grenada!")

Reagan's enemies in Congress were similarly embarrassed. For some, the days just before and after the invasion were times of almost acrobatic flip-flopping. House Speaker Tip O'Neill, for example, after a White House briefing, patted the president's arm and said, "God bless you, Mr. President." On the morning of the invasion, O'Neill told reporters, "It's not time for the press of America or we in public life to criticize our country when our Marines and Rangers are committed." But after fighting was over, O'Neill decided that he was against the invasion after all. "We can't go the way of gunboat diplomacy," he said. "[Reagan's] policy is wrong. His policy is frightening." Later, he would insist that Reagan ordered the invasion to divert attention from the massacre at the Marine barracks in Beirut. Still later, O'Neill said that the invasion was justified to save American lives.

Other congressional Democrats also expressed misgivings in the early going. Senator Charles Matthias of Maryland insisted that peaceful means had not yet been exhausted and that a "resort to arms" was not justified. Future presidential candidate John Kerry (D-MA) said that Grenada was "a bully's show of force against a weak Third World nation." One by one, the Democratic presidential candidates for 1984 took stands against the invasion.

Opposition from Reagan's enemies became far more muted, however, after the students returned home and kissed the ground. Even liberal Democrats began reporting that their calls were running 10 to 1 or better in favor of the invasion. Congressman Robert Torricelli (D-NJ) reported,

"I hardly get a call in my office about Grenada where people don't mention the Iranian hostage situation." Polls found that 65 percent of Americans favored the action, and, what is more important, 91 percent of Grenadians supported it, and 85 percent of Grenadians believed that the purpose of the invasion was to rescue Grenada from the Cubans.

Reagan took full advantage of the wave of favorable publicity. Two weeks after the invasion, Reagan hosted a group of the rescued medical students and some of the soldiers who rescued them. One of the students, who had been on TV kissing the tarmac, described how the experience had changed his political views: "Prior to this experience, I had held liberal political views which were not always sympathetic with the position of the American military. . . . I have learned a lot from this experience. It's one thing to view an American military operation from afar and quite another to be rescued by one."

Some of Reagan's enemies continued to react to the invasion, and to the American victory, with hysteria. I saw much of this hysteria firsthand. As an analyst for the Heritage Foundation, I made a number of media appearances in the days following the invasion. One professor from Howard University dismissed the joyous reaction of the Grenadians as evidence that the islanders had "internalized the oppressor." He described this as a sort of mass-induced Stockholm Syndrome, in which oppressed people decide that they really want to be exactly like those who keep them down. When I pointed out that the United States had never been the colonial master of Grenada and had never been aligned with the Bishop regime, which had done the actual oppressing, he replied that Grenadians could not be expected to understand that.

In other debates and radio call-in shows, a number of people objected when I said that the Grenadian people had welcomed the invasion. The Grenadian people, I was told, do not know what is best for them. The American students' joyous reaction was also dismissed. Many of the American students, I was told, were really CIA agents.

What impressed me most then, and many years later, was the near panic that accompanied leftists' consideration of what had just happened in Grenada. George Shultz may have had his spokesman declare that the invasion was not part of the East-West confrontation, but leftists in the United States knew better.

There was also a certain amount of hysteria and panic in Havana and Moscow. Caspar Weinberger described Soviet reaction as "intense and infuriated." Early reports on TASS, the official Soviet government news agency, showed maps of Granada, not Grenada, and suggested that American troops were invading southern Spain. *Pravda*, the Soviet newspaper, editorialized a few days later that the invasion of Grenada showed that the Reagan administration wanted "to introduce the methods of the American Wild West, when all problems are solved by the shot of a gun." Castro, after initially failing to believe the reports that the invasion was taking place, ordered his troops on the island to fight to the death, an order most of the Cubans disobeyed.

The Soviets soon seemed to accept the invasion as a fait accompli, muted their rhetoric about it, and even tried to suggest that the alliance between Grenada and the Soviet Union was not that strong. But for all of their apparent nonchalance, the Soviets knew that an important change in the global balance of power had just taken place, the ripple effects of which were incalculable, but clearly negative. The ripples were not long in making their appearance. Among the first actions of Paul Scoon was to break diplomatic relations with Cuba and the Soviet Union.

Before the second day's fighting was over, Cuba lost another potential ally in the region. Desi Bouterse in Suriname had recently expressed his admiration for "what the leaders of [Cuba and Grenada] are trying to do." He had also signed a mutual assistance treaty with Castro and had hired Cuban technicians to work in Suriname. On October 26, Bouterse gave the Cuban ambassador six days to leave the country and declared that henceforward, Cuba would have lower diplomatic status in Suriname. More than one hundred Cubans were expelled. Bouterse also suspended all Cuban aid projects, saying that "a repetition of developments in Grenada should be prevented here."

There was a flurry of speculation that the Grenada invasion was merely a warm-up for an invasion of Nicaragua. Had that been the case, the Sandinistas could have found very little comfort in the actions of some of their Communist "allies." Shortly after the invasion, the Soviet Union advised the Sandinistas that, in the event of an invasion of Nicaragua, they could not count on Soviet military assistance. Castro, for his part, decided to pull a substantial number of his advisors out of Nicaragua, without telling the Sandinistas. In late November, the Sandinistas asked the Salvadoran guerrillas leaders in Managua to leave the country.

The Grenada invasion yielded mountains of physical and documentary evidence supporting Reagan's beliefs about the dangers lurking there. The island was a virtual storehouse of weapons, from the most basic to the quite sophisticated. The Calivigny barracks alone contained enough weapons and ammunition to equip as many as ten thousand soldiers. More than 1 million rounds of ammunition were found under a false floor in the Cuban Embassy. Not only were the Cuban construction workers identified as Cuban regular army troops, but documents found on the island also pinpointed the units to which the 684 Cubans belonged. Besides the Cubans, there were 49 Soviets, 10 East Germans, 3 Bulgarians, 15 North Koreans, and 17 Libyans in residence.

American forces also found so many documents, from the Grenadian, Cuban, and Soviet governments that they had to account for them in tons, not pages. Never before had researchers had such a complete record of the Communist takeover of a country. The documents included five arms agreements, documentation on how greater restrictions would be placed on Grenadians, discussions of how to use friends such as Congressman Ron Dellums (D-CA) to mute criticism in the United States, plans for subversion of Caribbean neighbors, and even NJM ambitions involving mainland South American countries Suriname and Guyana.

The Reagan administration moved quickly to make the best use of this evidence. Members of Congress were invited to travel to Grenada and see the documents and weapons for themselves. Many of the weapons were brought to Andrews Air Force Base in Maryland, where anyone who wished to could ride a shuttle bus from the parking lot to the warehouse, as I did, examine the weapons, handle them, and peruse a selection of the captured documents.

For most of those who did so, the evidence was conclusive. One of Reagan's sharpest critics in Congress, Rep. Mike Barnes (D-MD), concluded after visiting Grenada that American citizens "were in danger or had a reasonable basis to believe they were in danger because a small group of hoodlums had taken over this country." Rep. Don Bonker (D-WA) added: "[The arms cache was] far more extensive that what I had expected, both in terms of the documentation, about the complicity of Cuba, North Korea, the Soviet Union." Pointing to the Cuban weapons, Sam Stratton (D-NY), another liberal critic of the president, admitted: "This alone justifies what Reagan did."

Still, some of Reagan's enemies refused to be persuaded. My liberal companion on my trip to Andrews Air Force Base insisted that the weapons might have been "planted" by the CIA. Liberal newspapers in the United States focused on what they saw as the illegality of the action. The *New York Times,* having called the invasion "a pathetic little war," editorialized, "[The invasion] demonstrates to radicals in Central America that only logistics, not laws or treaties, will determine the means the United States is ready to employ against them." The *Washington Post* added: "The United States has trampled on non-intervention, the doctrine that is the *sine qua non* of hemispheric relations." Liberal editorials also insisted on the equivalence between Grenada and Afghanistan. The *New York Times* said that "the cost [of the invasion] is the moral high ground: a reverberating demonstration to the world that America has no more respect for laws and borders, for the codes of civilization, than the Soviet Union."

What is most interesting, some liberal commentators implicitly supported the original State Department position that it would have been better to rescue the students and leave the Communist regime in place. The *Times* asked stiffly, even given a threat to the American students, which they were not willing to concede, "Could 1,000 troops not have seized the school or brought the students out fast? Rescue did not require occupation."

Sol Linowitz, a former Carter official, in an op ed piece in the *Wall Street Journal*, asked, "If there was evidence of a real threat to security and stability in the region, should it not have been put before the OAS for action pursuant to the provisions of the Rio Treaty?" In a similar vein, the *Times* said on November 10: "Cuban aggression to promote 'the export of terror' would indeed justify a vigorous response. A great power that wants respect for its values as well as its power would have marshaled its diplomatic and economic might to contain the threat." I believe these commentators wished that Reagan had dealt with Grenada the way that American presidents since Franklin Roosevelt had dealt with the Soviet Union: with containment.

Despite the comparisons between Grenada and Afghanistan, U.S. troops left Grenada on December 15, 1983, less than three months after they landed. (At the time, Soviet troops were about to begin their fifth year of occupation of Afghanistan). On December 19, Grenada held elections for a democratic government (something Afghans would not get to do until 2004.) Since 1983, Grenada has held four elections. In every case, the losing parties have turned over the powers of government without delay and without incident. Far from being a threat to its neighbors, Grenada no longer has an army, only a largely unarmed police force. Those neighbors, far from becoming dependent clients of the United States, are able to pursue their own destinies. Eugenia Charles was even able to force trade concessions from the U.S. government in the 1990s.

When the twentieth anniversary of the invasion came around, a number of retrospective articles appeared. One of Reagan's former critics paid such a visit to Grenada in 2004. He quoted a St. George's cab driver: "Please don't call it an invasion. It was a rescue mission. Mr. Reagan saved us." The author continued: "For the rest of the tour, [the driver] recounted horror stories of life and death under the Marxist academics and petty thugs whose best efforts had produced a bloody coup. He told of terror and mutilations, the rule of the machete, hunger, shots and screams, neighbors disappearing in the night. Every other Grenadian echoed the same thoughts. . . . Somewhere on Grenada, there may have been someone who didn't like Reagan, but I couldn't find him."

Reagan's willingness to use force had its most immediate impact in Central America. In El Salvador, the FMLN found that after October 1983, only forced impressments would fill their ranks. (For many of the Communists' potential supporters, fighting the Salvadoran military and possibly having to face U.S. Marines were two very different things.) With the rebels weakened and disheartened, the road to democracy seemed wider and smoother as El Salvador headed toward presidential elections in March 1984.

In Nicaragua, as we have seen, the Sandinistas faced abandonment from both of their Communist patrons, as well as a growing contra army and the genuine fear of a U.S. invasion. The government's first official reaction came within a week of the invasion, when Tomás Borge, the Sandinista interior minister, told the U.S. ambassador, "If the U.S. ever wants to get American students out of Nicaragua, please call me and I will facilitate their departure." Less glibly, the Grenada invasion prompted the Sandinistas to indicate a heightened interest in precisely what the Reagan administration saw as a basis for a political settlement.

But there was one front in the Central America struggle where the Grenada operation brought only a temporary and uncomfortable truce: the war within the Reagan administration. For the supporters of natural allies, Grenada was a triumph. But for the leveraged allies' side, the liberation of Grenada and its Caribbean neighbors from U.S. dominance was a setback, and one they did not intend to see repeated in Central America. In fact, those with a preference for leveraged allies did not immediately give up on Grenada. The U.S. Agency for International Development dawdled so much on finishing the Port Salines airstrip that it prompted even a member of McFarlane's inner circle to comment in a secret memo that "[AID's] heart is, in fact, not in it." In a January 25, 1984, memo to Shultz, McFarlane wrote: "I would like to discuss further with you the selection of the appropriate 'pro-consul' to fill this critical role [in Grenada]." McFarlane did not even bother to mark the memo "secret."

Thus, the struggle for power between the Reagan administration's "natural ally" faction and its "leveraged ally" faction extended to Grenada, before the shooting even stopped. The island quickly became a sideshow, however, as both factions of the administration set their sights on the opportunities for control or for freedom presented by the elections in El Salvador and the contra war in Nicaragua. The fortunes of the Reagan administration in the two countries were about to diverge.

7

Muddying (and Mining) the Waters, 1984–1985

All is not lost without a contra program. We still have leverage. . . . The amount the contras need is pitifully small. We should
keep working for the contra program but not be sanguine about
getting it. Things won't fall apart. It's not a catastrophe.

—*George Shultz*, June 21, 1984

If President Ronald Reagan thought that his success in Grenada would
quiet his critics on Central America, he was to be disappointed. While the
revelations of Soviet and Cuban activities in Grenada shocked Reagan's
enemies, and put them on the defensive for the remainder of 1983, the
start of the presidential election year brought new tensions and controversies over U.S. policy toward El Salvador and Nicaragua.

The year of Reagan's reelection, coincidentally the year that I was
most closely associated with Reagan's Central America policy, was a year
of triumph and defeat. In El Salvador, the long debate over America's
commitment to protecting the country's fledging democracy finally ended,
and in Reagan's favor. In Nicaragua, however, a series of devastating revelations about U.S. government activities, combined with ever more bitter
administration infighting, left the contras without U.S. aid and clinging to
life. In the fall, Reagan blinked during a confrontation and permitted the
passage of a new and stricter Boland Amendment. Daniel Ortega claimed
victory in a tainted election, and Reagan was reelected in a landslide.
Unbeknownst to the millions who voted in 1984, however, was that the
seemingly triumphant Reagan had started on a path that nearly ended

with his impeachment. The years 1984–1986 also saw the leveraged ally and the natural ally factions fight bloody bureaucratic and rhetorical wars.

Oddly enough, the wars were fought over some of the most innocent-sounding elements of the administration's Central America policy. At the time, a near-certain way to bore someone in a conversation about Central America was to bring up the Contadora process. Yet it was concerning this process, and how the U.S. government should respond to it, that sparked so much internal blood-letting at the Reagan White House. Constantine Menges, special assistant to Reagan for Central America on the National Security Council, opened his memoirs with a vignette about George Shultz and Caspar Weinberger getting into a near shoving match at a Cabinet meeting, just after Reagan left the room. The subject under discussion was Contadora.

Kissinger Makes His Report

Reagan's reelection year opened with the delivery of the report of the National Bipartisan Commission on Central America, at an East Room ceremony on January 9, 1984. The administration made every effort to insure a large and friendly crowd at the unveiling of the bipartisan report. Staff members from all over the Old Executive Office Building were invited (*summoned* would be a better word) to the East Room well before the scheduled start of the event. As my colleagues and I waited to hear from Reagan, Kissinger and others on the Commission, a certain restlessness came over the crowd. The scheduled start time came and went. In what I knew to be a bad omen, James Miller of the Policy Planning Office of the State Department came to the podium and began to speak about the international legal implications of the wars in Central America.

I had had a meeting with Miller in October, the day after the Grenada invasion. I had gone to his office at the State Department with the president and vice president of the Heritage Foundation, where I worked at the time. We had been invited to get a briefing from DOS officials. Since the Latin American bureau was no friend to Reagan's conservative supporters, I was surprised by the invitation.

Miller was the only official to speak, and he started on a discourse on the legal basis for the U.S. invasion. After a couple of minutes, it became clear that Miller's real talent was for talking interminably, without pauses, without paragraphs, and without providing any substantive information. The invitation to a briefing was evidently designed to keep us occupied for an hour, presumably to prevent the three of us from spending too much time talking to the press.

When this same Miller started talking in the East Room on January 9, I suspected there was some last-minute glitch in the Commission report. Whatever it was, it was finally smoothed over, and Kissinger came out to give his remarks. Reagan did not speak at all, usually a signal of disapproval. The president had reason to be hesitant about fully embracing the bipartisan report. The main outlines of the report were compatible with his policies in Central America, and in fact the Commission members called for a large increase in both military and economic aid to the region. However, the report also called for negotiations, both within Central American nations and between them and the United States, which was not in line with Reagan's policy. No one familiar with Reagan or Kissinger believed that the latter's report was anything more than a temporary cease fire in the bureaucratic struggle.

Progress in El Salvador

Confronting the Death Squads

Even after the first round of elections in El Salvador in March 1982, there was skepticism about the usefulness of democracy in El Salvador. For many Executive Branch officials, it was not realistic to even expect Salvadorans to embrace democracy. For others, the victory of rightist Roberto D'Aubuisson over the U.S.-favored José Napoleón Duarte was strong evidence that democracy was simply too risky. The change in Reagan's focus from defeating Communism to promoting democracy came gradually. It gained steam after the success of the March 1982 Salvadoran elections and accelerated further after Grenada was put on the path to democracy after the U.S. invasion.

But by promoting democracy, Reagan was also putting himself on a collision course with some U.S. officials, for whom the advantage of right-wing dictatorships lay precisely in their lack of popular support. The political isolation of a dictator like Anastasio Somoza, and the physical danger that often accompanied dictatorial power, made the dictator dependent on the goodwill and the largess of the U.S. government. One way for a dictator to maintain support among the country's elites is to permit corrupt uses of American aid. With enough U.S. money, even the masses can be mollified through public works projects or food subsidies.

The American success in Grenada changed the terms of the foreign policy debate. The U.S. invasion resulted not only in the complete defeat of the pro-Soviet government but also in the near certainty that the island would replace Communism not with fascism but with democracy, in a process overseen by the Grenadian governor-general and endorsed by the Reagan administration. The administration was also committed to helping to revive private businesses in Grenada, bringing the promise of relative independence to the island nation.

Applying the same policies to Central America, however, was another story. At the end of 1983, the internal war between the leveraged ally and natural ally factions was still raging in the Reagan White House. Yet there were occasional signs that Reagan was fully aware of the tension and planned to use both factions to further his policies in Central America. The visit to El Salvador by Vice President George H. W. Bush was an illustration of this and a political masterstroke by Reagan.

By late 1983, the Reagan administration was in serious danger of losing support for military aid to El Salvador, unless something could be done to improve human rights conditions in the country. Some in Congress wished to see all American assistance stopped and the fifty-five U.S. military advisors removed. For liberals in Congress, the risk of having pro-Soviet, Communist guerillas in El Salvador take over the country was less bothersome than having to explain to their constituents why they were voting to send U.S. dollars to a government that could not (or would not) stop private assassination. Reagan's enemies were also confident that if the worst happened in El Salvador, Reagan, and not Congress, would get the blame.

Since El Salvador's government could not defeat the guerrillas (supported by Nicaragua, Cuba, and the Soviet Union) on their own, substantial American assistance was necessary, at least in the short term. That meant Congress would have to be mollified, and that meant sending an unmistakable message to the Salvadoran government that human rights abuses had to stop. It was in this context that Reagan decided to send Vice President Bush to San Salvador in December 1983.

The original purpose of the visit was to have Bush meet with Salvadoran president Álvaro Magaña and explain to him the urgent necessity of reining in the death squads and making progress in the investigations of the murders of American citizens. Bush was exactly the right person to carry this message. Not only did his status as vice president add heft to the visit, but Bush was also well known to savvy Latin American politicians as a member of the leveraged ally faction of the U.S. government. Without saying a word, Bush was threatening Magaña. When Bush insisted that he and Magaña talk alone, the threat was palpable.

Magaña, for his part, wanted to test Bush's resolve and also to let Bush know what sort of people Magaña had to deal with on a daily basis. Unbeknownst to the American delegation, the Salvadoran president had invited the field commanders of the Salvadoran army to the presidential palace. He asked if Bush would be willing to speak to them directly. Bush agreed, and a very tense meeting followed. The generals, like most Latin American generals, saw themselves as keepers of the national dignity and independence. Being lectured by a foreigner on El Salvador's ethical and judicial shortcomings was abhorrent; being threatened with a cut-off of desperately needed U.S. assistance was humiliating. The generals learned what it was like to be on the wrong end of the leverage see-saw.

Reagan was playing with fire. It must have seemed to all the Salvadorans present that the leveraged ally faction was dominant in U.S. policy making on El Salvador. As word of the meeting leaked out, the guerrillas portrayed their countrymen's humiliation as an affront to patriotic Salvadorans. The nationalist business community, whose confidence in the future of El Salvador was vital to any kind of economic revival, had cause to wonder if the U.S. government would permit autonomous economic activity in the country. There was great danger that capital flight would continue, making El Salvador that much more dependent on economic aid from the United States.

But Reagan had to have sustained congressional support, and that meant mollifying the leveraged ally faction, which was dominant in Congress as well. By permitting Bush and his allies to think that they had the upper hand, Reagan was more likely to have their whole-hearted assistance in getting military and economic aid to El Salvador. However, the type of aid Congress provided, and the piecemeal method it used to distribute it, was designed to maintain U.S. leverage.

Even with this difficulty with the American aid, El Salvador could never be a natural ally of the United States if the guerrillas won. Reagan decided to use leverage to try to create a situation where the United States would no longer have leverage. In the short run, the strategy was successful. Death squad killings went down, and the Reagan administration received credit for standing up to the Salvadoran generals. What is more important, Congress was persuaded, by Bush's visit and the intense lobbying of the Kissinger Commission members to continue economic and military aid to El Salvador. To maintain leverage, Congress did place conditions on the aid and slowed its distribution. Congress extended the requirement that the administration certify that El Salvador was making progress in protecting human rights and seeking justice for the killers of American citizens.

A Democratic Breakthrough

After the confrontation between Bush and the Salvadoran generals, the administration benefited from some good news from El Salvador as 1984 opened. The Salvadoran army was steadily improving and demonstrating its ability to take the fight to the guerrillas. The FMLN, for its part, had to resort to kidnappings and forced conscription to fill its depleting ranks. Stories in liberal newspapers about the growing burden of refuges in El Salvador could not avoid mentioning that most of the refugees were fleeing rebel-held territory. The FMLN leadership announced its intention to try to disrupt the presidential election, scheduled for March 25. In so doing, the rebels seriously undercut their democratic credentials and made their supporters' job in the U.S. court of public opinion much more difficult.

The election was shaping up as a one-on-one confrontation between Roberto D'Aubuisson, an avowed rightist, and José Napoleón Duarte, a centrist with strong connections with Congress. As the long-time rivals became frontrunners, Reagan faced another harrowing choice. A victory by D'Aubuisson would almost certainly mean an end to U.S. military support for El Salvador, making a rebel victory more likely. D'Aubuisson himself admitted as much during the campaign, promising nervous Salvadorans that if he won, and the U.S. cut off funds, he could replace them with funds from right-wing Latin American governments. Moreover, D'Aubuisson backed free market economic policies that members of the natural ally faction were convinced would permit El Salvador to prosper.

Duarte, for his part, was the best face of Salvadoran democracy to put before the American people and their elected representatives. However, he favored the land reform program that would ruin agricultural exports in El Salvador, nationalizations that would frighten foreign investors, and other economic policies that would cement U.S. leverage in place. Moreover, Duarte was already identified as Washington's favorite Salvadoran. His election as president could embolden the rebels, who were already portraying him as a puppet.

In addition, Reagan had only one means of intervening in the Salvadoran election, and that was to provide money, clandestinely, to Duarte's Christian Democratic Party. The best mechanism for doing so was through an international organization of Christian Democratic parties, sponsored by the West German Christian Democrats. Should word leak out of American money going to Duarte, however, especially in a close election, Reagan's entire political investment in a democratic El Salvador could be wiped out. In short, Duarte was potentially dangerous to El Salvador's long-term future, but D'Aubuisson was unquestionably poisonous to its short-term future. Reagan decided to permit the CIA to transfer funds to Duarte, through the West Germans. A decisive victory by Duarte would permit the U.S. government to later contend that its intervention was not crucial to the outcome.

In pursuing this risky policy, Reagan knew he could count on the assistance of the foreign policy professionals. D'Aubuisson, with his talk of surviving without the United States and his commitment to economic policies that had proven successful elsewhere, was anathema to the leveraged ally faction. Its members were willing to do practically anything to harm him politically. Money laundered through West Germany would do so, while at the same time bringing Duarte to office in a weakened political condition. In such a condition, there would be insurance that Duarte would not suddenly change his mind about bringing statist economics to El Salvador.

At best, Reagan was postponing a showdown in his administration between the natural ally faction and the leveraged ally faction. But in the short term, Reagan could only hope that Duarte could induce Congress to provide enough military aid to remove a guerrilla victory from the list of realistic possibilities for El Salvador. This done, and with enough economic aid to prevent Duarte's socialism from resulting in economic collapse, Reagan and nationalistic Salvadorans could hope to muddle through to the next election, at which time a free market president could be elected. It was a gamble with the fate of a small nation at stake.

On March 25, Salvadorans proved that the huge, courageous turnout of 1982 was not a fluke. Over 80 percent of eligible voters braved the death threats of the FMLN to cast ballots. In spite of the problems, more than seven hundred international observers attested to the honesty and validity of the elections, and over one thousand foreign journalists chronicled the courage of the Salvadoran voters. As expected, Duarte and D'Aubuisson led the crowded field of presidential candidates, and as expected, neither gained a majority of votes cast. The stage was set for a run-off election on May 6. That election would largely determine the fate of El Salvador and Central America.

The first-round election was a complete triumph for Reagan. He had insisted that the people of El Salvador were eager for democracy, and events had proven him right. He had charged that the guerrillas in El Salvador were the enemies of democracy, and their murderous actions on Election Day had proven him right. He had contended that the military situation in the country was improving and was proven right by a larger turnout and fewer areas with no voting, than had been the case in 1982. Even the *New York Times* had to acknowledge that the election was a "vindication" of Reagan's policy and "cause for a new infusion of American aid."

The impact on Congress was immediate. Among those observing the election was a group of congressional Democrats. They returned to Washington and told their colleagues, and the media, that the size and enthusiasm of the voter turnout in El Salvador improved prospects in Congress for Reagan's request for emergency military assistance. Less than a week after the election, the U.S. Senate rejected a series of amendments offered by Democrats that would have placed onerous restrictions on military aid. The House seemed ready to follow suit, but with the requirement that the elected government of El Salvador attempt negotiations with the Communist guerrillas. As it happened, a mechanism for bringing about such negotiations already existed.

The Contadora Process

The Contadora proposal, adopted by the presidents of Mexico, Panama, Venezuela, and Colombia, contained twenty-one points, which were made public in early October 1984. The four Contadora presidents called for an end to all external support, the opening of negotiations, democratization, arms reduction, and economic assistance. The Contadora *process* referred to the necessarily prolonged and multistep phases that would be necessary to bring their lofty goals to reality. But the Contadora document raised more questions than it answered. What constitutes "external military support?" When are "negotiations" worthy of the title, as opposed to posturing or simply negotiating about negotiating? What exactly is "democratization?"

George Shultz, speaking for the Reagan administration, insisted that U.S. participation in the talks would require reciprocity, simultaneity, and verifiability. In other words, the U.S. government would, for example, back negotiations between rebels and government officials in El Salvador only if Nicaragua's Sandinistas agreed to negotiations with the contras. The end of U.S. aid to El Salvador and the contras would have to happen at the same time as the Soviets' cessation of their aid to the Sandinistas. International observers would have to certify that Soviet aid had, in fact, stopped and that it was not merely being replaced by Cuban aid.

By focusing on such esoteric issues, Shultz immediately accomplished two of his long-standing goals for Central America. First, he effectively destroyed the ability of anyone in the administration, except perhaps Reagan himself, to adequately explain U.S. policy in the region. If the talk about Central America revolved around a potential superpower confrontation, then the hardliners in the administration, and Reagan himself, would be the most compelling and credible advocates for a tough U.S. policy. But when the talk switched to meetings and conferences, resulting in diplomatic wrangling, only diplomats could discuss it, and the American people would tune out almost immediately. Second, by embracing such a hideously complex and uncertain course of action, Shultz insured that the State Department would be the lead agency implementing Central America policy.

To Reagan and the hardliners, the key issue in Central America, and the source of virtually all the trouble there, was the Sandinista regime. Its determination to spread Communist revolution throughout the region and its ties to the Soviet Union were for the Sandinista leadership, non-negotiable elements of their regime's very reason for being. (In the September 1983 issue of *Playboy* magazine, no less an authority than Tomás Borge was asked about Reagan's charge that the Sandinistas would spread revolution throughout the region. Borge replied, "That's one historical prediction of Ronald Reagan that is going to come true!") Reagan, for his part, was equally inflexible in his demands that the export of revolution stop.

Thus, there was never a realistic chance for a negotiated "solution" during the 1980s. It was evident that the Nicaraguan leadership would respond only to force, perhaps from the contras, perhaps from being starved of economic assistance, or perhaps from a U.S. invasion. Only under duress would Ortega's government loosen ties with the Soviet

Union, reduce support for Communist rebels in El Salvador and elsewhere, and permit Nicaraguans to exercise basic human rights.

Shultz and the leveraged ally faction agreed with Reagan up to this point. However, they had a major difference with Reagan over strategy. Shultz evidently believed that it was possible to stop Sandinista subversion and thwart the designs of the Soviet Union but still leave the Sandinista regime in place. But even if the Sandinistas made all of the reforms Reagan demanded, there was no guarantee that they would not reverse themselves once the outside pressure stopped. In fact, the Sandinistas' actions in 1979, when they made promises to the OAS to gain recognition, then broke them after recognition was conferred, argued strongly that the duress would have to be permanent.

In a word, Shultz and the Contadora nations were all proposing the *containment* of the Sandinistas, using some of the same tools that had been part of the U.S. containment policy toward the Soviet Union since 1946. Like the Soviet Union, Sandinista Nicaragua would be isolated diplomatically. Like the Soviets, the Sandinistas would be surrounded by U.S.-backed enemies. As with the Soviet Union, the United States would enter a "long, twilight struggle" against the Nicaraguan Sandinistas. And like the Soviets, the Sandinistas would be left in charge in Nicaragua to try to find ways out of the containment box.

Reagan had already rejected containment as the centerpiece of U.S. foreign policy toward the Soviet Union. Since the president believed he did not have to settle for permanent stalemate against a rival superpower with enough nuclear missiles to destroy the world, it was unlikely he would adopt containment toward a nation with 3 million people and an army one-thirtieth the size of America's. But with Shultz enthusiastically embracing the Contadora process, and thus committing the U.S. government to negotiations, Reagan faced a difficult choice. To repudiate Shultz on Contadora could bring about his resignation. This would, at best, paralyze U.S. foreign policy for weeks. A new set of confirmation hearings in Congress, following weeks of pious pronouncements about the tragedy of Shultz's departure, could spell political disaster for the administration. Needed aid for El Salvador would be, at best, delayed.

Reagan would have to temporize. He came more and more to use rhetoric that echoed his hard-line staffers, insisting that the Sandinistas "say uncle," for example, while he used the methods of the pragmatists, such as the economic embargo. Reagan never intimated that he wanted anything other than the replacement of the Sandinistas with a more democratic government. When he spoke of the need for elections, for example, it was with the confidence that if the Sandinistas ever held a free election, they would lose. By depending on officials in the State Department, CIA, and elsewhere who did not share his goals, however, Reagan was courting embarrassment, if not a more serious political wound.

Just as Reagan worked to take full advantage of the political victory that the election in El Salvador brought him, the dangers of depending on the foreign policy professionals threatened the entire democratic project in Central America.

Self-Inflicted Wounds in Nicaragua

Mining the Harbors

Since the middle of 1983, there had been rumors of explosive mines being placed in the main harbors of Nicaragua. In early April 1984, scattered reports of mines being laid turned into widespread reports that the ships responsible for the mines were owned and operated by the CIA. The *Washington Post* was first with the story, but the major networks and the other major daily newspapers ran follow-up stories immediately.

The apparent purpose of the mines was to disrupt ocean-borne trade to Nicaragua. The mines themselves were neither numerous nor powerful enough to blockade the harbors or to endanger very many ships. However, the very presence of explosive mines and the publicity that followed discovery of the CIA's role had the potential to create economic havoc in Nicaragua. The country depended on imports, largely due to the gross incompetence of the Sandinistas in trying to run a modern economy. Since 1979, domestic productivity had collapsed, and even basic foodstuffs had to be brought in by sea. Immediately after the *Post* story on the mines appeared, insurance premiums jumped on ships traveling to the ports of Potosí, Corinto, San Juan del Sur, and Bluefields.

Outrage in Congress and among the American people was immediate. Just days after the story broke, the Senate voted 84–12 to cut off all funds for the purpose of mining Nicaraguan harbors. Members of the House denounced the administration for what many Americans perceived as a sneaky, underhanded, and possibly illegal attack on a sovereign country that had not declared war on the United States. Members of Congress also publicly deplored the diplomatic protests that followed, many couched in decidedly nondiplomatic language, from Nicaragua's trading partners, including allies of the United States in Europe and Latin America. The French government went so far as to offer mine-sweeping assistance to the Sandinistas.

Much of the anger from Congress derived from the claim that the administration had deceived or, at the least, failed to inform the legislators about the mining program. However, even Congressman Edward Boland (D-MA) admitted that the House Intelligence Committee had been told of the program in January. Members of the Senate Intelligence Committee learned of the program at the same time. In fact, during the Senate's debate on additional money for the contras, Senator Joe Biden (D-DE), an Intelligence Committee member, told his fellow senators that they would vote against the bill, "if you knew what I know."

In Washington, when there is a "sudden" leak of information that has been available to the leakers for months, it means that someone considered the timing of the revelation. In this case, the timing of the mining revelations could not have been worse for Reagan. On the day before the story surfaced, the Senate had approved $21 million in CIA support for the contras. The contra forces had grown from fifteen thousand to eighteen thousand. An entire Sandinista brigade (more than two hundred men) had recently defected to the contra side. Administration officials seemed to be slowly but successfully making the case that the Sandinistas' interference with their democratic neighbors required a forceful response.

But with the success of the contras had come a fight within the Reagan administration over the relationship of the insurgents to the U.S. government. Reagan had repeatedly said that it was not the policy of the United States to overthrow the Nicaraguan government, directly or indirectly; rather, the contras' purpose was to prevent the Sandinistas from sending arms to the rebels in El Salvador. With this stated goal in mind, officials from the CIA pressed the contras to switch tactics from seizing territory to causing economic damage. U.S. aid, vital as it was to the contras, forced the contras to follow the lead of American officials. Indeed, the arrival of CIA employees coincided with the withdrawal of the Argentines and Hondurans, who did wish to see the Sandinistas out of power.

Once again, the decision to act covertly cost the Reagan administration the opportunity to defend itself in public. While the Sandinistas and their supporters in the United States were free to accuse the administration of violating international law, endangering innocents, intervening in the affairs of a sovereign nation, and various other crimes, administration officials had to respond by insisting that they could not comment on an ongoing intelligence operation. The sympathies of many Americans shifted to Daniel Ortega in a process that accelerated after Reagan withdrew the U.S. from the jurisdiction of the World Court, where Nicaragua had filed suit to seek condemnation of contra funding, harbor mining, and other hostile acts by the U.S. government.

In mid-April, Republican congressman Newt Gingrich exposed a letter written by ten members of Congress to Ortega, addressing him as "Dear Commandante." The letter was a mix of fawning respect for Ortega and abject apology for U.S. policy. It began: "We address this letter to you in a spirit of hopefulness and good will. As Members of the U.S. House of Representatives, we regret the fact that better relations do not exist between the United States and your country. We have been, and remain, opposed to U.S. support for military action directed against the people or government of Nicaragua. We want to commend you and the members of your government for taking steps to open up the political process in your country." The letter was an invitation to Ortega to bypass the president and negotiate with Congress directly. It ended: "We reaffirm to you our continuing respect and friendship for the Nicaraguan people, and pledge our willingness to discuss these or other matters of concern with you or officials of your government at any time." The signatories, all Democrats, included majority leader Jim Wright, Edward Boland, and the chairs of the House Intelligence Committee, the Latin America subcommittee and the foreign aid subcommittee. The twin revelations of the secret mining and the secret letter placed the administration on the defensive, and for a time it seemed that all funding for the contras would be cut off. In fact, there was even renewed danger to El Salvador's military aid.

Winning One Battle; Trying to Lose the Other

Reagan responded with a two-track strategy, designed to recapture the initiative and mollify both factions of his administration enough to keep them working together awhile longer. On May 9, he gave an Oval Office address to the nation on Central America. He had given the National Security Council the responsibility of drafting it, and it turned out to be one of the most bellicose speeches of his presidency. One sure sign that the speech was not drafted by the State Department was that Reagan used the words *Communism* and *Communist* twenty-six times. The following passage sets the tone: "[I]f we do nothing, if we continue to provide too little help, our choice will be a Communist Central America with additional Communist military bases on the mainland of this hemisphere and Communist subversion spreading southward and northward. This Communist subversion poses the threat that a hundred million people from Panama to the open border of our South could come under the control of pro-Soviet regimes."

Reagan minced no words in talking about the Sandinistas: "I want to tell you a few things about the real nature of the Sandinista regime in Nicaragua. The Sandinistas, who rule Nicaragua, are Communists whose relationship and ties to Fidel Castro of Cuba go back a quarter of a century. . . . The Sandinista rule is a Communist reign of terror." Reagan listed Sandinista human rights violations.

In a direct challenge to his critics in Congress, Reagan insisted that the Sandinistas were determined to export their revolution and cited their own statements as proof. He pointed out that the Sandinistas had come to power through "a negotiated settlement, based on power sharing between Communists and genuine democrats, like the one that some have proposed for El Salvador today." He invoked the memory of John F. Kennedy, who had warned of the menace of Cuban Communism. Reagan reminded his listeners of the Soviet role in supplying and supporting Communists in Central America and insisted, "If the Soviet Union can aid and abet subversion in our hemisphere, then the United States has a legal right and a moral duty to help resist it."

In the speech's peroration, Reagan set terms of debate that would frighten his political enemies: "The simple questions are: Will we support freedom in this hemisphere or not? Will we defend our vital interests in this hemisphere or not? Will we stop the spread of Communism in this hemisphere or not? Will we act while there is still time?"

There was a subtle shift in the president's rhetoric, perceptible at first only to careful listeners. Reagan spent relatively little time in the speech talking about El Salvador, which had been the main topic of his Joint Session address thirteen months earlier. Three days before Reagan's speech, his Central America policy received a huge boost from the victory of Duarte in El Salvador. One week after the speech, members of Congress cast what turned out to be the closest vote on aid to El Salvador of the decade, approving additional aid by a vote of 212–208. This vote would prove to be the turning point for U.S. foreign policy toward El Salvador. By the end of May, Duarte himself visited Congress ("conquered Congress" in the words of a *Washington Post* reporter hostile to Reagan) and won approval of even more aid. A congressional cutoff of El Salvador would never again be a realistic possibility. For all intents and purposes, the battle of El Salvador was over, and Reagan had won.

Reagan may have saved the country from a military victory by the Communists, but he had not yet saved El Salvador from the leveraged ally faction. However, given the other matters occupying his attention, there was little that Reagan himself could do to prevent officials from the State Department and elsewhere attempting to impose economic policies on El Salvador that would keep its economy from growing.

Thus, Reagan was correct to shift the focus from El Salvador to Nicaragua, because the core of the fight over Central America was far from being resolved. The natural ally faction in the Reagan administration, usually known as the hard-liners, understood that there could be no real freedom, no real security, and no lasting economic development as long as the military threat remained. Again, careful listeners heard a signal in Reagan's May 9 speech when he said that helping Central America meant doing "enough to protect the lives of our neighbors so that they may live in peace and democracy without the threat of Communist aggression and subversion." For the remainder of his administration, Reagan would be committed to finding a way to oust the FSLN.

But with the possibility of decisive action against the Sandinistas precluded, at least for the time being, Reagan was again forced to play for time. Again, he chose a risky and dangerous way of doing so. A dramatic diplomatic opening to Nicaragua could permit Reagan to shift the rationale for contra support from the very narrow purpose of stopping arms flows to El Salvador, to putting pressure on the Sandinistas to keep their 1979 promises of democratization and free elections. Reagan could build on the strength of his successful elections-centered El Salvador policy and argue that the contras would bring elections to Nicaragua.

The strategy also allowed Reagan to make use of George Shultz, who had been pushing for a face-to-face meeting with high-ranking Sandinistas for months. Though bitterly resisted by the hard-liners in the administration, Shultz won permission to set up a meeting, in the strictest secrecy. But there was danger to the strategy as well. No matter what Shultz and Reagan said about it, a meeting in which the United States took the initiative, and in which U.S. officials traveled to Nicaragua, instead of vice versa, would look like a victory for the Sandinistas. Moreover, it was unclear to everyone, except perhaps Shultz himself, exactly what Shultz planned to discuss with his Communist interlocutors.

To maintain secrecy until the last minute, Shultz decided to combine the Sandinista meeting with his trip to Central America for the inauguration of President Duarte in San Salvador. On the morning of June 1, El Salvador's new president was sworn in. That afternoon, after perfunctory "consultations" with the presidents of Nicaragua's threatened democratic neighbors, Shultz took off for Managua. His press secretary had invited American reporters, who flew with Shultz. (Shultz would later say that maintaining secrecy had been "miraculous." For most of the reporters present, however, a premature announcement could scuttle the trip, robbing the reporters of a story. Moreover, the mostly liberal reporters probably sensed that the trip would be an embarrassment to Reagan and would do nothing to jeopardize that embarrassment.)

Shultz was met at the Managua airport by Daniel Ortega, clad in his military uniform. Shultz stressed the Kissinger Commission report, which he compared to the Marshall Plan for Central America. These funds, Shultz said, would go to the other Central American nations, but not Nicaragua, unless reforms were made. The secretary of state told Ortega that "no pressure could be greater" on his regime than that of his neighbors moving toward democracy. Ortega responded, after reciting his usual list of American sins in Central America, by permitting the talks to go on. Shultz suggested that the talks be low profile, with little publicity. However, he had no problem with both sides keeping their "key friends" informed.

Stripped of the diplomatic language, it was clear what Shultz was communicating. Mentioning the Marshall Plan was an attempt to bribe Ortega with the possibility of aid funds from the United States. By calling the example of his democratizing neighbors the *greatest* pressure, Shultz was signaling that the contras were not intended to overthrow his regime. By agreeing that key friends could be kept abreast, Shultz communicated that he had no problem with the Sandinistas reporting to the Cubans and Soviets on the negotiations. These negotiations would be based on the Contadora principles, which were based on the assurance that no government in the region should have to worry about being overthrown. "At the end of the meeting," Shultz wrote later, "I felt that I had accomplished what I (sic) had set out to do."

U.S. allies in the region were aghast at the Shultz-Ortega meeting. The president of Honduras, in particular, feared that the resulting confusion would mean the breakup of the anti-Sandinista coalition in Central America. By acknowledging Ortega's importance, the Shultz meeting gave the unmistakable impression that Washington expected the Sandinista regime to last indefinitely. Given the poor record of the United States in supporting its threatened allies, and with the memory of Vietnam still fresh, there was incentive for Costa Rica, El Salvador, and others to make an accommodation with the Sandinistas. But since Ortega could restart subversion at will, once his regime was secure, his neighbors would be permanently dependent on the U.S. for economic and military aid. To underline the threat, Ortega left for Moscow soon after speaking to Shultz.

The administration hard-liners went into immediate damage control. Oliver North, John Poindexter, and Constantine Menges pressed Shultz to give the American diplomats new instructions. Shultz ignored their suggestions. Members of both factions of the administration had their eye on Congress, which was still considering $21 million in aid to the contras that the Senate had passed on the day of the mining revelations. The more conservative members of the administration predicted dire consequences if the contras were cut off. Some began toying with the idea of outside help for the contras.

Ortega Flexes His Muscles

The arguments over contra aid continued through the summer of 1984 and into the fall. The administration's early strategy was to insist that aid to El Salvador and aid to the contras be linked in the same bill. This effort was abandoned in late July, when it became obvious that the likely effect of the linkage would be to kill both forms of aid. In another defeat, the House at the start of August passed a new Boland Amendment, after stripping an intelligence bill of every cent of contra aid Reagan had requested.

Soon after this vote, another nail was put into the coffin of contra aid. The *Washington Post* reported that the contras were using a "guerrilla war manual" written by the CIA that included, among other things, instructions on the political use of assassination. The passage on "removing" political opponents was only one page of the manual, most of which was much more standard military advice about keeping a guerrilla army in the field and using it effectively. Nevertheless, the reaction in the media was to constantly refer to the document as a "CIA assassination manual."

The revelations immediately emboldened the Sandinistas. In mid-August, Nicaragua admitted that it was using Soviet aid and technicians to build a large airstrip, confirming a charge Reagan had made weeks earlier. The Sandinistas put new pressure on their opponents in Nicaragua.

La Prensa, the nation's single independent newspaper, was subjected to ever-tightening restrictions, in spite of Sandinista promises that press censorship would be eased. The Roman Catholic prelate of Nicaragua, Cardinal Miguel Obando y Bravo, was attacked by a Sandinista mob, and his sermons were regularly banned. When a public opinion poll in mid-1984 showed that the cardinal was the most popular man in the country (and that support for the Sandinistas was down to 30 percent), the regime responded by banning public opinion polls.

With a total cutoff of aid to the contras a near certainty, Ortega pressed on to the November election. Under the campaign rules drawn up by the Sandinistas, opposition parties would be given 15 minutes per day of radio and television air time. The other 23.75 hours would be, as they had been since 1979, given over to Sandinista propaganda. Rallies for opposition candidates and parties were frequently attacked by Sandinistas, in what came to be known as *las turbas divinas* (divine mobs).

For a short time, it looked as though Ortega might have at least one credible opponent. Arturo Cruz, a member of the original Sandinista junta, who had left the country under a death threat in 1982, returned in 1984 and said he was "exploring" the possibility of running for president. Cruz wanted to assure himself that the conditions existed for a free and genuine campaign and also that he would have the support of a broad spectrum of Nicaraguans. He was to be disappointed on both counts.

At the same time, Ortega and his colleagues had succeeded spectacularly in dividing their opposition, just as the Somozas had done for decades. Cruz's former association with the Sandinistas gave him considerable credibility in Washington but made him seem a traitor to some of his countrymen. In mid-September, Cruz dropped out. By that time, the outcome of the election was no longer in doubt. It was merely a question of Ortega's margin of victory. On November 4, he received just over 60 percent of the vote and began calling himself the president-elect of Nicaragua.

A Gift from Congress

The U.S. Congress handed Ortega even greater cause for celebration in the weeks before the election. The administration made a last-ditch effort to remove the restrictive Boland language that was included in an omnibus spending bill set for passage in early October. The Democrats' strategy was to place the Boland Amendment in a bill that Reagan could not veto without shutting down a sizeable part of the Federal bureaucracy.

The matter came to a head on October 11, 1984, probably the strangest day that I spent in the Reagan White House. In the morning, I was asked to be part of a delegation meeting the president in the Blue Room of the White House. Linas Kojelis, one of my colleagues in the Office of Public Liaison, had arranged for Reagan to spend twenty-five minutes with a group of heads of charitable organizations. A smaller group had shown up for the meeting than Kojelis expected, and Michael Deaver, keeper of the president's calendar, was known to exact revenge on White House staffers who failed to use all the time allotted to them. A number of us from the Old Executive Office Building were recruited to make sure Reagan had enough hands to shake.

While I was getting photographed with Reagan, Faith Whittlesey, head of the Public Liaison Office and a leader among administration hardliners, was frantically trying to get people to urge the president to veto the Omnibus Appropriations Act that was on his desk. Her efforts were focused on conservative congressmen, senators, and heads of large conservative organizations. By midafternoon, her efforts seemed to be having some effect. She called me and asked me to draft a veto message for her to give to the president if and when the time came. I started immediately, and after half and hour, I was ready to take the draft over to the West Wing. Before I could do so, another call came from Faith, saying that Reagan had decided to sign the bill.

None of us knew it at the time, but the course of Reagan's second term had largely been set at that moment. Either because he believed that he could successfully challenge the Boland Amendment in court or he believed that he could somehow get around it, Reagan permitted the restrictions to become law. Whether or not members of the Reagan administration violated the Boland Amendment was at the core of the whole Iran-contra scandal. With a stroke of his pen, Reagan could have avoided the scandal that nearly destroyed his presidency.

The Boland Amendment itself was open to interpretation. The amendment barred the use of funds available to the CIA, the Defense Department, and U.S. intelligence agency for "supporting, directly or indirectly, military or paramilitary operations in Nicaragua by any nation, group, organization or individual." This was not a comprehensive ban. The amendment did not mention the National Security Council, which is not an intelligence agency. Moreover, by listing certain Executive Branch agencies in the amendment, rather than simply saying that no federal funds could be used for the contras at all, its writers left open the possibility that other agencies were permitted to find money for the Nicaraguan rebels.

The outcome of the confusion over the Boland Amendment would be apparent later. In the short term, the passage of the giant appropriations bill, without a government shutdown, was the last significant obstacle to Reagan's reelection, and there was some sense of relief at the White House when the veto threat came to nothing. Reagan was overwhelmingly reelected on November 6.

New Term, New Problems

The Nicaraguan MiG Incident

One day after his reelection, though, a new problem arose. The administration announced that U.S. intelligence agencies were monitoring a Soviet ship headed to Nicaragua. The ship was being followed because there was reason to believe that MiG-24 airplanes were aboard. These very sophisticated jets were usually used as bombers, and they could be equipped with nuclear missiles. Stationing such weapons in Nicaragua would put them less than two hours' flying time from much of the southern and southwestern United States. Officials told the *Wall Street Journal* that air strikes to remove the MiGs were possible if they were deployed in Nicaragua.

Within a few days, it was clear that the Soviet ship was not carrying any jet warplanes. But it was carrying something far more dangerous: Soviet Mi-24 Hind helicopters. These state-of-the-art combat aircraft were extensively used by the Soviets in Afghanistan, and with deadly effect. Heavily-armored, and specially designed for use against insurgents, the weapon would soon be familiar to many Americans after being featured in the 1985 movie *Rambo*. At the time that the Hinds were landed in Nicaragua, the significance of their presence went almost unnoticed in the flurry of criticism leveled at the Reagan administration for raising a false alarm on MiGs. (Actually, the deployment of MiGs, at least in the mind of George Shultz, would have been a boon, since the Soviets would not dare use them, but their presence would prompt Congress to vote for money for the contras.)

Nicaragua Acquires New Friends

Daniel Ortega was inaugurated as president of Nicaragua on January 11, 1985. Ortega was overshadowed at his own inauguration by the unexpected arrival of Fidel Castro. Castro's presence demonstrated that the

Sandinistas were no longer concerned about publicizing their ties to international Communism. By the end of the month, the Sandinistas had broadened their circle of anti-American partners. Mir Hussein Moussavi, the prime minister of Iran, arrived on January 23. Moussavi pledged financial and diplomatic support and joined Ortega in a statement condemning the United States.

Sandinista ties with revolutionary Iran were not new. (In fact, this was the third meeting between Ortega and Moussavi.) In May 1983, Sandinista minister of culture Ernesto Cardenal traveled to Teheran and met privately with the Ayatollah Khomeini. Other contacts followed, and the Sandinistas announced a $23 million trade deal in March 1984. What did change in 1985 was the openness of the Iranians and Sandinistas about their relationship. Iran sent its deputy foreign minister to Ortega's inauguration, and the visit from the prime minister (identified by ABC news as the official in control of Iran's terrorist operations) followed less than two weeks later. Within days of the meeting, there were reports of two ships carrying arms leaving Iran and headed for Nicaragua.

Reagan used Moussavi's visit to highlight the growing support for the Sandinistas from Middle Eastern terrorists. The FSLN had a long-standing relationship with the Palestinian Liberation Organization (PLO) and, as early as 1978, had joined with elements of the PLO in issuing a "declaration of war" against the state of Israel. The PLO arranged contacts between the Sandinistas and Muamar Qaddafi, the Libyan dictator who openly proclaimed his support for international terrorism. In April 1983, four Libyan cargo planes were forced to land in Brazil for repairs. Brazilian authorities became suspicious of the pilots' claim that they were carrying medical supplies for Columbia. All four planes were loaded with weapons and bound for Nicaragua.

After the defeat of contra aid and the passage of the Boland Amendment, the Sandinistas made their ties with Libya more open. On September 1, 1984, Tomas Borge, the Sandinista interior minister who had made the first contacts with the PLO, traveled to Tripoli for the celebration of the fifteenth anniversary of Qaddafi's rise to power. The Libyan leader took the occasion to acknowledge his ties to Nicaragua's Sandinistas: "Libyan fighters, arms and backing to the Nicaraguan people have reached them because they fight with us. They fight America on its own ground." On January 16, 1985, the Sandinistas announced a trade agreement for Libyan oil. Soon after, police in Western Europe and Latin America found suspected terrorists carrying Nicaraguan passports. Violent groups such as the Basque ETA, the German Baader-Meinhof gang, and the Italian Red Brigades began to appear in Nicaragua.

Sandinista Internal Repression and Failure Continue

The prospect that the contra challenge would disappear emboldened the Sandinistas to further restrict human rights in Nicaragua. In February 1985, the country started a campaign against peddlers and small shopkeepers in Managua, calling them "speculators, profiteers, and hoarders." For the Sandinista leadership, the success of the shopkeepers was an embarrassment, since they were providing everyday necessities that the government was insisting had to be rationed.

Also by early 1985, the Sandinistas had completed their effort to establish Sandinista block captains throughout the country. Each neighborhood had a Sandinista official charged with assessing the loyalty of every member of the community and doling out rewards or punishments as appropriate. The most common form of punishment was withholding the government ration card, necessary for daily needs such as food, cooking oil, and toilet paper. It became customary for the block captains to distribute ration cards at Sandinista rallies, after watching carefully to see who cheered loudest or failed to cheer at all. In many cases, the Sandinista block captains were exmembers of the Somoza regime, hired for their reputation for cruelty.

The ration cards themselves soon became a symbol of the accelerating economic failure of the Sandinistas. In early 1985, the regime devalued the currency by 78 percent and warned that "new sacrifices" would be necessary. The devaluation still left a huge gap between the official dollar-peso exchange rate and the informal rate. Indeed, by 1985, one of the only reliable sources of hard currency for the regime was the requirement that passengers arriving at Sandino International Airport change sixty dollars in American money to Nicaraguan money, at the fictitious official rate. American journalists, including former supporters of the Sandinistas, wrote of the deterioration of Nicaragua since 1979.

"They are Our Brothers"

As conditions worsened for ordinary Nicaraguans, and the Sandinistas strengthened their ties with more and more of America's enemies, Reagan began a new effort to secure the repeal of the Boland Amendment and the passage of American aid for the contras. On February 16, he used his weekly radio address to urge Congress to renew support for the contras. Reagan used harsh language to condemn the Sandinistas: "The Sandinistas aren't democrats, but Communists; not lovers of freedom, but of power; not builders of a peaceful nation, but creators of a fortress Nicaragua that intends to export Communism beyond its borders."

Reagan also insisted upon a new term for the contras: "The true heroes of the Nicaraguan struggle—non-Communist, democracy-loving revolutionaries—saw their revolution betrayed and took up arms against the betrayer. These men and women are today the democratic resistance fighters some call the contras. We should call them freedom fighters." Later in the broadcast, he compared his actions to support freedom in Central America to the efforts of Lafayette, Von Steuben and Kosciusko during the American Revolution.

Reagan also made it clear that he would no longer describe the contras as simply a method of stopping Sandinista arms flows into El Salvador. He openly supported their efforts to bring liberty and democracy to Nicaragua. "They're fighting for an end to tyranny." He concluded, "They are our brothers. How can we ignore them?" He repeated this sentiment at the annual Conservative Political Action Conference: "They are our brothers, these freedom fighters, and we owe them our help. I've spoken recently of the freedom fighters of Nicaragua. You know the truth about them. You know who they're fighting and why. They are the moral equal of our Founding Fathers and the brave men and women of the French Resistance."

At a nationally televised press conference around the same time, Reagan was asked if his administration advocated the overthrow of the Sandinistas. Reagan said that the outright removal of the Sandinistas might not be necessary if the current government kept its promises and instituted true democracy. Reagan made it clear he believed that pressure from the contras and from the United States would be necessary, saying that all the Sandinistas had to do to relieve the pressure was "say uncle."

Secretary of State Shultz also sharpened his rhetoric concerning the Sandinistas, telling Congress that the people of Nicaragua had been dragged "behind the Iron Curtain" and that the United States had the moral duty to prevent the situation from becoming permanent. He later told the Commonwealth Club in San Francisco that if the contras did not receive aid to continue their fight, then Nicaragua would fall into "the endless darkness of Communist tyranny."

Mr. Ortega Goes to Moscow

At first, the heated words from Reagan and Shultz seemed to be having some effect. Members of Congress began discussing providing assistance to the contras. Daniel Ortega took notice of Washington's belligerence also. He announced an "indefinite moratorium" on acquiring new weapons systems and said that his government would send home one hundred Cuban military advisors. The moves were cosmetic (there were at the time nearly three thousand Cuban advisors in the country), but given Ortega's boldness only weeks before, it was evident that he believed he had to mollify his critics.

But just as Reagan started making progress, the major newspapers in the United States started publishing articles on alleged human rights abuses by the contras. The stories of contra brutality cost Reagan dearly in the public relations war over contra aid. Even as he formally made his request to Congress for $14 million in new funds for the contras, moderate Republicans were showing resistance. Senate Intelligence Committee chair Dave Durenberger (R-MN) used the National Press Club to urge Reagan not to ask Congress for contra aid. Durenberger, who had told the *Washington Post* in January that it was time to "chuck this thing [contra support] overboard," called the policy of supporting the contras an "illogical and illegal absurdity." House minority leader Robert Michel (R-IN) called Reagan's request "dead in the water."

By April, it was clear that military aid to the contras was out of the question, in large part because of the stories about contra human rights abuses. The Reagan administration decided to try for nonlethal aid, in the form of boots, blankets, medical supplies, and food. The compromise at least left the possibility that the contras could divert funds no longer needed to buy shoes to the purchase of weapons. Reagan was trying to find a way to keep the contras alive and in the field long enough to try again with Congress.

On April 24, 1985, even this watered down proposal was defeated in the House of Representatives, 303–123. For twenty-four hours, Democrats basked in the glow of giving Ronald Reagan a serious political defeat. During that time, the lopsided vote seemed to indicate that there was no chance of reviving the proposal at a later date. The day after the vote, however, Ortega announced that he would visit the Soviet Union at the end of April to discuss economic assistance. The day after Ortega's bombshell, embarrassed and disgruntled congressional Democrats met at the White House with Reagan to find ways to get another vote on the issue.

In the meantime, Reagan used the occasion of Ortega's friendly visit with Soviet leader Mikhail Gorbachev to inform Congress of his intention to order a complete trade embargo on the country. In his Executive Order imposing the embargo, Reagan said that the policies and actions of the Sandinista regime constituted a threat to U.S. security.

It is a sign of Reagan's near desperation that he resorted to an economic embargo, which is a quintessential tool for the creation of a leveraged ally. Less trade with Nicaragua meant less private economic development for the country. On the contrary, the embargo meant even more deprivation for Nicaraguans already suffering under Sandinista mismanagement and Communism. The longer the embargo was in place, the more the Nicaraguan economy would shrink, and the more dependent Nicaragua would become on outside aid, even in the event that the contras were to win the civil war. The embargo also meant even less clout for the beleaguered private sector in the country. Just days after Reagan's announcement, the largest private-sector group in Nicaragua denounced the embargo and asked that Congress pass legislation to overturn it. In May, Archbishop Obando y Bravo also came out against the embargo.

In the meantime, Daniel Ortega continued his tour of Communist capitals, with each stop making the revival of contra aid more certain. From Moscow, he went to Romania to meet with Nicolae Ceausescu, then on to Hungary and Czechoslovakia, where he asserted that most of Latin America supported him against Reagan. His last stop was Warsaw, where he met Polish military dictator Wojciech Jaruzelski. On the same day as his Polish stop, a group of Democratic congressmen introduced legislation to break the deadlock over contra aid and provide for more aid in 1985.

But the leveraged ally faction in the administration and Congress was hard at work on this issue as well. In June, Reagan reluctantly agreed to drop his insistence that the CIA continue to be the conduit for contra aid. Members of Congress, encouraged by George Shultz, were adamant that the spy agency be cut out of the process and replaced by the Agency for International Development (AID). This agency was part of the State Department, and thus under Shultz's direct control. The head of AID at the time was J. Peter McPherson, who was a strong believer in the usefulness of aid as leverage. Immediately, he placed restrictions on the aid, setting up obstacles that made any additional contra aid virtually unattainable by the contras. The incentive was still strong for the contras' friends to find other ways to support them.

On June 12, the House approved $27 million in nonmilitary aid, sending the measure to the Senate, which had already passed a larger amount. On the same day, the contra leaders announced that the various factions making up the armed resistance had agreed to form the United Nicaraguan Opposition (UNO) and coordinate their efforts to overthrow the Sandinista government. To a large degree, the formation of UNO also represented a victory for the leveraged ally side, since UNO included Eden Pastora. The former Sandinista had the smallest following of the three groups that merged, and he was generally recognized as the least active and least effective guerrilla leader. Nevertheless, he was closer to State Department officials than his counterparts, who had closer ties to the Defense Department, the CIA, and the NSC staff.

Still, the unity movement was a bit of good news for contra supporters, at a time when it was badly needed. More seemingly good news came from the State Department when Langhorne Motley resigned as assistant secretary for Latin America. Reagan replaced him with Elliott Abrams, who was known as more of a hard-liner than Motley. As assistant secretary of state for human rights and humanitarian affairs, Abrams had made a number of speeches denouncing Communist human rights abuses, especially in Cuba and Nicaragua. Conservatives hoped that Abrams would represent their point of view in the State Department and stand up to Shultz, at least on Latin American issues. For a time, Abrams cultivated the image of a lone, brave conservative fighting the State Department moderates.

The switch from the CIA to AID as the money conduit for the contras and the appointment of Abrams to replace Motley were mainly of interest to insiders. For most Americans, the real story of the summer of 1985 was the revival of contra aid, even if in nonlethal form. Beginning with UN ambassador Jeane Kirkpatrick, commentators began to refer to the Reagan Doctrine, referring to efforts by the U.S. government to support and fund anti-Communist guerrilla groups fighting Soviet-backed regimes. The best known example of such support was U.S. money and weapons to the Mujahedeen in Afghanistan, which had been fighting since the Soviet invasion of the country in 1979.

In July 1985, the U.S. House of Representatives began work on the Foreign Assistance Authorization Act, a usually obscure piece of legislation. The $27 million in aid to the contras was attached to this bill, along with an undisclosed amount for the Afghan resistance. It was clear that the idea of reversing Communist domination was beginning to take hold in the imaginations of the American people, perhaps because of the success of unabashedly patriotic movies such as *Red Dawn*, *Rambo*, and *the Hunt for Red October*. The tide on Capitol Hill was clearly flowing in the contras' direction. The question was, could they hold out long enough for Congress to provide enough for them to win? Some in the administration did not think so and began taking actions to funnel more cash to the Nicaraguan rebels.

Fall 1985—Harbingers

Interlude in El Salvador

On September 9, 1985, Inez Guadeloupe Duarte, the president's daughter, was kidnapped. The rebels also seized several of her friends, and in the days to come, they added twenty elected mayors to their collection of hostages. A week after Inez's capture, the FMLN demanded that thirty-four "political prisoners" be released in return for her safety. President Duarte, in the eyes of many Salvadorans, simply panicked during the crisis. He suspended all other government business, made no other decisions, and spent long hours alone. Finally, he made the barely face-saving offer to release twenty-three FMLN members, in return for his daughter, her friends, and the mayors. The trade took place on October 23.

Duarte's loss of self-control made the crisis seem worse than it actually was. In fact, the resort to high-profile kidnappings backfired badly for the rebels. Sympathy for President Duarte greatly increased his popularity. The FMLN leadership, for its part, had completely misread the loyalties of the Salvadoran people. In the early 1980s, before the country experienced free elections, the rebels could claim that all government officials were part of the repressive apparatus of the government. By 1985, however, mayors were popularly elected officials, and some of the twenty who were kidnapped had also spent time in jail under the military. Not only was the FMLN becoming less threatening, but it was also becoming less relevant to democratic El Salvador.

Another relic of El Salvador's recent past left the scene during the kidnapping drama. Roberto D'Aubuisson resigned as head of the Nationalist Republican Alliance party (ARENA) on September 28, ending his long and checkered career in Salvadoran politics. His departure made Reagan's job of getting sustained aid for El Salvador easier. Even better, from the point of view of the natural ally faction, D'Aubuisson was replaced by Alfredo Cristiani, a staunch free market economic conservative with no ties to death squads or other right wing violence. Cristiani's leadership of ARENA assured that the next election would be about El Salvador's economic future. It was a battlefield that Reagan's closest allies found favorable.

Ortega's Shopping Spree

In Nicaragua, in the meantime, President Daniel Ortega was becoming more and more repressive and unpopular at the same time. On October 15, he suspended what few civil rights still existed in Nicaragua, citing the "brutal aggression" of the U.S. and its "internal allies." Five days later, Cardinal Obando y Bravo, who had emerged as the main spokesman for the civilian opposition, said Mass in Estelí, Nicaragua's third-largest city. Outdoor masses were the only large gatherings still allowed in Sandinista Nicaragua, and Obando's drew several thousand people, in a scene reminiscent of Pope John Paul II's defiant outdoor masses in his native Poland.

Once again, Ortega did irreparable harm to his own cause. During a trip to New York to address the United Nations, Ortega and his wife did some shopping along Fifth Avenue. While hundreds of thousands of Nicaraguans were nearing starvation, Ortega spent $3,500 on a pair of designer eyeglasses. Many times in the 1980s, the issues surrounding Central America seemed abstract and esoteric to the average American. The purchase of eyeglasses that cost the same as the average used car, however, was a crystallization of the issue that even the most casual observer could understand. In ordinary Americans' minds, Ortega ceased to be a revolutionary hero at the moment he bought the bullet-proof spectacles. He became a selfish, uncaring dictator.

In both El Salvador and Nicaragua, the civil wars had entered new phases in 1984 and 1985. While many battles remained, political corners had been turned. El Salvador was no longer in imminent danger of acquiring a Communist government. The contras remained a going concern despite the cutoff of American aid (and some in Congress began to wonder how this was possible). Reagan made it clear that removing the Sandinista government, one way or the other, was a priority of his second term. Within his own administration, Reagan was continuing to pursue the risky policy of ceding short-term dominance to the leveraged ally faction, in the hopes that eventual freedom for El Salvador and Nicaragua would serve the goals of the natural ally faction.

As 1985 drew toward a close, Central America almost seemed destined to depart from the front pages, as the antagonists showed signs of either exhaustion or distraction. In the meantime, the world around El Salvador and Nicaragua was changing. By 1985, Honduras and Guatemala had both held democratic elections and were both showing some signs of economic improvement. In spite of the warm reception Ortega got in Moscow, Soviet leader Mikhail Gorbachev was rapidly losing his enthusiasm for supporting peripheral communist states.

But the region would not fade into the background just yet. There was one more portent in the fall of 1985. On September 15, Rev. Benjamin Weir, who had been kidnapped in Beirut, Lebanon, sixteen months earlier, was unexpectedly released.

8

The War at Home, 1981–1986

Ronald Reagan launched a massive propaganda offensive on behalf of U.S. aid to the rebels fighting to overthrow the Nicaraguan government. . . . To market U.S. intervention in Nicaragua, the president has set up a veritable propaganda ministry in the executive branch.

—*The Nation*, April 13, 1985

For eight years, the press called me the "Great Communicator." Well, one of my greatest frustrations during those eight years was my inability to communicate to the American people and to Congress the seriousness of the threat we faced in Central America.

—Ronald Reagan, 1990

Before continuing the narrative, which leads us next to the Iran-contra scandal, it is worthwhile to pause and look at the impact that the shooting wars in Central America and the bureaucratic wars in Washington had on the American people. Central America was constantly in the news during the 1980s, but few Americans, even to this day, realize the strenuous efforts that went into creating a particular context for news from El Salvador, Nicaragua, and elsewhere. This discussion will serve as necessary background to the events surrounding Iran-contra.

Setting the Terms of Debate

El Salvador Is Spanish for Vietnam

While opponents of the Reagan administration faulted it for seeing Central America as a Cold War battlefield, some of those same opponents insisted that the region would turn into another Vietnam. One of the more strained connections came in a *New York Times* editorial: "As construction crews prepare to break ground for a Vietnam War Memorial on the Mall, a different kind of remembrance of that conflict has taken shape here, a debate over whether United States involvement in El Salvador is leading toward a new Vietnam." Anthony Lewis titled one of his 1983 columns, "Why Are We in Vietnam?" and, a month later, came up with a new reason to worry: "[Reagan] has sent as Ambassador to neighboring Honduras an unreconstructed Vietnam hawk, John Negroponte, with the evident assignment of running the anti-Nicaraguan activities."

Closely connected with the Vietnam fear was the conviction that Reagan would eventually send U.S. combat troops into the region. When Secretary of State Alexander Haig told Congress that the Reagan administration would do "whatever is prudent and necessary" to prevent a Communist takeover of El Salvador, and spoke of "a line in the sand," some saw Haig's rhetoric as "the forerunner of sending American troops—to fight in partnership with a weak government and brutal extremists." William LeoGrande, an American University professor sympathetic to the FMLN, said that in trying to protect El Salvador from Communism, "Washington will be faced with only two options: allowing a victory for the leftist guerrillas or sending in ground combat troops on a large scale."

El Salvador Is Not a Democracy

Reagan's critics and opponents made no end of historical analogies to oppose U.S. action in El Salvador and, later, in Nicaragua. One of the most pervasive was dredging up the sordid history of U.S. intervention in Latin America and insisting that most, if not all, of those historical interventions were undertaken directly on behalf of U.S. business interests or to shore up a Latin American government likely to be compliant to U.S. businesses. In the anti-Reagan presentation of Latin American history, the continent had only two types of governments: oligarchies of the wealthy, backed up by the military; and romantic and idealistic revolutionary governments, either successful ones like Cuba's and Nicaragua's or those strangled by American might, like Guatemala's or Chile's.

El Salvador, Reagan's critics insisted, fit into the former category. Indeed, for the antiadministration forces, it was important enough to portray El Salvador as an oligarchy that they invariably simply ignored the October 1979 coup. This event brought a distinctly antioligarchy junta to power, made up of left-of-center civilian politicians and reformist military officers. When opponents of the administration acknowledged the October coup, they did so grudgingly and with the insistence that nothing had actually changed in El Salvador. The Salvadoran military was still really in charge.

One story, widely circulated even after Salvadoran junta leader José Napoleon Duarte denied it, told of how Duarte's torture under a previous military government had left his hands permanently injured. Duarte was said to have been walking into the presidential palace in San Salvador, where he saw the very military officer who had tortured him. Instead of ordering the man arrested on the spot, the story concluded, Duarte merely lowered his eyes submissively and walked on. (Actually, Duarte's hands were injured during an accident sustained while he was an engineer.)

The stereotype of El Salvador as an oligarchy-ruled banana republic persisted until the election of 1984. Prior to Duarte's 1984 election, most of the administration's critics loudly cast doubt on the usefulness of elections in El Salvador. Oddly, having repeatedly made the point that too many Latin American nations, including El Salvador, were governed by elites that ignored the will of the people, many of Reagan's opponents, most notably former Carter administration ambassador Robert White, promoted the idea of a coalition government for the country, rather than elections. Cloaking their preference in the mantle of "pragmatism," such critics argued that the U.S. government should broker a deal in which the FMLN rebels would be permitted a role in the Salvadoran government.

When Reagan made it clear that he and the Salvadoran junta rejected power sharing and would proceed with elections, Reagan's detractors argued that Salvadoran elections would either be fundamentally unfair or counterproductive or both. It seemed self-evident to many on the left that the only acceptable electoral result would be a victory for the guerrillas. When Salvadoran voters turned out in huge numbers and voted for the rightist ARENA coalition in the March 1982 elections those who had doubts about the wisdom of elections saw their worst fears confirmed. The *New York Times* wrote: "The large turnout in the Salvadoran election was a welcome victory for the democratic process. But it was a limited one, and a Pyrrhic one. . . . Whoever would have been the winner in that election, it was clear from the start that there was going to be one sure loser. That loser could only have been the United States."

Many of these "election skeptics" went beyond questions about the openness of the Salvadoran balloting and questioned whether or not Latin Americans wanted or needed democratic elections in the first place. One commentator condescendingly wrote: "To equate change with democracy misreads what is wrong south of the border. The continent's ills are economic; the system, for nearly a century closely identified with the U.S., simply does not work." Another skeptic added, with disdain: "[El Salvador] is an impoverished little country. . . . It would be nice if it were to become a democracy. That is also unlikely." In almost every case, liberals suggested that elections be replaced by power sharing, through an elite bargain negotiated by rebel and government leaders.

For Reagan and his supporters, the idea of power sharing between Communists and non-Communists was exactly what went wrong in Nicaragua in 1979. Democratic leaders made common cause with the Sandinistas to oust Somoza, only to find themselves ousted in turn as the Sandinistas traveled down the road to dictatorship and alignment with the Soviet Union. Put differently, it was the failure of power sharing that brought about the crisis in Nicaragua.

Nicaragua Is Not a Threat

Reagan's opponents, for their part, saw no danger in emulating Nicaragua's 1979 solution, since they saw no danger from Nicaragua to begin with. Liberals and other critics insisted that Nicaragua posed no threat to its neighbors, and certainly no threat to the United States. On some occasions, this conclusion was supported by visits to Nicaragua, as in the case of a *New York Times* letter writer: "Two weeks ago, I was in Nicaragua talking to leaders of that country's government as well as business managers. . . . The Nicaraguan government is determined to maintain the independence of Nicaragua from any outsiders." Other times, the Sandinistas' defenders downplayed or minimized the regime's dictatorial tendencies, using a very different standard than that applied to El Salvador. "Nicaragua's young leaders are intolerant but not yet ruthless" opined the *Times*. "Critics are harassed but not wholly silenced or tortured. . . . The relative civility of the revolution is among its vital assets."

On the issue of Nicaragua aiding the rebels in El Salvador and leftist guerrillas in Honduras and Guatemala, again their role was minimized. A Princeton University professor stated that "the Administration has yet to produce evidence that the flow of arms from Nicaragua has been of more than minor significance." Other Reagan critics went further. Long after even many congressional Democrats acknowledged the Sandinistas' interference with their neighbors, one columnist insisted: "There is no evidence that the Sandinistas give (sic) these movements [in El Salvador and Guatemala] material support." (The use of the present tense may have been intentional, since the column appeared during a lull in Nicaraguan arms shipments.)

Similarly, the same Princeton don defended Nicaragua's huge arms buildup in the early 1980s, calling it "scarcely an unnatural response" to U.S. hostility. Even acknowledging that the Sandinistas had many new weapons, there was no reason to worry about them. "The small democracy of Costa Rica, to the south, surely is immune to the Sandinist virus. Backward and under-populated though Honduras, to the north, may be, it would not be an easy conquest." From the safety of a New Jersey college campus, the fifty thousand Nicaraguans in the Sandinista army understandably seemed less threatening than they did to Salvadorans and Hondurans.

Beyond arguments over the strength and aggressiveness of Nicaragua was the antiadministration view that the Sandinistas brought the only real social, economic, and political progress happening in Central America. The Sandinistas, insisted Reagan's critics, were following a moderate revolutionary path and deserved patience and understanding, not threats. Decisions such as the one-year moratorium on strikes and a ban on the publication of "false news detrimental to the economy" were excused on the basis that Nicaragua was trying to recover from a civil war. (Liberals extended no such tolerance to El Salvador, also in the throes of a civil war.) Adolfo Pérez Esquivel, an Argentine Nobel Prize winner, wrote as late as 1985: "Yes, the Sandinistas have made mistakes—but they have also registered remarkable achievements that far outweigh their shortcomings."

What did not count as a shortcoming, to Reagan's opponents, was the failure of the Sandinistas to hold the elections that they had promised to the Organization of American States in 1979. The August 1980 FSLN decision to postpone elections for five years had to be seen in context, according to a liberal columnist: "The [Nicaraguan] government has taught the poor to read and inoculated them against disease and gives economic aid to them before giving it to the more financially stable. It is still planning to hold elections six years after its revolution, which beats the record of the United States, which took eight years to elect its first President." (That Americans voted for congressmen and local officials starting in 1776 is passed over.) Even after the Sandinistas held fraudulent elections in November 1984, Reagan's critics were eager to blame the United States, as an editorial from the time opened: "The most fraudulent thing about the Nicaraguan election was the part the Reagan Administration played in it."

It's Reagan's Fault

To the extent that liberals and Democrats saw hostility in the Sandinista regime, they were quick to pin the blame on Ronald Reagan. By expressing such harsh (and unfounded) hostility to the Nicaraguan revolution, Reagan was forcing the Sandinistas to turn to Cuba, the Soviet Union, and other U.S. enemies. Reagan, for example, failed to adequately reward the Sandinistas for a brief halt in arms shipments to the Salvadoran rebels, so "relations worsened, and Nicaragua is again accused of running guns to El Salvador. Thus did it turn to Libya." It was Reagan accusing the Sandinistas at the base of the problem; not the Sandinistas' actions.

A professor from Swarthmore College in Pennsylvania saw Reagan's actions as self-defeating: "[T]he irony is that Washington has created conditions that make it rational for the Sandinistas to engage in such [military] spending—and to turn to Havana and Moscow for help." Wayne Smith weighed in also, to defend Cuba: "Mr. Castro cannot loosen his relationship with Moscow so long as he is threatened by Washington." Most simply, a *Times* letter to the editor read: "Wouldn't you take aid from one devil if another were threatening to destroy your country?"

The administration was also headed for self-imposed defeat in El Salvador, according to its critics: "No one can guarantee that the [Salvadoran] revolution will not produce a left wing dictatorship" opined the *New York Times*. "But if Mr. Reagan pursues military options, Washington will inevitably guarantee that result." William LeoGrande agreed: "Washington's efforts to shore up the junta with increasing amounts of military aid has (sic) only deepened the war, and the Salvadoran military's brutality has become the guerrillas' best recruiter." Robert Feinberg of the Carnegie Endowment added: "In 1981, the Russians stepped in to provide grain we would not ship; in 1983, Algeria opened its market to sugar we would not longer buy; and several other donors—Mexico, Brazil, Guatemala, Sweden, Libya and the Soviet Union—have stepped in to replace blocked credits from international financial institutions."

Reagan's critics on Central America lost few opportunities to mention past U.S. sins in Latin America, particularly the role that the U.S. government played in the establishment of the Somoza dictatorship, but they did not limit themselves to blaming the United States for the crisis in Nicaragua. Russell Baker wrote in March 1982 that Fidel Castro "doesn't wish us any good. On the other hand, why should he? We financed an invasion of Cuba to throw him out and when that failed we tried to have him murdered by the Mafia." Another commentator, noting the thirtieth anniversary of the coup that ousted leftist Guatemalan President Jacobo Arbenz, titled his op ed, "Anniversary of Another Liberation . . . And Its Throttling by U.S."

Such self-flagellation was part of a larger effort by many who were opposed to the Reagan administration to place the United States on the same moral plane as the Soviet Union (sometimes referred to as the S.U. to heighten the mirror-image impression). Again, Russell Baker was most blunt: "[I]t would help if someone in Washington explained why it's all right for us to interfere in Poland, which is Moscow's territory, but all wrong for Moscow to interfere in Central America." In another editorial, the *Times* noted that the Soviets believed that their national interests were served by practicing covert activity in Central America, Angola, Syria, the Horn of Africa, Europe, Southeast Asia, and many other places, but noted that the United States did the same thing.

The 1984 CIA-assisted mining of the Nicaraguan harbors provided a rationale for more attempts to establish a moral equivalence between the United States and the U.S.S.R. I personally attended a "town hall meeting" run by liberal congressman Robert Edgar (D-PA) in July 1984, in which he asserted that the mining was no different than the September 1983 Soviet shoot-down of a civilian Korean Air Liner, in which one of Edgar's House colleagues was killed. Anthony Lewis made the same point in print when stories of the mining first appeared. "The Reagan Administration," he wrote, "has put heavy emphasis on the need to stop international terrorism, and just about every American would applaud that aim. But that same Administration engages in international terrorism, without apology, without shame."

Reagan's Friends Are Worse than His Enemies

For some on the left, insisting on moral equivalence was inappropriate because it was too charitable to the United States and its allies. Representative Tom Harkin (D-IA) told the House of Representatives, for example, "I agree [the Sandinistas] are not Boy Scouts. But compared to the Contras, whom we are supporting, they are Eagle Scouts." There was a sedulous effort on the part of Reagan's opponents to blame the anti-Communist forces in Central America for all the death and destruction that existed there. Former ambassador Robert White repeated a very common theme when he called government security forces "the chief killer of Salvadorans."

At the time that White spoke, the FMLN guerrillas themselves took credit for eighteen thousand deaths in the country, but this did not stop White and many others from insisting, repeatedly, that almost all of the forty thousand people killed in El Salvador by 1984 were killed by the Salvadoran army. (One would be tempted to believe, based on their assertions, that the Salvadoran guerrillas were the most ineffective guerrilla army in history.)

By contrast, Reagan's enemies spent his first term portraying the Sandinistas as the idealistic, misunderstood exemplars of progress, virtue, and charity. A Catholic priest used a letter to the *Times* to quote, without a trace of skepticism, a story about one of the most hard-line Sandinistas:

> Tomas Borge, a founder of the Nicaraguan Sandinista movement, was captured by the Somoza forces before the insurrection and so badly tortured that it was feared he would not survive. However, he recovered and was appointed Minister of the Interior. One of his first acts was to go to the prison where he had been held and where his principal torturer was now himself held. Borge said to him: "Remember when I told you I would take my revenge when I was free? I now come for my revenge. For your hate and torture, I give you love, and for what you did, I give you freedom." And he ordered the man set free.

The story originated with another Catholic priest, Sandinista foreign minister Miguel D'Escoto.

For Reagan's critics, the human rights violations of the Sandinistas, even when they were acknowledged, were either referred to as "mistakes" (this was especially true when liberals commented on the mistreatment of the Miskito Indians) or excused on the basis that Nicaragua had once been occupied by U.S. troops, that Somoza was a friend of the United States, that Reagan was implacably nasty to the Sandinistas, or that war in Nicaragua (but not in El Salvador) justified "mild" abuses of human rights.

Certain events in the 1980s brought out some of the more gushing pro-Sandinista statements from Reagan haters. In April 1984, for example, the FSLN appointed Nora Astorga ambassador to the UN. Astorga's chief qualification for the position was her success in luring a Somoza general into her bedroom, where he was ambushed and killed. Meeting liberals at the New York Athletic Club, Astorga prompted this reaction from political activist Susan Horowitz: "To try to get the guy to bed, then kill him! Fantastic. It's like a Western. That's my dream, to do that to Reagan, George Bush, go right down the line." The *Washington Post*, which ran Horowitz's comment, referred to Astorga as "a living, breathing, left-wing Dirty Harriet in the Age of Eastwood." (The paper never offered a word of disapproval of Horowitz's murderous hatred.)

Astorga got equally lenient treatment from other major media outlets. CBS' *60 Minutes* ran a friendly and sympathetic interview in October 1984 (days before a crucial vote on contra aid). Earlier, the *New York Times* compared her to "Lola-Lola, Shanghai Lily and X-27, a femme fatale." One letter writer complained, not because the *Times*' treatment was too biased, but because it was too flippant. "Rather than using comparisons to Lola-Lola and Shanghai Lily," she said, "you might better have read the Bible and then compared Senorita Astorga to Jael, who killed the general Sesira in her tent, or to Judith, who lured and killed the general Holofernes."

We Are Doomed to Defeat

By the end of 1983, some of Reagan's efforts in Latin America were beginning to bear flower, even if they were not yet bearing fruit. The immediate threat of a guerrilla victory was receding in El Salvador, the country was moving, albeit haltingly, toward democracy, and even the Sandinistas were acknowledging the strain that was resulting from the actions of the contras. It was at this point that Reagan's critics were most emphatic in their insistence that opposing Communism and supporting democracy was doomed to fail. Flora Lewis was eager to predict defeat in May 1983: "The question isn't whether the United States can really turn El Salvador around and achieve a peaceful, moderate solution. It is only whether collapse and leftist victory or a right-wing coup and bloodbath can be held off for a few more years."

In Nicaragua, anti-administration voices (the same voices that demanded that the contras not receive assistance in fighting the Sandinistas' twenty-thousand-man army) maintained that the war there was lost also. An editorial titled "The Contra Revolution Won't Work" compared support for the contras with the failed 1961 Bay of Pigs invasion of Cuba. In yet another effort to compare Central America to Vietnam, former National Security advisor McGeorge Bundy wrote in June 1985, as Congress voted to restore contra aid: "The House should reverse this vote on the simple and fundamental ground that this 'covert' operation will not work. I speak as someone with direct exposure to the ineffectiveness of covert operations." (It was almost stereotypical of Vietnam decision makers to assume that what they could not do simply could not be done.)

Sometimes the defeatism of Reagan's enemies took on apocalyptic overtones. A columnist wrote in August 1983: "Unless he is stopped by Congress—and only Congress and the force of public opinion can stop him—Ronald Reagan could plunge this country into the most unwanted, unconscionable, unnecessary and unwinnable war in its history, not excepting Vietnam." On other occasions, the predictions of defeat became laughable as the years refuted them. Alexander Cockburn, for example, asked in May 1984, "Who can doubt that Costa Rica is already on the Cambodian road to ruin, as this relatively tranquil and democratic country has, or soon will have, arms pressed upon it by the U.S. against nonexistent aggressors?"

Actions Speak Louder than Words

As powerful and influential as the words and ideas of the anti-Reagan forces were, the antiadministration leaders did not just write columns and make speeches. The 1980s saw a proliferation of forms of direct action. Some were symbolic; others sought to make a real difference. Some were traditional and familiar to veterans of the civil rights and antiwar protests of the 1960s; others were more innovative.

Demonstrations

As early as the spring of 1981, public protests against Reagan's determination to assist the government of El Salvador began to appear. On March

24, the first anniversary of the murder of Salvadoran archbishop Oscar Romero, there were demonstrations, hunger strikes, and candlelight vigils in various cities in the United States. Without exception, the sites of the protests were centers of liberal opinion. They included Boston, Ann Arbor, and the campus of the New York New School of Social Research. University students and faculty spearheaded the actions, and, for the most part, they made up the majority of the participants.

The coordination for this first set of public actions came from the Committee in Solidarity with the People of El Salvador (CISPES). The group was founded in 1980, during a trip to the United States by Farid Handal, brother of Salvadoran Communist Party founder Shafik Handal. CISPES had an unusually radical agenda for El Salvador. Whereas most administration critics sought the end to military assistance to the country, CISPES also deplored the provision of economic assistance. Where other liberals condemned violence on both sides of the Salvadoran conflict, CISPES sought material aid for the FMLN guerrillas and referred to the areas that the FMLN controlled as "liberated zones."

Public actions against the Reagan administration were usually staged at a place, or in a way, to attract media attention. In March 1981, for example, demonstrators in Chicago briefly took over the Senate office of Charles Percy (R-IL). (CISPES members took over a number of local congressional and Senate offices; in some cases, they declared during their occupation that the office had been renamed the "Oscar Romero Memorial Office" or something similar.) In New York on the same day, a march took place from the Argentine consulate to the Army and Marine Corps Recruiting Center.

After the U.S. invasion of Grenada in October 1983, fourteen demonstrators seized control of the U.S. mission to the United Nations. More demonstrators climbed to the top of the Statue of Liberty and unfurled a banner reading: "U.S. Marines out of Grenada." Some of the anti-Grenada demonstrations were organized by the hastily assembled Emergency Committee against the Invasion of Grenada. As with the 1981 protests, the real driving force was the leadership of CISPES.

July and November of 1983 saw two large anti-Reagan protests in Washington. In July, Central America was one of many issues protested by more than one hundred thousand people on the Washington, DC Mall and in the area around the Lincoln Memorial. In November, a smaller but still substantial crowd demonstrated on the White House ellipse and near the State Department. The gathered demonstrators heard folk music from Peter, Paul, and Mary and speeches by liberal Democratic presidential contenders. A smaller crowd gathered at the offices of the Immigration and Naturalization Service (INS). Again, the sites and the speakers were designed to maximize media coverage.

Many of the people who attended the demonstrations repeated the assertion that El Salvador was destined to become another Vietnam. Some, like Rev. William Sloane Coffin, had barely appeared in print or on television for nearly twenty years before the Central America issue brought them back into the news. While the demonstrators may indeed have wanted to prevent "another Vietnam," they seemed eager to reprise their own Vietnam history.

The Sanctuary Movement

Unlike the demonstrations of the Vietnam era, however, the rallies focusing on Central America had little lasting impact. It became clear by the end of 1983 that mass demonstrations had less impact that more specific actions, directed toward a more narrow audience. One of the more successful direct action campaigns of the 1980s, and one that had great success as a public relations ploy, was the sanctuary movement.

In March 1982, the Rev. John M. Fife of the Tucson Southside United Presbyterian Church declared that his place of worship was a sanctuary for refugees from El Salvador and Guatemala. Such sanctuary was needed, Fife said, because the U.S. government under Reagan was refusing to give political asylum to refugees from right-wing dictatorships in Central America. Claiming the ancient right of accused criminals to seek sanctuary in places of worship, Fife and his imitators vowed to keep the refugees safe in their churches until U.S. policy changed. By 1985, more than two hundred churches nationwide had followed Fife's example.

The movement received early backing from John Fitzpatrick, the Roman Catholic bishop from Brownsville, Texas. His "Director of Christian Services" said in 1984: "We do not feel we are breaking any laws. . . . We have no choice but to assist them for humanitarian reasons. No one denies the existence of death squads in El Salvador. This is the closest point on American soil to El Salvador." Another sanctuary leader told a judge that she felt she had not broken the law, but acted only under "biblical mandates."

The administration, for its part, contended that most of those who left El Salvador and Guatemala (and, usually, Nicaragua as well) were unable to prove that they had "a well-founded fear of persecution," which was the standard set down by the 1980 Refugee Act for claiming political asylum. In the early Reagan years, the administration view was usually given by Elliott Abrams, assistant secretary of state for human rights and humanitarian affairs. Abrams said that the Salvadorans and Guatemalans coming to the United States were economic refugees looking for jobs and thus not eligible for political asylum. Abrams told the *Washington Post* in 1985 that the State Department had attempted to track the fates of 482 Salvadorans deported in the previous few months. According to Abrams, DOS was able to confirm only one death among the deportees, and that death was due to the leftist guerrillas.

In 1984, a number of leaders of the sanctuary movement were indicted. Most of the attention went to Jack Elder and Stacey Lynn Merkt, both of whom were convicted but received lenient sentences: Elder had to spend 150 days at a "halfway house"; Merkt got probation. Both continued their activities after their sentencing. The indictments came after an investigation by the Federal Bureau of Investigation that included the use of infiltrators with tape recorders to document discussions of illegal activity. The operation resulted in sixteen indictments in January 1985.

For many of the enthusiastic supporters of the sanctuary movement, however, it had less to do with helping persecuted Salvadorans than with opposing Reagan administration policy in Central America. Joseph Azar, executive director of the Central American Refugee Center in Long Island, for example, said in June 1985, "Sanctuary is a very public statement that is more symbolic than it is designed to solve the direct needs of refugees . . . It is intended to make middle-class Americans ask the question, 'Why is my church in conflict with my government?' "

As a politically motivated movement, the Sanctuary Movement wanted nothing to do with refugees from the Sandinista regime in Nicaragua. An administrator at Azar's center insisted: "We have not come across many Nicaraguan refugees. . . . The refugees' churches are giving aid to people whose lives are in danger. You won't see the pattern of persecution among refugees from Nicaragua." In making this sweeping statement, the administrator took issue with Cardinal Obando y Bravo, who had by this point described the Sandinista regime as "totalitarian" and "an enemy of the church."

But the sanctuary movement did have some political influence. In 1984, Congressman Joe Moakley (D-MA) and Senator Dennis DeConcini (D-AZ) proposed legislation to give special status to fleeing Salvadorans. Under the legislation, which was never passed, Salvadorans would have occupied a new category in INS classification, the Extended Involuntary Stay category. In May 1985, a number of groups involved in the sanctuary movement filed suit in federal court to stop the Justice Department from instituting any new prosecutions of sanctuary members. The groups argued that the 1980 Refugee Act made their actions legal. The ultraliberal U.S. District Court in San Francisco, where the suit was filed, ruled in their favor, although the court's ruling was later overturned.

By 1986, however, the improving situation in El Salvador, and the unwillingness of the movement's organizers to extend their activism to include refugees from Nicaragua, led to a decline in the movement. In San Benito, Texas, near Brownsville, the city council voted in August to close a shelter run by the pro-Sanctuary Brownsville diocese of the Catholic Church. Approximately five hundred refugees were bused from the "Casa Oscar Romero" to the district office of the INS.

The "Sandalistas"

Opponents of U.S. aid to the Nicaraguan contras sponsored a large number of sight-seeing tours of Nicaragua during the 1980s. Particularly popular were coffee-picking tours. Most of the returning Americans told almost exactly the same story about their time in Nicaragua. (The Roman Catholic prelate of Nicaragua stated baldly, "The government here manipulates all the groups that come.") The common elements were: the sense of safety and well-being that the visitors found on arriving in the capital of Managua. Those visitors with experience in other Central American countries were quick to claim that Managua was a safer and happier city than San Salvador or Guatemala City.

Once in the countryside, the visitors would see health clinics, literacy centers, cooperative farms and Sandinista militia units, usually with women in prominent positions. The Nicaraguans would invariably tell the visitors of the atrocities of the Somoza regime and extol the Sandinistas' efforts to bring health care, education, and "dignity" to the countryside for the first time. Visitors would also hear, in dramatically hushed tones, of the attacks and abuses of the U.S.-supported contras, whom they would identify as members of the old Somoza National Guard. Very frequently, the clinics and schools would show signs of burning, which was attributed to the contras.

Another unvarying feature of the Sandinista tours was the obligatory vehicle breakdown, always in an area which the visitors' hosts would claim was rife with contras (which competed with Sandinistas' simultaneous claim that the contras held no territory in Nicaragua and were little more than a destructive nuisance). Many returning North American visitors would tell of their fear and apprehension, as their hosts strained to repair the vehicles (a task made difficult by the U.S economic embargo and the resulting shortage of spare parts) before the convoy was attacked by contras.

The tours provided the Sandinistas with two important assets. First, the tourists, like all other visitors to Nicaragua, were required to change sixty dollars in U.S. currency for Nicaraguan currency, at the official rate. Second, the returning visitors visited congressmen, talked to the media, and found ways to "spread the word" about the "Nicaraguan reality." A typical statement came from a returning pilgrim in February 1984: "I learned very quickly that the Nicaraguans love their North American neighbors, but with good reason they despise the American government." So many such visitors were processed through Nicaragua, wearing the same 1960s-style footwear, that Nicaraguans began to refer to them as the "Sandalistas." One expert compared the tours to the Potemkin village tours of Stalinist Russia in the 1930s, and referred to the Sandalistas as the new "political pilgrims."

The Role of the Mainstream Media

The debate over U.S. policy in Central America took place in an entirely different media era in the United States. In the mid-1980s, there were only three major news networks. Even the Cable News Network (CNN) was in its infancy, and the idea of a twenty-four-hour news cycle was still brand new. Almost two-thirds of Americans got their news from watching the nightly news programs on CBS, ABC, and NBC. When Reagan began his presidency, there were only three newspapers with nationwide reach: the *New York Times, Washington Post,* and the *Wall Street Journal. USA Today* did not begin publishing until 1982. There were three news weeklies, all with the same editorial slant.

For most Americans, the above list was the sum total of available news outlets. There were a few all-news or news and talk radio stations in the country, but these focused mostly on local issues. (Rush Limbaugh at the time was working for the Kansas City Royals.) Fox News, MSNBC, and CNBC did not yet exist. There was no such thing as the Internet, so there was no Drudgereport, or other alternative source of news. No one had ever heard the word *blog*. Media mistakes and distortions (unlike the forged National Guard documents story used by CBS against George W. Bush in 2004) for the most part went unchallenged.

Under these circumstances, the most significant role played by the media was that of "gatekeeper." Most nights the three major networks led their nightly broadcasts with the same stories. A few editors and news executives decided what was and was not news. If public demonstrations took place in Washington for and against U.S. Central America policy, for example, it was the network executives who decided which demonstrators, if any, received any media attention and whether or not the tone of that attention was favorable, unfavorable, or neutral.

Anti-administration leaders and movements sometimes received extensive and very favorable coverage in parts of the mainstream media, almost to the point where it seemed that a media outlet had "adopted" a part of the anti-Reagan coalition. The best example is the treatment that the *Washington Post* gave to the sanctuary movement. In 1984 and 1985, the *Post* published a number of lengthy articles about the movement, in which the illegal activities of its members were presented in the most favorable light possible. Given the outrage the same *Washington Post* would later express over alleged administration lawbreaking during the Iran-contra scandal, the paper's tolerant attitude toward the sanctuary movement is even more remarkable.

Debates about the liberal bias in the American mainstream media raged then as they do now, but the overwhelming weight of the evidence from the 1980s is on the side claiming liberal bias. The bias is perhaps best illustrated by what did not appear in newspapers, news magazines, or network news programs during the intense discussions of Central America while Reagan was president.

In April 1984, another Central American refugee arrived in Washington. But unlike most fleeing war and oppression in the region, this particular refugee was received at the White House and urged to speak to the media, to administration supporters, and to anyone else who would listen about the ordeal that prompted him to leave his home. The man's name was Prudencio Baltodano, once an Evangelical minister in northern Nicaragua. One day, while visiting members of his church, Baltodano ran afoul of a Sandinista patrol, who demanded his name and occupation. Upon learning that he was a minister, they told him, "You don't know what we do to the evangelical pastors. We don't believe in God."

Baltodano was tied to a tree and struck in the forehead with a rifle butt. His ears were cut off, and his throat was cut. All the while, his Sandinista captors mocked his religion and engaged in tormenting reminiscent of the passion of Christ. "See if your God will save you," the Sandinistas taunted. "See him?" they asked, pointing at the man who had struck him with the rifle, "He's God." Eventually, the Sandinistas left him for dead. Against the odds, Baltodano survived, was rescued by a contra patrol, and was brought to the United States.

On May 4, Baltodano told his story at the White House at a briefing for the press and for administration supporters. He spoke through a translator, pointed to the scar left on his neck from the bayonet, and removed the bandage so that the audience could see what was left of his ears. Speaking clearly and dispassionately, Baltodano told the story of other pastors and farmers who had undergone even worse mutilation by Sandinista soldiers. On May 5, not a single story appeared in any newspaper in the United States of America concerning Baltodano. Indeed, a search of every major newspaper in North America for the years 1984–1988 results in exactly two references to Baltodano, and one of these was a letter to the editor by an administration spokeswoman. Even today, a Google search of his name results in only 7 hits. By contrast, searching for Archbishop Romero results in 67,300 hits, and even limiting those to sites that also mention El Salvador leaves the researcher with 39,400 choices.

Similar silence greeted a visit to the White House by Costa Rican archbishop Roman Arrieta of San José, Costa Rica, in July 1984. Some days before his visit, the archbishop had just concelebrated a Mass with ten Roman Catholic priests who had been expelled by the Sandinistas. The archbishop said in his homily, "There were still in the world men and women of good will who did not believe a totalitarian regime had enthroned itself in Nicaragua." Then he said, "Now those people know the truth."

Americans would not have known about Arrieta's indictment of the Sandinistas had they depended on the mainstream media. A search of major news and business publications for 1984 reveals only two references: a letter to the editor of the *Washington Post* by an administration official, and another letter referring to the first one. Nor did the media take note of an even stronger statement by Nicaraguan prelate Miguel Obando y Bravo on July 11, 1984: "We want to state clearly that this government is totalitarian . . . [W]e are dealing with a government that is an enemy of the Church."

About the only way to compel coverage of Sandinista human rights violations, or credible anti-Sandinista statements, was for Reagan himself to include them in a nationally televised speech. Early in the administration, however, it became clear that Reagan could neither carry the entire burden of selling his Central America policy himself nor rely on the mainstream media to fairly or accurately report the evidence supporting that policy. Moreover, it was clear by mid-1983 that Reagan's enemies were dominating the debate. Public opinion polls showed support for the president's Central America policies to be extremely low, and, in many cases, poorly understood. If Reagan's hopes for Central America were to get a hearing, the effort would have to come from the administration itself.

The Administration Counteroffensive

The White House Outreach Working Group

In comparison to the numerous, well-funded groups opposing U.S. policy and the generally sympathetic portrayals that the anti-administration groups, and their opinions, received in the media, the efforts of the administration to break into the debate were small and shoestring affairs. One of the best examples of the ad hoc nature of the Reagan administration public relations effort on Central America was the White House Outreach Working Group.

Even the title of the group is somewhat misleading, in that it suggests a regular, ongoing effort to get the word out on administration goals and policies. In fact, the group was a loose coalition of friendly think tanks and pressure groups, some of which were one-person operations that did little more than create letterhead for quarterly fund-raising appeals. The Outreach Group was created in April 1983 by Faith Ryan Whittlesey, at the time Reagan's assistant for public liaison (in the hierarchy of the White House, the title *assistant to the president* denotes a member of Reagan's senior staff, just below the Cabinet level).

The job of the Office of Public Liaison was (and is) to maintain contact with the American people and explain and defend administration policy. Under President Jimmy Carter, Public Liaison was a much larger office, housing three full assistants to the president. Under Reagan, the office was staffed by about a dozen special assistants, all of whom had particular segments of the population as their responsibility. (To take one example, Linas Kojelis was responsible for maintaining links with ethnic organizations, labor unions, and conservative think tanks.) Public Liaison members did most of their work at the White House, frequently by providing briefings to groups visiting the White House. Under Faith Whittlesey, virtually every delegation that came to the White House received a talk on Central America, regardless of their primary reason for coming.

A number of our visitors were college students, and they became a particular specialty of mine after I joined the Office of Public Liaison as a consultant on Central America in December 1983. Dolf Droge, a veteran of the Johnson and Nixon White administrations, gave talks to groups outside of Washington that wished to have a White House speaker, although he spoke on many different topics other than Central America. In spite of the widespread perception that there was a "veritable propaganda ministry" in the White House, during 1984, I was the only White House staff member who worked full time on Central America. It was often frustrating, speaking to dozens of people in a White House briefing room when the administration's enemies got to speak to millions by gaining time on network news broadcasts.

My primary responsibility with the Working Group was to draft a newsletter, the *White House Digest*. These newsletters were short papers, photocopied and stapled together, providing information on some aspect of the Central America debate. After I drafted each paper, I had to send them to the State Department, the Defense Department, and the CIA to insure that the paper contained no potentially embarrassing or misleading errors of fact and to insure that the *Digest* was consistent with U.S. foreign policy.

In my experience, sending a draft *White House Digest* to the CIA and the Defense Department usually resulted in a reasonably fast turnover and changes that were limited to corrections of fact or citation. Dealing with officials at the State Department was an entirely different and more difficult matter. It was common for weeks to go by before I would get any response at all from State. When I did get a response, it was frequently to question whether or not there was any need for a White House *Digest* to be published at all.

The State Department officials also used a variety of classic bureaucratic maneuvers to retard clearance of the *Digests*. For example, during my first week on the job, I received word from my immediate superior in Public Liaison that the State Department Office of Public Affairs would not accept draft *Digests* directly from me. Instead, I had to send them to Constantine Menges on the NSC staff. Since Menges traveled a good deal, and had plenty of other tasks, this effectively meant delaying delivery of the draft for clearance.

Once Public Affairs did receive the draft, they sent it to every bureau and agency in the State Department imaginable, supposedly to get a wide variety of viewpoints. In effect, this again set up roadblocks and delays. It also made the paper almost untraceable from the White House. My only recourse was to call Public Affairs, talk to someone who frequently professed to have no idea what a *White House Digest* was, find the person who had sent it around for comment, and request that he or she try to hurry the officials purporting to check the draft for errors. After some weeks, the *Digest* would return to Menges' desk, usually with myriad comments and corrections. In many cases, the "corrections" were arguments against publishing any document at all on the subject.

I would then take the marked-up draft and rewrite it, taking the comments and corrections into account. Then, the entire process would begin all over again; the State Department insisted upon two clearance processes (which they called "informal" and "formal") before agreeing that the *Digest* could be published. After I did the second rewrite, the draft would go to the office of Richard Darman. Technically, the *Digests* were not a publication of the Office of Public Liaison, but rather of the White House Office of Media Relations and Planning. In the West Wing division of labor, this office reported to Darman, who, along with James Baker and Michael Deaver, were the highest-ranking moderates in the Reagan White House. Darman's final approval was invariably slow and reluctant.

Under these circumstances, I managed to get seven *Digests* published during the thirteen months I was at the White House. The first, on the persecution of Christian groups in Nicaragua, had already been through informal clearance when I started on December 1, 1983. However, the State Department Public Affairs office sent it through informal clearance again, suspecting (correctly, as it happened) that I would not realize this step had already been taken. It was not until February 29, 1984, that the *Digest* was published. The second *Digest* treated the mistreatment of Miskito Indians and told the story of how five thousand Miskitos, along with the bishop from eastern Nicaragua, had trekked hundreds of miles in December 1983 into Honduras to escape the Sandinistas. The goal of the White House Working Group was to publish this *Digest* as close to the events as possible. It was not published until April.

On two occasions, bureaucratic roadblocks forced me to abandon *Digests* altogether. When I arrived at the White House, my predecessor had already begun work on a paper on the refugee crisis that would result from serious and prolonged strife and warfare in Central America. At the time, El Salvador alone had five hundred thousand displaced persons, and a similar number had fled from Nicaragua. The paper speculated on what would happen if the crisis in the region spread to Guatemala and Mexico. At a time when the Reagan administration was looking hard for a way to increase awareness and concern among Americans about the stakes of the crisis in Central America, warnings about massive refugee streams into the United States seemed about the best way to do so. But, then as now, the issue of immigration was one that stirred deep passions.

The refugee *Digest* hit an impenetrable wall of opposition from those in Mike Deaver's office. In their view, any effort to warn about refugees would make the administration, and Reagan himself, seemed prejudiced against Hispanics. When I took over the *Digest*, I rewrote the refugee paper, making it clear that the administration's primary concern was for the displaced persons themselves. Central Americans, like most people, had a strong preference for being able to live at home, rather than the hardships that inevitably accompany becoming a refugee. Such arguments were of no avail. Even intervention by Faith Whittlesey failed to rescue the project.

In February 1984, Francis Mullen Jr., head of the Drug Enforcement Agency (DEA), testified before Congress on the growing involvement of the Cuban government and the Sandinistas in facilitating the smuggling of illegal drugs into the United States. Bob Reilly, special assistant to the president for public liaison, who directed the Outreach program, suggested that a *White House Digest* on the topic would help insure that Mullen's charges received more attention from the media and from members of Congress. I requested a draft *Digest* from DEA and added to it. Menges, per standard procedure, sent it to the State Department for clearance.

It was, I think, the only time that State responded quickly to anything from my office. The draft came back to me covered with markings, sarcastic questions, and entire paragraphs crossed out. I called an ally of mine in the Public Diplomacy office at the State Department, who had been helpful before in breaking things loose from the bureaucratic cement at Foggy Bottom. He had heard of the problem with the *Digest* on Cuban and Nicaraguan drug running, and was not sanguine about getting approval from the State Department. I pointed out that there was nothing in the *Digest* that had not already been said, in open congressional testimony, by the head of the DEA. He responded that Public Affairs' view was that Mullen should not have spoken of the allegations to start with. They did not dispute the accuracy of the DEA director's accusations, but rather said the charges were not "useful." Again, I had to drop the idea.

As with the aborted refugee paper, opposition from unknown persons in the State Department deprived President Reagan of the opportunity to demonstrate ways in which the spread of Communism would have a deleterious impact on Americans. Discussions about the global importance of Central America and of stopping Soviet Communism were usually effective in swaying audiences but not nearly as effective as talking about refugees coming across the Mexican border or about drug trafficking. On the latter issue, Senator Paula Hawkins (R-FL) attempted to raise awareness, but a freshman senator is simply not the draw of a document from the White House. At base, all of the efforts of the Working Group were intended to gain access to the media for the President's goals in Central America.

One of the Working Group's major events will illustrate the publicity problem for the administration. On July 18, 1984, the Outreach Group marked the fifth anniversary of the Sandinista takeover of Nicaragua. The afternoon's briefing featured Edgar and Geraldine Macias, two prominent members of the original Sandinista coalition. The couple had broken with the Sandinistas when the Sandinistas broke their promises to bring democracy, free elections and nonalignment to Nicaragua. Humberto Belli, an anti-Somoza reporter for the independent newspaper *La Prensa*, also spoke. The featured speaker, however, was Reagan himself, making his only appearance before the Working Group.

Coverage of the event was minimal. CBS did not mention the briefing at all. ABC gave it ten seconds, in which anchor Peter Jennings, with a smirk that nearly amounted to a wink at the audience, quoted Reagan calling Nicaragua "a totalitarian dungeon." NBC provided the most extensive coverage, just over a minute, and the network included two brief clips of the Outreach meeting. In the text of the NBC story, the narrator, referring to Belli and the Macias couple, said that anti-Sandinista spokesmen had been "produced" by the administration. The one reference on television to the *White House Digest* published that day was that it contained footnotes, citing "the same media outlets the administration says are not telling the truth about Central America."

In the face of such unabashed hostility, my colleagues and I had no choice but to try to reach more motivated, undecided Americans, by pursuing projects such as sending op ed replies to large city newspapers that published editorial attacks on administration policy. (I probably spent more of my time on this project than on any other.) Since our resources were so limited, we began by targeting wavering members of Congress, especially before important votes on aid to the contras, for example. Realizing that Congressman Dave McCurdy from Norman, Oklahoma, was a swing vote, for example, we would try to find radio stations or newspapers in central and southern Oklahoma willing to do an interview or publish an op ed. It often seemed like trying to turn back an incoming tide on the beach with a whiskbroom, but we occasionally had our victories.

The State Department Office of Public Diplomacy

Although I alone in the White House worked on Central America full time, there were others in the Executive Branch who were also in the struggle. Al Haig, Reagan's first secretary of state, expanded the Office of Public Diplomacy in the State Department Office of Public Affairs. Traditionally, this office had been almost completely reactive, responding occasionally to requests for interviews and publishing usually dense, fact-filled papers supporting administration policy. Under Haig, the office became much more aggressive in trying to get the word out on administration views of the Central American reality, both overseas and in the United States. In fact, the office was successful enough that some administration foes questioned whether or not its activities violated the law by spreading "propaganda" to the American people.

The head of the new office was Otto Reich, an immigrant from Venezuela who was fluent in Spanish and an effective public speaker in English or Spanish. Reich rarely turned down an offer to debate or be interviewed by any media outlet in the Western Hemisphere. Like the Outreach Group, he sought to bypass the mainstream media by getting into local newspapers, local radio and, especially, the growing Hispanic media. Reich took on Phil Donahue for an hour on one occasion and also did an hour-long interview on Sandinista radio (which he insisted on having broadcast live).

The Public Diplomacy Office also oversaw the publication of booklets and brochures about Central America, starting with a Central America "Background Paper," jointly published with the Defense Department, in May 1983. There followed publications on the Kissinger Commission Report, on the "Sandinistas and Middle Eastern Radicals" (August 1985), "A Special Investigator's Report" on the Sandinistas (February 1986), "Dispossessed: The Miskito Indians in Sandinista Nicaragua" (June 1986), "Attack on the Church: Persecution of the Catholic Church in Nicaragua" (July 1986), and two publications in August: "Crackdown on Freedom in Nicaragua and Profiles of Internal Opposition Leaders," and "Libyan Activities in the Western Hemisphere."

The publications were of uneven quality and sophistication. Some were little more than stapled fact sheets. Others were more glossy and attractive. The publication on Libyan activities, for example, had a cover picture of Muammar Qaddafi cutting a ribbon at a Managua factory dedication. Like the *White House Digests*, the publications were delivered to the media, to Capitol Hill, and to administration supporters. For the most part, they were ignored by the mainstream media, unless they contained an error of fact.

Administration Allies

Conservative think tanks and public interest organizations also helped to get the administration word out on Central America. Of the former, the Heritage Foundation was the largest and most influential. At the time when I worked there, Heritage actually had two people working on Central America, a luxury that most conservative think tanks could not afford. Heritage entered the public debate in two ways. First, the foundation published short papers titled *Backgrounders*, focused on a single issue and intended to inform and persuade. The main audience for these papers was congressional staff members, although copies went to the media, to many officials in the Executive Branch, to academics, and to the many financial supporters of the Heritage Foundation. The second way that Heritage sought to influence policy was having its analysts speak to interested groups about, among many other issues, Central America. The analysts also did as many radio and television appearances as possible.

Other private organizations devoted some or all of their resources to fighting Communism and left-wing movements in Central America, but many of these groups were very small (one or two people, in some cases) or were able to devote only a small part of their effort to Central America, and that only on occasion. To pool their efforts, they created an ad hoc organization of conservative foreign policy groups, the Staunton Group. Its representatives met every other week at the offices of the Free Congress Foundation, and Central America was on the agenda at practically every meeting during the 1980s.

Like the people in the White House Working Group and the Public Diplomacy Office, the experts at the Heritage Foundation and other conservative groups faced an uphill climb in trying to get their message into the mainstream media. A comparison with the press treatment of the Brookings Institution, Heritage's counterpart on the left, is instructive. During Reagan's presidency, the Heritage Foundation was mentioned in major newspapers and magazines 1,932 times. Brookings received 2,856 mentions in the same period. When Heritage was mentioned, it was identified as "conservative" more than half the time (when it was not described as "right-wing"). Brookings, on the other hand, was identified as liberal only about 10 percent of the time. (It was a running joke at Heritage to refer to Brookings simply as PBI, the "prestigious Brookings Institution," as it was often called in the mainstream media).

The same pattern held with two lobbying organizations, the conservative Council for Inter-American Security (CIS) and the liberal Council for Hemispheric Affairs (COHA). The former was mentioned in print 36 times during Reagan's eight years in the White House, in spite of its founder's friendship with many administration officials, which made him a potential source of news. COHA, for its part, received more than 100 mentions in print, and it was identified as liberal in fewer than 25. More frequently, liberal groups were titled nonpartisan or bipartisan, names that applied to Heritage and CIS also, although they were rarely used. In sum, when conservative groups spoke or wrote on Central America, Americans were told their political orientation with far more frequency than when liberal groups opined.

Making Headway

In spite of the David and Goliath nature of the two sides' public relations capabilities, there were definite signs by the beginning of 1986 that Reagan's view was starting to prevail. In El Salvador, four elections in a row (March 1982, March and May 1984, and March 1985) not only had been held in increasing peace and security but also had passed muster with thousands of international observers. A steady stream of visitors to El Salvador from the United States returned to attest to the desire of Salvadorans for democracy and their rejection of the extreme Right and Left. Convictions of some of the death squad killers gave Americans confidence that the rule of law was starting to take hold in the country. The departure of Roberto D'Aubuisson left El Salvador with a viable, nonviolent political Right, and essentially turned the nation into a two-party democracy, in which the FMLN guerrillas were becoming less and less relevant.

Indeed, in one of the most certain signs that things were changing for the better in El Salvador, the country began to disappear from major newspapers in the United States. One of the maxims of the American press is that good news is not news. In 1982, for example, the *New York*

Times index devoted seventeen columns to stories about El Salvador. By 1986, there were only three columns.

American attitudes toward the Sandinistas were also changing. To a large degree, this was due to the actions of top Sandinistas themselves. Ortega's April 1985 trip to Moscow, along with his purchase of bullet-proof sunglasses, and even the short-lived MiG scare, all served to sour some Americans on the FSLN. At the same time, the various contra factions united and significantly improved their public relations effort, emphasizing their commitment to democracy and the Sandinistas' failure to hold genuine elections.

A watershed event in changing U.S. public opinion was a widely quoted article in the October 9, 1984, edition of *The New Republic*. This liberal publication had strongly supported the Sandinistas during and after their rise to power. The author, Robert Leiken, was a Latin American expert who had made numerous trips to Nicaragua. His trip in September 1984, however, which prompted the New Republic piece, shocked him to the core. Where in 1979 he had found enthusiastic support for the new FSLN government from virtually all quarters of the Nicaraguan populace, in 1984 he found widespread discontent.

He also found increasing poverty. In 1979, he noted, most Nicaraguan children were barefoot. By 1984, many children were going completely naked because their parents had no clothes for them to wear. Malnutrition was beginning to appear. In spite of the claims of the regime's ballyhooed 1980 literacy campaign, Leiken found Nicaraguan "graduates" of the program who could not read their diplomas.

Most startling of all were the comparisons that Leiken made between the Sandinistas and the old Somoza regime. Both regimes, he said, used the same heavy-handed, sometimes brutal, methods to maintain control. Both censored the media. Both mistreated the Catholic Church. Both used neighborhood spies to watch over people and punish perceived expressions of disloyalty to the regime. In fact, Leiken noted that the neighborhood block commanders were, in many cases, ex-Somocistas doing the same job for a supposedly revolutionary regime. In the countryside, Leiken was shocked to find frequent expressions of support for the contras. He found large numbers of Nicaraguan peasants who affectionately referred to the contras as the "muchachos" (the boys), the same name peasants had used for the Sandinistas when they were the guerrillas.

Democratic staff members on Capitol Hill were stunned by the article, although the information it contained had been available to anyone attending the weekly briefings of the White House Outreach Working Group. Coming from a liberal commentator, however, in a liberal publication, the Leiken piece had inescapable credibility and made Sandinista bashing part of liberal rhetoric in the United States. For the Sandinistas' remaining apologists, there was not much to do except to attack Leiken personally, so he found himself fending off accusations that he was in the pay of the Reagan administration or of the contras.

In April 1985, the formerly pro-Sandinista editor of the *Miami Herald* wrote that he had begun hearing credible reports of political repression, economic hardship, and increasing discontent from Nicaragua. He decided to see for himself what was happening. "Three weeks ago," he reported upon his return, "I went to Nicaragua, hoping to discover whether my impressions from afar held true close up. They did. I wish they hadn't; that would have been far less disquieting than having them confirmed." He went on to say that his entire editorial staff was rethinking its opposition to aid to the contras. In June 1985, a *New York Times* poll showed progress for the administration as well. While a majority of 53 percent still opposed contra aid, this majority was shrinking. Moreover, support for the policy was highest among those most knowledgeable about the conflict.

Democratic members of Congress found it prudent to do some rethinking as well. Liberal senator Claude Pepper (D-FL), early in 1985 discovered something that Reagan had been talking about for four years: "[T]he government of National Reconstruction of Nicaragua has failed to keep solemn promises, made to the OAS in July 1979, to establish full respect for human rights and political liberties, hold early elections . . . and permit political pluralism. . . . The government of Nicaragua should be held accountable."

Events and apostasies such as these permitted the Reagan administration to try a "hard sell" of aid to the contras. Congress had set the date of March 19, 1986, for an up-or-down vote on a proposal to give the contras $100 million in military and humanitarian assistance. (The sheer size of the proposal, and the end of previous restrictions on using American money for contra arms, indicated the changing atmosphere on Capitol Hill.) On March 5, White House communications director Pat Buchanan, a vocal conservative commentator before he joined the administration, wrote an op ed for the *Washington Post*. In it, he presented the danger from Central American Communism in stark, challenging terms. "With the vote on contra aid, the Democratic Party will reveal whether it stands with Ronald Reagan and the resistance—or Daniel Ortega and the communists." The Reagan White House faced repeated charges of "red-baiting" and even the contention that Buchanan's op ed galvanized Democratic opposition. Liberal columnist Mary McGrory, for example, predicted when Reagan spoke to the nation on behalf of the contra aid package: "He will set aside the sandpaper for the silk. He will appeal for bipartisanship and sing the siren song of compromise."

Instead, Reagan used images and oratory nearly as stark as Buchanan's. He warned: "Using Nicaragua as a base, the Soviets and Cubans can become the dominant power in the crucial corridor between North and South America. Established there, they will be in a position to threaten the Panama Canal, interdict our vital Caribbean sealanes, and, ultimately, move against Mexico. Should that happen, desperate Latin peoples by the millions would begin fleeing north into the cities of the southern United States or to wherever some hope of freedom remained."

Reagan noted the international scale of the Sandinista threat, saying: "Gathered in Nicaragua already are thousands of Cuban military advisers, contingents of Soviets and East Germans, and all the elements of international terror—from the PLO to Italy's Red Brigades. Why are they there? Because as Colonel Qaddafi has publicly exulted: 'Nicaragua means a great thing: it means fighting America near its borders, fighting America at its doorstep.' "

Using the same facts that we in the White House Outreach Group had used hundreds of times, Reagan summed up the military and strategic threat to the United States:

> Through this crucial part of the Western Hemisphere passes almost half our foreign trade, more than half our imports of crude oil, and a significant portion of the military supplies we would have to send to the NATO alliance in the event of a crisis. These are the chokepoints where the sealanes could be closed. Central America is strategic to our Western alliance, a fact always understood by foreign enemies. . . . Today Warsaw Pact engineers are building a deep water port on Nicaragua's Caribbean coast, similar to the naval base in Cuba for Soviet-built submarines. They are also constructing, outside Managua, the largest military airfield in Central America—similar to those in Cuba, from which Russian Bear Bombers patrol the U.S. east coast from Maine to Florida.

Like Buchanan Reagan ended his speech with a challenge to his opponents. "My fellow Americans," he said, "you know where I stand. The Soviets and the Sandinistas must not be permitted to crush freedom in Central America and threaten our own security on our own doorstep. Now the Congress must decide where it stands."

The words of Buchanan and Reagan had the desired effect. After a frustrating series of delays, the entire $100 million aid package passed later in the spring. Reagan had won his greatest congressional victory on Central America and seemed poised to dominate action on the issue for the remainder of his presidency. The final vote took place on June 26; the new aid became available to the contras on October 1.

Five days later, a cargo plane carrying arms to the contras was shot down over Nicaragua. Three crewmen were killed and a fourth, Eugene Hasenfus, was taken captive by the Sandinistas. In the blink of an eye, anonymous Sandinista antiaircraft gunners changed history.

9

The Iran-Contra Scandal, 1986–1987

This is almost too absurd to comment on.

—Defense Secretary Caspar Weinberger, when first informed
of the NSC effort to contact "moderate" Iranians.

Legacy of Frustration

The series of actions that would eventually lead to the Iran-contra scandal began while President Ronald Reagan was sick. On July 18, 1985, Reagan was in Bethesda Naval Hospital, recovering from surgery. Then-National Security advisor Robert McFarlane came to the hospital with what Reagan described as "exciting" news. McFarlane told the president that he had been contacted by members of the Israeli government, who had given McFarlane a message from a group of Iranians who were anticipating the death of Ayatollah Khomeini.

These Iranians wished to start a quiet relationship with officials in the U.S. government, with an eye to reestablishing formal relations once the ayatollah was out of the way. Reagan possessed intelligence that indicated that the jockeying for power in the post-Khomeini Iran was already well under way. Reagan also knew the horrible toll that war with Saddam Hussein was imposing on the Iranian economy, and he had reports that the ayatollah was gravely ill.

With a population of 60 million, a large share of the world's known oil reserves, a large army and navy, a government with close relationships with innumerable anti-American terrorist groups, and two borders with the Soviet Union, Iran was not a country that the United States could afford to ignore. If there was indeed a looming power struggle, it would be the height of irresponsibility for the U.S. government to remain a spectator. McFarlane's talks with the Israelis seemed to provide an opportunity for the United States to be considerably more than that.

These large strategic issues, however, seemed to pale in Reagan's mind next to the tantalizing possibility that the "moderate" Iranians might be able to secure the release of seven Americans held hostage in Lebanon by terror groups affiliated with Hezbollah, which derived most of its funding from Iran. Indeed, if one element of Reagan's presidency can be singled out as the "cause" of the Iran-contra affair, it was his single-minded insistence that the U.S. government do more to free these seven people.

Just days before Reagan's 1985 cancer surgery, Reagan had faced his own hostage crisis, with the two-week ordeal of dozens of Americans who had been on a hijacked TWA flight from Greece. During the days of their captivity, Reagan felt the horrifying sense of helplessness, uncertainty, and pressure that comes from seeing, all too clearly, the limitations of American power. The June 1985 crisis ended largely through the good offices of Syrian president Hafaz Assad; Reagan was painfully aware of this.

Both Reagan and his close advisors have related that he began dozens of meetings of the National Security Council by insisting on an update on efforts to secure the release of the Beirut hostages. The answer, all too often, was that there simply was not much that the U.S. government could do, other than pay ransom, make political concessions, or attempt a dangerous and possibly disastrous rescue mission. Reagan himself had ruled out all three of these options, as well as a fourth option, which was to infiltrate terrorist groups to gain better intelligence. Reagan had signed an executive order prohibiting employees of the U.S. government from involvement in assassination. Terrorist groups, for the most part, require would-be members to commit murder even to be considered.

Given Reagan's persistent questioning of his NSC staff about the hostages, and their frustration at having to give him the same negative answers, it is perhaps not surprising that the hostages in Lebanon became part of McFarlane's discussions with the Israelis who claimed to be in touch with the Iranians interested in opening a relationship with the United States.

· The detailed story of McFarlane's dealings with the moderate Iranians, of how other U.S. officials got involved, of the weapons used by the United States as bait or as rewards, and of the failure of McFarlane's operation to free the seven hostages (only three were eventually freed), is beyond the scope of this book. This summary serves only as background to the Iran operation's sequel, the use of money from Iran to fund the Nicaraguan contras. To a large degree, the scandal occurred because Reagan was frustrated on a number of counts.

One area of frustration for Reagan was what he saw as the micromanaging interference in U.S. foreign policy by Congress. Reagan sometimes refers to Congress in his *Autobiography* as "a committee of 535" and laments the passing of the era in which "politics stopped at the water's edge." We have seen numerous examples in the earlier chapters of this book of members of Congress and senators second-guessing even the most sensitive foreign policy operations of the Reagan administration, carping after a foreign policy setback, and even offering foreign heads of state the opportunity to negotiate behind Reagan's back (most famously in the case of the "Dear Commandante" letter to Daniel Ortega). Even for the decisions that were popular with the American people, such as the invasion of Grenada, some members of Congress vilified the president and sought to place Reagan on the same moral plane as the leaders of the Soviet Union.

There was no area in which Reagan's policies were the subject of more interference than Central America. Yet, other than undermining the power of the Soviets, there was no foreign policy goal to which Reagan himself was more committed than thwarting the designs of Communists in Central America. This goal, it seemed at the time, was more important to Reagan than maintaining a correct, working relationship with Congress. If he had to forgo the latter to achieve the former, it seemed he would do so.

After Democrats in Congress won the October 1984 showdown over aid to the contras, Reagan made it clear, to his staff and to the American people, that he did not consider the verdict of Congress to be final. Somehow or another, Reagan was determined to keep the contras alive, in the field, and a part of the Nicaraguan political equation, until he could persuade Congress to reverse itself. The Cabinet and the NSC were told to find ways to keep the contras alive, with repeated admonitions to do nothing illegal. Reagan kept the pressure on his aides on this issue, as he did with the hostage issue. Under these circumstances, it is understandable that a member of his staff might try to find a way of achieving Reagan's goals in Central America and with regard to the hostages, even if it seemed shady.

Reagan's Management Style

None of the above, however, detracts from the central truth of the Iran-contra scandal: Reagan should have known better. Much of the blame for the crisis lay in the president's well-known management style, sometimes referred to as "hands off," sometimes as "detached," and sometimes as "irresponsible." Reagan himself acknowledges in his memoirs that he set the broad outlines of policy and then left the details to his staff. By itself, this is not blame-worthy; indeed, many respected experts on management suggest exactly this style. However, such experts add that it is absolutely necessary to have systems in place to oversee staff members and to insure that they are doing nothing that will reflect badly on the boss.

This is where, in my opinion, Reagan failed most notably. Reagan said later of his instructions to his staff about keeping the contras funded: "I repeatedly insisted that whatever we did had to be within the law, and I always assumed that my instructions were followed." A better plan would have been for Reagan to assign a different staff member, ideally someone from the attorney general's office, to check up on the foreign policy staff, so that he would not have to "assume" that his aides were remaining on the right side of the law.

Backing up a step further, Reagan plunged himself into the dangerous waters of covert, nongovernment funding in October 1984, when he failed to veto the appropriations bill that contained the Boland Amendment. With that veto, Reagan would have risked a partial government shutdown and the chaos such an interruption brings, less than a month before his reelection. He would have had to stake his political future on his ability to persuade the American people that the issue was important enough for a disruptive veto. But while Reagan was facing reelection, so was every member of Congress, and one-third of the senators. And unlike Reagan, most of them were not ahead twenty points or so in public opinion polls. Put differently, Congress had more to lose from a government-shutting confrontation than Reagan did. In the end, Reagan had to defend his Central America policies anyway to avoid the premature end of his political career, and he had to do so on terms largely dictated by his opponents.

Many of the analyses of the Iran-contra scandal focus on the role of the National Security Council and the wide powers it received during Reagan's presidency. The Tower Commission stated, for example: "The arms transfers to Iran and the activities of the NSC staff in support of the contras are case studies in the perils of policy pursued outside the constraints of orderly process." Later in the report, they placed the blame for the lack of order on Chief of Staff Don Regan, saying: "More than any other Chief of Staff in recent memory, [Regan] asserted personal control over the White House staff and sought to extend this control to the National Security Advisor. He was personally active in national security affairs and attended almost all of the relevant meetings regarding the Iran initiative. He, as much as anyone, should have insisted that an orderly process be observed."

Even Reagan's most ardent defenders do not claim that Reagan ran the White House staff well. But veterans of his administration assign the blame for a rogue National Security Council on different people. Constantine Menges pointed the finger at Shultz. The staff of the NSC is supposed to manage the paper flow on foreign policy matters and oversee the decision-making process. Menges insisted that only the NSC is structurally capable of acting as "honest broker" and insuring that the views of State, Defense, CIA, the Joint Chiefs of Staff and other foreign policy-making agencies are taken into account when decisions have to be made.

Starting in 1983, Shultz used Michael Deaver to bypass the National Security Council with increasing frequency. In his memoirs, Menges lists seven different occasions, just on Central America, in which Shultz or other officials in the State Department launched important foreign policy initiatives without going through the NSC. Shultz essentially did not believe in having an independent NSC staff at all. In Shultz's memoirs, he recounts suggesting that the NSC staff report to the secretary of state, instead of to the president. According to Casey, Shultz later used the Iran-contra revelations to try to have himself named National Security advisor while still serving as secretary of state.

These are not esoteric bureaucratic distinctions. Shultz's apparent goal was to render the State Department answerable to no one in the conduct of foreign policy. State should be not just the lead foreign policy agency, but the only foreign policy agency. He wanted to avoid scrutiny of his decisions by anyone from Defense, CIA, or another part of the Executive Branch. For Menges, it was Shultz who was the real "lone wolf" in the administration. Shultz, for his part, insists that having an agency other than the State Department involved in foreign policy led to the botched Iran initiative.

Both Menges and Shultz miss the point. Achieving a harmonious balance between State and the NSC, or between any other competing agencies of the Executive Branch is, unavoidably, the job of the president himself. As the Tower Commission put it, "The NSC system will not work unless the President makes it work." Reagan acted correctly when he directed McFarlane, after the latter had first broached the idea of using the Israelis to contact the Iranians, to inform Shultz and Weinberger of the plan and seek their input. But he waited too long to do so. By the time Shultz and Weinberger were brought in, Reagan was already committed to the plan as the best hope for freeing the American hostages.

Reagan made an even more basic mistake in not discussing the plan with any members of Congress. His reason for avoiding congressional leaders was that too much information was leaked from Capitol Hill. (This was a very legitimate fear. As the Iran-contra hearings were winding down, Congressman Les Aspin (D-IL), a member of the Armed Services Committee leaked sensitive information about U.S. dealings with Saudi Arabia. The ensuring outrage prompted some members of the committee to avoid briefings where Aspin was present to avoid being blamed for leaks that were his fault.) Both parts of the Iran initiative, influencing potential moderates and freeing the hostages, required absolute secrecy.

However, Reagan could have asked one or two conservative congressmen or senators to the White House and solicited their opinion. In so doing, Reagan could have gotten a feel for the potential political dangers in the initiative. As a matter of fact, such a meeting would likely have led to the demise of the initiative, since most conservatives on Capitol Hill would have seen it as a straight arms-for-hostages swap and argued forcefully against it. In the end, Reagan wanted the plan to work so badly that he evidently let the wish rule the thought.

The Background: Keeping the Contras Alive

At the time that Congress voted to cut off aid to the contras just before Reagan's re-election, the rebels in Nicaragua were becoming more successful. The establishment of UNO (United Nicaraguan Opposition) in 1984 resulted in more coordinated efforts in the field, and the assignment of Bosco Matamoros as the contras' permanent Washington representative kept the issue alive on Capitol Hill. At the same time, the rebels began to replace some former National Guard field commanders with former Sandinistas, improving their image both in Washington and in Nicaragua.

The confusing attitude of the Reagan administration toward the contras' cause was particularly damaging. While no one could doubt that Reagan was personally committed to aiding the rebels, his secretary of state said before the crucial October 1984 vote that losing funding would be "no disaster." Congressional aides spoke to me in late 1984 about officials of the CIA actively lobbying congressmen to cut off contra funding, or at least assign it to a different agency. With few exceptions, Cabinet officials spoke rarely, and often ineffectually, about the need for contra funding. In some cases, including meetings of the Outreach Working Group that I attended, ranking officials would refuse to discuss the contras, even after Reagan had committed his administration to their cause.

After the October 1984 contra aid cut off, some Reagan administration officials paid lip service to getting the funds restored but talked about funds for "buying out" or "phasing out" the contras. Menges reports that State's Latin America bureau "hoped for a compromise that would provide the Administration with what some termed a 'face-saving way of phasing out the contras in the context of a peace agreement.'" When additional contra aid came up on Capitol Hill in April 1985, McFarlane persuaded Reagan to announce that if the aid were approved, he would not spend any of it for sixty days, allowing time for a peace initiative to take place. Congressional Democrats took the offer as a sign of weakness and ended up voting for only $27 million, none of which could be used for arms. Even this smaller amount of aid was defeated on April 23 (by two votes). With this loss, McFarlane and Poindexter began looking for alternatives to congressionally voted aid. Another element of the Iran-contra scandal was in place.

Reagan's tragic misjudgments, which gave rise to the Iran-contra crisis, were his assumptions that first, Congress did not really mean to cut off the contras completely, and consequently left a loophole in the Boland Amendment for the NSC; and second, that even if Congress were serious, that the contras could be legally funded in some other way long enough for Reagan to persuade Congress to change its mind. Perhaps he believed in October 1984 that his coming landslide victory would be read as a mandate for his foreign policies, including aid for the contras.

Whatever Reagan's thinking, it became clear early in 1985 that getting off-the-books funding for the growing contra army would be a major undertaking. Moreover, it would be fraught with potential scandal, since administration officials would almost certainly have to engage in questionable financial transactions and deal with unofficial, shadowy arms suppliers. At the very least, members of the Reagan administration would have to turn a blind eye to such activities, while making sure the various congressional oversight committees were kept blind to covert contra funding as well.

No one with any experience in the workings of the U.S. government, and especially the workings of the leak-prone Reagan administration, could have seriously believed that millions of dollars could be raised, transferred, and spent on the contras' behalf and kept secret. Even had the administration kept its own secrets better, the contras themselves were certain to reveal that they were receiving funding. Indeed, to do their own fund raising, the contras would have to assure potential donors that they were still viable, in spite of the official U.S. aid cutoff. Such assurances would, necessarily, involve details of ongoing funding.

Early Reports of Continuing Funding

In April, Jack Wheeler, a globe-trotting expert on anti-Communist insurgencies, wrote an op ed for the *Wall Street Journal* titled "The Contras Can Still Win with Private Aid." In the piece, Wheeler called on Reagan to publicly and openly ask the American people to contribute money to organizations committed to help the contras. The *Washington Times* said in May 1985 that it would try to raise the entire $14 million just voted down in Congress. Putting its own money on the line, the paper pledged one hundred thousand dollars to "those seeking freedom" in Nicaragua.

On August 8, 1985, the *New York Times* reported that a hitherto unknown NSC aide, LTC Oliver North, had been involved in raising money for the contras and giving them military advice. The paper said that it received the information from "senior Reagan Administration officials and members of Congress." In retrospect, what is surprising is not that the information was leaked, but that it took ten months for the leak to appear.

The House Permanent Select Committee on Intelligence, chaired by Lee Hamilton (D-IN), opened an investigation, although in the same *Times* article, some congressmen said they doubted that any laws were being broken. In September, National Security Advisor Robert McFarlane met Hamilton in the committee's sound-proofed Capitol hearing room and offered repeated assurances that North had not given military advice, nor was he involved with soliciting funds. McFarlane repeated his "deep personal conviction" that no one on the NSC had violated the law in a letter to Hamilton. The committee dropped its investigation. Not all of Hamilton's Democratic House colleagues were so easily satisfied. Michael Barnes

(D-MD), the ultra-liberal chair of the Western Hemisphere Subcommittee of the House Foreign Affairs Committee, sent a letter to McFarlane later in August, demanding all records concerning North's involvement with the contras, their funding, or their military operations.

Reagan himself played an active role in efforts to find private and foreign contributors to the contras. Indeed, Reagan almost had to be personally involved, given the ambiguities of the Boland Amendment. Whatever agencies might or might not be restricted in their actions by Boland, one thing that was clear was that the president himself was not bound by it. But Reagan obviously could not handle the day-to-day management of whatever funds came from foreign governments. North later recounted how completely unprepared he was for such as assignment. He had to find out from Casey how to set up an off-shore account, what a wire transfer was, and how to keep track of the money going in and out. (At one point, Casey handed North a blank accounting notebook and said simply, "Keep good books.")

Officials of the Reagan administration were less circumspect in soliciting funds from foreign governments. The first such solicitation was from the Saudis. In February 1985, McFarlane met with Saudi prince Bandar bin Sultan, and told him that the contras needed money. The prince responded with a commitment of $24 million, although the contras actually received far less. The pledge itself, however, was useful in helping the contras raise money from other sources.

A process for Americans to give money to the contras also appeared after the congressional aid cutoff. Carl Channel, usually known as "Spitz," established the National Endowment for the Preservation of Liberty (NEPL) and the American Conservative Trust and worked closely with conservative groups and some officials of the Reagan administration. The NEPL was ostensibly designed to purchase nonlethal supplies for the contras, such as bandages and boots. Reagan was well aware of Channel's efforts. On January 30, 1986, Reagan met with eighteen donors to the NEPL in the Roosevelt Room of the White House. North and Elliott Abrams also appeared at the briefing, in which the donors were told that their money would be used to insure positive public relations for the Nicaraguan Resistance. Reagan did not deny helping Channel and the NEPL. In fact, he told reporters in May 1987, "As a matter of fact, I was very definitely involved in the decisions about support to the freedom fighters. It was my idea to begin with." Other administration officials dispute the last part of Reagan's statement.

The Resupply Operation

At the same time, stories of private gun-running began to come out. In late August, an American couple whose boat had engine trouble in the Gulf of Mexico was reported to have just ended weeks of detention in Nicaragua for suspicion of running guns to the contras. In early September, the role of retired army general John K. Singlaub became public. The general was arranging meetings between contra representatives and wealthy Americans who might be persuaded to contribute to their cause. Contributions were made to the World Anti-Communist League, which provided the funds to the contras. The significance of these episodes became clear, however, only after the NSC effort was revealed.

No one in the Reagan administration epitomizes the Iran-contra scandal more than Oliver North. In the mid-1980s, the ultimate proof that one was a true Washington "insider" was the ability to drop North's name in conversation. On some occasions, I heard people claim to have been with North on days when I knew he was out of the country. By people both inside and outside the administration, North was seen as someone who could cut through bureaucratic red tape and "get things done." His unbridled and unashamed conservatism, his contempt for the State Department, his stories of late nights in the Situation Room, and the hints and suggestions of secrets all made North a favorite of Washington's Reagan-era conservative community.

For some who worked closely with North, however, there were disquieting signs. (North himself says in his memoirs, "I knew nothing about covert operations when I came to the NSC.") Menges, for example, recounts a conversation in which North insisted that the role of the NSC staff was to give the president only those options that would insure that he went "the right way." At the same time, Menges says that soon after North got to the NSC, he would send memos to McFarlane from himself and Menges, without telling Menges he was doing so. Menges recounts a warning from a coworker that North was trying to get control of the NSC Latin America operation. In early 1985, Menges was excluded from the interagency team charged with getting contra aid restored. North was the NSC representative instead. (Conservatives' opinions of North shifted 180 degrees after his Iran-contra role became public. Menges, however, expressed only the most guarded opinions of North, while most DC conservatives lauded him.)

North's public activities at this time consisted largely of giving briefings to groups interested in Central America. I personally attended a number of such briefings, some at the White House, but most elsewhere in Washington. North's message was usually the same: the Sandinistas had betrayed their 1979 promises of a democratic and nonaligned government; they were working closely with the Cubans and Soviets to export their revolution, while at the same time harboring anti-American terrorists; the Sandinistas were abusing their own people, especially devout Catholics and Miskito Indians; and the contras represented hope for real change, if only they could weather the storm of the U.S. aid cutoff. I never heard North solicit funds, but his description of what was going on in Central America certainly left many of his listeners with a desire to assist the beleaguered Nicaraguan rebels.

While the funds were being raised, some American private citizens were working to help the contras make the best use of the money. Retired air force general Richard V. Secord and retired air force colonel Richard Gadd began looking for airplanes that could be used to carry supplies to the contras. They planned to use an airstrip in Costa Rica that would also be built with private funds. In early 1986, the contras were resupplied from the Illopango air base in El Salvador. Secord was involved in this part of the operation as well.

Secord was reluctant to get involved with the contras and did so only after he and North agreed that Secord would put aside his other business interests while helping the contras. Secord expected to make a profit from his assistance, and North admits that failing to agree upon a fee at the beginning of the resupply operation was a serious mistake. It is also a mistake that shows the pitfalls of running an intelligence operation with amateurs and self-interested parties. Whatever profits he made, Secord at least did provide assistance to the contras. His Project Democracy acquired ships and airplanes. It constructed airstrips and warehouses, along with maintenance and communication facilities. When the Soviets gave the Sandinistas armored attack helicopters, North and Secord bought Soviet SA-7 antiaircraft weapons from China. (At one point, Secord told North that some of the contra camps needed obstetricians.)

North relates an episode from 1985 in which beer magnate Joseph Coors was talking with CIA director Casey in the latter's office in the Old Executive Office Building. Coors expressed interest in giving money to the contras, and Casey took him to see North. Coors asked about various needs of the contras, and North told him of the usefulness of a small, four-seater airplane that the contras were using for medical evacuations and resupply. The plane's real advantage was its short runway needs. "All you really needed," North told him, "was a straight stretch of dirt road."

Days later, Secord received a check for sixty-five thousand dollars, which he used to buy a plane. For the remainder of the contra war, the plane flew with a Coors label on its tail.

It was the secondhand, aging planes used by Project Democracy that led to the disclosure of the operation. North tells of a mission in which the plane developed engine trouble over Nicaragua, and the crew had to dump cargo, including weapons, to stay aloft. The contraband was just what Nicaragua's leaders needed to prove that Americans were still involved with the contras. From that point on, all the Sandinistas had to do was to wait for a chance to shoot down a resupply plane and perhaps even detain a prisoner.

Leveraged Ally Redux

When North and Secord started Project Democracy, U.S. officials were in complete control of funds going to the contras. Even funds that contra leader Adolfo Calero and others raised on their own were supposed to go through North. Moreover, North insisted, repeatedly, that the contras buy arms from Secord, and only from Secord, even though he was charging substantially more than other arms dealers. Caspar Weinberger and North both recount an offer from retired Gen. Singlaub. Weinberger expresses incredulity that North did not take the general up on his offer. North insists that working with Singlaub would have been too public. Other, less expensive arms dealers had, in North's words, "unsavory reputations."

At the very least, the North operation was woefully inefficient, especially given the contras' need for value from every dollar. The departure of the CIA meant that the contras had to provide communications, training, and intelligence on their own. To maintain leverage, the CIA officials had never taught them how to do any of these things. North quotes a CIA agent: "I taught them [the contras] everything they know. But I didn't teach them everything I know." When North was ordered to facilitate the Saudis' contributions, Casey told him to make monthly payments. "That will give us more control," Casey said.

A $10 million contribution from the sultan of Brunei was simply lost when North (or perhaps his secretary, Fawn Hall) gave the donor the wrong account number. Americans contributed another $10 million in 1985 and 1986, of which less than half actually got to the contras, according to the Congressional Joint Committee report. Of the $18 million received by overcharging the Iranians for weapons, the contras received only $3.8 million.

I attended meetings in which Bosco Matamoros, the contras' Washington representative, visibly chafed at the heavy-handed leverage exercised by U.S. officials. The contras were told what targets to attack in Nicaragua, what to say to the press in Washington, and what leaders to follow. At a meeting at the offices of the American Security Council that I attended, a staff member for Sen. Jesse Helms (R-NC) demanded that Matamoros get the contras to become more active in southern Nicaragua. Failure to do so, the staffer threatened, would mean the contras would "never get another cent from the U.S. Congress." North relates that Casey was the driving force behind the formation of UNO and that later an assistant secretary of state came to a meeting on contra funding with a list of new leaders for the contras.

At the same time, no one except Reagan, occasionally, and the more conservative members of his administration, quietly, ever expressed the hope that the contras would win. Until September 1986, when CIA funding was restored, discussions of the contras revolved around how to keep them in the field and keep the destructive and divisive war in Nicaragua going. A prolonged war, which left the Sandinistas in place, provided the best opportunities for continued and enhanced U.S. government leverage. Nicaragua would remain a threat to its neighbors, who would depend more on U.S. aid. Nicaragua itself, potentially a prosperous country, would see economic recovery put off indefinitely.

Parts of the resupply operation are difficult to understand without assuming that greater American leverage was the goal. The case of the Soviet antiaircraft missiles is a case in point. When the Soviets began deploying Hind-24 helicopters in Nicaragua in November 1984, North said that he and Secord agreed that giving the contras U.S.-made Stinger missiles was "politically impossible." Presumably, North was convinced that his role in getting Stingers to the contras would become public. Instead, North went to the Communist Chinese to get Soviet SA-7 missiles. Not only are SA-7s not nearly as reliable as Stingers, but also North was actually increasing the chances of a leak by involving an enemy of the United States in the transaction. (The Chinese enmity toward the Soviet Union was no incentive to keep the operation quiet; it was just the opposite, in fact.) The only perceptible advantage was that North and only North could give SA-7s (and, afterwards, ammunition and spare parts) to the contras.

The Iran Initiative Becomes Public

On November 4, 1986, the American media picked up a story initially published in *al-Shirra*, a pro-Iranian newspaper published in Lebanon. The release of Donald Jacobsen, according to *al-Shirra*, occurred in return for shipments of arms, mostly TOW antitank missiles, from the United States to Iran. As this shocking news was breaking, it was overtaken by a political upheaval in Washington. After six years out of power, the Democrats retook the U.S. Senate. The two events would prove to be a poisonous combination for the Reagan administration. The news on the hostages cried out for a congressional investigation, and that investigation would now be led by Reagan's political enemies.

The administration's response to the news from Lebanon and Iran was ineffectual. Reagan himself was convinced that more hostage releases were soon to come, and he begged the media not to speculate on what else might be going on until the hostages were released. In fact, on November 7, Jacobsen appeared with Reagan in the Rose Garden, where the two men talked to the reporters who were demanding answers about the Iran initiative. Reagan said: "Anything that we tell about all the things that have been going on in trying to affect [his] rescue endangers the possibility of further rescue." Jacobsen then gave the reporters his own tongue-lashing: "Unreasonable speculation on your part can endanger their lives. . . . And in the name of God, would you please just be responsible and back off?" One reporter's reply to this plea was illustrative: "Mr. Jacobsen, how are we to know what is responsible and what is not?" Both men assumed, wrongly, that American reporters would view the release of more American hostages as a more important goal than hurting a Republican president.

As the scandal took Washington over, the glee among media representatives was unbridled. My own work often took me to the Hart Senate Office Building, where the media was "camped out" to speak to the senators who came rushing back from their Thanksgiving break to be in on the action. Almost without exception, the reporters, usually a dour and bored-looking group, were wreathed in smiles and high-fiving one another.

Reagan clung to the belief that more hostages might be coming out and pressed for secrecy. Poindexter argued at NSC meetings that the whole thing would simply blow over if everyone in the administration kept quiet for a few more days. He might have been right, but in the event,

Shultz and Weinberger made their opposition to the entire idea known to anyone who would listen. Interestingly enough, however, at a National Security Planning Group meeting on November 10, Shultz argued in favor of keeping the contacts going, although he insisted that all future contacts with Iranians be coordinated through the State Department.

The Other Shoe Drops: Funds for the Contras

When it became clear even to the most optimistic members of the administration that the scandal was getting worse, not blowing over, Reagan took steps to insure that there would be no repeat of the Nixon Watergate coverup. Reagan asked Attorney General Ed Meese to question the officials involved and develop a chronology of exactly what happened. This inquiry was to take place over the weekend of November 21–24.

On Saturday, Assistant AG William Bradford Reynolds and Meese's chief of staff John Richardson were in North's office in the Old Executive Office Building. They discovered a memo from North to Poindexter in which North said: "$12 million [of the money from Iran] will be used to purchase critically needed supplies for the Nicaraguan Democratic Resistance forces." This memo would be the scandal's smoking gun. On Sunday, Meese showed North a copy of the "diversion memo." North, according to Meese's account, was visibly surprised that the memo had survived being shredded and asked Meese if the cover sheet, which would have showed the routing of the memo, was with it. Such a memo would have shown who saw the memo and signed off on it. Its absence means that, to this day, no one knows if Reagan approved the diversion or not.

Meese reported to Chief of Staff Don Regan on Monday morning. The latter knew immediately that the Iran scandal has just gotten much, much worse. According to Regan's own account, he sat at his desk with his head in his hands while he listened to Meese's report. Meese told Reagan about the diversion late Monday afternoon. Stated most simply, the Iranians had been charged $30 million for $12 million worth of weapons. Almost all of the $18 million difference was unaccounted for. Meese and Regan describe the president as shocked, with his normally ruddy skin turning "pasty white" at the news. Both men were convinced that Reagan's violent reaction was evidence that he had no idea about the diversion beforehand. The White House went into full damage-control mode, with Regan in charge.

The chief of staff decided upon a three-pronged response. First, both North and Poindexter would be fired. Second, Reagan and Meese themselves would break the news before any of the administration's innumerable leakers got the story out. Third, Reagan would be portrayed as outraged and determined to get the facts out. As proof of his determination, Reagan would appoint a special bipartisan commission, made up of former senator John Tower (R-TX), former national security advisor Brent Scowcroft, and former secretary of state and senator Edmund Muskie (D-ME). Regan scheduled a press conference for Tuesday afternoon, November 25.

Before the press conference, Regan went to Poindexter's office to ask him, point blank, why he did not stop North from using the residual funds in this way. Poindexter calmly responded, "I felt sorry for the contras. I was so damned mad at [House Speaker] Tip O'Neill for the way he was dragging the contras around."

At the press conference, Reagan announced what Meese had found. He said that he had accepted Poindexter's resignation and that LTC Oliver North, whom most Americans did not know, was to be "relieved of his duties at the National Security Council" and "reassigned" back to his Marine infantry unit. The reporters shouted questions, only one of which Reagan answered, insisting he had not made a mistake sending arms to Iran. Within days, the new Democratic majority leaders in the Senate, and their counterparts in the House, announced that there would be a full congressional inquiry. The word *impeachment* began to appear more and more frequently in the writings and statements of politicians and political pundits.

But as devastating as the contra element of the Iran-contra scandal seemed, it may actually have helped the president. Reagan biographer Lou Cannon states, correctly, that Americans were much angrier about sending arms to Iran than about efforts to get money and arms to the contras. Cannon adds that once North's diversion of the Iran money was revealed, all Reagan had to do to survive politically was to insist, and keep insisting, that he did not know what North was doing. For a time, this might make Reagan look out of touch, but such impressions would divert Americans' attention from the actions that Reagan did authorize.

Cannon does not comment on a deeper aspect of the affair. Reagan's congressional enemies were determined, right from the start, to turn the Iran-contra scandal into another Watergate. With this determination in mind, they focused almost entirely on the funds diversion, which was the part of the Iran-contra scandal that was most likely to include outright lawbreaking. Had Democrats been as eager to engage the Reagan administration in a policy discussion, concerning the opening to Iran, and kept the discussion revolving around the arms-for-hostages deal, they might very well have had Reagan's resignation. (Indeed, a *New York Times*-CBS poll on December 2 showed that Reagan's approval rating had dropped from 67 percent before the revelations to 46 percent. This was the largest one-month drop in the history of the *Times*-CBS poll.)

For weeks after Reagan and Meese appeared before the press, the attention of the media was almost wholly devoted to the funds diversion. While few Americans accepted North's characterization of the diversion as "a neat idea," there were plenty of Americans who cared a lot less about shaking down the Iranians for money than about selling them weapons. Moreover, the administration moved very effectively to portray North as a loose cannon, in which effort they (for once) had the full cooperation of the mainstream media. Articles appeared about North's marital problems, his supposed combat fatigue, and his reputation for embellishing stories to the point of self-delusion. With the press vilifying North, and the administration acting as though they had never heard of him, Reagan was becoming more and more insulated from the details of the scandal.

The first three months of 1987 were the dark days of the Reagan presidency. Having ceded the public relations battle to his enemies in the first days of the scandal, Reagan tried and failed repeatedly to regain the initiative. Each day seemed to bring new revelations of shady and disreputable actions on the part of his staff, with the net of accusation and suspicion drawing closer and closer to Reagan himself. Some White House insiders even suggested that Reagan became withdrawn and barely functional during this period. (One account has Reagan barely coherent during a question-and-answer session with the Tower Commission members.)

The public record does not support charges that Reagan became dysfunctional in the weeks following his November 25 press conference. First, no one with frequent, direct access to the president at that time made any such charge at that time. Had congressional Democrats, for example, been able to portray Reagan as losing his grip, the argument for impeachment would have been strengthened. None offered such a portrayal at the time. Second, the public papers of the president show a reduced number of public statements, but this is attributable to the political impact of the Iran-contra mess and does not indicate any diminished capacity on Reagan's part to act.

His January 27 State of the Union Address was compelling and delivered in Reagan's clear and forceful style, as were his remarks to the antiabortion march, the February National Prayer Breakfast, and his

February 10 speech to the American Legion. Indeed, one of the remarkable elements of the Iran-contra scandal is how little impact it had on Reagan's policies, foreign and domestic, even in the face of major staff changes. In late 1986 and early 1987, Reagan hired a new chief of staff, a new National Security advisor, and a new CIA director, with barely a ripple in either his domestic or foreign agenda.

The scandal entered a new phase on February 26, when the Tower Commission issued its report. While the lengthy report was long on criticisms of the president's staff structure, management style, and policy decisions, its authors confirmed that they found no evidence that Reagan had any knowledge of the funds diversion to the contras before Ed Meese told him about it on November 24. While blasting Reagan for his administration's dealings with Iran, the report exonerated him of the part of the scandal that was most likely to lead to actual criminal proceedings.

Reagan spoke to the nation on March 4 and admitted his culpability in the Iran part of the scandal: "A few months ago I told the American people I did not trade arms for hostages. My heart and my best intentions still tell me that's true, but the facts and the evidence tell me it is not. As the Tower board reported, what began as a strategic opening to Iran deteriorated, in its implementation, into trading arms for hostages. This runs counter to my own beliefs, to administration policy, and to the original strategy we had in mind. There are reasons why it happened, but no excuses. It was a mistake."

Later, he added: "It's clear from the Board's report, however, that I let my personal concern for the hostages spill over into the geopolitical strategy of reaching out to Iran. I asked so many questions about the hostages' welfare that I didn't ask enough about the specifics of the total Iran plan." Reagan went on to tell the American people that neither he nor the Tower Commission knew where all the extra money from Iran had gone but expressed his confidence that the special prosecutor and the congressional committees would eventually find out. At the end of the speech, he expressed his determination to learn from his mistakes and move on, insisting that that was what members of Congress from both parties wanted, along with the American people.

By admitting bad judgment in trading arms for hostages, Reagan effectively removed that issue from discussion. There was no need to convince anyone that the Iran deal had in fact been an arms-for-hostages swap after Reagan acknowledged it. By admitting that he did not know what happened to the money destined for the contras, he made this issue the focus of the continuing investigations. By speaking of his determination to continue the work of his administration, he subtly put pressure on his opponents to complete their investigations quickly or face an increasingly impatient American public.

Nonetheless, congressional Democrats did not seem to be in a hurry. After agreeing to merge the House and Senate committees into a single select committee, the legislators took their time assembling data and preparing to call witnesses for what promised to be the most-watched congressional hearings since Watergate. Democrats believed that their best chance of reaping political rewards from the scandal was to keep it going, long enough to have an impact on the 1988 presidential election. They further believed that their best chance of implicating Reagan, directly or indirectly, would be during the testimony of former National Security aide Oliver North. His testimony, many Democrats believed, would be the scandal's turning point.

They were right.

"Olliemania": A Show Trial Goes Wrong

By the early summer of 1987, the House and Senate committee investigating the Iran-contra affair had been making headlines for weeks. Among the star witnesses were Fawn Hall, Oliver North's secretary; Elliott Abrams, assistant secretary of state for Latin America; Richard Secord; Robert McFarlane; George Shultz; and Caspar Weinberger. Senator Daniel Inouye (D-HI), a veteran of the Watergate hearings, presided over the questioning with a constant, and photogenic, air of indignant disbelief. At times, the testimony was explosive; at other times, it was stunningly boring. For many Americans, and seemingly for many members of the Joint Committee, all the witnesses were mere preliminaries to the main event, which was the testimony of LTC Oliver North.

At times during the spring and early summer, there was some doubt over whether or not North would ever testify. On the advice of his legal counsel, North was saying nothing, and he made it clear that, unless the Joint Committee granted him immunity from prosecution, his testimony before the committee would consist of little more than him taking the Fifth Amendment. Finally, in June, North's lawyer, Brendan Sullivan, reached an agreement with the committees that provided North with the immunity he wanted.

But as part of the agreement with Sullivan, the Joint Committee made what turned out to be a fatal error. They agreed to permit North to testify before appearing for a deposition. Although most Americans were not aware of it, all of the previous witnesses had provided step-by-step previews of their testimony to the committee before they ever got in front of the television cameras. Thus, when the committee members questioned Fawn Hall, or Abrams, or any of the others, the committee members knew all the answers to the questions ahead of time. In fact, members of the Joint Committee sometimes went over the depositions and decided who was going to ask which questions during the televised hearings.

North's lawyer refused to have his client deposed, and thus the Joint Committee members would be hearing his testimony for the first time as he gave it, starting on Tuesday, July 7, 1987. The negotiators for the committee may have believed that a Marine lieutenant colonel could not possibly be the intellectual or rhetorical match for twenty-six U.S. senators and representatives, not to mention the committee's expert counsel. Moreover, committee Democrats may have believed that North would place the blame for the scandal on Reagan and thus may have been so eager to get North to the stand that they neglected to insist upon a deposition. Whatever the reason for the omission, it served only to draw more attention to North as he prepared to testify just after the Fourth of July weekend (the timing was another tactical error on the part of the Joint Committee).

From the beginning, the members and employees of the Joint Committee overplayed their hand. Just after North was sworn, ramrod-straight and in uniform, creating an image that would dominate American perceptions of him for years, Inouye refused to waive a rule requiring opening statements to be submitted forty-eight hours in advance. In fact, Inouye attempted to use North's request to again portray North as a renegade: "Here once again, the witness is asking us to bend the law and to suggest that he may be above the law."

There followed a series of objections from Sullivan, all before North spoke at all. First, Sullivan described his efforts to gain access to the written materials that the committee possessed from North's time in the White House. He wrote to the committee in March and received no reply to his request until June 30. On that day, the committee did indeed deliver the written records, which, stacked up, stood seven feet high. Sullivan displayed a photo of North standing next to the paperwork to the Committee and to the American people. Moreover, Sullivan pointed out, the papers were "shuffled by date and subject matter so that one could not even begin to understand what those records said, much less read them all." Sullivan's initial task, to portray his client as a persecuted victim of a biased committee, was well under way.

North's lawyer received considerable assistance in this portrayal from Chairman Inouye. Rather than referring to the substance of Sullivan's objection, he primly asserted: "Under our rules it is your responsibility to advise your witness, your client, not to advise the Committee." He then proceeded to overrule Sullivan's objection. In fact, Inouye overruled every one of Sullivan's objections, usually with statements indicating that the committee was doing North a favor by even permitting him to have counsel present during the questioning.

After the initial sparring between Inouye and Sullivan, the House Committee chief council, John Nields, asked North one of the few direct questions of the proceedings: "Colonel North, were you involved in the use of the proceeds of sales of weapons to Iran for the purpose of assisting the contras in Nicaragua?" North, as expected, refused to answer, citing the Fifth Amendment. Inouye provided North with immunity and directed him to answer all questions put to him by the Joint Committee. Sullivan acknowledged receipt of the necessary court documents, and the questioning resumed. However, Nields then put a different question to North: "You were involved in two operations of great significance to the people of this country, is that correct?"

One can only speculate on why Nields changed the question. Had he reiterated his initial question, North would have had to answer in the affirmative, and the Joint Committee would have had what they insisted they wanted, in the first minutes of North's testimony. To close observers, the new, and more general, question for Nields indicated that the committee was planning to expand its questioning of North to a number of other areas than the diversion of funds to the contras. To more casual observers, more apparent unfairness to North was soon in evidence. Nields began reading from the transcript of a tape recording that had been provided to North's lawyer just minutes before. Once again, Inouye overruled Sullivan's objection.

North pressed his advantage. He told the committee and the American people: "I came here to tell you the truth—the good, the bad and the ugly. I am here to tell it all, pleasant and unpleasant, and I am here to accept responsibility for that which I did. I will not accept responsibility for that which I did not do." Once again, Inouye made the wrong response. He insisted that North's statement had to be from a verbatim text and asked North to produce it. By insisting on this, Inouye tacitly acknowledged that neither he nor his colleagues would have been able to come up with compelling phraseology on the spur of the moment, as North just had.

Throughout the first day of the proceedings the committee members and counsel seemed shocked that a Marine officer could reply so effectively and so articulately to their questions. As it became evident to the Joint Committee that their early attempts to browbeat North might backfire on them badly, they permitted North to speak longer and longer without interruption. If they thought this tactic would result in North making exploitable verbal mistakes, they were again disappointed. North responded forthrightly and compellingly, with statements that were easily understood by those watching the hearings live and easily made into sound bites for those who would watch the evening news broadcasts.

Even Inouye's decision to deny North the opportunity to make an opening statement until the third day of the hearings backfired. By Thursday, July 9, the "Ollie" phenomenon had already begun, and North had already captured the sympathy of many Americans. The television audience for the hearings was considerably larger on Thursday than it had been on Tuesday. Moreover, the Oliver North who appeared on Thursday was, in the eyes of many viewers, a courageous solider, standing virtually alone against the overwhelming odds brought to bear against him. It was with this additional sympathy, and additional interest, that North finally got to deliver his opening statement.

This statement was alternatively personal and self-congratulatory. On the first day of the hearings, it would have been seen as just that. On the third day, however, it came across as a sincere and heartfelt self-introduction by a man who was forced to suffer fools and scoundrels. Moreover, after his statement, North was questioned by George Van Cleve, who was counsel for the Republican minority. Not surprisingly, Van Cleve's questioning was far more friendly and gave North more opportunities to present his actions in the most favorable light possible.

The committee chair also used the "security" excuse to prevent North from giving his Central America slide show briefing, which some Republican committee members suggested he do. The slide show, Inouye insisted, would require lowering the lights in the committee room, which would be unsafe. Aside from the fact that the Russell Senate Office Building was heavily guarded, and the hearing room even more heavily guarded, the only "security threats" that had appeared by that point were two young women wearing anti-North t-shirts.

The discomfort of the Democratic committee members continued. After Van Cleve completed his questioning, North's next inquisitor was Arthur Liman, a world-famous litigator from New York City. Liman had

the well-earned reputation of being able to coax information from anyone on a witness stand and to embarrass anyone who tried to evade his
relentless questioning. But Liman, too, made mistakes. He took North to
task for consulting a book of notes before answering a question. Sullivan
responded angrily:

> I think it should be fully understood by the Committee that
> Colonel North has been struggling here for 2 ½ days to tell the
> truth and the whole truth. He's also exercising great care in addi-
> tion to telling the truth, because, Mr. Chairman, this body had
> created an independent counsel, which occupies an office down
> the street and he's like a separate "super Justice Department" to
> those of us that work in the defense of citizens. He has 100 people,
> you have 125, he's got 100 people down there looking at Colonel
> North and everything that he did, just as your staff is. He's got
> 26 bright lawyers, 35 FBI agents, 11 IRS agents, four customs
> agents, investigators, and they're all pouring over the testimony.

Liman, however, continued to belittle North. He referred to North
as "Lieutenant," prompting North to remind him of his correct rank. He
also asked North a number of hypothetical questions, prompting another
outburst from Sullivan, this one directed toward Chairman Inouye and
designed, again, to portray North as the underdog:

> Sullivan: "Those kinds of [hypothetical] questions, Mr. Chairman,
> are wholly inappropriate. . . . Come on, let's have, Mr. Chair-
> man, plain fairness, that's all we're asking."
>
> Inouye: I'm certain counsel realizes that this is not a court of law.
>
> Sullivan: I—believe me, I know that!
>
> Inouye: And I'm certain you realize that the rules of evidence do
> not apply in this inquiry.
>
> Sullivan: That I know as well. I'm just asking for fairness—fairness.
> I know the rules don't apply. I know the Congress doesn't recognize
> attorney-client privilege, a husband-and-wife privilege [a member
> of the Committee had earlier suggested that North's wife be sub-
> poenaed to corroborate parts of her husband's testimony], a priest-
> penitent privilege. I know those things are all out the window.

Inouye: We have attempted to be as fair as we can.

Sullivan: As we rely on just fairness, Mr. Chairman, fairness.

Inouye: Let the witness object, if he wishes to.

Sullivan: Well, sir, I'm not a potted plant. I'm here as the lawyer; that's my job.

Knowing that North had repeatedly been threatened by terrorists, the committee displayed a large copy of a letter to North, complete with his home address. On the third day of the hearings, North and his wife went to the balcony of the small holding room allotted to them during the breaks. Thousands of well-wishers were gathered in the street below, and Col. and Mrs. North greeted them. The image of the Norths waving from a balcony made every network news broadcast. The following day, North reports, the door to the balcony was bolted shut, with headless screws. Yet again, whatever power on the Joint Committee had the door bolted, the action insured that only the first, positive image of Col. and Mrs. North would be seen.

North maintained that using Iranian money for the contras was not illegal, since the U.S. agencies involved were fully paid for the weapons, and since statutes like the Boland Amendment applied only to U.S. government money. While strongly disputing this claim, the Joint Committee also sought to indict North as personally corrupt and noted that he had accepted a security fence for his home from Richard Secord. (In fact, accepting the fence would be one of the only actions for which North would be convicted in a court of law.)

But even attempting to pin North down about the fence backfired. He insisted that the fence was to provide security to his family, which had been threatened by terrorists. Indeed, on one occasion some months earlier, FBI agents intercepted terrorists on their way to North's home, forcing him to move his family to a secure military base for a time. Continued threats, North said, came from Palestinian terrorist Abu Nidal. The issue gave North the opportunity to make one of his most dramatic statements of the hearings: "I want you to know that I'd be more than willing . . . to meet Abu Nidal on equal terms anywhere in the world. There's an even deal for him. OK? But I am not willing to have my wife and my four children meet Abu Nidal or his organization on his terms."

By Friday, newspapers across America were commenting on "Olliemania." Young conservative men were going to barber shops to get "Ollie cuts." (North's Marine crew cut was contrasted with the truly awful haircuts of Nields and Liman.) *USA Today* opened a telephone hotline, which by Friday had received sixty-six thousand calls. Nearly fifty-nine thousand of these applauded North. White House spokesman Marlin Fitzwater said operators there fielded two thousand phone calls about North, eighty-three of which were critical. Donations poured into both the Oliver North Defense Fund and the conservative organizations that pledged to get the money to the contras. Even the ultraliberal Massachusetts state legislature and the Boston City Council barely defeated resolutions honoring North.

Two weeks running in mid-July, North was on the covers of all three major newsweeklies. *Time* ran a detailed tour of the six rows of ribbons on North's uniform. He was the lead story night after night on all three networks and occupied the front pages of almost every newspaper in the country. Only a week after his testimony ended, Pocket Books published a verbatim account of the hearings, with a huge initial printing run. Hollywood talent agents predicted that North could draw twenty-five thousand dollars for a speech and $1 million for a book deal, about a quarter of the money he had funneled to the contras.

Some commentators sought to minimize North's impact on the hearings' huge television audience. Sen. Warren Rudman (R-NH), for example, sniffed that the hearings ran at the same time as many popular soap operas and probably drew many soap opera viewers who would, he said, be taken in by the good guy versus bad guys story line. Liberal TV mogul Norman Lear insisted it was all about image: "TV eats up moist eyed people. People like Jackie Gleason, Carroll O'Connor and Ronald Reagan. . . . TV loves moist. The camera loves moist." Still other "media experts" noted that the committee camera angles put viewers eye-level with North, looking up at the committee members sitting on the dais.

Other North critics focused on other parts of the North image and testimony. His Marine uniform was, in the view of some observers, a "chilling" suggestion that civilian control over the military was in jeopardy, especially when coupled with the fact that North's boss was *Admiral* John Poindexter. For others, North's waving from the balcony was reminiscent of Juan and Evita Perón in Argentina. North was routinely referred to as fascist, Nazi, or demented. (Interestingly enough, the Sandinista official newspaper used many of the same terms.)

North did more, however, than simply prompt a few people to get crew cuts. What is most important, North had an effect on public opinion on Central America. For many of the hearings' viewers, North's testimony was the first they had heard of such matters as the Sandinistas' connection with international terrorism, their internal repression, their support for Communism elsewhere in Central America, and their close ties to the Soviet Union.

In a *Wall Street Journal* / NBC poll published a week after the hearings, support for aid to the contras was at 40 percent, with 43 percent against. While hardly a ringing endorsement, these numbers were substantially improved over polls just weeks earlier. A *Los Angeles Times* poll also found proponents and opponents of contra aid tied, at 42 percent. Even a Harris poll that showed 61 percent opposed to contra aid was down from 74 percent opposed earlier. More revealing than any single poll, however, is the fact that during the whole of the Iran-contra crisis (November 1986–August 1987), there were no serious attempts to rescind the $100 million in aid for the contras approved in October 1986.

North's newfound popularity was not lost on the committee members either. Moderate Republican senator Paul Trible of Virginia said, "Oliver North has won the hearts and minds of the American people." As the colonel's popularity soared, and public regard for Congress in general, and for the Joint Committee in particular, plummeted, Joint Committee members reacted in three different ways. Some made the almost laughable complaint that the hearings had turned into a circus and suggested that the American people were not sophisticated enough to understand what was going on. Not surprisingly, such arrogance did little to restore public affection for the committee.

Other congressmen and senators began arguing among themselves and with the committee's own counsel. (As they did so, Sullivan whispered to his client, "This case is closed.") The arguments were over the amount of time that committee members would have to question North. For nearly two full days, Democrats on the committee finally found a way to silence North: not to ask him any questions. Instead, members used their allotted "question" time to lecture North, their fellow committee members, the news media, or the American people. North sat silently, poker-faced.

Finally, Daniel Inouye, politically tone-deaf to the end, read a closing statement in which he compared North to the Nazis at Nuremberg who defended themselves by saying they were just following orders. This was too much for Sullivan, who angrily protested and insisted that the hearings not end on such a note. Inouye simply responded, "May I continue with my statement?" When Sullivan pointed out that another twenty thousand telegrams of support had arrived overnight, Inouye was equally unimpressed.

Inouye's failure to understand the North phenomenon was inexcusable. Oliver North had given dozens of briefings on Central America just in the DC area over the previous three years. He was a frequent guest at the White House Outreach Working Group meetings that I arranged, and he spoke at many other gatherings as well. Yet I cannot remember a single instance of a Democratic senator, representative, or congressional staff member attending any one of these briefings. Had they done so, they would have known of North's eloquence of ability to capture and hold an audience. North's would-be antagonists paid a heavy price for their willful ignorance.

The "Crisis" Peters Out

As the glow of Olliemania faded, which it did almost immediately after North ceased to appear on television every day, the Joint Committee and the American people finally took note of the substance of North's testimony. North had said nothing that implicated Ronald Reagan in the diversion of Iran arms funds to the contras. However, he insisted repeatedly that he had authorization for everything he did, and he described the voluminous paper trail that he created, seeking permission to proceed with various elements of the Iran-contra operation, keeping his superiors up to date, and asking questions. He also candidly described how much of that trail he later destroyed.

Ex-National Security Advisor John Poindexter took center stage later in July. Occupying the stand for five days, Poindexter gave testimony that was the epitome of anticlimax. He insisted, fervently and repeatedly, that he never told Reagan about the funds to the contras. His reasons for not doing so varied. At one point, Poindexter said that he did not need to ask the president since he was sure Reagan would say yes, and silence would give Reagan "plausible deniability." At other points, Poindexter admitted he did not know how Reagan would react, but he decided to go ahead, since Reagan had said he wanted the contras kept alive.

But with Poindexter's bland statement, on July 15, that "the buck stops with me on this," the Iran-contra scandal, as a threat to the presidency of Ronald Reagan, came to an end. Talk of impeachment left the mainstream and became the stuff of small-circulation left-wing newsletters and publications. Reagan's job approval ratings began to revive (this had started even before North testified). Democrats' poll numbers started slipping as the possibility of impeachment faded.

Moreover, other matters were distracting Americans' attention from Iran-contra. Domestically, Americans watched the contentious confirmation hearings of Robert Bork for the U.S. Supreme Court and the October stock market crash. Pope John Paul II came to the United States, amid extensive media coverage. The Reagan administration remained busy in foreign affairs as well. In June, Reagan had gone to Berlin and given his famous speech in which he commanded: "Mr. Gorbachev, tear down this wall!" Preparations were under way for another summit with Gorbachev, in which he and Reagan would sign a treaty dismantling an entire class of nuclear weapons. September saw a U.S. air strike in the Persian Gulf and the decision to "reflag" merchant vessels as U.S. ships to deter attacks and keep the Gulf open to civilian ship traffic.

Perhaps most significant, Reagan began a new peace initiative in Central America, while the congressional hearings on Iran-contra were still going on. As the scandal wound down, policy makers began to realize that during the year and a half that the contras did not receive any U.S. government money, their army had grown exponentially. In October 1984, there were eight thousand contras in the field; by August 1987, that number had grown to more than twenty thousand. For most of the first six years that Reagan was president, he and his administration had to deal with problems related to the fact that the contras were too weak.

Now, for some in the administration, there was a new and more vexing problem: the contras were too strong.

10

Another Year, Another Peace Plan, 1987

When persecution of religion has ended, and the jails no longer contain political prisoners, national reconciliation and democracy will be possible. Until this happens, "democratization" will be a fraud. And until it happens, we will press for true democracy by supporting those fighting for it.

—*Ronald Reagan*, to the United Nations, September, 1987

The Speaker Speaks Out

Pundits commenting on the Iran-contra scandal give different dates for when the scandal ended. Some, like Reagan biographer Lou Cannon, say it was when Reagan admitted to trading arms for hostages in his speech on March 4, 1987. Others believe that it was during the testimony of NSC aide LTC Oliver North and the ensuing "Olliemania." Still others believe it was when Reagan and Soviet leader Mikhail Gorbachev signed an arms control treaty in December 1987. I think the best date to assign to the end of the Iran-contra scandal, as a threat to the Reagan presidency, is August 5, 1987. On that day, Reagan appeared at the White House with House Speaker Jim Wright (D-TX) to announce a bipartisan peace plan for Central America.

For most of his presidency, Reagan had expressed the desire for bipartisanship on foreign affairs in general and for Central America in particular. Votes in Congress on crucial parts of Reagan's Central America policies were usually razor-thin, such as the four-vote margin on aid to El Salvador in May 1984, and the six-vote win for $100 million in contra aid in September 1986. For the president, the opportunity to work with, rather than against, the Democratic majority (now in charge of both the House and the Senate) was attractive. The promise of bipartisanship was even more attractive given Reagan's weakened political standing in 1987, the result of the prolonged Iran-contra scandal. When Reagan's aides brought him word of a potential deal with the House Speaker, Reagan was immediately attracted, if somewhat wary.

For his part, Wright fancied himself an expert on Latin America, although his experience with the region was quite limited. In fact, Wright had considerably more contact with Hispanic North Americans than he did with actual Latin Americans. He had never been any more than an extremely reluctant supporter of aid to the Nicaraguan contras, although he was a strong proponent of aid to El Salvador, at least after José Napoleón Duarte was elected president.

To any genuine expert on the region, Wright's pronouncements on Latin America seem almost touchingly naïve. He wrote in his memoirs, for example, that he did not believe that the Ortega brothers (Daniel, president of Sandinista Nicaragua, and Humberto, the country's defense minister) were Marxists. From 1979 to 1987, both brothers had repeatedly proclaimed their adherence to Marxism-Leninism. Nevertheless, Wright believed that he knew them better than they did themselves, saying: "Most [junta members], including the Ortega brothers, were homegrown nationalists, inexperienced in governing, suspicious of imperialism, and groping for the best path to economic development."

Nor was Wright's faith in the Ortega brothers' good intentions shaken by the fact that, by Wright's own account, Daniel Ortega had repeatedly lied to his face. Wright met with the Sandinista leadership in June 1980 as part of a U.S. congressional delegation. Rep. Bill Alexander (D-AR) asked Daniel Ortega if the Sandinistas would guarantee freedom of speech, freedom of the press, and freedom of assembly. Ortega replied, "All of these things are being guaranteed in our new constitution." Wright says he asked if Nicaragua would become socialist under the Sandinistas. Ortega told him, "We want private business to be in private hands. We want them to be successful. We want private citizens to own land. We want *more* of them to own land, and own businesses. We want *more* of our people to be capitalists" (emphasis in original).

It was with such questionable "expertise" that Wright entered the fray on Central America. The genesis of Wright's intervention (or interference, for some) was a meeting with Sandinista ambassador Carlos Tunnermann. Wright had told Tunnermann "not to be so sure [that] contra aid would not be renewed." This story is almost certainly disingenuous. First, the Speaker was relatively new to his job and had no idea if he would be able to deliver sufficient Democrat votes to pass contra aid. Second, and more important, it is extremely doubtful that Tunnermann needed any information from Wright on the likely future actions of Congress. The thoroughness and depth of the Sandinistas' knowledge of Capitol Hill were bywords in the 1980s. Wright's actions may have had more to do with wishing to regain the initiative on contra aid from the U.S. Senate (a likelihood evidenced by the strongly negative reaction of many Democratic senators to his initiative).

Wright had little difficulty in securing a meeting with Secretary of State George Shultz to go over the basic points of a bipartisan peace plan for Nicaragua. The Speaker and Secretary Shultz wished to build on the foundation that Costa Rican president Oscar Arias had laid when he called for an end to external military assistance to Central America and the advance of democratization. Wright and Shultz settled on a deal in which the United States would suspend aid to the contras in return for a simultaneous halt of aid to the Sandinistas from Cuba and the Soviet Union. Also simultaneous with the end of contra aid would be the immediate restoration of all "civil rights and liberties" in Nicaragua, whose government would promise to establish an "independent, multiparty electoral commission" to prepare for elections "to be supervised and guaranteed by an international body such as the OAS."

With few modifications, this was the plan put forth by Reagan and Wright at the White House on August 5, 1987, just two days after the Iran-contra Joint Committee wrapped up its work. Reagan was clearly trying to regain some control over the country's foreign policy, and he was also eager to demonstrate that he could still work with the Democratic congressional leadership. Both Reagan and Wright were also determined to maintain a strong U.S. role in the region, mindful of the fact that the five Central American presidents were due to meet in Guatemala the coming weekend to discuss a plan based on President Arias' proposals.

Reagan's conservative supporters were outraged by the terms of the deal. (*The Wall Street Journal* called the Reagan-Wright plan "Ronald Reagan's Bay of Pigs.") With the $100 million that had been voted in by Congress and had started flowing to the contras in late 1986, the Nicaraguan rebels were having the most significant battlefield successes of the war. Pressure on the Sandinistas was growing; the government was becoming somewhat less secure. Moreover, public support for the contras in the United States was at the highest point it had ever been, largely due to the testimony of Oliver North. Congressman Jack Kemp (R-NY), for example, believed that it was time to press for a huge increase in contra aid, not a reduction, and certainly not a suspension.

Even more ominous to the contras and their supporters was the shoddy treatment the contras received while the Wright-Shultz discussions were going on. Shultz met with the contra leadership the night before Reagan and Wright made their announcement and said nothing to the Nicaraguans about the discussions going on over their heads. Moreover, an appointment for the contras with Reagan on August 5 was postponed until after the Reagan-Wright appearance. At that point, the contras' complaints about aspects of the plan were met with administration officials' response that the matter was a "done deal."

Changing Conditions

Many pages have been written by experts attempting to discern Reagan's "true" intentions in appearing with Wright to endorse his plan and later embracing (albeit tentatively) the Arias plan for peace in Central America. Many observers, mostly those critical of Reagan, insist upon an almost unprecedented level of cynicism from Reagan in his dealings with Wright and with the Central American presidents. From the point of view of these observers, Reagan completely changed his policies and goals for Central America, and especially for Nicaragua, and was trying to hide the fact that he was doing so. Conservatives, normally supportive of Reagan, were no less convinced that Reagan was up to something that was at best naïve and at worst was cynically deceptive.

Both liberals and conservatives based their criticism of Reagan on a false premise: that Reagan saw the contras not just as an instrument to bring democracy to Nicaragua but also as the only instrument to do so. Both liberals and conservatives believed Reagan wished for nothing other than a triumphal march of the contra army into Managua. There is no compelling firsthand evidence to support this premise. In Reagan's innumerable statements on the contra issue since 1982, he was remarkably consistent in what he saw as their purpose: to stop the flow of arms to El Salvador and to force the Sandinistas to fulfill the promises of democracy, nonalignment, and economic freedom that they had made to the OAS in 1979.

For Reagan's liberal critics, his embrace of the Wright plan was an attempt to preempt the Central American presidents and maintain American supremacy over the decisions made about the region. Many critics believed that Reagan thought that the Central American presidents would postpone their Guatemala meeting or suspend serious discussions long enough to study the Reagan-Wright plan. While they were studying the plan, the critics contended, Reagan would find some way to permanently displace the Central Americans as prime movers in the region. According to this scenario, Reagan was shocked and dismayed when the Arias plan was adopted, and his administration's halting and half-hearted endorsement of the plan was based on nothing more than short-term political thinking.

For the president's conservative critics, by far the more vocal and angry of the two sides, the Reagan-Wright plan and the Arias plan were borne of either a loss of nerve on Reagan's part or the successful manipulation of his thoughts by George Shultz, Chief of Staff Howard Baker, or in some cases, Nancy Reagan. Indeed, for almost the remainder of the Reagan administration, some conservatives would insist that decisions of the Reagan administration were not made by Ronald Reagan. Conservatives had good reason to suspect Shultz's motives. Former Senator Howard Baker was a moderate Republican who thought little of conservatives. There was reason for suspicion of him as well.

The loss of faith in Reagan himself among conservatives is harder to fathom but much easier to find. During the Iran-contra scandal, there were rumors that Reagan had gone into a deep depression and nearly ceased to function as president. Conservatives outwardly rejected such rumors but seem to have internalized them in their reaction not only to the Reagan-Wright plan, but to many of Reagan's foreign policy decisions in 1987 and 1988. Liberals, for their part, had long since adopted the image of Reagan as an "amiable dunce," as Clark Clifford had once said.

Yet for all of this unflattering characterization, Reagan seems one of the few observers of Central America in 1987 who fully realized just how drastically conditions had changed in the previous eighteen months. Conservatives and liberals, still scarred from the contra battles of the first six years of Reagan's presidency, acted as though no part of the contra debate had changed since before the Iran-contra scandal broke. Like soldiers emerging from the jungle years after a war has ended, both sides expected to see the same world that existed when they entered the jungle.

But the late summer of 1987 presented quite a different world. One difference was the increased effectiveness of the contras themselves. As one analyst pointed out at the time, the $100 million that the contras had received in October was more than the nation of Honduras spent on its entire military in a year. The appropriation amounted to almost seven hundred dollars per contra, per month. The funds permitted vastly improved communications equipment, which allowed contra task forces to coordinate their attacks and to get word when the Sandinista army was approaching. It permitted more frequent and reliable resupply from bases in Honduras and El Salvador.

What is most important, the military aid in 1986 included, for the first time, U.S. Stinger antiaircraft missiles. When he was trying to coordinate irregular funding for the contras in 1985 and 1986, North had always wished for Stingers, since they were much more effective than SA-7s, but he was unable to secure them on the international arms black market. With these in hand, the contras in 1987 shot down nineteen of the frightening Soviet Hind-24 helicopters. Up until 1987, the Sandinistas' most significant advantage over the contras was air power. The contras were redressing the imbalance.

In so doing, the contras were also accelerating a growing split between the Sandinistas and the Soviet leadership. As early as June 24, the Soviet government newspaper *Izvestia* estimated that the "war zone [in Nicaragua] embraces two-thirds of the republic's territory—the only exception is the relatively quiet Pacific strip." The Soviet reporters added that the economy was a shambles as well. "The majority of the stalls at the large central market in Managua are empty. There is no rice, meat, poultry or eggs. The price of tomatoes and potatoes has gone up several times in the last year." The only suggestion that *Izvestia* made to its Nicaraguan wards was to redouble their internal repression.

As the Soviets digested this gloomy picture, Sandinista defense minister Humberto Ortega announced the day before the Reagan-Wright announcement that he was proceeding with plans to receive MiG fighter jets from the Soviet Union. "We have the airfield; we have the men," Ortega boasted. He claimed that only technical glitches in the advanced navigational systems needed for the MiGs had prevented their deployment. In fact, the Soviets were dragging their feet on keeping the commitment to supply MiGs to the Sandinistas. As early as 1984, Reagan had made it clear that fighters capable of hitting the United States were unacceptable and hinted that such planes could provoke an American air strike or even invasion. During the 1984 presidential campaign, Democratic nominee Walter Mondale had threatened to respond vigorously to any deployment of MiGs in Central America.

Of far greater impact was another broken Soviet promise, concerning oil. Of all the multiplying crises that the Sandinistas faced in the late 1980s, this was perhaps the most serious. As late as 1986, the Sandinistas had expected, and counted on, significantly increased shipments of Soviet petroleum to keep the domestic economy moving and to carry out operations against the contras. As Gorbachev, pressed by the economic pressure of the West, started looking for ways to economize, he dispatched Boris Yeltsin, then first secretary of the Moscow Communist Party, to Nicaragua to find out what use the Sandinistas were making of past Soviet largesse. Yeltsin was shocked to find that Nicaraguans paid only ten cents a gallon for gasoline, and he recommended that Gorbachev demonstrate his displeasure by reducing their oil exports.

The Sandinistas were compelled to seek other sources. But trips by Sandinista officials to Iran, Algeria, Libya, Mexico, Venezuela, Peru, and Indonesia resulted in almost no help at all. The Sandinistas found that revolutionary solidarity, which they could offer, was far less attractive than hard currency, which they could not offer. Even pleas to Western European and Latin American states went unheeded. Eventually, the Soviets would provide only a two-month supply of oil and would wait until September to do so. Even then, the fuel they supplied was of such low quality that cars were emitting thick, black smoke and crop-dusting planes were crashing when their engines gave out in midflight.

The Sandinistas' oil crisis was largely the result of the U.S. embargo, although the Sandinistas' own inefficiency and mismanagement certainly made the problem worse. The United States closed off the most economically attractive source of oil, which was U.S. oil companies. The embargo also starved Nicaragua of hard currency by cutting off its exports, making it impossible for the Sandinistas to pay for oil on any but the most generous terms. Finally, the Reagan administration's public diplomacy operation had succeeded in souring segments of European and Latin American public opinion toward the Sandinistas, making governments in those regions less willing to help. Indeed, Sandinista officials themselves cited the country's economic crisis as one of the reasons they were willing to talk peace.

In the meantime, military pressure on the Sandinistas continued. In July, the contras launched a series of attacks in central Nicaragua, mostly directed against government militia, but occasionally engaging regular soldiers of the Sandinista army. In every case, the contras pulled back when government reinforcements arrived, evidence of their increased ability to communicate and coordinate. Also in July, the rebels taunted the Sandinistas by occupying La Palma, a medium-sized town on a major east-west highway, for eight hours. Only a few miles away, soldiers in two major Sandinista military bases stayed put, fearing an ambush.

As the Reagan-Wright plan was being unveiled in Washington, American journalists discovered that the contras had, finally, achieved an internal base of support in Nicaragua. The peasants of Chontales province, on the eastern side of Lake Nicaragua, actively and willingly gave their support to the contras. According to the *Wall Street Journal*, in a story later confirmed by other sources, young Nicaraguans from the province joined the rebels by the hundreds, and hundreds more residents gave the contras food, shelter, and information. The Sandinistas themselves acknowledged the contras' successes in the province but chalked them up to the fact that Chontales was dominated by "large landowners, conservatives, and politically backward people."

The situation was bad enough that the Sandinistas had to stop delivering boots and batteries to Chontales, since the peasants gave the boots to the contras and used the batteries to listen to clandestine contra radio broadcasts. The rationing only served to further alienate the local population from the Sandinista regime. In other provinces, the contras had less success, but this was due in part to more successful Sandinista counterinsurgency operations. Since many of these operations included forced relocations, the Sandinistas were undercutting their support and further damaging the economy at the same time.

The contras, and the U.S. officials in contact with them, also found that humanitarian aid was nearly as useful to the rebels as military aid. While there are no substitutes for Stinger missiles, the contras were increasingly able to supply themselves by raiding government arsenals, dealing with corrupt government officials, or most frequently, trading their food and medicine with Nicaraguan peasants for militia weapons. As the economy of Nicaragua worsened, the contras found that food was a very valuable trade commodity.

The Sandinistas would, of course, learn that weapons intended for the local militia had been given away. The rumors of food availability alone insured that, and the local state security chiefs would often exact a terrible revenge on anyone caught dealing with the contras. Such repression made the contra cause more popular and made people more eager to deal with the contras. In some cases, peasants found themselves caught between contras, who would punish them for dealing with the government, and government officials who would punish them for dealing with the contras. But the rebels were itinerant; the government, represented by the state security watchdogs, was there all the time. As 1987 progressed, it was the Sandinista government that, fairly or not, received most of the blame for the wretched conditions in the Nicaraguan countryside.

The Opposition Opens a Second Front

The final wall in the box that was slowly but surely closing in on the Sandinistas was the growing boldness of the internal, democratic opposition to the Sandinistas. To the extent that the Arias plan had a salutary effect on the Nicaraguan struggle, it was primarily in providing opportunities for the Sandinistas' civilian opponents. On August 3, seven opposition political parties, from right wingers to Communists, met in Madrid and declared that they too must be part of any discussion on the political future of Nicaragua. Ridiculing the Sandinistas as a "Bonapartist" dictatorship, the opposition figures agreed that the contras, far from being a creation of the CIA, were a creation of the FSLN's repressive policies.

Deteriorating conditions inside Nicaragua also emboldened the internal opposition, making it grow exponentially. For most Nicaraguans, 1987 was a terrible year. Coffee, oil, and beer all disappeared nearly completely. Inflation in 1987 ran into five figures. (A pair of shoes cost twice the average worker's monthly salary.) At the same time, Nicaraguans began to see that not all Nicaraguans were suffering. Near the barren public markets were what Nicaraguans came to call the "diplos." These were originally secret stores, started for the convenience of the Soviets and their families. By 1987, their existence was notorious, since the Sandinistas opened them to anyone with dollars to spend.

Further hatred for the Sandinista regime resulted from the compulsory military service law, which undermined support for the Sandinistas among population groups that had once been their strongest supporters. Sandinista women's groups saw their membership decrease as women joined organizations of bereaved mothers. Young people, who had only vague memories of a time before the Sandinistas, saw their friends and brothers taken away for military service. Businesspeople, some of whom had been favored by the regime in an attempt to split the business class, became united in their opposition to the draft, since it robbed them of their labor force. As with the economic hardships, the pain of the draft was not evenly spread. Favoritism and corruption determined who got drafted and who did not.

Thus, while many contemporary accounts of the Arias plan focused on Reagan's alleged weakness, the crucial reality of 1987 was the Sandinistas' undeniable weakness. It was against the backdrop of the Sandinistas' declining fortunes that the tangled machinations of the various peace plans would take place.

Implementing the Arias Plan

The Devil Is in the Details

Of all the provisions of the Arias plan, none was more important to U.S. officials than the difficult and diseuphonious concept of simultaneity. In his memoirs, George Shultz is almost single minded in his attention to this detail. He assured Reagan, after a lengthy and seemingly defensive description of the Arias plan, that the multifaceted and highly complex proposal was a "victory" for the United States, because "to our relief and astonishment, its measures have simultaneity."

The greatest fear for the contras and their supporters was abandonment, that the aid to the rebels would be cut off in return for Sandinista promises. The rebels would consequently cease or curtail their operations, the pressure on the Sandinistas would thus be relieved, and the Sandinistas would, yet again, break their promises. Shultz seemed to be of the opinion that words on paper, committing the Sandinistas to simultaneity, and the possible opprobrium that would come from breaking their commitments, would be sufficient to insure Sandinista adherence to the Arias plan. The contras' conservative supporters, for their part, seemed to believe that only military pressure would compel Sandinista good behavior.

Reagan evidently did not subscribe to either view. For the president, the contras' military success, the Soviets' second thoughts about providing support, the economic deterioration and consequent loss of support among the Nicaraguan people, the pressure he was putting on Democrats in Congress not to abandon the contras, and the world's expectation that they would adhere to the Arias plan would all, in combination, bring about the outcome that Reagan most desired. This was the holding of free and fair elections in Nicaragua.

Much more important, Reagan evidently saw one feature of the Reagan-Wright plan as crucial. The House Speaker had signed on to a plan that linked contra aid to democratic reforms in Nicaragua and insisted on the latter. Wright had also committed to lining up his fellow Democrats to support democratization as well. While most commentators focused on the details of the plan, and on issues such as when the administration would be able to ask for more contra aid, they missed the fact that, for the first time since 1978, Democrats in Congress had agreed that democratization in Nicaragua meant free and fair elections in Nicaragua. From Reagan's point of view (which history showed to be correct), such elections meant the end of the Sandinista rule. Put differently, Reagan had gotten the House Democratic leader to adopt regime change in Nicaragua as official U.S. policy.

There is no doubt that Reagan would have preferred a well-funded, well-armed contra army, capable of bringing the Sandinistas to the bargaining table sooner, rather than later. However, Reagan was convinced by the summer of 1987 that substantial amounts of contra aid from Congress were simply not in the realm of possibility. This conclusion is the most important difference of opinion between Reagan and Washington conservatives, and the difference was the root cause of the unpleasantness between the president and his erstwhile supporters.

Closely connected to this was another difference of opinion over how long "Olliemania" was likely to last. Conservatives believed that Reagan should have demanded more aid, while public opinion was with him. I believe that many Washington conservatives, unaccountably, forgot just how skilled the Democratic majorities were in postponing votes that they did not wish to cast. Had Reagan made a new contra aid request in July 1987, while North was dominating the news, it probably would not have come up for a final vote until October, at the end of the fiscal year. Events have proven that support for the contras was back to pre-Ollie levels by then. Moreover, Reagan's proposal would have been delayed without any matching concession from the Democrats.

Lacking the political clout (or, to quote conservatives, the political will) to successfully fight for a large infusion of military aid to the contras, Reagan decided, no doubt reluctantly, that he would have to settle for keeping the contras in the field and keep them together as an armed and fighting force. He and the Nicaraguan people would have to wait longer, perhaps considerably longer, for the accompanying pressures on the Sandinistas to force them to open the polling booths.

To this end, Reagan spent considerable time, effort, and political strength in 1987 and 1988 fighting for contra aid. At a White House meeting in June 1987, Reagan told President Arias that he would not hesitate to seek more aid for the contras. Reagan dropped subtle reminders from time to time that neither the United States nor the contras was a party to the Arias plan, so neither was committed to ending U.S. contra aid. He also insisted that both the Reagan-Wright plan and the Arias plan include a provision compelling the Sandinistas to open direct negotiations with the contras, in spite of adamant refusals from Sandinista officials.

Reagan also insisted that a cease fire with the contras be accompanied by a reduction in the Soviets' aid to the Sandinistas and by such immediate democratization steps as a general amnesty for contras willing to lay down their arms, restoration of civil liberties, suspension of the 1982 emergency law, and establishment of an electoral commission. The Sandinista leadership had rejected every one of these concessions, repeatedly, prompting some observers to conclude that Reagan had only embraced Wright's proposal because he expected the Sandinistas to balk yet again and hoped to gain a propaganda advantage from their intransigence. Some liberals saw the entire Reagan-Wright exercise as a ploy. "Every time a contra aid vote comes up, they dangle something," said Sen. Tom Harkin (D-IA), "and nothing happens." Sen. Ted Kennedy (D-MA) added, more bluntly, "It is a sham from beginning to end."

If the Sandinistas did agree to the plan, the Reagan administration promised to end the trade embargo and make Nicaragua eligible for U.S. foreign aid on the same basis as other countries in the region. It is possible that Reagan might have permitted the inclusion of these economic carrots to insure that the leveraged ally faction of his administration was fully supportive of the initiative. If this was the case, then it is more likely that Reagan did not wish the plan to succeed, since he was not in the habit of granting real power to the leveraged ally faction if he could help it. I believe the most likely explanation is that Reagan never liked the embargo to start with, knew that foreign aid could always be adjusted later, and was willing to promise a lot to get Jim Wright to embrace regime change in Nicaragua.

The Arias Plan Takes Center Stage

To the surprise of absolutely no one, the Sandinistas immediately dismissed the Reagan-Wright plan. To the calls for a reduction in Soviet aid, the Sandinistas simply replied that their foreign relations were not the business of the United States. To calls for democratization, Daniel Ortega replied that such demands were interference in Nicaragua's internal affairs and that "We [the FSLN] have been developing democracy in Nicaragua since the revolution." The Sandinistas' foreign minister added mockingly that he might have some suggestions on how to improve U.S. democracy as well. Once again, talks with the contras were loudly rejected.

One day after rejecting the Reagan-Wright plan, Ortega signed the Arias plan, which had many of the same features. The Sandinistas agreed, at least on paper, to an amnesty for government opponents; a cease-fire in the contra war; a series of democratization measures, including complete freedom of the press, political freedom for all groups and free and fair regular elections under international monitoring; and an end to external funding for insurgents. The measures in the agreement, alternatively called the "Arias plan" or "Esquipulas II," were to take effect "simultaneously and in a public form" within ninety days.

There were two differences between the Arias plan and the Reagan-Wright plan, neither of which had much to do with the substance of what the Sandinistas had agreed to do. First, the Arias plan did not forbid Nicaragua from continuing to receive military aid. As we have seen, however, changing Soviet priorities, much more than pieces of diplomatic paper, were already reducing Soviet aid. Second, the Arias agreement was multilateral rather bilateral. For many Reagan critics, this second difference was the crucial one. Reagan is often pictured in the press (by his opponents) as enraged and shocked that the Central American presidents created an agreement without U.S. direction.

This image if Reagan is not based on any firsthand evidence, and it is at variance with Reagan's known political preferences and management style. Reagan did not mind when allies with an interest in common with the United States acted on their own initiative. While he strongly, and sometimes overbearingly, protected U.S. interests, Reagan happily deferred to Margaret Thatcher, Helmut Kohl, Pope John Paul II, Eugenia Charles, and others when they undertook policies and initiatives that Reagan supported. Indeed, one of Reagan's most often-quoted sayings was, "It's amazing what you can accomplish if you don't care who gets the credit."

Such delegation was also consistent with Reagan's management style. As he had done many times during his gubernatorial and presidential administrations, Reagan set broad policies and allowed others to work out the details. In the case of Central America, and especially Nicaragua, Reagan's broad policy was to deny the Soviets a strong ally and to protect and promote democracy in the region. If Wright would do some of the heavy lifting to bring these goals about, so much the better. If the democratically elected Central American presidents were willing to be out front putting pressure on Ortega to democratize, better still.

Moreover, there is every reason to believe that Reagan and the U.S. power he administered were a large part of the Esquipulas negotiations, even if no official U.S. representatives were there. First of all, the contra leadership was present, a not-so-silent reminder that, six years after they appeared, and in spite of the Sandinistas' massive military buildup, the contras were making steady, sometimes spectacular, military progress. Second, Arias himself said, "I was able to persuade my colleagues that either we reach an agreement today [August 7] or there will be an escalation of war." He added that Ortega had agreed, as did El Salvador's Duarte, because he was "quite desperate."

The Sandinistas Make Concessions, and More Concessions . . .

The Reagan administration's reaction to the Arias plan was cautious. (Some officials, like Secretary of Defense Caspar Weinberger, were completely opposed to the plan.) Reagan released a statement that said, in part: "The United States will be as helpful as possible consistent with our interests and the interests of the Nicaraguan resistance who have already stated their readiness to take part in genuine negotiations for peace and democracy in Nicaragua." The Sandinista leaders, for their part, left Guatemala immediately after the Arias plan was signed, to avoid answering any questions about it. One of the questions they wished to avoid was whether or not they had just agreed to negotiations with the contras, as the latter insisted. The plan called for national cease fires and committed each nation "to carry out all the actions necessary to achieve an effective cease-fire." It was unclear how the Sandinistas could do this without speaking directly to the contras.

Perhaps feeling the trap starting to close in, Ortega tried delay and temporizing media shows. The Tuesday after the peace summit in Guatemala, the Nicaraguan president met with Cardinal Miguel Obando y Bravo and representatives of eleven opposition political parties to talk about creating the National Reconciliation Commission. Ortega had less than three weeks to establish such a commission, and he probably hoped to either catch the opposition parties off guard by moving fast or to exploit what he expected to be bitter disputes among the eleven parties over which ones would be represented.

By the time the meeting was over, Obando had deviated from the script enough to get Ortega to agree to the reopening of Radio Católica. And instead of haggling over seats on the Reconciliation Commission from the political leaders, Ortega reportedly heard a chorus of demands that the other democratization provisions of the Arias plan be implemented, starting with the lifting of the Emergency Law and complete freedom of the press. Instead of gratitude for holding the meeting, Ortega got criticism. "It was a publicity show more than anything," said one democratic leader. President Arias supported the opposition leaders, saying that the peace plan could not work without press freedom in Nicaragua.

The day after the meeting, Ortega made an unannounced trip to Cuba to meet with Fidel Castro. Although the Cuban dictator expressed his support for the Arias plan, and ostensibly made plans to reduce the number of Cubans in Nicaragua, he gave scant material support. Castro himself was being squeezed by the Soviet Union, and he was not in a position to do much for Ortega. Similarly, Gorbachev's support was becoming more symbolic than substantive. With great fanfare, Ortega bragged in September that had been invited to Moscow for the celebration of the seventieth anniversary of the Russian Revolution. He ended up coming home two days early, before the celebration actually took place, and he came home empty handed.

In late August, Ortega was on the defensive again. He announced that the National Reconciliation Committee would include three opposition figures: Cardinal Obando y Bravo; Mauricio Diaz, president of the opposition Social Christian Party; and an Evangelical Christian leader. The Sandinistas would have one representative. Ortega took the unprecedented step, after five years of referring to the contras as "mercenaries," of admitting they were "Nicaraguans after all."

At the same time, probably to insure Obando's service, without which the commission would have no credibility, the Sandinista president announced that two banished Catholic leaders would be permitted to return. Bishop Pablo Antonio Vega and Monsignor Bismarck Carballo had been expelled in 1986 for their outspoken criticism of the regime. (Carballo had been attacked and stripped by a Sandinista mob in a clumsy attempt to frame him for sexual misconduct.)

The Sandinistas were playing for time, though, at a point in the struggle in which time favored the contras. Even while making concessions that were alternatively cosmetic and substantive, the Nicaraguan leaders were promising the Sandinista faithful that they were not serious about negotiating with the rebels, and even less serious about ever giving up power. Bayardo Arce spoke to a Sandinista party conference in November promising that there would never be "direct or indirect political dialogue with the leaders of the counterrevolution."

More Battles over Contra Aid

When the Arias plan was unveiled in August 1987, American conservatives warned that Democrats in Congress would use it as an excuse to delay any vote on contra aid well past the September 30 date in the Reagan-Wright plan. Even Vice President Bush, always reluctant to voice even the slightest hint of public disapproval of Reagan's actions, said that the United States should not let the contras "twist slowly in the wind." On this point, the conservatives were correct. Wright, abandoning his own plan less than seventy-two hours after it was announced, said that he saw little reason to vote on further military aid while the peace process in Latin America was going on.

However, Wright left a huge loophole in his statement. The Speaker said that he would have no objection to continued humanitarian aid to the contras for the interim period, during which time the Sandinistas' adherence to the plan would be assessed. As we have seen, by 1987, humanitarian aid was almost as useful to the contras as military aid, and it certainly permitted the rebels to remain in the field. As long as they were a viable force, they still constituted a source of fear to the Sandinistas.

The Sandinistas played the only card left in their hand: to insist that more contra aid would mean abandonment of the entire "peace process." Nicaraguan Vice President Sergio Ramirez fired the opening salvo in mid-August. "If President Reagan says he supports the Guatemala agreement, but does not end the counter-revolution, he is sinking the agreement." The Sandinistas also asserted that the terms of the Arias plan required that high-ranking American officials open direct talks with the Sandinistas. This claim was pure bluff, since the United States was not even a party to the Esquipulas agreement and thus was not bound in any way by its terms, even if those terms could be interpreted to require bilateral U.S. talks with Nicaragua.

Unaccountably, however, the Sandinista position was echoed by Philip Habib, the U.S. special envoy to Central America. He had reacted to the Arias plan by publicly calling for U.S. involvement in peace talks with Nicaragua. Since 1984, Reagan had said that such talks would only take place if the Central American democracies were part of the process as well. Habib's idea was rejected, and the special envoy interpreted the rejection as evidence that the hard liners had reasserted control over Central America policy. He announced his resignation, and Congressional Democrats were quick to sing his praises, to lament his departure, and to charge that Reagan was not serious about peace in the region. After Habib's resignation, a spokesman for Wright warned Reagan that an aid request on October 1 would be voted down, "even if there is no cease fire" in place at the time. "The vote would be pretty clear," he said.

Reagan had to reset the terms of debate. The issue, he reminded the press and other Americans, was democratization in Nicaragua. This goal was embraced by the Speaker on August 3. Regardless of the machinations of negotiations, statements, peace plans, and contra aid votes, it was this goal, and nothing less, to which Reagan was committed. He and his aides started using the words *verifiable* and *irreversible* as the measures of democratization steps undertaken by the Sandinistas. For Reagan, military pressure from the contras was absolutely indispensable in bringing about true democratization in Nicaragua. For Reagan, a democratic Nicaragua was the only guarantor of peace in the Central American region. In statements throughout August, the president made it clear that he would not be deterred from seeking new contra aid.

Reagan's statements also made clear that he rejected what some prominent foreign policy figures were touting as a compromise outcome. Former Carter officials such as Viron Vaky, assistant secretary of state for Latin America in the previous administration, suggested that the Sandinistas could be left alone if they ceased getting aid from the Cubans and Soviets and stopped threatening their neighbors. Shultz had been angling for such an outcome for years. In effect, it amounted to containing the Sandinistas but allowing them to remain in power indefinitely. But such a guarantee for the Sandinistas would leave all their neighbors threatened, since U.S. commitment to containment could wane over time. It would make the four Central American democracies permanent leveraged allies. A new political war was on, with fronts in Washington and Central America.

The administration began by recalling all its ambassadors from Central America for new instructions and talking points on the Arias plan. They were told that while the Guatemala accords were a good beginning, they were only a framework for further discussion. Such further discussion had to include verification of cease-fires and democratization. Elliott Abrams summed up the administration attitude: "We're working with the agreement, not against it. But in our view that means keeping your hand on your wallet."

Reagan met with the contra leadership in Los Angeles. The meeting was intended to reassure the contras, their conservative backers, and members of Congress that no abandonment was in the works. Reagan agreed to make a broadcast over Radio Liberación, the contras' clandestine station. In the broadcast, which was made on August 24 and 25, Reagan told Nicaraguans that "the journey's end is Nicaragua libre." He referred to Sandinista promises about democratization, saying, "[T]he Sandinistas have told us that before, but no one believes the Sandinistas anymore." The United States would support the contras "until the people of Nicaragua are guaranteed basic liberties." Unfortunately, the White House press office released a transcript of the broadcast before it actually took place, and the Sandinistas jammed the transmission. Word of mouth, however, got the message to most Nicaraguans. The very gesture of speaking for the contras' radio, which was unprecedented, spoke louder than Reagan's words.

Once again, the Sandinistas chose the worst possible moment to underline the need for skepticism about their commitment to democracy. While the U.S. ambassadors were meeting in Washington, Sandinista police raided the headquarters of the Permanent Commission on Human Rights using electric cattle prods and German Shepherds. Lino Hernández, the head of the commission, and Alberto Saborio, a leader of the opposition Conservative Party, were arrested; files were seized; and onlookers were assaulted. Hernández and Saborio were sentenced to thirty days for "disturbing the public order."

Conservatives in Congress responded to the attack by pressing for a large contra aid package. On the Republican side, Reagan was assisted by the jockeying for position going on among those vying for the 1988 Republican Presidential nomination. As we have seen, George H. W. Bush spoke out more strongly than usual on the issue, and on August 31, Senate Republican Leader Bob Dole (R-KS) led a delegation of senators to Central America. During the group's stop in Managua, Dole engaged in a public argument with Daniel Ortega. Dole confronted the Nicaraguan leader with his dependence on Moscow, his disregard for civil liberties, and his dependence on Communist advisors. Dole certainly realized that nothing would endear him more to conservative Republican primary voters (who were extremely skeptical of him) than shepherding a contra aid bill through the Senate.

The month of August, which had included so much political and diplomatic maneuvering, ended with a very effective ten-day offensive by the contras. Especially satisfying for the contras and their supporters were the images of Soviet helicopters destroyed by U.S. missiles. In addition, the contras claimed 483 Sandinista casualties during the late summer offensive. The Sandinista defense minister, for his part, discounted the rebels' successes and insisted that they already faced "strategic defeat."

As 1987 neared its close, Reagan spoke more and more forcefully on the need for more contra aid and his determination not to abandon the resistance. Reagan promised, "We will not accept a mere semblance of democracy." He quoted Arias, who had said repeatedly that peace would not come to the region until Nicaragua achieved "true democracy." Reagan also asserted that any progress that had been made in Nicaragua was due to the efforts of the contras. His speech to ranking administration officials included a blunt warning: "If the recent peace agreement does not work, let's resolve that [the contras] will be able to count on our continuing assistance until Nicaragua is a genuine democracy." The following day, Reagan had Shultz carry a proposal for $270 million in aid for the contras to Capitol Hill.

The new contra aid request kicked off the most intense lobbying effort that the administration had ever made on the issue. When the Democratic leadership in Congress delayed the request until February 1988, a long battle over Central America was inevitable. The White House girded for the coming political war by holding daily meetings, chaired by National Security Advisor Colin Powell and Elliott Abrams, to go over strategy for getting the contras more money.

One of the early fruits of these discussions was a meeting between Powell and moderate Democrats, in which Powell got a crucial concession from the group. The National Security advisor proposed that some of the humanitarian aid that Congress had provided, and was still willing to provide, might be used for "maintenance of the contras in the field." Powell also referred to the contra army's "deferred maintenance expenses." He was really referring to the helicopters and supply trucks that the contras used to get humanitarian and military aid. The same helicopters were used to transport troops and scout Sandinista positions. The gambit was successful, and it bought valuable time for the contras.

Reagan also recognized early on that much depended on the continued role of Obando y Bravo. Only the Cardinal could put enough pressure on the Sandinistas, and retain enough global credibility in the process, to prevent the Sandinistas reneging on their commitments. The president even used a private meeting with Pope John Paul II in Miami to ask the pontiff to reduce Obando's ecclesiastical duties so that he could spend more time monitoring and mediating the peace talks in Nicaragua.

The Sandinistas, for their part, continued efforts to make contra aid seem to be the one roadblock in the way of peace in the region. Returning early from a trip to Moscow in November, Ortega seemed to promise several large steps forward. He said he would begin indirect talks with the contras, free thousands of political prisoners, and lift the state of emergency. He then added that none of this would be possible without an end to contra aid.

Now it was the contras' turn to be ingenuous. Their leadership simply ignored Ortega's demand that contra aid be stopped and announced that they were thrilled to hear that the Sandinistas had finally agreed to indirect talks. "We consider this a triumph for the resistance," said Alfonso Robelo, one of the contras' six directors. Alfredo César, another contra director, crowed, "[Ortega] went to Moscow, and there, I am sure, Gorbachev told him he had to negotiate. Ortega went home and told them they had no choice but to do it." Talks were set for the first week in December in the Dominican Republic.

Military successes, especially against the Sandinistas' air force, emboldened the contras' political leaders to take a harder line in their talks with the government. While the Sandinistas insisted that the talks in the Dominican Republic were only about the technicalities of a ceasefire, the contras handed the government representatives a document demanding political concessions. These included disbanding the Sandinista mobs, lifting the state of emergency, and ending the draft, an issue that would bedevil the Sandinistas. Obando prevented a threatened Sandinista walkout by promising the gathered international media that there would be more talks between the two sides, before Christmas.

The civilian opposition to the Sandinistas also took a hard line. A united group of fourteen political parties grew bolder in denouncing the Sandinistas and demanding such political concessions as limiting the president to one term and separating the army and the police forces from the Sandinista party. All the while, internal opposition was growing as the Nicaraguan economy continued its collapse and the Sandinistas blatantly insulated themselves from the suffering accompanying that collapse. The Sandinistas' neighbors were also growing more hostile. In spite of the opposition of President Arias, for example, the Gallup poll found that 77 percent of Costa Ricans favored U.S. military aid to the contras.

The Sandinistas' prestige and credibility took a further tumble with the defection of Major Roger Miranda, who left Nicaragua in October, after serving as a close aide to Defense Minister Humberto Ortega. When he arrived in the United States, Miranda was carrying documents that showed the Sandinistas to be engaged in a massive, long-term military buildup that would result in over half a million Nicaraguans serving in the armed forces. The huge army was to be backed up with advanced Soviet weapons, including MiGs, and provided with plans for attacks on neighboring countries.

The threat of spectacular charges coming from the Reagan White House, based on Miranda's revelations, prompted Defense Minister Ortega to preempt Reagan by describing the proposed military buildup himself, in a speech on December 13. Ortega confirmed everything that Miranda charged, even admitting that the future Sandinista army would be larger than Miranda's claims by almost one hundred thousand. Ortega also confirmed that his government was seeking Soviet MiGs and other advanced weapons, and he was defiant in his speech to a picked audience in Managua: "[Self-defense] is a right that we are not going to renounce, whether Mr. Reagan likes it or not."

Ortega made a crucial mistake in his speech, however. He reported that the Sandinistas were counting on a cutoff of U.S. aid to the contras, after which they anticipated defeating the contras, by 1989 at the latest. The huge army, however, would not be in place until 1990. In other words, the Sandinistas themselves acknowledged that they were not putting six hundred thousand men in uniform to defeat the contras. The unavoidable conclusion was that the Sandinistas were not committed to democracy, not committed to peace, and therefore not negotiating in good faith.

Only sustained pressure could keep the peace process moving forward. Daniel Ortega made an even more revealing comment, saying the huge army would remain even if relations with the United States were "normalized." "We are not defended by any military pact," Ortega complained. "The United States can do anything it wants against Nicaragua and nobody is going to defend us." If any Americans harbored doubts that relations between Managua and Moscow had changed, Ortega's perhaps unwitting revelation put them to rest. At the same time, other reports from Nicaragua spoke of ammunition shortages among government soldiers and growing frustration among Sandinista leaders with their increasingly undependable Soviet suppliers. High desertion rates forced the Sandinistas to hold soldiers' family members as hostages during their military service.

The Miranda revelations were an embarrassment for the opponents of contra aid. Liberal Senator Chris Dodd (D-CT) fumed, "Obviously, this doesn't help. The timing wasn't very good at all." House Speaker Jim Wright dismissed news of the proposed buildup as "preposterous" at the time and later suggested that the Miranda disclosures were nothing more than a fantasy of Frank Carlucci, Reagan's new defense secretary. He never mentioned that no less an authority than the Sandinista defense minister confirmed every claim that Miranda made. For more moderate Democrats, less committed to either a single peace plan or to insuring a defeat for Reagan, the Miranda disclosures were food for thought.

On December 20, the contras launched a new series of attacks. Some seven thousand contras, the largest contra force mobilized at one time in the war, attacked the gold-mining areas of eastern Zelaya province and the landing strips that served as the only reliable transport in and out of the area. In addition to the gold mines, the area contained huge Sandinista munitions stockpiles and radar and tracking stations that the government forces used to attack incoming rebel supply planes. The contras also destroyed a hydroelectric facility used to run the mines and process the gold.

The spectacularly successful attacks hurt the Sandinistas in three vital areas. First, by severely interrupting gold mining operations, the contras cut the Sandinistas off from the one asset that they might have used to increase arms supplies from the Soviet Union. By late 1987, the USSR itself was in serious economic trouble and would certainly have been tempted to accept gold as payment for arms. Second, by capturing most of the munitions dumps intact, the contras were able, for the first time in the civil war, to match the Sandinistas in weaponry, at least for awhile. The Sandinistas' draftee army was short of weapons for some time, hurting morale and fighting efficiency. Third, by destroying the radar tracking system, the contras were able to insure their own supply line.

In addition to all this, the contras found that the eastern part of the country was most severely affected by a nationwide drought, allowing the contras to trade food with the local peasants for information. Sandinista duplicity in dealing with the locals was also made obvious. The contras found depots containing fifty tons of food, of which the starving local people were not even aware.

At the end of 1987, the momentum was with Reagan and his request for contra aid. On December 12, the Senate approved $12 million in nonmilitary aid and used an unusual "standing vote" procedure to do so. Before approving the aid, the Democratic-controlled Senate rejected an amendment that would have placed the funds in escrow. As a result of Powell's dealings, the Senate package also included funds to transport the aid. House Democrats, for their part, settled for the completely symbolic and, in the words of one congressman, "seismically unconstitutional" ban on Reagan's soliciting other governments for contra aid.

A Battle Is Won, and Another Battle Is Postponed

Reagan finally threatened to veto any deficit reduction package that did not contain contra aid. His threat bore fruit just before Christmas when the administration and congressional leaders agreed upon $8.1 million in nonlethal aid to the contras. Under the complex agreement, Congress appropriated both humanitarian assistance and the means to transport it to the contras. In addition, previously authorized military aid, left over from the $100 million the contras received in 1986, could be delivered to the contras, "commingled" with the new aid, until January 12, 1988. For the following week, during which time the Central American presidents would hold a previously scheduled meeting to assess the progress of the Arias plan, no U.S. aid could be delivered. Commingled aid could resume, if there were no cease-fire in place, until February 4. On that day, Congress would hold an up-or-down vote on further aid to the rebels.

The compromise gave both sides something to use to claim victory. Reagan got aid to the contras, the release of more military aid, transport funds, and the certainty of a vote on the matter early in 1988. The Democrats got six additional weeks for the shock of Miranda's revelations and the Ortega brothers' statements to wear off. On balance, Reagan got far more of what he wanted than the Democrats did, but at the cost of a considerable loss of momentum. Democrats may have calculated that the unusually effective White House public relations effort could not last long.

It is important to note that Reagan got at least half a loaf on contra aid when he threatened to veto a major spending bill. Veterans of the Washington political wars over Central America could not help but remember that Reagan had had the chance to use similar political muscle in October 1984 but refused to do so. Instead, he committed his administration to secret, off-the-books funding for the contras, with consequences that were nearly disastrous. Had Reagan shown the same resolution three years earlier, his administration might never have been damaged by Iran-contra, the United States would have been spared weeks of political trauma, and the contras might have brought the Sandinistas to the bargaining table three years and thousands of lives earlier.

The last year of the Reagan presidency would bring new battles for contra aid, but with a new feature: a definitive timetable for Congress to consider the matter and vote. Under the December agreement between the administration and Congress, the legislators would return to Washington on January 25 to hear Reagan's State of the Union Address. He would then have two days to decide whether or not to request more contra aid. Once he made the request, the House of Representatives would vote in early February. A senior administration official called the vote, "very, very critical." He added that if the administration failed to win the vote, lethal aid would be "over," and with it, the entire contra program.

The official would be proven wrong on this last point.

11

Endgame

My fellow Americans, there can be no mistake about this vote: It is up or down for Central America. It is win or lose for peace and freedom. It is yes or no to America's national security.

> —*Ronald Reagan*, February 2, 1988, the night before a
> congressional vote on aid to the contras.
> (The major networks refused to carry the speech.)

A New Contra Aid Battle

As 1988 opened, the stage seemed set for a resumption of military aid and a huge victory for President Ronald Reagan. The contras were enjoying significant military success. The Sandinistas were having no end of difficulties with the Soviets, with their internal civilian opposition, and with the peasants in the countryside, not to mention a terrible drought and the ravages of their own corruption and mismanagement. Revelations by a Sandinista defector portrayed the government as committed to aggression and an arms buildup. Even Costa Rican president Oscar Arias, whose peace plan seemed destined to lead to the end of contra aid, was having political problems at home, as his countrymen, confronted with plans for a six-hundred-thousand-man Sandinista army, grew skeptical about the ability of paper documents to hold back such an army.

Events in other parts of the region were also progressing in Reagan's direction. In El Salvador, negotiations between the government and the Communist rebels, mandated by the Arias plan, were proceeding, and real progress was being made. The government was releasing political prisoners, and regional cease fires were in place. Human rights abuses were declining, and more parts of the country were returning to something approaching normality. The election campaign for president and national assembly members was getting underway. In Honduras, the government's earlier declaration that it would close down contra bases was quietly reversed in the wake of the revelations about Sandinista military intentions (and in the wake of the delivery of new U.S. fighter planes).

Yet for the opponents of contra aid, and for the leveraged ally faction of the Reagan administration, all of the above meant looming disaster. The contras seemed to be having enough success to actually threaten the Sandinista government. A substantial portion of the Democrats in Congress and a significant part of the administration wished to see the Sandinista government left in place. For the moment, aid was coming from the Soviet bloc, but with Mikhail Gorbachev having his own problems, it seemed just a matter of time before the Sandinistas needed a replacement for Soviet aid. At the same time, the Sandinistas would still be enough of a threat to their neighbors to make those neighbors also dependent on a continued U.S. presence.

As expected, the Reagan administration made its request on time, in accordance with a 1987 agreement between Reagan and House Speaker Jim Wright (D-TX). In a move calculated to inform the leveraged ally faction that no interference from them would be tolerated this time, Reagan largely kept Shultz off the scene and gave the job of shepherding the aid request to Elliott Abrams and Colin Powell. Both had had considerable success on Capitol Hill.

Opponents of contra aid, however, presented a vote in favor of contra aid as a vote to prolong the Central America controversy. A "no" vote, however, would bring an "end" to the entire bitter contra argument, at least for the remainder of the Reagan administration. (No one on Capitol Hill believed that either Vice President Bush or any Democratic president would give the contras the priority that Reagan did.) Those who desired to leave the Sandinistas in power found a persuasive cloak for their intentions. A vote against contra aid, in their view, was a vote for "peace."

The administration's lobbying effort opened in mid-January with a tour of Central America by Assistant Secretary Abrams and National Security advisor Powell. In meetings with the presidents of the four democratic Central American countries, Powell urged the leaders to lobby Congress for contra aid. The aid was vital, Powell told them, because only the necessity of fighting the contras was restraining the Sandinistas from attacking their weaker neighbors. To this point, Powell was only putting long-harbored fears into words, and his message was straightforward enough. However, he went on to make the highly questionable statement that, in the event the Sandinistas did become aggressive, the democracies could not count on any help from the United States.

Not surprisingly, such a heavy-handed threat had exactly the opposite effect. The Central American presidents complained, made the threat public, and caused Powell and Abrams to be accused of clumsy and ignorant diplomacy. The trouble with these charges is that neither man was clumsy or ignorant. Both were veterans of high-level meetings with heads of state, and both were known for their rhetorical skills. Abrams had been to the region repeatedly, over several years; it is inconceivable that he did not anticipate that any threat made under the circumstances would backfire.

Abrams and Powell's motives, on which only speculation is possible, range from the ingenious to the disingenuous. On the one hand, they may have wanted a negative reaction, in the hopes that the administration would have to settle for a smaller or more temporary aid package, thus keeping the war going, to maintain U.S. leverage. Moreover, they may have deliberately shown the Central American presidents what the naked face of U.S. leverage looked like, to induce them to join Reagan in seeking to remove the source of that leverage, which was the Sandinistas. In the event, the Abrams-Powell tour represented a serious setback in the administration's efforts.

An even more serious obstacle appeared days later, wrapped in a hopeful disguise. Daniel Ortega made a dramatic announcement on January 16. At the end of a summit of the five Central American leaders, the Sandinista president said that he was lifting the state of emergency. In addition, he revealed plans for the first direct talks with the contras on a cease fire and a partial amnesty once the cease fire was in place. Ortega also promised to move forward on elections.

There was considerably less to these statements than met the eye. Ortega proposed to talk to the contras only about the technicalities of a cease fire. Such talks had already taken place and ended when the Sandinistas refused to discuss democratization. The Arias plan called for a complete amnesty, not a partial one. The only elections Ortega mentioned were for the Central American Parliament, which had not even been formed yet. Upon closer inspection, the Sandinista president's pledges seemed more designed to thwart Reagan on contra aid than to effect reconciliation in his own country.

In this regard, Ortega was successful. Congressional Democrats embraced his "opening" as a reason for voting against contra aid. Indeed, Ortega suggested that all of his "concessions" could be withdrawn if the rebels started getting U.S. military aid again. His hints were echoed by more blunt statements by his aides. Liberal media outlets praised Ortega for his efforts to "keep the peace plan alive." Even a cynical comment from a Sandinista official that his government had to keep the peace plan alive to stop contra aid did nothing to dampen enthusiasm for what some were already calling a "breakthrough." The *Chicago Sun-Times* cast Reagan as the obstacle to peace, writing that he was "defying" Ortega's peaceful intentions by making the request for contra aid.

Both the Reagan administration and the contras insisted upon face-to-face negotiations, with a neutral mediator, and they insisted that the talks, once convened, deal with "the roots of the Nicaraguan conflict." These demands were exactly what Wright had agreed to the previous summer and the sort of negotiations that Democrats had said for years were exactly what they wanted. But by refusing to acknowledge any difference between the cosmetic changes Ortega suggested and genuine concessions to democracy, Reagan's enemies managed to turn the debate into one in which Ortega represented peace, and Reagan called for more war. Rep. Lee Hamilton (D-IN) fretted that more contra aid might induce the Sandinistas to "desert the peace process."

Some congressional Democrats went beyond cheering Ortega from the sidelines. Speaker Wright led a delegation to San José in January to confer with the Sandinistas on strategy. Rep. David Bonior (D-MI), an outspoken liberal critic of the contras, reportedly told the Sandinistas exactly how to defeat contra aid in Congress without fully complying with the peace plan. After the meeting, Bonior had nothing but praise for Ortega's flexibility and sincerity. Perhaps at Bonior's suggestion, Ortega proposed January 26–27 as dates for the talks with the contras. These were the days on which Reagan had to present his contra aid request. On the same day, Ortega announced fulfillment of his promise on a partial amnesty by releasing seven opposition leaders from jail. Thousands more remained. One day after the seven were released, twelve other opposition leaders were arrested. Even with the lifting of the state of emergency, political prisoners were told only that they could now receive a trial. Release was still up in the air.

Reagan responded with one of the few tools still in his possession. He officially certified to Congress on January 19 that he did not believe that the Sandinistas were acting in good faith to comply with the Arias peace plan. That presidential certification allowed the United States to resume shipments of military supplies to the contras. Democrats were quick to spin the action as proof that Reagan only wanted to prolong the war. "Basically, it proves that the White House does not want peace in Central America," said one leading Democratic liberal. Sen. Chris Dodd added, "Every time the Sandinistas make a concession, the White House sees it as a major setback."

By the time of his State of Union Address, Reagan was visibly back-tracking on contra aid. The previous fall, Shultz had suggested that the administration would ask for $270 million in military and humanitarian aid. By January 21, the request had been trimmed to something "in the ballpark of $50 million" and Reagan assured Congress that most of the assistance would be in the form of nonlethal aid. Congressional Democratic leaders saw these concessions as signs of weakness and began to talk about defeating contra aid altogether. In fact, some congressional staff members began to speculate that the administration might withdraw the request. Administration officials emphasized that the lower request was proof that the contras were doing fine without so much military aid (which they were), but such truths were lost in the political maneuvering.

Rhetoric on the issue from the White House escalated. Taking the unusual step of rebuking a legislator by name, Marlin Fitzwater told the press, "Chris Dodd and others—they want a surrender, and they think a surrender is the best way to achieve peace. We disagree." Fitzwater went on to deflect criticism that he was "red baiting" by pointing out the harsh and vituperative oratory coming from the Democrats. Such a defense, at a time when there were more press outlets, might have been more effective. As it was, the major media showed only Fitzwater's criticism and permitted Dodd to respond. Fitzwater ended up looking more desperate than righteous. Senate Republican leader Bob Dole suggested it might be a good idea to delay the vote, scheduled for February 3. Democrats, sensing victory, insisted on the agreed date.

The Sandinistas also sensed victory and were emboldened enough to send the government mobs to attack opposition offices with rocks and bottles. Uniformed Sandinista police did nothing to stop the violence as the gathering broke up in panic. Ortega, still skillfully playing both good cop and bad cop, followed up this domestic intimidation by sending a letter "of peace and friendship" to Reagan on January 23. The Sandinista president told reporters that his letter contained "assurances" about U.S. "security concerns" in Central America.

Within days, the administration request was scaled back again and accompanied by the assurance that no more than 10 percent would be for military aid. Democrats in Congress responded to this further sign of weakness by insisting that any aid be immediately withheld, until such time as Congress voted again to release it. Retreating still further, the administration set to work finding a formula for releasing the aid that was mutually acceptable.

A crippling blow was delivered to Reagan's contra aid package on January 27. Rep. Tony Coelho (D-CA), the House majority whip, publicly promised that, if the administration's contra aid request were defeated, House Democrats would come back with their own proposal to provide humanitarian aid to the rebels. "We think once the February 3 vote is over, we will put something bipartisan together," Coelho said. "February 3 is a new beginning for us. We don't intend to turn our backs and run away." The proposed bipartisan plan gave moderate Democrats cover to vote against the president, while insisting that they were still supporting the contras.

Reagan, for his part, was saving one of the more powerful arrows in his quiver, an address to the nation on the subject. White House aides planned the speech for February 2, the eve of the vote.

Meanwhile, the long-awaited direct talks between the contras and the Sandinistas opened in San José, Costa Rica, on January 28. Three ranking Catholic officials were to serve as observers. (Obando was in Rome.) The contra leadership sought to underline their common cause with the civilian opposition by promising that no contra leader would serve in the Nicaraguan government or in any interim government that might be formed as a result of the talks. At the same time, the contras insisted on a prominent role for the representatives of the civil opposition and repeated their demand that Obando mediate the talks. *Achieving national unity* became the contras' new catchphrase.

The talks broke no new ground. The contras insisted on linking a cease fire with democratization in Nicaragua, as called for in the Arias plan. The Sandinistas called the proposal "absurd." The chief Sandinista negotiator wanted to talk only about the size and location of cease fire zones and methods of disarming the contras. It soon became clear that both sides were awaiting the outcome of the congressional vote.

As the showdown neared, it often seemed as though the entire previous seven years of debate and strife on Capitol Hill were being reprised in a matter of days. Halls of the congressional office buildings were crowded with citizens seeking to lobby their representatives and senators. Sandal-wearing religious leaders repeated ancient charges against the Somoza government and attacked U.S. foreign policy. Antiadministration visitors to Capitol Hill predominated, and Reagan's opponents grew more confident, as moderate Democrats lined up to support the promised "bipartisan plan." Only the possibility that Reagan would sway the nation with his televised speech gave them pause.

They need not have worried; most of the nation, including the nation's capital, never heard or saw Reagan's speech. In a stunning display of raw political power, all three of the broadcast networks refused to air the presidential address. An ABC official sniffed, "The thinking is, his remarks on this subject have been made many times before." Other network executives insisted that there had been enough debate on the issue, a statement belied by the fact that all three morning news shows featured debates on the issue the morning after the presidential address. Reagan in his diary called the networks' censorship "an unprecedented affront [which] reveals where their sympathies lie—right with the Communist govt of Nicaragua."

Only the Cable News Network ran the speech live. Since Washington, DC, did not have cable at the time, no one in Washington saw the speech. In most of the nation, cable was still not available either, and, in any event, the people of the United States had not yet acquired their taste for cable news. ABC, CBS, and NBC were still most Americans' source for news. Reagan appeared only in excerpts, and only at 11:00p.m.

It will never be known whether or not Reagan would have changed any minds or any votes had he not been censored by the networks. While the network officials were correct in saying that Reagan's speech did not contain much that was new, it might very well have been given to a new audience, since there had never been a presidential address on Central America that had received as much advance buildup as this one, on a vote that was widely perceived to be the final showdown on contra aid of the Reagan administration. Moreover, Reagan had always been his administration's most potent and most persuasive speaker. The officials who appeared on the morning shows the next day were considerably less persuasive.

When the End Is Not the End

When the votes were counted in the U.S. House of Representatives on February 3, Reagan and the contras came up short, 219–211. Eight votes separated Reagan from victory. After the vote, Speaker Wright smugly promised to get to work on a package of "truly humanitarian aid." Had Reagan had all the members of his own party behind him, he would have won. Forty-seven Democrats voted for the aid package.

After the initial heartbreak of defeat in the House began to wear off, however, the White House began to see bits of evidence of a silver lining in the dark cloud. The first of these was the closeness of the vote itself. The second was the surprisingly large number of Democrats who voted for the full Reagan package, with military aid, even with the assurance that they would be able to vote for solely humanitarian aid in short order. A third bit of silver lining occurred on the following day when the Senate voted 51–48 to support the president.

It began to occur to observers in the United States and in Nicaragua that the phrase *final vote* is meaningless on Capitol Hill. Especially in an election year, chances were good that another vote could occur. Indeed, only days after the vote, White House sources told the *Chicago Sun-Times* that Reagan could renew his request by having a Republican member of Congress attach it to an appropriations bill and thus bypass the committee process. While most analysts downplayed the possibility of any aid renewal, they agreed that a sudden change of course from Managua, which looked like a betrayal of the Arias peace plan, could change the atmosphere instantly.

Ortega himself acknowledged that the "no" vote from Congress did not relieve the pressure on his regime. "The President [Reagan] will try to change the vote," Ortega said the day after the Senate vote. "This is not a closed matter." House Majority Whip Coelho agreed: "We'll have ten votes on contra aid this year. This thing's not over with yet." Even the *New York Times*, perhaps the contras' worst enemy, editorialized, "It feels good to say [no], but that can't be the last word."

Having said this, there is no doubt that both Reagan and the contras would have preferred a positive vote from Congress. Having failed, they had to put the best face on what happened and make the best use of what they had. What Reagan had, first and foremost, was a contra army that was still in the field and, thanks to leftover supplies from the 1986 money, was in a position to keep fighting for nearly a year without more military aid from the United States. (However, the contra force could probably not grow any larger during that year.) That reality alone forced the Sandinistas to remain on a war footing, keep the draft in place, continue to beg the Cubans and Soviets for aid, and maintain at least the pretense of reforming the regime. The box that surrounded the Sandinistas was no larger, nor any more porous, than it had been before the vote. The contras themselves defiantly vowed to continue fighting.

Reagan also had a commitment from Speaker Wright to bring a package of humanitarian aid to the House floor as soon as possible. Wright was receiving pressure to keep his promise not only from the White House but also from a substantial number of his colleagues who were worried about their upcoming reelection campaigns. An aide to one moderate Democrat told the *St. Louis Post-Dispatch*, "We want to keep the contras as a stick, to help insure serious negotiations." A nonlethal aid package would help do that, especially since money for one purpose would free up money for another purpose.

Liberal Democrats in Congress knew that any aid from the U.S. government would permit the contras to use money from other sources for weapons. Reagan's opponents were also caught off guard when George Shultz refused to rule out soliciting aid from third countries. But with the elections coming up, even liberals recognized the potent threat of seeming too soft on the Sandinistas. Sen. Chris Dodd floated the possibility that a new aid package could actually contain military aid. Perhaps belatedly, Democrats realized that their future was tied to the behavior of a Communist dictator.

One week after the "final" rejection of contra aid by the House, it was the congressional leadership that came to Reagan with a plea that he and Shultz get involved directly in negotiations over the replacement package of humanitarian aid. In what must have been a jarring show of strength, the White House spokesman replied, "We want to see what their [the Democrats'] proposal is before we make a commitment to support it. They rejected our plan, and now the American people have a right to see what they offer the resistance." Days later, Wright had to suddenly cancel a roll call on a Democratic plan to provide humanitarian aid when it became clear he could not deliver enough Democratic votes, and Republicans refused to make his task any easier.

Exploring the Political Road

The Civilian Opposition Comes to the Fore

For all the silver lining, however, with the cutoff of direct military aid to the contras, it was clear that they were not going to win an outright military victory. There would be no triumphal entry into Managua like the Sandinistas had in 1979. The path to democracy in Nicaragua would be a political one. The Sandinistas' civilian opposition would have to come to the fore, with the contras acting as the "stick" to prevent the Sandinistas from reinstituting oppression. Refusing to permit the opposition to speak out would have led to huge protests that would have required heavy-handed and highly visible tactics to overcome. Even the Scandinavian countries, the only non-Communist friends the Sandinistas had left, would have punished such repression severely. The only conceivable way for the Sandinistas to regain the initiative was with massive Soviet support. Gorbachev, trapped in his own box and desperate to maintain a relationship with Reagan, was in no position to anger the American president by sending arms to Nicaragua, even assuming that the Soviet leader had any desire to do so.

Within hours of the February House vote, the civilian opposition became vocal. A leader of the Social Christian Party, considered closer to the Sandinistas than some of the other opposition parties, explained, "Congress has voted for the political option in Nicaragua, and that gives us more responsibility to take on the Sandinistas. We do not seek to overthrow them. We only want democratic reforms that allow us to compete on equal terms." The leaders of a coalition of fourteen parties marched to the National Assembly with a list of demands. They included an end to Sandinista control of the army, the judiciary, and the electoral process; a bar on consecutive presidential terms; and abolition of open-ended security laws. The democratic coalition, recognizing one of the roots of Sandinista power, also insisted that their power over food rationing be discontinued.

The Sandinistas had never taken the civilian opposition seriously. On the one hand, as unarmed supplicants, the opposition leaders not only could be safely ignored but also could be easily threatened. But as the Sandinistas' arms caches grew smaller and smaller, with no sign of an end to the contra war, or any certainty of replacements, the Sandinista leadership had to be wary about provoking a violent confrontation that they might not be able to control. On the other hand, the Sandinistas were confident that they could take steps, such as favoring one party with membership in the reconciliation commission, to induce disunity among their opponents.

To the Sandinistas' surprise, however, the coalition did not fall apart. In fact, it was the Sandinistas who had to repeatedly deny rumors of internal strife. In most accounts, Interior Minister Tomás Borge wished to crack down on internal dissent, while others were more concerned about the political ramifications of such an action.

The civilian opposition was also becoming bolder, and its representatives used language unthinkable only months before. "We have the Sandinistas cornered," gloated a prominent business leader. "They've made too many errors, and now they have to pay the price." On February 8, riots over the draft took place in Monimbó, a small town in southern Nicaragua that had been the center of the first large anti-Somoza demonstrations in 1978. Even a local vendor of the official Sandinista newspaper joined in the protests. A store owner lamented that her store still had a pro-Sandinista mural on one side. "I'd paint over it," she said with disgust, "but there's no paint!"

Amidst such growing signs of defiance, the Sandinistas and contra representatives restarted their discussions in Guatemala in mid-February. With Obando y Bravo again serving as mediator, the talks revolved around cease fire proposals. Obando was now insisting, however, that any definition of the term *cease fire* would have to address political issues as well. Obando said that the Sandinistas should free all political prisoners, reopen the dialogue with the civilian opposition, and end the draft. In return, the contras would gather into cease fire zones for a thirty-day truce.

The Sandinistas walked out of the negotiations rather than broaden their subject matter, but when Obando publicly criticized them for doing so, they quickly backtracked, complaining that Obando was moving too quickly. The cardinal was indeed trying to force the pace, and he also embarrassed the Sandinistas by rejecting their proposal that one of their North American lawyers draw up a cease fire plan. At this point, it was the supposedly nationalistic Sandinistas who wanted American involvement in the peace talks.

Face to Face at Last

Obando's growing prestige and the spreading impression that he was indispensable to the credibility of the peace talks profoundly threatened the Sandinistas. Ortega needed a dramatic method of shoving the Cardinal aside, and on March 2, he unveiled it. The Sandinista president proposed direct talks between the Sandinistas the contras, with no mediator. To induce the contras to agree, he said that the talks would take place in the town of Sapoá, inside Nicaragua. For Ortega, this was a major concession. He and his Sandinista colleagues had always insisted that they would never talk directly to the contras and would certainly never do so in Nicaragua. (The Sandinistas had always demanded that Washington be the venue for the talks.) Ortega may have thought that the contras would refuse to talk without Obando present. By giving in on the site, Ortega could make the contras seem obstructionist, on the eve of another congressional vote.

Ortega's gambit was successful in the short run, since Congress did vote against contra aid on March 3. However, members on both sides of the aisle pressed for another vote as soon as the March 3 vote was taken. In the meantime, Ortega's proposal for talks was soon perceived to be his effort to "fire" Obando y Bravo. As such, it cost Ortega more than it cost either the contras or Obando. Nor would Ortega rid himself of the "troublesome priest," since the contra leadership, in accepting Ortega's proposal for face-to-face meetings, insisted on inviting the cardinal as a "witness for the Nicaraguan people." One contra called the cardinal's presence a "sine qua non condition for further negotiations." Among other things, the presence of Obando at negotiations inside Nicaragua would prevent the Sandinistas from throwing the entire contra leadership in jail before discussions even started.

The Sandinistas, bowing to international pressure, soon agreed to Obando as a witness and added the head of the Organization of American States (OAS) as a second witness. The contras had now achieved another historical irony; it was the OAS that negotiated the Sandinistas' entry to power nine years earlier.

As well as things were progressing in the prenegotiation political jockeying, things were not going well for the contras in the field. The Sandinistas, determined to maximize their strength before the negotiations, launched a major offensive at contra strongholds in northern Nicaragua. By the middle of March, the contras themselves acknowledged severe losses and admitted that most of their forces had been driven back across the Río Coco into Honduras. The Sandinista army pursued the rebels into Honduras and seized large contra supply stockpiles.

This proved to be another glaring political mistake for the Sandinistas. The Reagan administration immediately seized upon the Sandinista troops in Honduras to call the operation an invasion of a democratic, neutral country. Some White House sources suggested that Reagan was prepared to send the Eighty-second Airborne Division into combat to dislodge the Sandinistas from Honduras. As these plans were leaked, the Sandinistas waited for outrage and consternation from Americans.

To the horror of the Nicaraguan leadership, however, the response was muted. Many of the Sandinistas' best and most loyal supporters evidently believed that this new outrage, like so many others coming just after a congressional vote, was the last straw. Even worse, the invasion caused such strong international pressure that the Sandinistas had to stop short of the contras' main Honduran base camps. Thus, the offensive failed both militarily and politically.

In perhaps the most remarkable turnaround, the ultraliberal editorial page of the *Washington Post* excoriated the Sandinistas for the invasion and also excoriated Democrats for their failure to condemn the invasion strongly enough. Writing as though there had previously been some distinction between the *Post* and the Democratic leadership, the editorialist fumed, "Rather, Ortega is again faulted not for his policy but for his poor 'timing.' He is made to appear not hardheaded but hapless, not as a leader of a regime which just may give its neighbors the creeps, but as some sort of exasperating klutz." The same editorial went on to endorse a resumption of military aid to the rebels.

At home, the Sandinistas reacted with near-panic to the dispatch of thirty-one hundred American soldiers to central Honduras. Warning that a full-scale U.S. invasion of Nicaragua was imminent, they called upon their followers to deploy into the local militia brigades. The *Washington Post* called the exercise a "nationwide civil defense drill." What the *Post* did not report was that the drill was largely a failure. Even the threat of having their ration cards discontinued was not enough to draw many Nicaraguans from their homes. Those who did turn out, as often as not, used the occasion to denounce the Sandinista draft and make additional antiregime statements. When no U.S. invasion took place, the Sandinistas' credbility at home suffered another decline.

On Monday, March 21, the jockeying, symbolism, and gamesmanship were finally replaced by the long awaited face-to-face talks. The discussions were described as "frank and cordial" and had one immediate result. The two sides agreed to a cease fire in place while the three-day session was going on. The Sandinistas, for their part, still insisted that the Sapoa talks were only about military questions revolving around a more permanent cease fire. To that end, they sent their top military leaders to Sapoa. In the meantime, however, the FSLN reopened political talks with the civilian opposition in Managua. The civilian leaders, for their part, insisted that political issues be part of both negotiations, and the Sandinistas agreed. At the end of a single day of negotiations, civilian opposition leaders had gotten the Sandinistas to agree to a national dialogue, based on the seventeen points of democratization that the opponents of the regime had proposed months earlier.

The contras agreed to a sixty-day cease fire, to start on April 1, and to move into "cease-fire zones" too wide and too large for the Sandinistas to surround them. The talks produced an agreement from the Sandinistas to start freeing political prisoners and gradually to grant amnesty to political opponents. The two sides agreed to resume the talks on April 6 in Managua, a site the Sandinistas had always said was off limits for contra negotiations. In yet another reversal, Daniel Ortega himself showed up in Sapoa at the conclusion of the talks and signed the cease fire document on behalf of the government. His presence gave the contras another propaganda boost: a picture of Ortega face-to-face with Aldolfo Calero and the other contra leaders. Within minutes, the photo was broadcast all over the world. In addition, the government agreed to lift restrictions on the Nicaraguan media, so the picture of Ortega and Calero was soon available to Nicaraguans as well.

When the contras had organized their first political directorate, the Sandinista newspaper ran photos of the contra leaders, under the headline, "These Beasts Will Never Return." Tomás Borge had once stated that rivers would reverse their flow before any contra walked the streets of Managua. Bayardo Arce was the first of many Sandinistas to refuse to talk to the contras, saying, "We want to talk to the owner of the circus, not to the clowns." Borge, Arce and even the chief of the security police not only acceded to the accords with the contras; they took part in the discussions.

Back in Washington

The cease fire produced bipartisan agreement that more aid, at least more humanitarian aid, should start flowing to the contras again. Some moderate Democrats even spoke of including military aid, subject to a quick congressional vote on its release, should the ongoing peace talks in Nicaragua break down. In describing the need to have a well-fed and equipped contra force, to make sure that the Sandinistas kept negotiating, and negotiating in good faith, even liberal Democrats such as Jim Wright echoed what Reagan had been saying since 1983. The issue had come full circle; Reagan had won the argument. The aid package was ready by the end of March. Reagan's only concession was having the money administered by the State Department's Agency for International Development, instead of the CIA. The final vote in the Senate was 87–7. The House vote was 345–70.

Some important issues were left out of the Sapoa and Managua agreements, such as a promise by the Sandinistas to stop receiving aid from the Soviet bloc. The Sandinistas also did not agree to stop the growth of their military. They did not promise to send the Soviet and Cuban advisors home. They did not agree to power sharing. These omissions promoted some commentators, such as Constantine Menges and conservative columnist Charles Krauthammer, to describe the Sapoa talks as the contras' "surrender." Such pessimism was understandable at the time, since in the spring of 1988, the Berlin Wall was still solid, and talk of the fall of the Soviet Union was still reserved for dreamers. In retrospect, it is reasonably clear that Soviet arms supplies did not come up for the simple reason that the Sandinistas had almost no chance of getting any more. Without weapons, Soviet and Cuban advisors were not threats. And as to the growth in the Sandinista military, this was the issue that would eventually defeat the Sandinistas.

In the meantime, the political pressure on the Sandinistas was unrelenting. The two parts of the opposition to Ortega had become two claws of the same vice, slowly but surely moving together. They were a symbiotic pair. The contras could not overthrow the Sandinistas militarily, and the civilian opposition could not keep Ortega at the table making concessions without the shadow of the contras visible. That an organized, courageous, and effective civilian opposition still existed in 1988 was remarkable, after nine years of sedulous Sandinista attempts to supplant all "nonrevolutionary" political movements in Nicaragua. For the Sandinistas' defenders, the existence of the civil opposition was proof that the Sandinistas were not the Sovietlike totalitarian rulers that Reagan and other conservatives made them out to be.

Such apologias do not square with the facts. The clearest view of the Sandinistas' true intentions is what they actually did from 1979 through 1982, when they were without an effective armed opposition, or times since 1982 when they believed that they had the contras beaten. During all such times, the FSLN tried to eliminate a free press, tried to marginalize independent churches (and even to replace them with state-sponsored churches), destroyed free labor unions, persecuted Indians, postponed elections, and made innumerable other attempts to insure that only the Sandinista Front had political or military power in Nicaragua. Had the

Sandinistas had the leisure to do away with the opposition political parties that played key roles in the negotiations of 1988–89, they would have done so. Most civilian leaders themselves attributed their existence in 1988 to the preoccupation of the Sandinistas with the contras.

Having survived long enough to see the FSLN come to them with proposals on democratization, the opposition parties, to their credit, were ready. They remained united, they recognized their mutual dependence on the contras, and they kept their eyes on the political prize: free elections, preceded by a free campaign.

Repression in Nicaragua Grows Worse

The on-again, off-again talks took place against a backdrop of growing unrest in Nicaragua and growing uncertainty among the Sandinistas that the domestic violence could be contained. In February, for example, three zeroes were dropped from the Nicaraguan paper money, as the country seemed headed for Weimarlike inflation. In addition, February saw rumors emerge in Central America that the Reagan administration had sought cooperation from Panamanian dictator Manuel Noriega in a U.S. invasion of Nicaragua. Such rumors had appeared many times, but with Reagan's presidential term winding down, the Sandinistas were forced to consider the possibility of dramatic actions by a lame-duck president with nothing to lose.

By May, the high hopes generated by the Sapoa talks and cease fire agreement had largely been dashed. With the U.S. Congress still unwilling to give the contras military aid, with the contras themselves refusing to disarm (and supported in that refusal by the Reagan administration), with more rumors of an invasion, and with U.S. presidential election polls favoring the Democrats, the Sandinista leadership concluded in late spring that they had a free hand to reestablish their authority. They took a much harder line in their talks with the contras, who walked out of the negotiations at the end of April. When a new round of talks began, the Sandinistas pressed hard for the contras to disarm and gather into detention areas.

On May 4, three radio stations in Nicaragua were prevented from broadcasting to suppress news of a widespread hunger strike against the government. On the same day, twenty-five opposition leaders were arrested to stop a planned anti-Sandinista march. Perhaps not coincidentally, this was the same day that Soviet leader Gorbachev announced that

Soviet troops would soon be leaving Afghanistan. The Sandinistas, and the rest of the world, must have concluded that if the Soviets no longer intended to defend a pro-Soviet government on their own border, they were certainly not going to extend assistance to a pro-Soviet government half-way across the globe.

Throughout the year, the fortunes of ordinary Nicaraguans seemed closely tied to the public opinion polls in the United States When Democratic presidential nominee Michael Dukakis, a harsh and consistent critic of the contras, was leading in the polls, repression at home and a harder line abroad were the hallmarks of Sandinista actions. On July 10, thirty-nine people were arrested in Nandaime, about twenty miles southeast of Managua, during a peaceful demonstration. The arrests were accompanied by severe beatings, leaving some of the arrested demonstrators in critical condition and without access to medical care.

The following day, Catholic Radio in Managua was closed for what the government called "inciting to violence, disorder and lack of respect" for the Sandinista government. On the same day, the Sandinistas expelled the U.S. ambassador and seven other U.S. diplomats, saying that the officials had been illegally helping the contras and inciting people to revolt against the government. Reagan responded by expelling the Nicaraguan ambassador and seven of his colleagues.

The increased repression and the diplomatic flap with the United States made contra opponents on Capitol Hill increasingly nervous about the potential political cost of their seeming support for the Sandinistas. House majority leader Tom Foley took to the House floor to warn the Sandinistas that their actions could strengthen the president's hand if another vote on contra aid came up. Typically, Foley did not so much condemn the actions of the Sandinistas as their timing. Costa Rican president Oscar Arias was less circumspect, condemning Sandinista human rights abuses in no uncertain terms.

Events proved that Foley's warning to the Sandinistas was well taken. The House and Senate voted for a new aid package for the contras in August. Once again, it included only humanitarian assistance, but once again, it came with the written guarantee from House Speaker Wright and Senate Majority Leader Robert Byrd that military aid could be included if the Sandinistas failed to live up to the terms of the Arias peace plan. As they had been since the end of the Iran-contra scandal, the Sandinistas were living under the constant threat of renewed contra aid.

Unity at Last

One of the reasons that the threat was more immediate and disquieting in 1988 was that, since the focus on democratization in Nicaragua took center stage, divisions within the Reagan administration were far more muted. Both the leveraged ally and the natural ally factions of the administration were, finally, on the same page on Nicaragua. The leveraged ally faction had been studiously ambivalent about contra aid as long as its members perceived that the aid was for the purpose of overthrowing the Sandinistas. When it became clear that an outright military victory was nearly impossible, the leveraged ally faction became much more enthusiastic about contra aid.

In part, this change in attitude had to do with bureaucratic infighting. Shultz, for example, was likely to be enthusiastic about any plan that included giving the State Department's Agency for International Development (AID) the job of distributing contra aid. For Shultz, such an arrangement increased his clout as against that of the CIA director. In addition, putting AID in charge conjured up what were, for the secretary of state, extremely pleasing visions of contra leaders coming to him, hat in hand, begging for the aid. At the same time, Shultz could use his control over contra aid in his dealings with the Sandinista government. He would have leverage over both sides.

As the Soviets pulled out of Central America, Nicaragua would find itself destitute and bereft of friends. Its desperation would create an opportunity for the United States to step in with aid and create permanent leverage over the country. At the same time, since no one was pressing the Sandinistas to fundamentally change the socialist direction of their economy, U.S. officials could be reasonably certain that the Nicaraguan economy would not recover for an indefinite period. The *New York Times*, often the voice of the leveraged ally faction, started using the word *mature* to describe the Sandinistas' purportedly new attitude toward democracy and pluralism. The paper made it clear that a compelling sign of this maturity was the willingness to accept aid from the United States.

For the natural ally faction, the dream of the contras marching into Managua died hard, but by early 1988, it was obvious that keeping the contras alive and in the field was the best they could do. Natural ally faction members placed their hopes, albeit reluctantly, in the possibility that a combination of contra military pressure, internal dissent, and international scrutiny would eventually force the Sandinistas to hold a free election.

The leveraged ally faction also looked forward to a Nicaraguan election. The issue that really separated the two factions was what they thought would be the outcome of an election in Nicaragua. For the natural ally faction, elections would surely bring the downfall of the Sandinistas and the election of an anti-Communist government. The leveraged ally faction was equally certain that the Sandinistas would win, either because they rigged the election or because they really had a strong base of support in the country. (Democrats in Congress largely believed in the latter possibility, based more on their own ideology than on any evidence from Nicaragua.) Shultz insists in his memoirs that he believed one election would be enough to finish the Sandinistas, but he wrote this after the election had been held. Reagan, by contrast, exuded confidence in elections in Nicaragua from the start.

With the two factions in the administration, and many Democrats in Congress, all in agreement with Reagan (finally) that the contras could push the Sandinistas toward elections, the debate over contra aid in the last year of the Reagan administration was less rancorous than in previous years. Jim Wright, however, initiated a controversy over alleged CIA funding of opposition groups in Nicaragua. It was a short-lived flap, but a revealing one. Wright's only reasonably plausible motive for discrediting the Nicaraguan internal opposition was to insure that if there were an election in Nicaragua, the Sandinistas would be more certain to win. Put differently, Wright was evidently not convinced that the Sandinistas could win without his intervention.

Climbing into the Hand Basket

Meanwhile, conditions in Nicaragua continued to deteriorate. In spite of all their problems, the contras were still armed and still in the field. As long as that was true, Ortega had to keep looking like a peacemaker. As summer turned to fall, the prospect of a Dukakis victory faded. Such an outcome had been Ortega's last hope for a return to what he would have considered normality. Low on supplies, and with the Sandinista draft meeting more and more resistance from Nicaraguans, Ortega unilaterally extended the April cease fire to include all of June, then all of July, then all of August. On August 10, the U.S. Senate approved more contra aid.

When the Sandinistas and the contras renewed their talks in Guatemala in September, the government still did not have the upper hand. On the contrary, the rural-based contras were becoming a less pressing problem than unrest in the cities of Nicaragua. The international press ran stories throughout 1988 about the growing prevalence of malnutrition and outright starvation in Managua and other major cities. Media sources in Florida began running stories about the waves of Nicaraguan professionals who were leaving their homeland for the United States. In many cases, these were government bureaucrats, ex-security officials, and other Nicaraguans who were inclined to favor the Sandinistas. By late 1988, the exodus from the country accelerated enough for U.S. immigration officials to propose limiting the number of Nicaraguans allowed into the United States.

Economic disasters were replacing military disasters for the Sandinistas in the fall of 1988. On October 1, two Nicaraguan economists were arrested for being in possession of "state secrets." The contraband turned out to be government economic forecasts that are public information in most countries. Later in the month, Hurricane Joan pounded the east coast of Nicaragua for five days, leaving more than one hundred dead and thousands homeless. Such was the Sandinistas' collective loss of credibility that only a handful of nations, not including the United States, extended emergency aid. Most national leaders, like Reagan, believed that the Sandinistas would misuse the money. The cycle was complete. Somoza had lost his credibility over a natural disaster sixteen years earlier.

As economic disaster spread across Nicaragua, the Sandinistas' political enemies lost more and more of their fear and reticence. International pressure for the release of political prisoners had its effect. Three were released on November 17 and then a few more days later. On December 7, all the remaining opposition leaders were released on the order of a Managua judge. It was also one more signal that another branch of the Nicaraguan government was losing its fear of the Sandinistas.

Handing over the Baton

On October 12, Reagan announced that he would not seek military aid for the contras before the Congress adjourned. While the president added that he would not hesitate to call Congress back to session if the Sandinistas broke the crease fire, this announcement meant that Reagan would never again ask for contra aid while president. The future of the contras, and of Nicaragua, was passing out of his hands.

As the Reagan administration drew to a close, the president could be satisfied that Nicaragua never became a base for advanced Soviet warplanes, that its Sandinista leaders never managed to establish a full-fledged dictatorship, that he had kept the contras alive and fighting despite titanic odds, and that three of the other four Central American countries had become democratic on his watch. Reagan accomplished many of the goals he had for the region when he took office, ten days after the Salvadoran guerrillas' "Final Offensive."

There were, however, horrible costs. Far from the prosperous and economically independent states that he hoped to leave behind in the region, all four Central American democracies were heavily dependent on U.S. aid, which meant that they were dependent on the leveraged ally faction. Worse, Reagan had every reason to believe that this faction would become dominant in the new Bush administration. Bush's early Cabinet selections included James Baker as secretary of state, whose commitment to maintaining U.S. leverage over poor countries was even stronger than that of George Shultz.

Nicaragua, at the end of the Reagan administration, had achieved the near impossible: a per capita GDP and standard of living below that of Haiti. Ten years of Sandinista ideology, corruption, and mismanagement had reduced the once-prosperous regional power to an economic basket case, in which more children starved to death every year. With the added burdens of a civil war and a government seemingly determined to sever every international relationship that it had (except with the equally destitute Castro), Nicaraguans suffered to a degree barely known outside of sub-Saharan Africa. Reagan had the plight of Nicaragua on his mind during a speech that I heard him give at the University of Virginia on December 16. Reagan said, "Congress' on-again, off-again indecisiveness on resisting Sandinista tyranny and aggression has left Central America a region of continuing danger."

Reagan could not help, however, but reflect on his own role in the outcome. His early support for the contras was tentative and defensive, and officially secret, even long after the word was out that U.S. officials and American money were assisting the rebels. When he had the chance to call the bluff of Congress over aid to the contras in October 1984, he put his dreams for a landslide victory first and signed a spending bill that included the Boland Amendment. Not only did this decision lead directly to the Iran-contra scandal, but it prolonged the Sandinista regime by years, leaving the Nicaraguan people to the incompetence and repression of their leftist government.

Reagan's policies had also insured that, at least for the foreseeable future, Nicaragua would be economically dependent. Had a democratic government been elected in Nicaragua on the day that Reagan left office, that government would have had no choice but to come begging for aid from the U.S. State Department, whose officials could be relied upon to try to make the need for aid permanent. To save Nicaragua from Communism, which is what Reagan set out to do, he ended up surrendering it to the leveraged ally faction of his administration. Only when that faction was reasonably sure that even a non-Communist government would be a needy aid recipient did it willingly join in the fight to remove the Sandinistas from power.

Still, except for the grievous tactical mistakes I have examined, Reagan deserves more praise than blame for what he did in Central America. In El Salvador and Guatemala, harsh dictatorships were replaced by democratic governments. More to the point, within months of Reagan's departure, both countries had elected leaders who were fully aware of the twin-bladed nature of U.S. aid and determined to pursue policies that would strengthen their own economies and reduce the need for outside aid. In El Salvador, Alfredo Cristiani, elected in March 1989, gave a new, charismatic, and progressive face to the ARENA party and used policies much like those of Reagan himself to hasten his country's economic recovery. By 1989, a free election in El Salvador, complete with a turnover of power, was no longer even newsworthy.

This, perhaps, is the best way to consider the Reagan legacy in Central America. He gave the people of the region the chance to create their own destiny, under difficult circumstances and often seemingly insurmountable odds. Even with all of the obstacles Reagan faced, he prevented what would have been the most irrevocable outcomes in Central America: the rise of fully-consolidated, pro-Soviet regimes. Such regimes would have closed off any chance at all of a Cristiani being elected or indeed of free elections of any kind. As he contemplated the negative part of his Central America legacy, Reagan could console himself with the thought that none of those negative elements had to be permanent. The people of Central America, including the people of Nicaragua, had their destinies largely in their own hands, thanks to Ronald Reagan.

12

Reagan's Legacy

My friends: We did it. We weren't just marking time. We made a difference. We made the city stronger. We made the city freer, and we left her in good hands. All in all, not bad, not bad at all.

—*Ronald Reagan*, Farewell Address

After Ronald Reagan left office on January 20, 1989, political observers focusing on Reagan's legacy in Central America can be excused for focusing on the negative. In El Salvador, the war between the U.S.-backed government and the Communist guerrillas still went on, even though violence was at a much lower level. In Nicaragua, the Sandinistas seemed as well entrenched as ever, while the contras, in spite of Reagan's determined backing for virtually his entire presidency, seemed to be headed for ignominious dissolution. Indeed, the influence of the U.S. itself seemed to be at low ebb in Central America, with much of the discussion of the region's future revolving around a peace plan authored by the president of Costa Rica.

Reagan himself, speaking just weeks before he left office, named his failure to win consistent support for the Nicaraguan contras as his greatest disappointment. Even to Reagan's supporters, it appeared that he had little if any permanent worth to show for all the pain and controversy he had endured to pursue his vision of a free and prosperous Central America.

Such pessimistic analyses of Reagan's Central America legacy have not stood the test of time. Reagan's legacy on Central America came in two waves. The immediate results, while not visible when Reagan left office, became obvious later in 1989 and 1990. The broader and more permanent

Reagan legacy manifested itself in the administration of George W. Bush, especially after the terrorist attacks of September 11, 2001.

Central America after Reagan

In a truly ironic sense, the Salvadoran guerrillas had been right in 1980, when they announced their "Final Offensive." The January 1981 attacks by the Salvadoran FMLN represented the last forward movement by a proxy of the Soviet Union anywhere in the world. Having been met with force, the guerrillas retreated. The FMLN would never again come so close to taking power in El Salvador, nor would any other Soviet ally anywhere in the world make any significant advance after January 1981. By the time Reagan left office, the idea of the Soviet Union being able to fund a successful guerrilla army anywhere was almost pathetically laughable. The FMLN's final offensive really was the final offensive.

Had Reagan remained in office just one more year, his administration would have witnessed the liberation of Eastern Europe, and the Berlin Wall would have come down on his watch. Reagan could have received the credentials of an ambassador from a free Poland and would have waved farewell to the last ambassador from East Germany. With one more year, Reagan would have had a role in rebuilding the world after the Cold War, whose end he did so much to bring about. As it happened, the task of dealing with a new political world, and with new political realities in Central America, would be left to someone fundamentally unsuited and unprepared for it.

George H. W. Bush's Inaugural Address included a plea for bipartisanship directed to House Speaker Jim Wright. As the latter listened impassively, without the slightest sign that he shared Bush's desire to suspend partisan warfare, some observers wondered what Bush's extended hand would mean for the resolution of some of the outstanding issues of the Reagan administration, including Central America. Before long, Bush would face decisions about aid to the government of El Salvador and to the Nicaraguan contras, as Reagan had so many times in the previous eight years.

There would be one notable difference between the two administrations, however. While Reagan was president, the leveraged ally faction of the U.S. government had to operate largely under the radar, since Reagan himself was committed to creating natural allies in Central America. Many of the top decision makers in Reagan's administration, such as

Defense Secretary Casper Weinberger and CIA Director William Casey, shared the natural ally views of their boss. Those in the Reagan Cabinet who desired leveraged allies, such as Secretary of State George Shultz, had to hide that preference.

By contrast, Bush's foreign policy cabinet was filled with men wholly and unashamedly committed to using economic power as political leverage and to encouraging economic stagnation to insure that U.S. political leverage remained in place. Bush's secretary of state was James Baker, who had invariably sided with the leveraged ally faction while chief of staff and secretary of the treasury under Reagan. In the White House, foreign policy was overseen by National Security Advisor Brent Scowcroft, yet another champion of leverage.

The only reliable friends that the natural ally faction had in the Bush administration were Defense Secretary Dick Cheney, who was not inclined to intervene in discussions of Central America, and Vice President Dan Quayle, who would spend much of his time in office fending off public ridicule. They were, at best, uncertain allies.

Nevertheless, during his eight years in office, Reagan had hired hundreds of conservative staff members to work in various parts of his administration, including in the foreign policy apparatus. Many of these had become Foreign Service officers and stood ready to continue to work for natural allies, even with Reagan back in California. In the Bush administration, it would be the natural ally faction members who had to lay low, work beneath the radar, and try to nudge U.S. foreign policy in what they considered the right direction.

Elections in El Salvador: Unwelcome Outcomes?

As Bush took office, El Salvador prepared for its third presidential campaign since 1982, when Reagan had ignored those who had insisted that democracy would never work in that country. President José Napoleón Duarte was banned from seeking another term, but his Christian Democratic Party had designated Fidel Chavez Mena as its candidate. The hand-picked successor of Duarte promised to continue his policies of reconciliation with the guerrillas and of nationalization of the Salvadoran economy.

The opposition candidate was Alfredo Cristiani, who had wrested control of the conservative, free-market ARENA party from its longtime leader, Roberto D'Aubuisson. Under Cristiani, the party had become far more supportive of democracy and focused on economic reform and fighting corruption. It was evident that the ARENA party wished to move past issues directly related to the war.

That war, however, was not yet quite ready to go away. In January, the FMLN guerrillas launched yet another final offensive. This time, the guerrillas' violence was largely directed toward elected mayors and officials in charge of running elections. The actions of the guerrillas came to resemble single acts of terrorism much more than sustained guerrilla war, however, and the shift to "soft targets" such as mayors and city halls was a clear indicator that the FMLN was nearing the end of its tether. With supplies from Nicaragua no longer reliable, the guerrillas desperately needed time to regroup and reequip.

With this in mind, the guerrilla leadership offered President Duarte a cease fire proposal on January 23. In return for a six-month postponement of the scheduled March elections, the guerrillas offered to take part in those elections and abide by the results. In addition to the postponement, they wanted what they called "security guarantees," which referred to safe areas in the country where they would be unmolested by Salvadoran troops. Duarte responded almost immediately, rejecting the rebels' offer as a "proposal for war." The guerrillas' political arm could take part in the March elections if it wished, Duarte said, but negotiations toward that end could resume only after the FMLN renounced violence.

In a clear sign which faction was running El Salvador policy in Washington, the State Department reacted favorably to the rebel proposal, one day after Duarte had rejected it. For the leveraged ally faction, a six-month postponement of the elections would give the rebels the time they needed to continue to threaten the Salvadoran government, while events in Nicaragua and the Soviet Union made it a near certainty that the FMLN could never actually overthrow the democratic regime. In other words, a breathing space for the rebels would perpetuate El Salvador's need for U.S. assistance. The Baker State Department also published a report on El Salvador that was unusual in its gloomy assessment of conditions there. It referred to "systematic terror" from the left and right, ignoring the underlying reason for the rebels' switch from guerrilla to terrorist tactics.

With the leveraged ally faction rising, President Bush also attempted to forestall any attempt by natural ally factions to create a split in his administration. He sent Vice President Quayle to El Salvador to deliver the message that the U.S. administration wanted the FMLN proposal to get a fuller and more sympathetic hearing. By doing so, Bush insured that Quayle would become a spokesperson for the administration's policy of conciliation with the FMLN, rather than a critic of it. Duarte, whose party faced stiff opposition in the coming elections, no doubt explained to the vice president that his flexibility in dealing with the rebels was limited. He knew Washington did not wish to see Cristiani elected, and both sides knew that too many concessions on Duarte's part could make that outcome a near certainty. Nevertheless, the urging of an administration holding the purse strings could not be ignored, so Duarte consented to negotiations with the rebels. The talks began on February 20, in San Salvador. Bowing to U.S. pressure, Duarte proposed that elections be postponed for six weeks, rather than six months, and that a cease fire go into effect immediately. The State Department said that Duarte's proposal represented the best hope for ending the civil war.

As it happened, both the FMLN and the ARENA party rejected Duarte's proposal out of hand. In so doing, the ARENA leadership signaled that it did not consider itself beholden to Washington and would not necessarily respond to Washington's urgings. Indeed, Cristiani's ARENA party had been endeavoring to make clear its independence from the U.S. government for some time. Its declaration of independence was central to the party's electoral strategy.

While vowing to take a tough line with the guerrillas, Cristiani and his colleagues advised Salvadorans to think about the post–civil-war situation in their country. Once the shooting stopped, El Salvador would still be poor and would still be relying on the U.S. government for handouts. Cristiani described a future in which that would not always be the case. Much of the blame for the country's economic malaise, he suggested, lay with the Christian Democrats' misguided economic policies. He rarely failed to remind audiences that officials in the U.S. government had insisted on some of these policies.

Cristiani promised that there would be no extension of land reform in his administration, describing the U.S.-backed plan as a serious check on the country's agricultural progress. He added that he would not undo the land reform that was already in place. Instead, he promised to move expeditiously to distribute full legal titles to those currently being compelled to live in rural cooperatives. ARENA also promised to privatize the country's banks, which had been nationalized at the insistence of the United States. The coffee marketing board, established at the behest of the U.S. State Department, would also be dismantled.

Chavez Mena, the Christian Democrat candidate, promised to proceed with the long-postponed phase 2 of the land reform program. This part of the program would have totally disrupted production in the cotton and coffee sectors, the country's two largest foreign exchange earners. He also promised to create 160,000 new government jobs in the countryside. He hinted that more sectors of the nonfarm economy might be nationalized under his administration.

Cristiani's appeal was a clever mix of conservative, Reaganlike economic policies and nationalism. Cristiani openly predicted victory, telling audiences in El Salvador, "Every indication is that ARENA will be chosen to lead the way. Yet, it is said, such a vote will not be welcomed by many in the United States." He rejected as unconstitutional the suggestion that the elections be postponed. Unlike former leader D'Aubuisson, who denounced the United States in fiery terms, Cristiani merely suggested that not all Americans had Salvadorans' best interests at heart. Compared to D'Aubuisson, the 1989 ARENA candidate was able to present a more moderate image, without retreating from the party's commitment to free market economics and a tough prosecution of the war against the guerrillas.

Cristiani's predictions of victory came true. His party won 54 percent of the vote on March 19, leaving the once-dominant Christian Democrats with barely half the votes they had received (with U.S. government assistance) in 1984. For the first time in modern Salvadoran history, a candidate for president won an outright majority, with no need for a runoff. Cristiani's other prediction also came true. American newspapers were filled with commentary, both from journalists and from unnamed administration officials, that the election results were a huge setback for U.S. goals in El Salvador.

In fact, the win by ARENA marked the beginning of El Salvador's transition from leveraged to natural ally of the United States. Almost from the moment of Cristiani's ascension to power on June 1, 1989, the economy of the country began to pick up, and the civil war began to wind down. Targeted with a vigorous prosecution of the war, but without the human rights violations that had played into the guerrillas' hands, the FMLN became less and less effective. With farmland back in private hands, the country became more productive and gained the ability to earn its own income. Salvadorans who had left during the 1980s began to return, and some of those who did not return began to allow their money to return, in the form of investments in the country. By 1995, El Salvador was the recipient of only a token amount of U.S. aid.

In the meantime, the democratic processes that Reagan protected so ferociously took root. The country has had regular elections, on schedule, up to the present day. Eventually, former members of the FLMN were permitted to take part. On one occasion, a leftist nearly won the election, and his near victory made barely a ripple in the U.S. media. None of this progress has made El Salvador a less reliable ally of the United States. On the contrary, El Salvador's government has been a consistent supporter of U.S. foreign policy. Reagan's policies, often undertaken over the objections of his own Cabinet members, and sometimes nearly invisible to the untrained eye, had helped to save El Salvador from both Soviet and American domination.

Stumbling toward the Future in Nicaragua

While President Duarte was holding firm, albeit with some reluctance, on the date of the upcoming elections, his Sandinista neighbor was making a major concession to the democratic opposition. Daniel Ortega advanced the election date from November to February 1990 to demonstrate his commitment to democracy. (It is worth noting that the armed opposition in Nicaragua wanted elections brought forward. In El Salvador, the armed opposition wanted them postponed.) To minimize domestic fallout, Ortega made the announcement in San Salvador, where he was meeting with the other Central American presidents.

The advancement of the election came amidst new signs of pending economic and social collapse in Nicaragua. U.S. officials, especially in Florida and Louisiana, were becoming increasingly alarmed about the flood of refugees from Nicaragua, and the officials commented on the number of refugees from all walks of life. Just before Ortega's announcement on elections, he initiated a series of tough austerity measures, including the firing of thirty-five thousand public employees. He also admitted that economic recession was forcing him to cut the number of soldiers in the Sandinista army.

But even as Ortega was giving these unmistakable signs of weakness, his fellow Central American presidents seemed determined to make his work easier by orphaning the contras. They offered Ortega normalization of relations and an end to support for the contras (which as a practical matter meant an end to contra bases in Honduras, Costa Rica, and El Salvador), in return for greater political freedoms inside Nicaragua. Again, Ortega seemed poised to receive immediate concessions from his enemies in return for vague promises for actions sometime in the future.

The plan, however, was a dead letter as soon as it was written. The contras vowed to resume their war inside Nicaragua, whether or not they were forced out of neighboring countries. Moreover, no one in Central

America had any certainty that Honduras, Costa Rica, or El Salvador had either the military force or the political will to forcibly remove the contras (and they would need both). By pointing out the long record of the Sandinista's broken promises, the contras and their conservative supporters in the U.S. Congress were able to induce Ortega to make some immediate concessions of his own. Days after the Central American summit, Ortega announced the pardon of nearly two thousand former National Guard members, most of whom had been in jail since 1979. In addition, the Sandinistas lifted the ban on Radio Católica and permitted the return of ten Catholic priests who had been expelled for "subversive" activities.

Contra supporters were also able to place enough pressure on the Bush administration to prevent a premature embrace of the "peace process," such as had happened in August 1987. In March, the administration requested that Honduras permit the contras to remain in their bases in the country for one more year. By that time, administration officials assumed, the world would know whether or not the Sandinistas had held the promised elections of February 1990. At the same time, Bush's commitment to bipartisanship bore its first fruits, in the form of an agreement to continue to provide humanitarian assistance to the contras until February 1990. In May, Soviet leader Mikhail Gorbachev informed Bush that he had stopped sending weapons to the Sandinistas.

In the meantime, opposition Nicaraguans of both the armed and unarmed variety continued to work together and continued to realize that they needed one another to face their common enemy. In April, representatives of the civilian opposition, taking advantage of liberalized travel rules, went to Guatemala City to meet with contra representatives. The purpose of the meeting was to map out a common strategy for the upcoming campaign.

A united front would be absolutely necessary, since Ortega and his colleagues, having announced elections, kept trying to tamper with the rules for campaigning. Issues such as access to media, permission to hold rallies, voting rights for Nicaraguans living abroad, campaign financing, and the makeup of the supreme electoral council (which would determine the implementation of the rules) separated the Sandinistas and the opposition. A key opposition demand was the end of the military draft, which the Sandinistas were using as a tool to control dissent among the young.

As the negotiations over the election rules dragged on, it became more and more plain that the Sandinistas saw the election as simply a method of remaining in power and gaining legitimacy. At no time before

February 1990 did any leading Sandinista admit, even in the most general or abstract terms, to the possibility of defeat. Thus, the apparent goal of the government negotiators was to concede only what was necessary to preserve appearances. Indeed, some Sandinistas admitted during the negotiations in May that what concessions the opposition received were largely due to the fact that Ortega was on a European fund-raising trip. Put differently, the apparent concessions had little to do with evolving ideological flexibility and everything to do with accelerating economic deterioration.

Since economic need was what was driving the Sandinistas to make concessions, the partnership between the contras and the civilian opposition continued. The nightmare scenario for the opposition was that the Sandinistas would make just enough temporary concessions, and gain just enough economic breathing space, to win the election (or to persuade outside observers not to watch the election too closely) and then reimpose the political restrictions. With the contras still in place, and still a threat, however, the Sandinistas could not afford to ease up their military buildup, which remained a source of discontent among Nicaraguans. In the event, Ortega announced a "suspension" of the draft in August but said that conscriptions would start again after the election.

Through much of this maneuvering by Nicaraguans, the Bush administration remained largely in a passive, observer mode. Other than preparing to provide funds to the civilian opposition political parties in the coming campaign, the administration did little to advance or retard the halting progress of democratization in Nicaragua.

Nicaragua Holds Elections, Finally

The Opposition Acquires a Face

As 1989 progressed, the Sandinistas' hopes for remaining in power were suspended from three increasingly slender threads. First, the U.S. and/or the Central American democracies could give up on the contras and insist that they be immediately disbanded. Without the continued threat of the rebels, the Sandinistas could postpone the elections to late 1990 and perhaps even beyond. In the interim, the end of the war might bring enough foreign economic aid to allow the Sandinistas to win an election. Even if an outright victory were not possible, improving conditions, plus a healthy dose of voter fraud, might permit the ruling party to continue in power.

The second hope was that the Sandinistas could convince potential donors in Western Europe or Latin America to contribute enough economic aid to start a public works program, subsidize basic foodstuffs, or control inflation sufficiently to make it appear that things were getting better in Nicaragua. Again, any improvement was likely to bring political benefits, and perhaps enough to make an election close enough for the Sandinistas to win or to steal.

The Sandinistas' third way out of the crisis seemed to be their best hope. Their opposition consisted of both armed and civilian segments, and the civilian segment was a diverse collection of political tendencies. It was reasonable to expect that this varied lot would not be able to agree upon a unified platform, or a single candidate, for the February 1990 election. In a two-way race, the Sandinistas would lose. In a three- or four-way race, however, they stood a fair chance of winning.

As summer gave way to fall, each one of these threads of hope seemed on the point of snapping. Eager as Costa Rican president Oscar Arias was for the contras to turn over their weapons and fade into oblivion, they refused to do so, and the Bush administration seemed in no hurry to force the contras to disband. Bush had recently gotten approval for enough humanitarian aid to keep the contras alive through the February elections. As long as the rebels held together, the Sandinistas would have to keep their huge army in place, maintain the draft, and continue to postpone economic improvements. Europeans, far from extending economic aid, were generous only in their advice to Ortega about the economic changes he ought to be making, changes that Ortega could not make without repudiating the entire Sandinista revolution. Ortega's fellow Latin American presidents, for their part, were unsure about the attitude of the Bush administration toward friendly overtures to the Sandinistas, so they adopted a wait and see attitude.

The Sandinistas' third and seemingly best hope died on September 3, when the opposition parties announced that they had a single candidate, behind whom they would join under the banner "United Nicaraguan Opposition" (UNO). As discouraging as this news was, the identity of the candidate was even worse. Violeta Chamorro was the widow of Pedro Joaquín Chamorro, former editor of La Prensa, an opposition newspaper that had angered both Somoza and the Sandinistas. Chamorro's murder in January 1978 had galvanized the civilian opposition to Somoza and prompted it to join forces with the armed Sandinistas. His widow could similarly bind the civilian opposition together and cement its relationship with the contras.

The reaction of the Bush administration to the selection of Chamorro is instructive. Initially, Bush and members of his administration welcomed Chamorro's nomination and called her the best candidate possible to unify the opposition and present Nicaraguans with a genuine choice. Bush's embrace of Chamorro, however, soon got too close for comfort. The administration immediately announced plans to contribute $9 million to the Chamorro campaign, through the National Endowment for Democracy.

The announcement was almost certainly disingenuous. No one in the U.S. government with more than a passing knowledge of Latin American politics could have doubted that the Sandinistas would attempt to portray Chamorro as a puppet and instrument of the U.S. government. Thanks to the Bush administration, Chamorro had to begin her campaign fending off exactly those charges. It is inconceivable that the administration did not foresee the firestorm that was ignited by its offer of money.

On the one hand, the people of Nicaragua might react negatively to a candidate who got most of her funds from the United States, in which case the Sandinistas would win. On the other hand, if Nicaraguans elected Chamorro, then the new president could be reminded of the role that American money played in her victory. Post-Sandinista Nicaragua would, in any event, need substantial assistance to overcome the ravages of civil war and Sandinista rule. Either way, the leveraged ally faction of the U.S. government was likely to add to its influence and power in Central America. Even with only a rudimentary political sensitivity, Chamorro should have realized that the Bush administration was a potential threat to the eventual independence of her country.

Revolution in Managua

The most likely design on the part of the Bush-Baker foreign policy team was to ensure that the U.S. government would not be blamed for what it foresaw as an inevitable loss by Chamorro. Indeed, few observers foresaw anything other than a resounding win for the Sandinistas. On the surface, the ruling party seemed to have all the advantages. During the campaign, the FSLN granted the UNO coalition the right to time on radio and television, but more than twenty hours each day were still given to programming created and cleared by the Sandinistas. The Sandinista neighborhood defense forces still existed and still used ration cards and occasional brute force to keep the population in line. Every imaginable organizational and financial advantage rested with the Sandinistas.

In addition, the ruling party took significant steps to insure that the issues of the campaign broke their way as well. The Sandinistas continued to portray themselves as the nationalist party, fighting for Nicaraguan sovereignty and respect in the face of U.S. aggression and arrogance. Their ties to the Soviets and Cubans were minimized and, indeed, seemed less significant in the light of epoch-changing events in Eastern Europe and the Soviet Union itself. The Sandinistas insisted that Chamorro herself was either a well-meaning political ingénue or a knowing agent of the North American colossus.

Near the end of 1989, the Sandinistas took three further steps intended to remove any lingering doubt about the likelihood of their victory. First, Ortega announced that he would end the cease fire with the contras and begin attacking their positions again. This move was designed to convince voters that the Sandinistas intended to rid themselves of their armed enemy before the balloting took place. With the leverage of the contra threat removed once and for all, the Sandinistas could rig the election or, if necessary, ignore the results, with confidence that Americans would fail to give President Bush sufficient support for any effort to continue the pressure for democracy in Nicaragua, assuming that the Bush administration itself had any stomach for doing so. By going back on the offensive against the contras, Ortega was warning the domestic opposition that there would be no one to protect them if they tried to claim victory.

The Sandinistas' second move to insure victory was to give the vote to members of the military. These were mostly young men, and in most cases, they were young enough not to have any clear memory of a time before the Sandinista revolution. Moreover, they were closely watched by their officers and political commissars. The ruling party believed it to be a near certainty that soldiers would vote overwhelmingly for the FSLN.

The party's third decision sought to exploit even further the perceived loyalty of young Nicaraguans. In the weeks before the election, the legal age for voting was lowered from eighteen to sixteen. In addition, the Sandinistas made overt appeals to young voters based on sex and self-indulgence. Sandinista youth rallies featured rock music, free condoms, and the undisguised suggestion that sex would be free and plentiful under the Sandinistas but restricted and difficult under the overtly

Catholic Chamorro. When the votes were finally cast on February 25, 1990, the Sandinistas suffered a complete repudiation. In spite of all their advantages and tools of intimidation, the Sandinistas gained less than 40 percent of the vote. Except for one voting place on a military base near Managua, the ruling party lost every precinct in the country. After ten years of insisting that the FSLN had won the hearts and souls of the people of Nicaragua, Sandinista defenders were rendered speechless by the Chamorro victory.

Explaining the Outcome

For such an earth-shaking event to take place, a unique combination of circumstances must exist. Three major factors contributed to the Sandinistas' defeat. First, not even the entire weight and might of the Sandinista propaganda machine could hide the fact that the FSLN had failed, and failed horribly, in the eleven years that it ran the country. The continuing war, the economic collapse, the diplomatic isolation, and the social upheaval all took their toll on a population abused by decades of dictatorship even before the Sandinistas came to power and disillusioned by the Sandinistas in power. By the end of the campaign, the Sandinistas themselves were tacitly acknowledging their failure. Their last campaign slogan was "Todo se mejorarán" (Everything will be better.)

Second, the Sandinistas (and most Americans) never fully understood the power of Chamorro's promise to end the draft. No issue illustrated the hardships and sacrifices of the Sandinista regime better than the onerous and detested national conscription law, put into place in 1985. For all of his sins, Anastasio Somoza had never had a draft, except in the last, desperate days of his regime, and even then, the Somoza draft affected very few Nicaraguans. The Sandinistas, by contrast, had made enemies of tens of thousands of young people and hundreds of thousands of parents, either by drafting their sons or by making them fear that their sons would soon be drafted. After four years of conscription, there were thousands of young Nicaraguans telling stories of brutal discipline, political indoctrination, and official corruption, incompetence, and cowardice. The army abandoned the Sandinistas on Election Day and persuaded many more Nicaraguans to do the same.

A third factor was the U.S.-led invasion of Panama in December 1989. The Sandinistas reacted in horror to the invasion. On the one hand, ousted dictator Manuel Noriega had been a supporter, supplier, and middle man to the Sandinistas since the mid-1970s, and the Sandinista leadership could not help but wonder exactly what secrets the Americans would uncover once they started examining Noriega's files. On the other hand, the invasion placed more than twenty-five thousand American troops within easy striking distance of Nicaragua, even though the logistical and tactical problems of moving the army from one place to the other were considerable. Moreover, the relative efficiency of the Panama invasion demonstrated that the Americans had learned important lessons from the mistakes of the Grenada invasion six years earlier and that the U.S. Army was a more formidable weapon than the Sandinistas had believed.

Worst of all, from the Sandinistas' point of view, was the lack of any sustained or significant diplomatic uproar over the invasion. Ortega and his colleagues hoped that the overt use of American military power in Central America would lead to loud protests and perhaps even to diplomatic sanctions. While some Latin American capitals experienced anti-American protests in the wake of the invasion, there was nothing approaching the general uprising that Ortega (and Noriega) desired.

The Sandinistas could not help but wonder if perhaps Bush might try what Reagan had never dared and send U.S. troops to Nicaragua. Moreover, Bush rationalized Operation Just Cause by accusing Noriega of ignoring the will of the Panamanian people as expressed in a free election. Not only that, but Noriega had been a CIA informant while George Bush was head of the CIA, providing information on Soviet activities and drug running in Central America. If President Bush was willing to send American troops after a former employee, there seemed little reason to believe he would not do the same to sworn enemies, if the proper rationale could be found. There is no evidence that Bush himself saw Panama as a dress rehearsal for an invasion of Nicaragua, but Ortega did not know that.

After Operation Just Cause, if the Sandinistas desired to either cancel or rig the February 1990 election, they knew they faced unacceptable risks in doing so. Thousands of international monitors were coming to observe and certify the balloting. Thousands of international media representatives would also be present. Then again, it is entirely possible that Ortega never gave serious thought to cancellation, since he was convinced his party was going to win.

Carter in Charge, Again

On election night, Reagan placed a phone call to Chamorro to congratulate her, but she gave the former president only a couple of minutes, saying that more important matters were pressing. She might have done better to converse with Reagan longer. Unfortunately for the Nicaraguan people, Reagan was not on the scene when they made their stand for freedom and self-determination; Jimmy Carter was. Perhaps because no one in the Bush administration expected the UNO coalition to win, the White House had failed to place any high-ranking officials in Managua on election day or even to have the secretary of state, or assistant secretary ready to fly to Managua to take part in the postelection aftermath. The most prominent American in Managua on election night was the former Democratic president, who immediately appointed himself an informal advisor to president-elect Chamorro. His influence was nothing short of catastrophic for Nicaragua.

On Carter's advice, Chamorro cancelled plans for a victory celebration on the night of February 25. Such a public demonstration, Carter cautioned, might prompt the Sandinistas to stage a military coup and nullify the elections. Chamorro herself might be in danger of arrest, exile, or possibly even assassination, the former president warned. Carter's counsel was devastating to UNO supporters, many of whom felt cheated of their well-deserved victory celebration. Their anger was directed toward Chamorro, causing a split in the UNO coalition just as victory was being achieved. Within days of the Sandinistas' repudiation, Chamorro announced, again at the prompting of Jimmy Carter, that Humberto Ortega would continue to serve as defense minister and commander in chief of the Sandinista army.

For many Nicaraguans, the fruits of their hard-fought victory were being negotiated away, based on fears that had little basis in reality. It borders the inconceivable that the Sandinistas would have attempted a bloody military crackdown on election night, with so many neutral international observers in Managua ready to report on their actions and with the example of the U.S. invasion of Panama so close at hand. To deny UNO supporters the chance to celebrate permitted the Sandinistas to continue to claim a high level of popular support. Even after the reporters and vote counters left Nicaragua, it is doubtful that the Sandinistas would have called on the military to crush the country's budding democracy. Like every other segment of Nicaraguan society, the army had rejected the Sandinistas. Ortega would not have dared to mobilize the army, for fear of mass insubordination, which would have meant the end of his political influence. At best, Carter was making decisions about Nicaragua in 1990 that were every bit as ill-informed as the ones he had made in 1978 and 1979.

In 1990, as in 1979, the Sandinistas responded to peaceful overtures from Jimmy Carter and their democratic opponents with rapid and effective moves to consolidate and protect their power. During the two months between the election and the actual transfer of power, the Sandinistas appropriated houses, cars, farms, factories, and innumerable other government assets. The lame-duck Sandinista National Assembly then passed a series of laws legalizing the takings. At the same time, it distributed weapons to its supporters to defend its new property. The Sandinistas labeled the theft of state property "delayed compensation" for the years of tireless effort that the revolutionaries gave to the country. For most Nicaraguans, however, it was known as the "*la piñata.*"

The defeated FSLN evidently understood the importance of privatization to an effective transition, and its members strove untiringly to prevent any significant transfer of land or other property to private hands. There is no other issue on which the Sandinistas have fought harder to prevent change. The FSLN leadership has acquiesced to reversals of its policies in many other areas, including the size of the army and control of the police, but it has fought to prevent any rollback of the *piñata*. The government of President Violeta Chamorro unfailingly backed down in the face of Sandinista threats to use violence to protect their appropriated property, in spite of increasing evidence that the FSLN was losing support, and losing it because of the venality displayed by the *piñata*. The FSLN's intransigence, abetted by Chamorro's compliance, delayed real economic reform in Nicaragua for years.

Chamorro had run on a platform promising to make privatization a priority. Her actions after her inauguration drove a wedge between her and the UNO coalition. In fact, in October 1990, Chamorro created a de facto coalition government with the defeated FSLN. Faced with Executive Branch reluctance, members of UNO tried to act on their own, through their majority in the National Assembly, to reverse the *piñata* and begin significant privatization. Chamorro responded by vetoing the legislation, again in the face of Sandinista threats of violence. Privatization became a solely Executive Branch function; the National Assembly was excluded altogether.

A sign of the divorce between Chamorro and the political backers who helped defeat the Sandinistas was the bad blood between Chamorro and Virgilio Godoy, UNO vice president and a champion of privatization. On the day of Chamorro's inauguration, after a ceremony in which the Sandinistas were given an equal number of seats as the winners, Godoy was stopped at the door of the national palace and told he had no duties and no role in the new administration. Godoy was not even allowed inside the palace; he eventually rented office space from the Liberal Party.

Chamorro's break with her political partners represented an enormous victory for the leveraged ally faction of the U.S. government. With no significant privatization, there would be no rapid or even appreciable economic progress in post-Sandinista Nicaragua. The country would remain an economic basket case, heavily dependent on U.S. aid, and with a president who would come to depend on U.S. officials to protect her from the frequent encroachments on her power by the Sandinista holdovers. Repeatedly during the Chamorro administration, the FSLN would launch crippling strikes and other job actions, all with an eye to sabotaging the economy and causing Nicaraguans to long for the days of Sandinista rule. Damage to the economy, the Sandinistas knew, also perpetuated Chamorro's dependence on the United States.

Taking the Long View

The February 1990 victory over the Sandinistas, however, was not in vain. After taking the oath of office on April 25, Chamorro kept a campaign promise and ended conscription. The remaining contras turned in their arms to her representatives on June 25, 1990, and Nicaragua knew internal peace for the first time in nearly fifteen years. In other areas, Chamorro also made a difference. Political indoctrination ceased in the army and in the schools. The police forces were purged of Sandinista leaders and made subordinate to civilian command. The army, while still loyal to the FSLN and to Humberto Ortega, was cut by more than half. The few Soviet military advisors remaining in the country were sent home, along with most of the Cuban advisors. As in El Salvador, Reagan's actions had left Nicaraguans with the chance to construct their own destiny.

That destiny moved in agonizing fits and starts while Chamorro was president. Chamorro's major accomplishments were preventing a Sandinista coup (having empowered the Sandinista army in the first place) and seeing her way to the end of her term in 1995. She also used the generous assistance of the U.S. government to buy back hundreds of thousands of weapons from private citizens, reducing the level of violence in the country.

The legacy of Chamorro's decision to permit the Sandinistas to thrive under her presidency has cast a long shadow over the country.

Chamorro's successor was Arnoldo Alemán, who promised to pursue free market reforms. To a certain extent, Alemán did so, but he also set new standards for corruption in the country. Alemán was eventually convicted on multiple corruption counts and sentenced to twenty years in prison. Due to alleged health problems, Alemán was permitted to serve his prison time under house arrest, and he continued to run his party while supposedly under confinement. In 2005, Alemán started making an arrangement with Daniel Ortega to return the latter to the presidency and return numerous Sandinista supporters to government offices, in a process that President Enrique Bolanos called "a coup in slow motion." After a highly suspicious Supreme Court decision striking down Alemán's corruption convictions, the "coup" moved to fast motion. Ortega was reelected president on November 6, 2006. Seemingly, all of Reagan's work against the Sandinistas had been undone.

But Reagan's legacy is also visible, even in the tortured political history of Nicaragua since 1990. Daniel Ortega, even as the elected president, does not have a fifty-thousand-man army behind him anymore. He does not have the power to suppress opposition parties. There are no neighborhood watch committees anymore, and certainly no Cuban, Soviet, Bulgarian, or Palestinian interlopers. Ortega can make decisions that harm the economy of Nicaragua and make common cause with Hugo Chavez of Venezuela, but he cannot do so with impunity. His election is in no way evidence that democracy has not worked in Nicaragua. It is evidence that a freedom-loving people have been mercilessly and repeatedly betrayed by their own elites.

Reagan's goal was for a Nicaragua freed from totalitarianism and no longer a threat to the United States. These goals were achieved. There is no chance of 1980s-style Sandinista rule returning to the country. Even with an alliance with Chavez, Nicaragua is in no position to threaten the security of the United States, even indirectly. The Nicaraguan economy, while seriously hampered by the failure to take actions that would permit economic growth, is nowhere near the rock-bottom, basket-case status where it could be found in 1990. Nicaraguans have made some poor choices, and, more often, have had poor choices imposed upon them. But it was to establish the principle of popular choice, and to insure some respect for popular will, that Reagan and his supporters worked so hard during his administration. It was for this same goal that the contras fought and the anti-Sandinista civilian leaders worked and suffered.

Finally, it is important to note that the fate of Sandinista Nicaragua was tied to the fate of Soviet Communism. Reagan's actions on the global stage played a crucial part in hastening the end of the Soviet Union. Even before the fall of the U.S.S.R., Reagan's forceful actions to challenge the Soviet Union made it more and more costly for the Soviet leaders to continue their risky support for the Sandinistas. Whatever plans the Soviets may have had for using Nicaragua to take offensive actions against the United States (and Grenada demonstrated that such actions were probably being contemplated), such plans never came close to fruition. Soviet influence retreated from its high water mark in 1981, when the U.S.S.R. had partners in Southeast Asia, Southwest Asia, the Middle East, the Horn of Africa, Southern Africa, and the Caribbean. The failure of the Salvadoran Final Offensive was the turning point.

Central America was the site where the Cold War began its long, slow fade into oblivion. It was where the seeds of our own post–Cold War world were sown. Central America has departed center stage, as our world copes with new problems, challenges, and opportunities. But without the actions of Reagan and hundreds of thousands of freedom-loving Central Americans, our world, as we know it, would not exist.

Central America and the War on Terror

I urge you to beware the temptation of pride—the temptation of blithely declaring yourselves above it all and label both sides equally at fault, to ignore the facts of history and the aggressive impulses of an evil empire.

—Ronald Reagan, March 1983

States like these, and their terrorist allies, constitute an axis of evil, arming to threaten the peace of the world.

—George W. Bush, January 2002

Back to the Future

Twenty years after the fall of the Berlin Wall and the collapse of the Soviet Union, it is tempting to minimize the significance of events in Central America in the 1980s. The Reagan-era warnings about hostile governments in Nicaragua or El Salvador and danger to the United States seem almost quaint in retrospect, something like nineteenth-century warnings to American pioneers about Indian attacks. The nightmare scenarios of the 1980s, such as Soviet missiles in Nicaragua, or floods of refugees from a civil war–torn Mexico, did not come to pass, so there is a natural tendency to believe that such threats never really existed. Reagan's critics are particularly smug in their self-assurance that Communism never really threatened the United States and that if the Soviets ever were a threat, they were certainly not a threat in Central America. The Central

America controversy of two decades ago, for such critics, is an episode of American history best forgotten.

There are at least four good reasons, however, for remembering the Central American crises of the 1980s. First, while it is easy now to scoff at the idea of superpower confrontation over Central America, many of Reagan's critics were making dire predictions about Central America twenty years ago and placing the blame on Ronald Reagan. Walter LaFeber, for example, said in 1982 that Reagan's Central America policy was "the diplomatic counterpart of trying to use gasoline to extinguish a gasoline fire." Senator Chris Dodd (D-CT) insisted that Reagan's efforts to fight Communism in Central America showed "desperation." The following year, Sen. Gary Hart (D-CO) compared Reagan's policies to "pushing a stick of dynamite closer to a lighted match." The senior editor of the *New York Times* warned, "Unless he is stopped by Congress—and only Congress and the force of public opinion can stop him—Ronald Reagan could plunge this country into the most unwanted, unconscionable, unnecessary and unwinnable war in its history, not excepting Vietnam."

It is, of course, impossible to disprove a counterfactual. One cannot ever say with certainty what would have happened had the guerrillas prevailed in El Salvador, for example. But it is also impossible to dispute that El Salvador was the final battleground of the Cold War, the last place in which proxies of the United States and the Soviet Union would face off during that "long, twilight struggle." In El Salvador, the Soviets met determined (even if uneven) resistance to their hopes to see a new anti-American government challenge the supremacy of the United States in the Western Hemisphere. It is also impossible to dispute that the Soviets, having seen their allies thwarted in El Salvador early in 1981, spent the remainder of the 1980s in retreat. That this retreat accelerated beyond anyone's imaginings in 1988 and 1989 hides the true starting point of the USSR's retrenchment and ultimate collapse.

The multiple elements of Reagan's offensive against the Soviet Union (such as the deployment of medium-range nuclear missiles in Europe, the Strategic Defense Initiative, a targeted economic boycott, and a determined psychological attack) serve to mask the importance of Central America. Even some of Reagan's supporters believe that it was the U.S. military buildup, the repair of the NATO alliance, assistance to the Afghan rebels, or even the American economic boom of the 1980s that ultimately felled the Soviet Union. In *Reagan's War: The Epic Story of His Forty-Year Struggle and Final Triumph over Communism*, Peter Schweizer makes probably the most explicit argument that Reagan's policies brought the Cold War to an end. Schweizer, however, barely mentions Central America in his treatment.

Such analyses neglect the comprehensive nature of Reagan's challenge to the Soviet Union. Sharp rhetoric alone would not have changed Soviet behavior, nor simply the threat of a defense against Soviet nuclear weapons. Only by challenging the Soviets around the world, at virtually every opportunity, did Reagan succeed in exerting enough pressure to force cracks in the Soviet system. These cracks were barely noticeable at first but became unmistakable soon after Reagan left office. Central America was where the first tiny fissures opened up.

Still Geopolitically Important

The second reason to understand the Central America of the 1980s is the ongoing geopolitical importance of the region. It is still on the North American mainland, and still within easy distance of the still-vital Panama Canal. Civil strife in Mexico, with an accompanying flood of refugees into the United States is still to be feared. A single hour spent listening to various talk show hosts decrying Mexican immigration to the United States, absent any crisis in Mexico, and at a time when illegal immigration to the United States is actually declining, gives an idea what the reaction would be if the thousands coming across the southern border turned to millions. The Gulf of Mexico is still important to the economy of the United States as the disruption in the wake of Hurricanes Katrina and Ike amply showed.

Moreover, not only the geography of Central America has remained constant. In some significant ways, the politics of the area has not changed so much either. In April 2006, Oscar Arias, best known as the author of a Central American peace plan in the 1980s, returned to the presidency of Costa Rica. A few months later, ousted Sandinista president Daniel Ortega was reelected president of Nicaragua. While both men have changed in twenty years, as have the countries they lead, their simultaneous reappearance emphasizes the essential continuity that underlies the many important changes that have occurred since Ortega and Arias last held power. If Ortega can no longer look to the Soviet Union for support, he can look to Venezuelan president Hugo Chavez, who is actively trying to build an anti-American alliance in the Western Hemisphere. If the threat of Soviet missiles in Central America has gone the way of the dodo, the threat of al-Qaeda terrorist cells using the isthmus as a base against the United States is a serious one.

Since the beginning of the war on terror in 2001, the attention of U.S. citizens and policy makers has been drawn, understandably, to Afghanistan, Iraq, Iran, and elsewhere, much in the same way that policy makers in the early years of the Cold War focused on places such as West Germany, Czechoslovakia, and Korea. In part, it was the long neglect of Central America by the United States that made the area ripe for anti-American movements in the 1970s and 1980s. Similar disregard for the Western Hemisphere now could bring a similarly rude awakening.

Nicaragua and Iraq

The war on terror itself, and especially the war in Iraq, is the third reason for studying the debates over U.S. policy toward Central America in the 1980s. To a striking degree, the debates over Iraq policy mirrored the issues and copied the rhetoric of the Central America debates of twenty years earlier. In both cases, a Republican president was singularly unsuccessful in convincing a majority of Americans that forceful action was necessary. In both cases, the president at the time acted alone, arguing that an immediate danger to U.S. national security made such action necessary.

Indeed, Bush's reasons for invading Iraq were virtually the same as Reagan's reasons for opposing the Sandinistas. Bush worried about Iraq acquiring weapons of mass destruction; Reagan expressed concern that Nicaragua could become a base for advanced Soviet weaponry. Bush recounted Saddam Hussein's aggressions against its neighbors; Reagan portrayed Nicaragua as a threat to its democratic neighbors. Bush charged that Saddam's Iraq was involved in international terrorism; Reagan asserted that Nicaragua was becoming a base for the PLO and various Latin American terrorist organizations. Bush reminded his critics of the promises that Saddam had made to the UN; Reagan had used the Sandinistas' promises to the OAS against them. Finally, both Reagan and Bush denounced their opponents' dismal human rights records.

Both Reagan and Bush did persuade Congress to give vague and grudging approval to the broad outlines of their actions. Later, however, Democrats and some Republicans would publicly regret their support and find ways to cast subsequent votes against the policy that they had earlier approved. Most famously, Sen. John Kerry (D-MA) reassured a town hall meeting, "I actually did vote for the $87 billion [for Afghanistan], before

I voted against it." Opponents of the Reagan administration, while often underlining their distaste for the Sandinista regime of Daniel Ortega, insisted that his regime did not constitute a danger to Americans. Bush's critics used the same argument about Saddam Hussein. In the 1980s, some of the more liberal members of Congress traveled to Nicaragua to meet with Ortega and to undermine Reagan administration foreign policy. In 2002 and early 2003, similarly liberal members of Congress went to Baghdad to meet with Saddam. (In some cases, it was the same members.)

In both cases, administration opponents remained stolidly unconvinced by evidence of the aggressive intentions of Ortega or Hussein. Satellite photographs were deemed unclear. Intercepted phone calls and other electronic evidence were doubted. Openly aggressive statements by Ortega and Hussein were minimized. Administration opponents maintained that containing Ortega or Hussein was preferable to more aggressive action. Democrats twenty years apart demanded that only economic weapons be used. Administration critics, both times, dismissed democracy as either unrealistic, inappropriate for the county in question, or simply a convenient mask for more nefarious administration goals. Opponents of democracy in Nicaragua seemed to find vindication in the difficulties of the administration of Violeta Chamorro, much in the same way that Bush's critics insist that nothing has improved for Iraqis since the overthrow of Saddam Hussein.

When administration opponents failed to derail Reagan and Bush from their determination to confront Ortega and Saddam, some of those opponents spoke of impeachment. Once again, the parallels are striking. Both Reagan and Bush were accused of lying to the American people, of disregarding international law, of damaging America's reputation around the world, and of making a bad situation worse (the Cold War then, the hatred of Islamic fundamentalists now). Congressional critics spoke of Americans' lives being endangered needlessly; both Nicaragua and Iraq were frequently compared to Vietnam. Both Reagan and Bush saw Republicans lose control of the Senate in their sixth year in office, in large part because of dissatisfaction over their respective administrations' foreign policy. George Shultz and Colin Powell, secretaries of state thought to be skeptical of their presidents' aggressiveness and less "hard line," were spared the harsh media treatment given to their colleagues.

Like all historical parallels, that between Central America and Iraq has its limits. Reagan never sent American troops to Central America in a combat role, and the Bush administration never faced a scandal even remotely similar to Iran-contra. There was a Cuban-built airfield in Grenada; there were no weapons of mass destruction in Iraq. In addition, Reagan was far superior to Bush in diverting the focus from the most contentious policy of his presidency. (In part, this was because Bush never copied Reagan's model for an Office of Public Liaison.) Nevertheless, the similarities between the two prolonged and bitter foreign policy controversies call for close study of the Central American imbroglio. Moreover, the place of Central America as the first stepping stone in the eventual victory of the United States in the Cold War is worth noting now, as the United States confronts another determined global enemy.

Leveraged and Natural Allies Redux

One particular subtext of the Central America controversy provides the fourth reason to study events in the Isthmus in the 1980s, to gain a better understanding of U.S. foreign policy under George W. Bush. As I have shown in the preceding pages, the political war between Reagan and his opponents outside of his administration was only a part of Reagan's challenge in dealing with Central America. The war within his administration, between the leveraged ally faction and the natural ally faction, provides vital clues to understanding how and why many crucial decisions were made.

In this regard, there are two noteworthy differences between the Reagan and Bush administrations, which, while significant, should not distract from the essential continuity of the clash between those who favor leveraged or natural allies. First, the Bush administration was far more disciplined and internally loyal than the Reagan administration. There was nothing in the Bush administration to compare with the bitter (and public) feud between George Shultz and Caspar Weinberger. Even given the explosion of media outlets in the first decade of the twenty-first century, the Bush administration was remarkably leak-free. Stories of backbiting and internal rivalries were rare in Bush's Administration. To a large degree, this was because Bush's Chiefs of Staff were Bush loyalists.

The second difference is more important: in the Reagan administration, most top officials, and the great majority of Cabinet and sub-Cabinet-level officials, were of the leveraged ally faction. Reagan himself preferred natural allies, but he started his Presidency without a cadre of like-minded people qualified for high public office. Moreover, Reagan was extremely reluctant to fire or discipline members of his own Administration who disagreed with him. By contrast, Bush surrounded himself (with some exceptions, such as Colin Powell) with officials committed to creating natural allies. In the main, these officials were veterans of the Reagan Administration, and thus well-versed in the stakes of the struggle. In the Bush Administration, it was the leveraged ally faction that had to work behind the scenes and in the shadows. For the most part, disaffected Bush Administration foreign policy makers (mostly long time Foreign Service officers) had their say in public, but had as much difficulty getting media attention as the natural ally faction did in Reagan's time.

The Natural Ally Faction Rising

The attacks of 9/11 reignited the factional struggle over foreign policy. The decisions of President George W. Bush in the immediate aftermath of 9/11 provided plenty of political and bureaucratic battlefields for the leveraged and natural ally factions, which reappeared almost before the flames at Ground Zero and the Pentagon were extinguished. Indeed, understanding this internal struggle is key to understanding the foreign policy decisions of the Bush administration, just as it was while Reagan was president. To a large degree, the issues driving the wars over Central America are reappearing in the global war on terror. To chronicle the infighting of the leveraged and natural ally factions in the Bush administration would require another book. Instead, we can focus on some significant examples of both rhetoric and policy to demonstrate the parallels with the Reagan administration.

Differences in Rhetoric

From the very start of Bush's response to the attacks of September 11, it was clear that his approach to war, at least in Afghanistan, would reflect the views of a dominant natural ally faction in his administration. (Most pundits, unaware of the leveraged ally/natural ally split, refer to the natural ally faction in the Bush administration as the "neoconservatives" and the leveraged ally faction as the pragmatists or the professionals.)

From the time of his candidacy in 1999–2000, George W. Bush used language in his speeches on foreign policy that clearly indicated his preference for natural allies. For example, in a campaign speech at the Reagan Library, Bush said: "We have partners, not satellites. Our goal is a fellowship of strong, not weak, nations. And this requires both more American consultation and more American leadership. . . . The support of friends allows America to reserve its power and will for the vital interests we share." Later, he added: "Let us not dominate others with our power—or betray them with our indifference. And let us have an American foreign policy that reflects American character. The modesty of true strength. The humility of real greatness. This is the strong heart of America."

The most sriking similarity with Reagan was the paucity of references to stability in Bush's statements on developing countries, and the much more frequent use of words like *freedom* and *liberty*. It was rare, even after September 11, for any member of the Bush Administration to speak of the necessity of bringing stability to the Middle East, to the Islamic world, or to the developing world. Bush's critics, for their part, focus on stability almost exclusively.

What was true for Bush himself was also true for members of his administration. During her confirmation hearings, Secretary of State-designate Condoleezza Rice openly rejected past U.S. policy: "In the Middle East, President Bush has broken with six decades of excusing and accommodating the lack of freedom in the hope of purchasing stability at the price of liberty." Rice dismissed the theory that stable regimes are preferable to democratic ones. Like Bush, Rice has been much more likely to describe democracy, or freedom, or liberty as the goal of U.S. policy toward Islamic countries. Many additional examples exist in the speeches of Vice President Dick Cheney, Defense Secretary Donald Rumsfeld, Undersecretary of Defense Paul Wolfowitz and other members of the Bush "war cabinet."

Differences in Policy—Afghanistan

In one of the more revealing indications that U.S. policy was in different hands, then-National Security Advisor Condoleezza Rice went to Rome to visit with the exiled King of Afghanistan before the U.S. military attack on the Taliban commenced on October 11. That a U.S. administration official was willing to consult with a leader who was not a creation of the U.S. government, and who owed nothing to the U.S. government, was striking enough. That a ranking U.S. foreign policy official was willing to go to the king, rather than summoning him to Washington, was an unmistakable signal that the U.S. government was willing, even eager, to make common cause with independent, nationalist political figures.

It was also eyebrow-raising that the U.S. administration showed itself willing to work with the Afghan Northern Alliance during Operation Enduring Freedom. The United Islamic Front for the Salvation of Afghanistan, as the Alliance is formally known, was neither the creation of the U.S. government nor particularly pro-U.S. in its actions before the September 2001 terrorist attacks. The Bush administration stepped up contacts with the Northern Alliance immediately after 9/11, at a time when the group was reeling from the assassination of its leader by the Taliban.

Had the leveraged ally faction been making the policy, Washington would have taken advantage of the leadership vacuum to install its own preferred leader of the Northern Alliance, much as the State Department under Reagan did with José Napoleón Duarte in El Salvador. Instead of working with and supplying all of the factions of the Northern Alliance, as the Bush administration did, the U.S. government would have selected one faction, christened it a "moderate" or "pragmatic" faction, and assisted only that faction. Almost certainly, U.S. officials would have selected a small or weak faction to supply, to insure gratitude and subservience.

With the natural ally faction in charge, however, the U.S. military played a largely supporting role in the war to overthrow the Taliban in Afghanistan. Such a policy also helped, for a time, to keep the United States out of the complex ethnic politics in Afghanistan, which leveraged ally officials would have seen as the perfect opportunity to play divide and conquer. After the defeat of the Taliban, the Bush administration supported the presidency of Hamid Karzai, who was a supporter of the exiled King, and no more a creation of the U.S. government than the King himself. Indeed, Karzai is best likened to El Salvador's Alfredo Cristiani, whom the leveraged ally faction undermined at every opportunity during the Reagan years.

Again, no parallel is perfect. Afghanistan's progress since the overthrow of the Taliban has been, to put it mildly, uneven. This is especially true if it is compared to El Salvador's history since the end of its guerrilla war. In this regard, it is important to bear in mind that El Salvador had never undergone the wholesale political, economic and social destruction that the Taliban, civil war or the Soviets had wrought in Afghanistan. Parallels between Afghanistan's heartbreakingly difficult recovery and that of post-Sandinista Nicaragua are more useful. Nicaragua suffered from warfare and from economic mismanagement almost as badly as Afghanistan, and has had similar difficulties with corruption since regime change took place.

A second important difference is the significant (albeit often invisible) influence of the leveraged ally faction in the Bush Administration. As noted earlier, Bush surrounded himself with natural ally supporters, but did nothing to purge leveraged ally supporters from middle-level positions in his Administration. Thus, while the war to overthrow the Taliban and destroy the Afghan-based al-Qaeda organization was in its early stages, top level officials were in charge, and strong evidence of a preference for natural allies dominated. When the focus turned to rebuilding Afghanistan, however, Bush, Powell and Rice turned to middle-level foreign policy and foreign aid professionals to do so. Evidence of a preference for a leveraged ally in Afghanistan was clearer during this latter phase of the Afghan war.

Differences in Policy: Iraq

Since the beginning of the war in Iraq in 2003, most of the commentary has focused, understandably, on the intelligence failures that preceded the war and the military failures that have impeded the war's progress. These are vitally important discussions, to be sure, but they distract from an examination of the relative weight of the leveraged and natural ally factions in the Bush administration. As noted above, Presidents Reagan and Bush had parallel difficulties in convincing their critics that U.S. national security was threatened at all. Reagan's opponents eventually acknowledged the Sandinistas' sins, but still opposed forceful action to correct them. Critics of the war option in 2002 and 2003 all expressed their repugnance for Saddam Hussein, but went on to advocate leaving him in power. Some Bush critics insisted that Hussein was unlikely to use weapons of mass destruction, even if he had them, and advocated containing the dictator, rather than overthrowing him.

While the huge cost of the Iraq war has made such critics look like prophets, most would have opposed the overthrow of Saddam Hussein even had they been assured it would be quick and easy. For those preferring leveraged allies, dangerous, aggressive dictators like Saddam serve to push their neighbors toward more dependence on security guarantees from the United States. With Saddam Hussein in power, Kuwait, Saudi Arabia, Turkey, even Iran all had someone on their border to fear. Kuwait and Saudi Arabia, impervious to economic leverage, were forced to permit a seemingly permanent U.S. military presence on their soil. This presence, along with the repressive nature of the Kuwaiti and Saudi regimes, guaranteed enough angry opposition that the relationship between the two countries' ruling cliques and the U.S. government became symbiotic.

This situation exactly parallels the process through which El Salvador, Guatemala, and Costa Rica were forced to accept U.S. aid, with strings attached, to respond to the threat of an aggressive Nicaragua under Daniel Ortega. Just as the leveraged ally faction saw no need to upset the Middle Eastern apple cart in 2002 and 2003, their counterparts of twenty years earlier saw nothing but disadvantage in removing the Sandinista threat in Central America.

It is also enlightening to compare U.S. military actions in Iraq in 2003 with those during Operation Desert Storm twelve years earlier. In January 1991, the first President Bush opened the war with a forty-day bombing campaign. Only after Iraq's infrastructure was pulverized did Bush order an offensive with ground troops. During the air campaign, the Saddam Hussein regime was able to sabotage oil wells in southern Iraq and in the Persian Gulf. By contrast, the 2003 Iraq war started with a simultaneous air and ground campaign. In 1991, only about 15 percent of the bombs dropped on Iraq were guided (either by laser or by an imbedded Global Positioning System). In 2003, almost 90 percent of the explosives used by the U.S. military were guided to a specific target. In the first case, collateral damage was extensive; in the latter, it was minimal. In 1991, residents of Baghdad lost power in the first minutes of the war. In 2003, U.S. bombs and missiles were so specifically targeted that the lights in the capital stayed on until retreating Hussein loyalists destroyed the power plant as the Saddam Hussein government was collapsing.

Because U.S. and British troops entered Iraq immediately in 2003, the oil wells in the south and in the Gulf were taken intact. In addition, American troops seized Iraqi missile bases in western Iraq, protecting Israel from the missile threats it had endured in 1991 (and which, incidentally, also increased Israel's dependence on U.S. Patriot missiles). In 1991, the senior Bush had every intention of leaving Saddam in power, which left Kuwait, Saudi Arabia, Turkey, and Jordan (and Israel) in danger. In addition, Saddam Hussein's army, intelligence services and police forces were left in place. George W. Bush removed the Saddam threat permanently, both for Iraqis and for their neighbors.

The above does not excuse the tragic errors in planning and execution of the current Iraq war. But it does indicate that the second President Bush possessed a keen understanding of the goals and desires of the leveraged ally faction and that he intended to create a postwar Middle East in which threats to the United States, to its allies and to its interests would be permanently reduced or eliminated. Bush acted forcefully against what he perceived as the region's central threat in the same way that Reagan acted against the most dangerous threat in Central America.

Turning Points

Twenty years from now, perhaps, the world will know whether or not Operation Iraqi Freedom was a turning point in the war on terror. Perhaps the next generation will also see the end of the war between the natural ally and leveraged ally factions, although that is extremely unlikely. Major eras like the Cold War or the War on Terror may come and go, but the basic disagreement over whether the United States should make requests or issue commands to its allies will probably remain a pivot point of U.S. foreign policy.

There can be little doubt, however, that Reagan's actions in Central America were a historic turning point in the Cold War. After January 1981, no Soviet-backed movement would ever again take the offensive against an American ally. After 1981, the developing world, which had hitherto been a breeding ground for pro-Soviet armed movements, would become instead a breeding ground for anti-Communist guerrilla movements. From 1981 onward to the fall of the Berlin Wall, the power and influence of the Soviet Union would steadily decline.

Turning points rarely seem as crucial at the time that they occur as they do in retrospect. This is especially true in the minds of the eventual losers. Great Britain's leadership was just as confident in its ability to crush the colonial rebellion in North America after the Battle of Trenton as they were before. Napoleon probably did not that know his cause was lost after the Battle of Trafalgar. If the papers of Jefferson Davis are any guide, the Confederate president saw no reason to despair after Gettysburg. The Japanese high command did not know that their advance on Guadalcanal would be the last Japanese land offensive of the war. And there is nothing to indicate that the Soviets saw any irony in the Salvadoran guerrillas' "Final Offensive" of 1981.

Even two decades later, when Reagan and his administration are widely acknowledged to have brought about the end of the Cold War, the pivotal role of Central America is not generally recognized. But Central America was the central, fighting front of the Cold War in the 1980s. Other Reagan-era policies certainly played their part, such as building up the American military, starving the Soviet Union of hard currency through the pipeline boycott, threatening to build a missile defense system, supporting the resistance in Afghanistan, and challenging the fragile psychology of the Soviet leadership.

All of the above policies, however, were directed toward the middle and long term. Reagan and his supporters knew that none of these policies would have an immediate effect on Soviet strength or on the global correlation of forces. In Central America, however, Reagan acted within days of becoming president to blunt a determined Soviet-backed offensive in El Salvador. What had seemed like a sure victory for a Soviet-backed group turned into a wholly unexpected defeat. Reagan had demonstrated American resolve in the Western Hemisphere, which was essential to the continuation of his other anti-Soviet policies. Reagan became president less than six years after the American humiliation in Vietnam, and just minutes after the end of the Iranian hostage crisis. America's allies (and potential allies) around the world needed convincing that a U.S. Administration would take risks to counter Soviet advances. Determined action in Central America provided the proof.

Reagan's tough anti-Soviet rhetoric would have seemed, at best, a poor joke had Reagan not supplemented the rhetoric with tough actions in Central America, where the Soviet threat was most immediate. Thirty years earlier, after all, President Dwight Eisenhower's administration talked of rolling back the Soviet empire, but the language of "rollback" was coupled with passive inaction when the Soviets invaded Hungary in 1956.

U.S. policymakers had concluded just after World War II that the Soviet system had to keep expanding in order to survive. This conclusion formed the basis of the containment policy that every post-war president followed, from Truman to Carter. The invariable Soviet response to containment, however, was to seek an opportunity to expand in some part of the world where it was difficult for the U.S. to respond. Thus, while the United States was ostensibly "containing" the Soviet Union, Moscow created new satellites in North Korea, Cuba, Vietnam, Angola, Mozambique, Ethiopia, South Yemen, Afghanistan, Nicaragua, and Grenada.

The essence of any successful "containment" policy, therefore, was to effectively counter the Soviets at the periphery of their empire, no matter how imperfect the non-Communist government was, how many logistical difficulties there were to sending military aid, or how unpopular the cause may have been with American editorial writers. In blunting the Salvadoran guerrillas' "Final Offensive," Reagan did just that.

But had Reagan settled for mere containment of the Soviets in Central America, he would have merely continued history; he would not have changed it. Containment is, at base, a reactive and defensive policy. Reagan went on offense in Central America, on both the military and the political playing fields. Militarily, he gave the Soviets a long-overdue taste of their own medicine by supporting a guerrilla war in Nicaragua. Politically, Reagan put the United States unmistakably on the side of democracy in Latin America, for the first time since the Jefferson administration. The impact on Soviet strength was immediate; their setback in El Salvador, coupled with new challenges in the region, compelled the Soviets to reconsider their entire strategy in Central America.

Faced with long-term deterioration of their global position because of the West's hostility, the Soviet leaders decided that they could not afford to abandon their Central American allies. Under compulsion, they made the tactical decision to devote precious material and political resources to a battle in America's back yard, gambling that the United States would not have the will to continue the fight. Thus, it was not only Reagan's quick actions in 1981 that made a difference, but also his stubborn determination to stay the course in Central America, even in the face of repeated setbacks, administration infighting and a crippling scandal.

Less than ten years after Reagan predicted it, the Soviet Union was indeed consigned to "the ash heap of history." Stunned political commentators spent most of the early 1990s trying to figure out how the seemingly impossible had happened. They should have been looking at Central America. In the early 1980s, the Soviets' commitment to the Sandinistas and the Salvadoran guerrillas seemed like a show of strength. In fact, it was an act of desperation, brought on by a shift in the global balance of power that almost no one perceived. Only by the end of the decade, with the Berlin Wall down and the Soviet Union itself reeling, did the real turning point of the Cold War reveal itself.

Index